NETWORKS IN MARKETING

To my mother, Sandy; my late father, Tony;
my stepfather, Chuck; Toni, Julie, Simona, and T&G.

NETWORKS IN MARKETING

DAWN IACOBUCCI
EDITOR

SAGE Publications
International Educational and Professional Publisher
Thousand Oaks   London   New Delhi

For information address:

SAGE Publications, Inc.
2455 Teller Road
Thousand Oaks, California 91320
E-mail: order@sagepub.com

SAGE Publications Ltd.
6 Bonhill Street
London EC2A 4PU
United Kingdom

SAGE Publications India Pvt. Ltd.
M-32 Market
Greater Kailash I
New Delhi 110048 India

Printed in the United States of America

Library of Congress Cataloging-in-Publication Data

Main entry under title:

Networks in marketing/ editor, Dawn Iacobucci.
    p. cm.
    Includes bibliographical references.
    ISBN 0-7619-0139-6 (acid-free paper).—ISBN 0-7619-0140-X (pbk.:
acid-free paper)
    1. Communication in marketing. 2 Business networks. 3. Public
relations. I. Iacobucci, Dawn.
  HF5415.123.N48 1996
  658.8'02—dc20   96-10122

96 97 98 99 00 01 02 10 9 8 7 6 5 4 3

Sage Production Editor: Vicki Baker

Contents

Part V: Consumer Networks

Part VI: Final Issues

Acknowledgments

I have had the absolute pleasure of working with the contributing authors for this book. Each of them enthusiastically agreed to participate and each produced fine efforts on behalf of a belief in networks in marketing. I thank them all for making this a rewarding experience.

My colleagues at Northwestern are an amazing source of inspiration. I am particularly grateful to Sid Levy, Jim Anderson, Bobby Calder, Anne Coughlan, Dipak Jain, Phil Kotler, John Sherry, Lou Stern, Brian Sternthal, Alice Tybout, and Naufel Vilcassim for encouraging me to enter their world of marketing and for their continuing support, encouragement, and feedback. Colleagues who have been in other departments have been equally important to me, including Max Bazerman, Jeanne Brett, Jenny Chatman, Paul Hirsch, Maggie Neale, Denise Rousseau, Mark Satterthwaite, Joel Shalowitz, Eitan Zemel, and Don Jacobs. I have also appreciated the friendly support of Kellogg administrative people such as Carole Cahill, Cathy Grimstead, Kathy Nickolopoulos, and Lucy Vandenburgh. All these people have made NU a lively and interesting place to work—as the ad says, "it's not just a job. . ."

I have also been blessed with close relations with many of our doctoral students over the years whose interactions I have also treasured. These classes have included the wonders of Alexa Bezjian-Avery, Kent Grayson, Gerri Henderson, Nigel Hopkins, and Amy

Ostrom, as well as Nancy Artz, Pablo Azar, Bridgette Braig, Rick Briesch, Jennifer E. Chang, Jill Grace, Sonya Grier, Deb Heisley, Jonathan Hibbard, Prashant Malaviya, Eyal Maoz, Ramya Neelamegham, Seong-Yeon Park, Laura Peracchio, Lisa Scheer, Jakki Thomas, Dan Turner, and Phil Zerrillo in marketing; and Zoe Barsness, Joe Baumann, Brenda Ellington, Etty Martzke Jehn, Claus Langfred, Peter Kim, Mike Lounsbury, Charles Naquin, Jared Preston, Sandra Robinson, Ann Tenbrunsel, Melissa Thomas, Cathy Tinsley, Kathleen Valley, Kim Wade-Benzoni, Marvin Washington, Jim Westphal, and Sally White in organizational behavior.

If my colleagues are the present, and the doctoral students are the future, my mentors were exceedingly important in my past. I am grateful for the training, advice, and intellectual models of Phipps Arabie, David Birch, Lloyd Humphreys, Larry Jones, Ledyard Tucker, and Stanley Wasserman in quantitative psychology; Chuck Hulin and Fritz Drasgow in industrial/organizational psychology; Gordon Greenberg (for my first stats course); Harry Hake, Sam Komorita, and Robert Wyer.

I am extremely grateful to the National Science Foundation (Grant No. SES-9023445) for the past five years of generous research support. I also thank Rick Bagozzi, Steve Brown, Dipankar Chakravarti, Wayne DeSarbo, Linton Freeman, Joe Galaskiewicz, Håkan Håkansson, Larry Hedges, Mike Houston, Larry Hubert, John Lynch, Lars-Gunnar Mattsson, Mike Mowkwa, Peter Reingen, Mary Roznowski, John Saunders, Jag Sheth, Terri Swartz, Bart Weitz, and Dave Wilson for their help and encouragement over the years.

I am also grateful to Lars-Gunnar Mattsson for arranging that the Stockholm School of Economics host my visit in 1992. It was a pleasure to experience an entire marketing department steeped in network thinking. About that time, I had a conversation with Håkan Håkansson in which we were commenting on how nice it was that the study of relationships was currently in vogue in marketing, but it was his remark that it does not really matter, for when the interest of others eventually drops off, we "real" network marketers will continue to study the structure of relationships in marketing, and be perfectly happy doing so. Here's to happy network researchers!

And last, and most. . . . When I finished teaching my last MBA class meeting in the fall of 1987 (my first teaching quarter), I remember that as I was packing up my papers to head out of the classroom, I distinctly heard the "Hallelujah Chorus" go off in my head—funny and quite suitable if one's life has a soundtrack. When I finished this book, I remember hearing the gentler and quieter, but probably more heartfelt dismissal in the Lutheran liturgy in which the pastor says to the congregation, "Go in Peace. Serve the Lord." And the congregation responds with joy, "Thanks be to God."

—DAWN IACOBUCCI

 Introduction

The term *network* has come to have many meanings. Colloquially, networking is a verb used to describe the initiation and sustenance of interpersonal connections for the rather Machiavellian purpose of tapping those relationships later for commercial gain. Although this definition may sound harsh or extreme, much of network research does investigate the integration of social and business ties. For example, one might rely on one's social ties to obtain a job (e.g., Granovetter, 1973), to cross-consult on boards of directors (e.g., Galaskiewicz, 1985a), or to sell consumer goods (e.g., Frenzen & Davis, 1990). Leveraging interpersonal, social ties for commercial access, however, is only one application of networks.

As a noun, a network describes a collection of actors (persons, departments, firms, countries, and so on) and their structural connections (familial, social, communicative, financial, strategic, business alliances, and so on). Social networks traditionally were those networks whose relational ties were primarily social in nature (e.g., interpersonal liking, respecting, communication patterns, and so on), developing largely within the discipline of sociology. The term "social networks," however, is often used when "networks" would suffice. For example, there may be both business and social components to the network under study and there is no reason the modifier social should supersede that of business. Furthermore, sometimes there is no apparent social component at all, except to the extent that the network researcher is using relational analogies in the business setting (e.g., "partnerships"). Accordingly, I thought it proper that this book be titled *Networks in Marketing* to represent the study of structural links of any sort including, but not limited to, social ties as applied to problems within marketing. In addition, the actors described in the chapters contained herein vary from consumer to business-to-business and other constituent networks, a distinction that further generalizes the applicability of networks and the study of interconnections in business and marketing (Arabie & Wind, 1994; Iacobucci & Hopkins, 1992).

Network research has also come to represent the toolbox of techniques for analyzing data describing interconnected actors. Classic data sets, such as those obtained from survey or experimental studies, result in observations-by-variables data sets in which the focus of the analysis (e.g., regression, factor analysis, and so on) is on the relationships among the variables, and the respondents are assumed to be independent. For dyads or networks of interconnected actors, their very connections violate assumptions of independent units of observations. The network methodologies share the goal of analyzing such interrelated data; Kenny and Judd (1986) capture the spirit of this goal best when they state that sometimes the lack of independence is not simply a statistical nuisance that must be overcome, but rather, sometimes the interconnections are the very thing of interest in the research study. Clearly, appropriate methods are required to elicit from the data descriptions and inferences of the structural interconnections. Many of the early analytical approaches are matrix based, drawn originally from graph theoretical mathematics, although more recent methods rely on stochastic modeling (e.g., Hopkins, Henderson, & Iacobucci, 1995; Iacobucci & Hopkins, 1992; Knoke & Kuklinski, 1982; Wasserman & Faust, 1994).

Finally, perhaps the reference to networks as a paradigm is the most comprehensive use of the word. *Paradigm* may be an overused term, but it is fitting here in describing an approach to studying relational phenomena and the structural analysis of interconnected actors. This use of the term paradigm is captured in the subtitle of Axelsson and Easton's (1992) book, *Industrial Networks: A New View of Reality*. Networks as a paradigm subsumes network logic, methodology, data structure, and relational theory tests. Each of these uses of the term network is reflected throughout this book; some chapters focus on social ties, others on methodology, and so on, but all share the common theme of attempting to understand patterns of connections through the paradigm of networks.

The goal of researchers working within the network paradigm is to understand structures of relationships: Who is connected to whom? What is the nature of their relationship? How long has it lasted? How frequently is it activated? How satisfying is it to the involved parties? Who else is affected by the actors and their relationship? Are we studying a series of independent dyads (e.g., manufacturer-distributor pairs) or many actors and dyads embedded in a larger network frame (wherein each actor may relate to all others)? What groups of actors might be identified as functioning subsets of the larger network? How do those groups interrelate? Which actors appear to be similar in their relational behavior? Are there actors that are functional replicates that might, for example, serve as multiple informants on the relationship? Is the structure of the network the same when it is observed for objective ties such as business contracts as on subjective properties such as trust or reciprocal cooperation? Are interpersonal relations similar in structure to those between businesses? How do networks appear to change over time? How do the actions of a single actor ripple throughout the network via its immediate and more distant linkages? These are but a subset of research questions that have been, are being, and will continue to be addressed by network researchers. The chapters in this book span the range of these questions.

Even given the breadth of the network paradigm, the logical argument of this book is simple:

Much of marketing is relational.

Networks are an excellent means of studying relational phenomena.

∴ Networks are an excellent means of studying much of marketing.

The first two sections of this book illustrate the first two premises, and the remainder of the book explores the richness of the deduction.

To support the first premise, that it is important to study relationships in marketing, I asked two stellar marketers scholars (Stern and Spekman) to contribute minichapters that would reflect their own research interests and expertise (even though their work has not relied on network concepts). To support the second premise, that networks are useful as a perspective in studying relationships, I asked several stellar network researchers (Galaskiewicz, Burt, and Krackhardt) similarly to write from their own perspectives (even though their work has not directly addressed marketing problems). To demonstrate the deduction, the richness of the possibilities of networks in marketing, I asked approximately a dozen excellent scholars whose network research in marketing I have long admired to participate. Their contributions appear as the main research chapters in Parts III, IV, and V in this book, and together these chapters illustrate the vast diversity of issues in which networks and marketing overlap. Although these researchers share an interest in studying marketing networks, there their similarities end. This is an interesting collection of contributors; we have diversity in representing U.S. and international researchers; established researchers who can speak with perspective on the field, as well as several researchers at the beginning of their careers who can point to new trends; writers presenting managerial, methodological, or conceptual and theoretical chapters, and so on. Thus, these researchers differ on many interesting dimensions that should make the book a strong case for the wide array of research questions one might address via a network perspective in marketing. As a whole then, it is my intention that this book, like Figure 0.1, represent many perspectives on the overlapping themes of networks, relationships, and marketing. Let me now describe each section in somewhat more detail.

In Part I, "Marketing Is Relational," the chapters by Stern and Spekman demonstrate that business-to-business connections comprise a critical enterprise for marketers. Stern compares the concepts of cooperation, competition, and conflict in marketing relationships, and he urges relational marketers to go beyond studies of dyads. Spekman uses the buying center literature to explore how transactions develop toward long-term relationships, further to partnerships and alliances, further still to intricate networks of interconnections. In such relational development, he argues for the importance of understanding the management of relationships and how alliances become true competitive advantages.

In Part II, "The Network Paradigm Allows the Study of Relational Phenomena," the chapters illustrate the unique insights networks can lend to the study of relationships and patterns of interconnec-

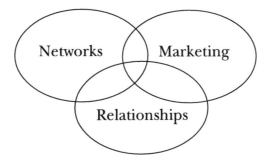

Figure 0.1. The Interrelationships Among Marketing, Networks, and Relationships

tions. Galaskiewicz describes current trends in network studies, including moving beyond description to providing a context in which to test theoretical propositions, and viewing networks not as environmental constraints in which a firm functions but rather as rich opportunities to be explored, and means of achieving organizational goals. Burt and Janicik compare cohesion (actors related to other actors) and equivalence (actors similar to other actors with respect to their ties to others) as a means for effective influence. These comparisons are made among three illustrative settings: corporate officers, political lobbyists, and physicians. Krackhardt explores the structure underlying word-of-mouth and diffusion networks. He models networks with different structural properties and demonstrates how those properties yield different diffusion patterns, thereby making explicit a means of studying diffusion as a process.

The chapters in Parts III, IV, and V begin to demonstrate the diversity of research topics currently being approached using the logic, paradigm, or methods of networks. Part III, "Theoretical Concepts of Networks for Marketers," begins with a chapter by Araujo and Easton who provide an overview of the many types of theoretical approaches that have either fallen under the rubric of networks or have provided classic comparison cases for the network approach. In a detailed analysis, these approaches are compared along a number of distinguishing criteria to explore their similarities and differences, thus providing a thorough introduction to theoretical aspects of networks. Håkansson and Sharma examine the development of the network perspective, focusing particularly on a firm's position in a network vis à vis strategic alliances. They contrast this network view with transaction cost analysis and they emphasize the dynamic nature of relationships and networks in such alliances. Campbell and Wilson take the practical stand that networks will exist and succeed to the extent that the structure of interconnections raises overall performance and lowers costs of the involved players. They emphasize the value-adding nature of networks and propose the concept of a "network captain," an actor responsible for coordinating and integrating network activities. Ford, McDowell, and Tomkins also consider some practical issues, including questioning how business accounting systems must be modified to determine and incorporate relational value. These authors describe how much more complicated decision making can become when managers are concerned not just with short-term, but also long-term outcomes, and not just as affecting one's own firm, but also affecting one's firm's relationships with other firms.

Part IV, "Dynamic Networks and Market Structure," begins with a chapter by Hertz, who considers the likely nature of network changes—changes in relationships are most often subtle and gradual, and market structural differences may not be easily visible in gross observations of phenomena. As illustrated through several detailed case analyses, we see that gradual changes may be advantageous in that they allow for a flexibility between the involved players, and tentative changes may also signal impending changes of a more radical nature. Hertz's cases also illustrate how the bounds between networks may be fluid in that as a firm drifts toward another, the firm is also drifting away from a third, for example. Zerrillo and Raina also consider dynamic effects emanating from a source actor. In particular, they describe how extant network structures may impede the introduction of new products; a firm wishing to enter a new market must consider the possible resistances of potential channel members given the status quo of the embedded sets of present connections. Iacobucci, Henderson, Marcati, and Chang analyze brand switching data that describe purchases in the automobile industries in France and the United Kingdom over a period of 4 years. They compare various network methodologies for sensitivities to detecting network structure and network change. In a companion chapter, Marcati focuses on the managerial implications of changing market structures having identified certain network characteristics and properties of the various automobile manufacturers. In particular, he illustrates how the identification of actors with equivalent patterns of ties to others in the network might be an especially useful tool in studying competition.

Part V, "Consumer Networks," begins with a chapter by Ward and Reingen, who explore how the cognitive belief systems of consumers might be integrated with their social ties. In an analysis of patronage segmentation of a health food store, they describe cognitive associations motivating the health food store purchases that differ for animal rights activists versus consumers seeking macrobiotic diets. Furthermore, they show that there is little social connection between groups even though both are engaged in the same behavior of making purchases at the same health food store. The chapter by Grayson introduces the concept and structure of network marketing organizations, those known for predominantly relying on the personal ties of the sales force to enhance further purchasing (like that of the MCI "Friends and Family" campaign described by Arabie and Wind, 1994, or the Tupperware sorts of home parties described in Frenzen and Davis, 1990). Grayson describes the industry and clarifies misconceptions regarding illegal versions of the multilevel marketing structure. In his chapter, the voice of participants in such networks is used to describe, for example, the role conflicts they experience, their personal styles of selling, and the like. Much has been said of the usefulness of weak ties, and this chapter makes the clever point that sometimes the strength of weak ties is simply due to the fact that they outnumber the strong ties. The chapter by Martin and Clark explores the various forms of connections customers might have with each other. Their discussion broadens the consideration of customer relationships far beyond the standard notion of word-of-mouth networks; for example, they consider how customer connections affect customer satisfaction and other indicators of interest to the marketing manager. Bagozzi, Henderson, Dabholkar, and Iacobucci apply network methods to means-ends causal goal chains to examine the cognitive connections within a hierarchy of specific to abstract goals. The causal chains representing beliefs held by recyclers were compared to those held by nonrecyclers. The research explores whether structural differences in the cognitive networks might explain why the behaviors of the groups differ.

Finally, we close with Part VI, "Final Issues." Iacobucci and Zerrillo describe the methodological challenges of studying networks as units of analysis, compared with studying individual actors, or subgroups smaller than the whole network, such as cliques of actors. Relational data on samples of actors, or even dyads, are easier to obtain than for multiple networks, yet statistical tests of theoretical positions require replications. The chapter considers such issues and proposes solutions.

This collection of chapters is intended to demonstrate the utility of networks in marketing. Technical aspects of networks are explained where required, but this book is intended neither as an introduction to network philosophies and paradigms nor as a methodological primer. Excellent introductory and methodological material exists: Burt and Minor (1983), Knoke and Kuklinski (1982), Scott (1991), and Wasserman and Faust (1994). Collections of research similar to the current book but not aimed at marketers would be those by Mizruchi and Schwartz (1987) and Nohria and Eccles (1992), who focus on organization behavior and management applications; and Wasserman and Galaskiewicz (1994) and Wellman and Berkowitz (1988), who focus on sociological and other behavioral network research, not particularly intended for management audiences.

It is my hope that various chapters in this book will be of interest to different communities of marketing academics, including relationship marketers, business marketers, consumer marketers, and methodologists. Networks are relatively new enough (at least to business school researchers) that little has been written, so perhaps this book can begin to fulfill this need. Similarly, perhaps these chapters may interest organizational networkers and traditional social networkers, such as the readers of the journal *Social Networks* who themselves are diverse. I believe that this volume is exciting and timely and I hope that readers will agree.

PART I

Marketing Is Relational

Relationships, Networks, and the Three Cs

LOUIS W. STERN

There can be little doubt that the concept of "networks" is central to marketing, and yet it is surprising to find such a paucity of empirical research addressing it. There are, of course, a number of published works that outline the dimensions of networks and the potential impact of different kinds of relationships among parties in networks. But there are relatively few scholars in marketing who have been willing to brave the profound theoretical and measurement issues associated with testing hypotheses using network frameworks. Perhaps this hesitancy stems from the fact that, historically, a great deal of the empirical network research that has been conducted came from the field of sociology. The likely genesis of this work can be found in sociometric analyses of opinion leadership. There, the notions of "central" and "marginal" members of the network are critical to the understanding of, say, the diffusion of innovations. Unfortunately, that research and much of the research that followed it was and has been virtually devoid of theory or a strong theoretical foundation. Rather, it has focused mainly on a description of properties of the network and the elements within them.

The research on networks that seems to have most promise disaggregates networks into dyads and examines the effects on dyads that are connected, negatively or positively, to other nodes in the system. The work of Emerson and Cook and their students is a case in point. But the insight having the most impact, from a methodological standpoint, is that the dyad remains the fundamental unit of analysis.

Whether this is due to tractability or the existence of theory relative to dyads or some other reason is not certain.

If dyadic analysis is critical to the understanding of networks, the major research question seems to be: How do elements of the network in which the dyad is embedded affect the sentiments, behavior, and performance of the members of the dyad? To uncover hypotheses about these phenomena, it is important to analyze the dyad's relationship with its environment in terms of the three Cs—competition, conflict, and cooperation.

Returning to the mother discipline of network analysis, it is possible to define these constructs sociologically as follows:

Competition is behavior that is goal or object centered, based on scarcity, indirect, and impersonal, in which a third party controls the goal or object.

Conflict is behavior that is opponent centered, very direct, and highly personal, in which the goal or object is controlled by the opponent.

Cooperation is behavior that involves joint striving for a goal or object, is direct or indirect (explicit or implicit), and personal, in which the goal or object that is controlled by a third party can only be secured if the focal parties coalesce.

Identifying cooperative behavior is relatively uncomplicated. It is much more difficult to separate competition from conflict, and vice versa. The easiest way to understand the difference between competition and conflict, as defined above, is to think in terms of sporting events. All field events in a track meet (shotput, discus, javelin, high jump, and so on) are purely competitive, as are all swimming events (with the exception of water polo). The object is to throw, jump, or swim as far or as fast as one can so that he or she has a chance to win the gold medal, which is in the possession of the Olympic Committee (the third party, in this case). There is no interference with anyone else. The competitors focus on the finish line; it's individual performance that counts.

In conflict sports, interference (opponent-centered behavior) is critical to success. Unless one competitor "destroys" the other or somehow impedes the other from winning, there is no hope of victory. Basketball, football, soccer, and hockey are obvious examples. But even tennis is a conflict sport. All of these sports call for direct efforts to overcome the opponent, and each is personal—the specific identity of the opponent is very important.

Applying the three Cs to marketing situations is relatively simple. Let's use distribution channels as an example (surprise, surprise!). Taking the end-user's perspective first (which is what we have been taught), the shopping process for a specific good or service is always enhanced when there is a choice of "places" from which to purchase. The "places" can be different types of retail outlets (discount or full-service) in the case of consumer goods, and different salesforces (company-employed or distributor-employed) in the case of business-to-business markets. The "places" represent bundles of service outputs. Obviously, end-users' needs often vary over time; therefore, they may prefer one bundle on one occasion and another bundle on another, depending, in large part, on such factors as time pressure, income levels, and a whole host of exogenous variables. Therefore, on any given purchase occasion, end-users prefer to self-select, based on their requirements at that moment in time or on their projected requirements over time.

Competition is key to the availability of a variety of service output bundles. To win the "gold medal" (the end-user's patronage), each marketing channel must engage in a "beauty contest" on each purchase occasion. Interference with others is likely to be wasteful of the resources required to be highly attractive over all purchase occasions. Clearly, the third party (per the definition of competition above) controlling the goal or object (the gold medal) is the customer.

Conflict among marketing channels is likely to be destructive and self-defeating, both from the perspective of end-users and suppliers. It is also likely to generate dysfunctional conflict between channel members within any given channel dyad. Conflict occurs when end-users cannot distinguish among channels relative to service offerings. When the "places" are identical in terms of what they can provide, then the only way they can win the end-user's patronage is to become opponent centered and disparage the ability of rivals to deliver on their promises. Assuming that the end-user is shopping for a particular brand, rational behavior on his or her part in such a situation will be to try to play one "place" off against another. But in the process, given the heightened level of conflict that emerges (i.e., the extent and nature of opponent-centered behavior), the end-user becomes increasingly uncertain about the efficacy of the entire shopping process for the particular brand as the opponents undermine one another.

The cause of the conflict in this situation is the redundancy with respect to the bundles of service outputs that the supplier of the brand has created by its selection of duplicate channels. The end-user is confused, and channel actors become increasingly frustrated with the supplier for having put them in such a predicament. They find that they must expend significant resources in nonproductive, combative activities. ("Unfair competition," a term used in antitrust enforcement, can sometimes be applied to the kind of opponent-centered behavior that occurs in channels.) Therefore, to prevent dysfunctional channel conflict, it is important to limit the redundancies in channel systems. This is accomplished by designing channels for each trading area so that each "place" offers end-users unique bundles of service outputs.

Unfortunately, in the world of business, managers have misunderstood these concepts. What they generally mean when they use the term "channel conflict" is, in reality, "channel competition." For example, in the marketing of personal computers, when a company-employed salesforce competes for a customer's order with a dealer's salesforce, they call this "channel conflict" and become highly anxious over its potential long-run effects. But, in fact, it is not conflict, but competition, that is taking place. And, as long as the competition conforms to a 100 meter dash where both runners stay in their lanes and run as fast as possible to secure the gold medal, everyone will benefit, especially the customer. It's redundancy that converts good, healthy channel competition into inter-channel conflict. This, in turn, will tend to breed dysfunctional intrachannel conflict within the dyad, and the entire network may start to unravel.

As has been argued and demonstrated repeatedly, however, intrachannel dyadic conflict is part of the fabric of the dependency relationships between channel members. Just as members of a family disagree, channel members will disagree—and the disagreements can produce new understandings, positive change, and enhanced benefits. The real trick, of course, is keeping the conflicts within bounds, that is, of preventing the conflict from becoming dysfunctional.

The key is the third C—cooperation. It is only through cooperation that suppliers can be assured that customers will be given a choice of service output bundles and that, when selected, the appropriate bundle will actually be delivered. In other words, cooperation is critical to strong, functional competition. Some of the major elements leading to dyadic cooperation are (a) the creative use of positively valanced influence strategies, (b) commitment on the part of channel members, and (c) an atmosphere of trust. These are the means for building effective relationships. The end result are high performance dyads that will form the core of the networks in which they are located.

A Reflection on Two Decades of Business-to-Business Marketing Research

Implications for Understanding Marketing Relationships and Networks

ROBERT E. SPEKMAN

I have been asked to reflect on my research over the past 20 years and relate it to the primary themes of this volume— marketing relationships and networks. This is an opportunity for me to build bridges between the themes of my academic work and the major themes captured in the various chapters written here by my colleagues. As I look back, I have always viewed marketing relationships as important, but they often appeared as the subtext in my empirical analysis. That is, I only rarely dealt with marketing relationships explicitly. In fact, in my early work I tended to speak about these buyer-seller relationships as adversarial in nature. The purpose of this chapter is to discuss the importance of relationships in marketing within the context of my own research. I will develop my presentation by tracing the various themes of my work over time beginning in the mid-1970s.

ORGANIZATIONAL BUYING BEHAVIOR AND THE ROLE OF THE PURCHASING MANAGER

My early research focused on organizational buying behavior and the role played by the purchasing manager as a buying center member. The buying center represented a decision-making unit in which different organizational actors participate, often on an informal basis, in a particular purchase decision. Although there was an implicit internal network of formal and informal ties among the various decision-making participants and the purchasing manager (my focal person), I examined the decision-making influence of the purchasing manager and the various externalities that contributed to his or her "power." This work represented the confluence of three separate streams of research. I was influenced by Sheth (1973), and Webster and Wind (1972), who were early proponents of models of organizational buying behavior in which a number of task and nontask-related factors were shown to affect the purchasing decision-making process. I was affected also by the contingency theorists in organizational behavior who demonstrated that decision-making processes in the firm were influenced by structural and process-related factors that, in turn, were affected by the degree of environmental uncertainty. Organic organizations (i.e., those that responded to environmental changes) were more likely to make "better" decisions because they were more adept at gathering and processing relevant external information. Finally, I was greatly influenced by Louis W. Stern, my mentor, and his work on power and conflict in distribution channels. From these streams of research it is no wonder that power in decision making and the factors that contribute to it were an important focus of my efforts. Interestingly, during this period Bobby Calder, a colleague at Kellogg Graduate School of Management at Northwestern, and I began to develop a very preliminary network approach to buying center activity. Rather than ask the question of "who had decision-making power relative to whom," we began to address the question of "what were the patterns of interaction among buying center members?" We never progressed, however, beyond the conceptual stage in our many conversations.

For the most part, this early work was driven by managerial concerns that converged on the marketers' need to better understand the buyers' decision-making processes so that marketing resources could more effectively be targeted to the influential members of the buying center. At no time did the intent of this work attempt to build bridges between marketers and buyers. Sadly, I admit that an "us versus them" mentality framed my early buying center work. This more adversarial orientation was most apparent in the companion articles that were written for the purchasing professional. Here, a series of articles (e.g., Spekman, 1979) emphasized that purchasing professionals needed to better manage their vendor base if they were to contribute to the productivity of their firm. Relationships were viewed as important internally because purchasing managers were advised to better align themselves with other functional managers. I was less concerned with external, market-based relationships. The goal of these very normative articles was to propose ways to enhance the organizational status of purchasing managers and to improve their ability to contribute to the strategic goals of the firm. Again, relationships were defined by relative influence both within the buying organization and between the buyer and the seller. It is important to note that cooperation was not a key concern. Buyers were advised to be prepared to deal with a seller who was often more skilled. Although not exactly Machiavellian in content, the prince was alive in spirit!

FROM BUYING CENTER
TO SELLING CENTER

In the early 1980s my work with Johnston (Johnston & Spekman, 1982; Spekman & Johnston, 1986) and Gronhaug (Spekman & Gronhaug, 1984) began to change its perspective and began to look at the relationship between buyer and seller. In particular, we argued for the need to align buying centers and selling centers. These articles implied that relationships between firms were important, and that buyer and seller needed to align their businesses as is illustrated by early just-in-time inventory systems and other information linkages between trading partners. Our objective was to discuss approaches to examine the complex interaction that typifies the business-to-business marketplace. Influenced to some degree by the Industrial Marketing and Purchasing (IMP) project in Europe, we began to discuss the importance of networks and their ability to explore evolving relationships between firms. It should be noted that the implicit focus of this work was dyadic in nature and did not reflect the fact that ties between buyer and seller can extend to other firms who also are partners in the full network linking all parties. For instance, one can easily point to the network of subtier suppliers who feed the automotive and aerospace industries and visualize a pattern of relationships that span a number of different firms at different levels in the production process.

PARTNERSHIPS: A NEW FORM OF
INTERACTION AMONG FIRMS

About this time, Halberstam (1984), Piore and Sabel (1984), and others observed a significant change in organizational form. No longer was the vertical integrated firm seen as a paragon of virtue and Alfred Sloan's view of hierarchy was challenged as the model of organizational effectiveness. Williamson's (1975) work on markets and hierarchy became the platform on which marketers build a conceptual base for examining the emerging organizational form that linked buyer and seller. Growing from earlier work by Schumpeter (1934), Williamson argued that new organizational forms require the flexibility that is lost on market failure. Williamson has had a significant impact on research beginning during the mid-1980s and contributed to an understanding of why firms might wish to form more collaborative relationships and what factors help to facilitate these more cooperative linkages between trading partners. For example, research with colleagues (e.g., Frazier, Spekman, & O'Neil, 1986; Sriram, Krapfel, & Spekman, 1992; Spekman & Salmond, 1992) attempted to better understand the nature of close ties between buyer and seller and reflected the influence of Williamson's transaction cost analysis approach. In one instance, data were collected from both sides of the relationship to gain an appreciation for a shared perspective between buyer and seller. Here, we were influenced also by both resource dependency and social interaction paradigms. One of our goals was to understand the degree of consensus between buyer and seller.

Although this work focuses on relationships between trading partners, it falls short of understanding fully the norms and values that link these firms. Nor does this work attempt to understand the impact of such relationships and assumes that outputs (e.g., satisfaction, profits, lower costs) are enhanced by such relationships. More recent work (Mohr & Spekman, 1994) has attempted to link outputs to partnership formation. This phase of my research again focused

indirectly on marketing relationships and has attempted to understand the factors that facilitate partnership formation. Satisfaction
was partly a function of one's relationship with one's trading partner.
It is important to note that there has been a noticeable gap in an
attempt to understand how to manage these marketing relationships
over time. To be sure, the work described thus far has reflected a shift
from transactions to relationships. Nonetheless, the full effects of
relationship management tools and techniques has not fully been
demonstrated.

FROM PARTNERSHIP FORMATION
TO ALLIANCE MANAGEMENT

Webster (1992) states that marketing cannot be the sole responsibility of a few specialists and that everyone in the firm must be
charged with developing and contributing value to the customer.
Implicit here is the need to develop and nurture mechanisms for
bridging the gaps between firms and for managing effectively the
nexus between firms. Marketing linkages are one set of ties and are
often complemented with a series of cross-functional linkages.
Health care, airlines, telecommunications, and multimedia are only
a few of the industrial sectors in which alliances are the mechanism
through which value is being created in the marketplace. Academic
research is just now beginning to develop and employ paradigms and
tools to investigate these emerging organizational networks and
relationships. To be sure, work by Iacobucci (Iacobucci & Hopkins,
1992), Anderson (Anderson, Håkannson, & Johanson, 1994), and
others are laudable attempts to clarify research approaches and
techniques.

My colleagues and I at the Darden Graduate School of Business
(e.g., Spekman, Forbes, Isabella, & MacAvoy, in press) have been
engaged in a multiyear project funded by an international consortium of companies in which we attempted to understand better how
alliances develop over time and what are the requisite skills needed
to manage these relationships as they evolve. We have engaged in
both in-depth case studies of a small number of alliances and have
collected survey data on a set of 43 alliances. Although not marketing
focused per se, a number of these alliances were driven by market

and marketing-related factors. In all cases, our alliances were the product of the new competitive realities (see Best, 1990). Our primary focus is on the process of alliance management and how one manages close, cooperative relationship over time. To some degree, our work was influenced by Senge's (1992) view of the learning organization in which alliances and networks are mechanisms for facilitating the transfer and creation of knowledge aimed at gaining a competitive advantage. One of our key findings is the central role played by the alliance manager who sits at the nexus of the relationship and manages the interchange among partners. Thus, we take both a macro and a micro perspective to our analysis and extend the more traditional view of alliances to the importance of developing strategies for the implementation of a viable partnership. Our position is that many intelligent alliances fail because they were badly executed.

WHAT'S NEXT?

The new world order suggests that network-linked organizations are the emerging organization form. Terms such as virtual corporation are used to reflect these corporate entities. Ironically, scholars in entrepreneurship have examined networks for several years. They argue that for the small, emerging business such networks are an economic necessity (e.g., Larson, 1992). I believe that the work summarized here reflects a number of relationships described by Webster (1992). I have attempted to discuss briefly different streams of research that reflect a transition along Webster's continuum from transactions to long-term relationships to partnerships/alliances to networks.

It is almost passé to say that relationships are important. Equally as important is an understanding of the structures and processes by which those relationships can be nurtured and managed. For the marketer who develops alliance strategies to better meet the needs of his or her customers, it is essential that the relationship appear seamless. This is a nontrivial issue as the effort devoted to managing an alliance is considerable. We often do not acknowledge, or appreciate, the resource commitment that alliances demand. By focusing future attention on the management of alliances one understands quickly the importance of management time, personnel allocation, and other scarce resources. Because a network contains many more linkages the management challenges are significantly greater and require even more attention.

There are a number of unanswered questions suggested by the previous discussion. First, we need to question the implicit paradigm by which we discuss alliances. We tend to use marriage analogies and much extant research has used literature taken from work in interpersonal relationships. Thus, we have truncated a number of alliance relationships and have limited our inquiry to the dyad. Although many alliances are dyadic, there are many that extend to groups of firms joined together for mutually beneficial gains. It is here that the marriage analogy no longer applies. The question becomes what is the appropriate analogy? Is it the family, the extended family, the clan, or the tribe? The point is that our models must be adapted to accommodate the realities of more extensive relationships among firms. For example, we do not know whether the development of trust and commitment between husband and wife is similar to how trust and commitment develop in a clan, or a tribe.

Second, we need to question the methodological approaches used in network research. A great deal of network research has used methods that examine centrality, connectivity, and other measures that describe the structure of the network. Although such findings are useful, there are a number of important questions about the relationships among the constellation of firms that comprise the network that remain unanswered. For example, such information fails to provide insight into the level of trust within the network, how the network norms evolve, and how commitment to the network is nurtured and sustained. Borch and Arthur (1995) argue that networks consist of fine, delicate ties well hidden behind the material aspects of the exchange relationship. Two points should be noted here: (a) alliances comprise both a business relationship and an interpersonal relationship— both are important; and, (b) hard quantitative data might not fully describe the complexities of alliances and networks in particular. My colleagues and I have come to rely on surveys and case studies in our study of alliances and urge that greater insight can be gained from a multimethod approach to the study of multifirm alliances.

Third, we need to question what motivates our research. If we are driven by questions related to understanding the nature of alliances, I feel that this ground has been covered. There is more to be gained from research that asks questions related to the management of alliances. Despite the exponential growth of alliances in recent years, the landscape is littered with failures; the data suggest that as many as 60% of alliances fail (e.g., Bleeke & Ernst, 1993). It would appear that although academics purport to understand the concept of alliance formation, the practice of alliance management continues to pose a significant challenge. I believe that we can contribute to both theory and practice by focusing on alliance management problems.

As a final question, I would ask that greater attention be given to learning how alliances create and sustain knowledge. Quinn (1993) suggests that a firm's ability to learn faster than its rivals is ultimately a primary source of competitive advantage. An alliance is a journey; it is not the destination. The destination is how best to create an agile, effective learning organization. Alliances are a mechanism by which knowledge can be transmitted among partners. One problem is how to ensure that partners mutually achieve their learning objectives. A second problem is that partners learn at different rates. Such a differential might cause friction as one partner might gain competencies at a faster rate than another. Research is needed to assist managers in better understanding the complex interplay between cooperation and competition and how one can effectively manage this tension.

PART II

The Network Paradigm
Allows the Study of
Relational Phenomena

The "New Network Analysis" and Its Application to Organizational Theory and Behavior

JOSEPH GALASKIEWICZ

Researchers in a number of the social and behavioral sciences are now routinely using social network analysis to study behavior, and the field of organizational studies is no exception. Beginning with the Hawthorne Studies (Roethlisberger & Dickson, 1939) up through the present, students of formal organizations at both the micro and macro levels have used such concepts as density, connectivity, centrality, cohesion, and social distance in studying interorganizational relations, labor markets, intraorganizational conflict, morale, power, turnover, decision-making, job satisfaction, and a host of other topics.

The purpose of this chapter is not to provide an overview of the organizational research done from a social networks perspective (for reviews of the networks and organizations literature, see Knoke & Guilarte, 1994; Nohria, 1992; Powell & Smith-Doerr, 1994), but to highlight three changes in the field. I will argue that these changes have helped to differentiate a "new" form of network analysis from more traditional approaches. To summarize, there was a shift from detailed formal descriptions of network structures to testing substantive theory using network variables on both the right- and left-hand sides of the equation. There was a move away from looking at networks as constraints on action and determinants of behavior to viewing them as opportunity structures that actors can use to further their own self interest in a variety of ways. Finally, researchers have begun to look at network organizations, that is, purposeful efforts to use networks to accomplish organizational goals. Previous work framed social networks as "informal social structures" that operated "in the shadow" of formal bureaucratic structures. Now networks are looked at as alternative governance structures.

NETWORK ANALYSIS:
THE BASICS

The appeal of network analysis lies in its focus on relational systems as opposed to individual actors. Granovetter (1985) argued that both rational choice theory and structural functionalism portrayed social actors as autonomous, independent, and solitary. The only difference was that the former saw social actors as active, strategic, self-serving, and "undersocialized"; whereas the latter portrayed social actors as passive, adaptive, manipulated, and "oversocialized." Actors' relationships with others (e.g., friends, neighbors, family, workmates, superiors, and acquaintances) were incidental and supposedly inconsequential (Galaskiewicz & Wasserman, 1993, p. 5).

In contrast, network analysis begins with the assumption that actors, whether they be natural persons or corporate actors, are embedded in a myriad of social relationships, and it is impossible to understand their behavior without understanding the relational context in which they function (Granovetter, 1985). Furthermore, we assume that actors and their actions are interdependent rather than independent, the relationships that actors have with others are channels or conduits through which resources flow, and an actor's position in these networks defines both the opportunities and limits on its subsequent action (Wasserman & Faust, 1994, p. 4). Thus network analysis studies not only actors and their behaviors but also their relationships to other actors. This brand of network analysis has been very popular, because studying, for example, the correlates of actor centrality or homophily within dyads dovetails nicely with more traditional approaches in the social and behavioral sciences which have individuals or isolated pairs of individuals as the units of analysis.

Network analysis, however, has another dimension. It describes and analyzes the configuration of nodes and relationships that constitute the structure of the network. It assumes that social relationships are perduring, lasting, and can be aggregated into something that is more than the sum of the parts. In other words, one can take the social relationships established at the dyadic level and aggregate them into something that is a meaningful social fact worthy of study in its own right. This is not a trivial assumption and in fact quite controversial. It presumes that some social entity can exist without the actors who are part of that entity agreeing on its boundaries, recognizing it as a meaningful reality, or even realizing that the entity exists. Yet network analysts often argue that this makes network analysis all the more appealing. Through the manipulation of relational data and the application of mathematical formulae, analysts can see or discover social realities that are unrecognizable to those who are embedded within them.

From the very beginning to the current period, researchers have studied actors, dyads, and the structure of networks. This is true for the field as a whole as well as for organizational researchers. This has not changed, nor do we expect it to. Studying all three levels is part of doing network analysis, and, of course, studying their interrelationship is part of the agenda as well.

FORMAL DESCRIPTIVE NETWORK ANALYSIS VERSUS MODEL BUILDING AND HYPOTHESIS TESTING

The first change is the shift away from research that applied formal mathematical models to network data to research that operationalizes network variables for inclusion in substantive models and hypothesis testing.

The Formal Network Approach

Equipped with a toolbox of sophisticated methods, organizational sociologists and social psychologists in the mid-1970s endeavored to map the networks of ties within and among organizations. These efforts, which we will label the formal network approach, provided rich, detailed, and provocative descriptions of the structure and differentiation within networks using quantitative methods adopted from graph theory (Harary, Norman, & Cartwright, 1965), psychometrics (e.g., multidimensional scaling), and later formal algebra (White, Boorman, & Brieger, 1976).

Mizruchi and Galaskiewicz (1994, p. 233) distinguished between studies that applied "relational techniques" and "positional techniques." Examples of the former included Levine's (1972) spherical mapping of broad interlocking ties among U.S. firms using multidimensional scaling, Sonquist and Koenig's (1975) analysis of the interlocks among large U.S. firms using graph theoretical techniques, and Laumann and Pappi's (1976) mapping of overlapping memberships among organizations using smallest-space analysis. Research using positional methods (e.g., blockmodeling) included Allen's (1978) factor analysis of interlocking directorates among firms, Knoke and Rogers's (1979) blockmodel analysis of public and private agencies, and Knoke and Wood's (1981) blockmodel analyses of networks of money, information, and support among social influence organizations. The agenda was to identify the formal properties of networks, ignoring the content and substantive context, and to look for similar patterns across different networks.

Model Building and Hypothesis Testing

Although this literature produced a number of interesting findings, it was apparent that the field would not be content with simply describing networks; researchers wanted to know "so what?" (Laumann, Galaskiewicz, & Marsden, 1978). In response, analysts turned to the literature on interpersonal relations and small groups and addressed the "so what" question by generating and testing hypotheses using network variables. One popular strategy was to identify actors' formal position in networks (usually centrality) and correlate this with a litany of outcome variables. This was a common practice both in the interorganizational literature (e.g., Boje & Whetten, 1981; Galaskiewicz, 1979; Knoke, 1983; Laumann & Knoke, 1987; Laumann & Pappi, 1976) as well as the intraorganizational literature (e.g., Brass, 1984; Brass & Burkhardt, 1992, 1993; Burkhardt & Brass, 1990; Fombrun, 1983; Tushman & Romanelli, 1983). Studying homophily in dyads and the effects of social proximity on subsequent behavior also became fashionable. For example, researchers looked at proximity in networks and the subsequent formation of coalitions (Laumann & Pappi, 1976; Thurman, 1979). Cook's (1977) often cited article on power dependence, interorganizational relationships, and network centrality illustrates nicely how much this literature was influenced by small groups research, power theories, and social exchange theorists like Emerson (1962) and Blau (1964).

By the late 1970s the agenda shifted slightly, and organizational theorists were beginning to incorporate network or relational variables into their own theories. For example, network ideas and relational analysis were central in Pfeffer and Salancik's (1978) formulation of resource dependency theory and in their empirical work, for example, Pfeffer and Salancik's (1974) study of university budget making and Pfeffer and Leong's (1977) study of resource allocation to United Fund agencies. Burt's (1983) *Corporate Profits and Cooptation* was another example of how network ideas could be used to test hypotheses derived from resource dependency theory.

Other theories followed suit. In DiMaggio and Powell's (1983) classic statement on institutional theory, network imagery and relational ideas were prominent but again were used by the theory for its own purpose, that is, to explain isomorphism in organizational fields. Researchers testing transaction cost theory conceptualized the make-or-buy decision in relational terms and used relational data to test the theory's central hypotheses (e.g., Noordewier, John, & Nevin, 1990). Political sociologists studied the role of social networks among organized interest groups in terms of collective action theory (Laumann & Knoke, 1987; Laumann & Pappi, 1976). The same trend was happening in micro-organizational behavior. For example, Krackhardt and Brass (1994) show how equity theory, the job design literature, the social information processing model, and the leader-exchange model have or could benefit from adopting a relational or network perspective.

Although used to answer theoretically driven questions, network analysis was used almost exclusively as a metatheory, that is, a sensitizing paradigm that alerted researchers to the importance of social relations in explaining individual and organizational behavior, and a methodology, that is, a set of quantitative measures to describe actors' positions in these networks and the networks themselves. It clearly was not a theory that *explained* what happened within and between organizations (see Salancik, 1995). This is not surprising, because network analysts, with a few notable exceptions, were slow to develop models that had any explanatory power. When they did try to explain their findings, they turned to existing theories, for example, exchange theory, resource dependency theory, collective action theory, or transaction cost analysis, but once they did, they surrendered the high ground and soon network analysis became the handmaiden of organizational theory instead of its master.

NETWORKS OF CONSTRAINT
VERSUS NETWORKS OF ENABLEMENT

A second change was a shift away from viewing networks as constraints on action, behavior, or both to viewing networks as opportunity structures that can enable social actors to realize their own interests.

Networks of Constraint

When researchers began to tackle the "so what" question, they often found themselves answering this question by testing models and showing results that demonstrated that the behaviors of actors who were embedded in social networks were constrained or even determined by network position (Nohria, 1992, p. 6). For example, this line of argument was standard in the resource dependency literature. Burt (1983) argued that the industry in which a firm was embedded was itself embedded in a larger network of inputs and outputs. Some firms had less autonomy than others by virtue of their industry's dependency on other business sectors for inputs and sales and the degree to which these other sectors were organized. He showed that firms that were vulnerable responded by engaging in different interorganizational strategies, for example, acquisitions, interlocking directorates, and so on. The assumption was that firms were all profit maximizers who were equally risk averse, saw and defined the situation from their position in the network, and would do what was necessary to overcome their vulnerability.

The social influence (or contagion) models also took this approach. The received wisdom argued that firms in direct contact with each other would influence each other's behavior and that ideas, technologies, and practices would diffuse throughout organizational fields through direct contacts (Galaskiewicz & Wasserman, 1989). Burt (1987) challenged this argument and posited that organizational players would mimic those who are their structural equivalents. To maintain their status or reputation in organizational fields, firms will imitate their competitors. Studies showed that direct contact or structural position affected dyads' likelihood of quitting a job (Krackhardt & Porter, 1986), scheduling job interviews with the same firms (Kilduff, 1990), interpreting organizational events similarly (Rentsch, 1990), evaluating nonprofit organizations seeking corporate contributions the same (Galaskiewicz, 1985b; Galaskiewicz & Burt, 1991), and making PAC contributions to the same candidates (Mizruchi, 1992).

Both of these examples depict the social actor, whether it be an individual or organization, in a passive role surrounded by all these social relationships that are influencing its behavior. It may respond in one way or another, but the reason for its response is found in the social structure in which it is embedded and not in the initiatives of players in the network.

Networks of Enablement

Analysts are now beginning to look at networks not as constraints but as opportunity structures. Coleman (1988) and Granovetter (1985) have argued that social networks should be viewed as a kind of social capital that ego can use to further its own interests. For example, an actor's weak ties (i.e., casual acquaintances) can be an important source of information on possible jobs (Granovetter, 1995). An individual's chances of securing a more attractive job depends on the information that his contacts have on the job market. Although ego's strong ties were likely to have the same information as ego on the environment, his or her weak ties should have information that ego typically does not have access to. Thus the more weak ties in ego's personal network, the more new information ego has; and the more information ego has, the more likely ego will achieve his or her goals (see Granovetter, 1995 for a review of the research on this topic). Burt (1992) extended this argument in his discussion of structural holes. He argued and showed how being linked to disconnected others gives ego a strategic advantage as ego is in a position to bridge or negotiate

discourse between disparate and disconnected actors/cliques. Structural holes are then good for ego if he can provide the linkage that
fills the hole; whereas they are bad for ego if ego is the one disconnected from others and dependent on others to bridge the gap.

Family ties and strong ties can also be useful in finding out who is
trustworthy and this can be important in overcoming the problem of
opportunism in market settings (Granovetter, 1985; Powell, 1990).
As described by Galaskiewicz and Wasserman (1993),

> Social networks provide detailed, rich information on others. Not only
> does recurring interaction provide information on your friends, work-
> mates, neighbors, and family, and some idea about how they will behave
> in the future, but your friends, workmates, neighbors, and family can
> testify on behavior of others in your network as well as others outside
> your network. They can tell you who to trust and who to distrust.
> Granovetter argues that networks give information on how some alter
> might treat a particular ego; he is less interested in information on
> alter's general reputation. Still, to the extent that alter's prospective
> "partners" are in close social proximity, ego can have confidence that
> alter will continue to behave as it has in the past, so as to insure the
> integrity of its reputation as a trustworthy player. (pp. 13-14)

Although empirical work is scant, some interesting studies have
been done. For example, Stearns and Mizruchi (1993) showed that
firms will choose debt financing that is consistent with the type of
financial institution represented on its board, Kilduff and Krackhardt
(1994) discussed the way actors can enhance their reputations by
strategically choosing their network contacts, and Baker (1990) described the way that corporations directly manipulate the number
and intensity of market ties to pursue the objectives of independence,
uncertainty reduction, and efficiency.

INFORMAL SOCIAL STRUCTURE
VERSUS THE NETWORK ORGANIZATION

Perhaps the biggest change in the organizational field over the
past 15 years is the shift away from studying social networks as
informal social structures to studying social networks as a governance
structure that is a legitimate alternative to bureaucratic hierarchies.

Networks as Informal Social Structures

Organizational research has long recognized that there is an informal network or social structure within organizations that functions in the shadows of the formal division of labor and hierarchy of control (Bacharach & Lawler, 1980; Mintzberg, 1983). This network is marked by face-to-face contacts between individuals who find one another attractive for one reason or another. The content of the relationship varies. Actors may be seeking advice, giving advice, or both; exchanging technical information; exchanging gossip about others in the organization; making loans/collecting interest; giving or receiving moral support in a time of crisis; sharing affections; or sharing secrets. The bond between these actors is particular to the dyad, the relationship between these actors persists as long as the actors find it advantageous, and there are few if any legal recourses to enforce promises made by parties to the relationship. This informal relationship becomes a network when the parties involved give each other access to their other friends and acquaintances. At times, these networks can harden into cliques or coalitions.

Most organizational scholars depicted these informal structures as either subverting bureaucratic goals or furthering private agendas at the expense of the larger collective good. Some thought this was bad; others thought it was good. Roethlisberger and Dickson (1939) concluded that the informal network among workers at the Hawthorne plant was a hindrance to productivity, whereas Gouldner (1954) saw these informal structures as a way for workers to resist managerial dictates. Researchers found such deviant forms of social organization interesting, because they challenged the conventional wisdom that both internally and in relations with others in their environment, organizations behaved and were structured rationally, oriented toward the attainment of stated collective goals. Yet Powell and Smith-Doerr (1994) argue that more often than not the formal and informal structures shaped and complemented one another as much as they subverted the other's purpose.

Researchers have continued to find that informal structures are very important in explaining how work actually gets done. As noted by Powell and Smith-Doerr (1994, p. 380), "Industries as diverse as construction, book publishing, architecture, the diamond trade, and the film industry rely, to a very considerable extent, on stable and enduring personal networks, based on loyalties and friendships, cemented over time." Within organizations, project-based work depends on workers' ability to build and operationalize social networks, mobility within internal labor markets is a function of informal ties between super and subordinates, and the quick concentration of the right knowledge or information at the right time and place requires that organizational players have extensive network ties.

Network Organizations

The network organization (sometimes called the virtual organization in the popular press) is now being viewed as a legitimate alternative to the traditional hierarchy (see Granovetter, 1985; Powell, 1990). Nohria (1992, p. 2) argues that one of the reasons why management theory is so interested in networks today is because of the emergence of what he called "the New Competition." To quote,

> This (refers to) the competitive rise over the last two decades of small entrepreneurial firms, of regional districts such as Silicon Valley in California and Prato and Modena in Italy, of new industries such as computers and biotechnology, and of Asian economies such as those of Japan, Korea, and Taiwan. . . . If the old model of organization was the large hierarchical firm, the model of organization that is considered characteristic of the New Competition is a network of lateral and horizontal interlinkages within and among firms.

Baker (1992) gives the essential elements of this new form: "an organization *integrated* across formal groups created by vertical, horizontal, and spatial differentiation for any type of relation." Ibarra (1992, p. 169) defines it "as characterized by lateral or horizontal patterns of exchange, interdependent flows of resources, and reciprocal lines of communication." At the macro level the image of an organizational field (DiMaggio & Powell, 1983) is an attractive one. At the center is a relatively small organization structured in a unitary manner with minimal layers of hierarchy specializing in a given product or service. This organization has a set of relationships with a cluster of suppliers that is long term and mostly (but not completely) exclusive, a set of customers that is also long term and even intimate, and investors who have a long-term commitment to the management of the firm. Relationships with competitors is not cut-throat or zero sum, but rather there is a friendly, even cooperative atmosphere where personnel and information flow back and forth freely among competitors. Powell (1990, p. 302) characterizes relationships as indefinite, governed by norms, mutually supportive, trustworthy; the relationship is valued in and of itself, debts and obligations tend to be long term, resources are pooled, and players are oriented toward achieving mutually desirable goals.

Although network forms of organization were quite common in premodern economies and were popular in the delivery of public services in the 1960s and 1970s (see Mulford, 1984; Rogers & Whetten, 1982), network forms of economic organization are just catching on. The appeal of these organizations lies in their greater flexibility and adaptability and their capacity to circulate know-how or tacit knowledge (Powell, 1990). Powell and Brantley (1992) see them as facilitating organizational learning. A combination of small size and ample technology to facilitate communication and coordination make these organizations, to use Powell's (1990, p. 303) colorful imagery, "lighter on their feet" than traditional hierarchies.

Research on these new organizational forms is also scant, but some observers have already noted some problems. Often entrepreneurs in the West who adopt the network form selectively mimic their neighbors in the Far East and southern Europe. For instance, often flexibility is achieved by outsourcing services and even production, firing middle managers and decentralizing authority, hiring temporary workers or paying minimum wage and benefits, being antiunion, and subjecting workers to arbitrary rule making by throwing out standard operating procedures (Clegg, 1990). Relations to other firms in the network may be cozy and comfortable, but relations to workers are tense and hostile.

Also, it is not clear how much of the network organization is emergent or prescribed (Ibarra, 1992, p. 167). This is a crucial question, because once a network is planned and implemented from above, there always is the threat that actors will create their own network, which may work better for them although not necessarily for the firm or its partners. Thus one ends up with two networks: the official one and the shadow network existing alongside. To truly create a network organization, there has to be a continual adjustment of the formal configuration of roles and procedures to actual patterns of interaction (Ibarra, 1992, p. 167). This asks a great deal of management, because the structure of the network organization has to mirror the initiatives of those who are engaged in production, sales, R&D, purchasing, and so forth, not necessarily the outlines of strategic plans.

PROSPECTS FOR THE FUTURE

What can we expect in the near future? Where are networks and organizations going to be in the next 5 years? We can only speculate, but there are a few glaring holes in the literature that need to be filled.

Researchers have to begin to take change seriously. In his provocative essay, Salancik (1995) accuses network researchers of paying too much attention to the structure of ties as is and not enough attention to why a network looks like it does, why it changes, and why it does not. Almost every network study in the organizational literature is a snapshot of a relational field at one point in time. In almost every study the network is taken as a kind of social fact that has a persisting or perduring quality about it. Although there is some evidence that networks do not change (e.g., Burt, 1988) and that broken ties are replaced (Palmer, Friedland, & Singh, 1986), analysts should not take comfort in these studies. The phenomena they are studying are vulnerable to change. Not only is the population constantly changing, but the relationships among actors can also change. Econometric models, event history analysis and panel studies in sociology, and cohort analysis in demography put the field of network analysis to shame. Compared to the other social sciences and subfields within sociology, dynamic modeling of social networks lags far behind.

Network analysts must be ready to take into account the larger context in which social networks are embedded. Powell's (1990) descriptions of various network organizations caught everyone's attention, because he drew on the social, political, economic, and cultural context to help us understand why these network organizations were so successful. Works by Warren, Rose, and Bergunder (1974) on social delivery systems, Alford (1975) on health care delivery systems, Gerlach (1992) on business networks in Japan, and Gereffi (1994) on global commodity chains have done the same. Clearly this means that researchers need to refamiliarize themselves with qualitative methods and methods for comparative research. Given the complexity of contemporary organizational life, any network analysis that ignores the "big picture" will provide only partial explanations.

CHAPTER 4

Social Contagion and Social Structure

RONALD S. BURT

GREGORY A. JANICIK

It is widely understood that social contagion, the process by which a person catches an idea or behavior from another person, is a function of social structure. Network measures of cohesion and structural equivalence operationalize the two social structural conditions in which ideas and behaviors are contagious. Both conditions are circumstances in which people are expected to see themselves as socially similar, and so believe that they should find value in the same ideas and behaviors. By cohesion, contagion occurs between people in the same primary group in the sense that the recipient has a strong relationship with the source. By structural equivalence, contagion occurs between competitors in the sense that recipient and source are defined by the same pattern of relations with friends, clients, and enemies. This chapter is not the place to belabor the distinction between cohesion and structural equivalence. That is done elsewhere (Burt, 1982, Chap. 5; Burt, 1987), and evidence of contagion by cohesion versus structural equivalence is debated in articles by diverse authors.

Our purpose in this brief chapter is to argue that social contagion processes, via cohesion or structural equivalence, are contingent on the broader social structure in which they occur. More complex social structures obscure the social frame of reference responsible for contagion. As relational complexities allow for individuals to become more structurally unique, the need to compare and resolve differ-

32

ences from others' ideas and behaviors becomes less important. Hence, where it is difficult to answer the question "Who is like me?" social contagion effects are restricted.

The chapter is in four parts. We describe contagion in three social systems; a system of corporate officers, a system of lobbyists, and a system of doctors. We conclude by describing how the strength of contagion in the three systems covaries with the relative complexity of their social structures. For the purposes here, we defer to other publications for discussion of statistical issues and technical details of the network theory.

INTERORGANIZATION CONTAGION

We begin with a moderately complex social structure. The study population is corporate philanthropy officers in large corporations in the twin cities of Minneapolis and St. Paul around 1980. The study population is described in Galaskiewicz (1985a, and a follow-up survey is described in Galaskiewicz, 1995). Galaskiewicz and Burt (1991) analyze the relative importance of cohesion and structural equivalence for contagion processes among the officers. Figure 4.1 is a summary of social structure and contagion among the officers.

The Social Structure of Corporate Officers

Social structure is based on sociometric citations among 61 officers. Interviewed officers were presented with a list of all publicly held companies in the Twin Cities area and asked to "check off those firms in which you know personally individuals involved in corporate contributions, that is, on a first-name basis, would feel comfortable calling for lunch or drinks after work, and so on." Their responses define a (61 by 61) choice matrix. The bar graph in Figure 4.1 shows close connections between the officers (16% direct citations, and another 33% indirect connections through one intermediary) while also displaying the existence of distinct groups among the officers (there is no chain of intermediaries that connects 34% of the officer pairs).

Routine structural equivalence analysis reveals a center-periphery structure; a social hierarchy stratified across six positions. Relations

60 corporate philanthropy officers in a hierarchical center-periphery contact structure evaluating the merits of specific donee organizations (3.0 perception exponent v; .33 mean structural uniqueness ω_{ii})

29%	contagion variance (28.1% SE, 0.9% Coh)
17%	additional for personal differences
6%	additional for contagion slope adjustments
48%	residual variance

Y	1.00		
SE	0.54	1.00	
Coh	0.22	0.34	1.00

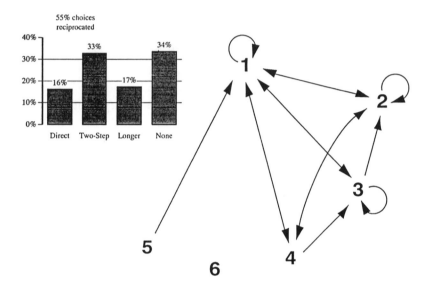

Figure 4.1. Interorganization Contagion

within and between positions are summarized in the sociogram in Figure 4.1.[1] Numbers identify sets of structurally equivalent officers, and arrows indicate choice densities greater than average. Officers at the top of the hierarchy, Position 1, have strong contacts with one another and dense contacts with other positions. All individuals in Position 1 are officers in the largest firms. All but two of these firms have their headquarters in Minneapolis or its suburbs. The officers in Positions 2, 3, and 4 form a hierarchy of decreasingly prominent positions below the top position. Positions are linked to geographic boundaries. Officers in Positions 2 and 4 are principally affiliated with firms headquartered in Minneapolis and its suburbs. Officers in Position 3 are all affiliated with firms headquartered in St. Paul and its suburbs. There are two positions at the bottom of the hierarchy. Position 5 is a satellite to the most prominent officers. Officers in Position 5 have little contact with one another, but claim to have contacts with the officers at the top of the hierarchy, in Position 1. Contact with other positions is minimal. These officers, with only one exception, are all affiliated with a small firm. Finally, there is an isolate position—officers in Position 6 have no contact with one another and little or no contact with officers in other positions. They are a heterogeneous group, drawn from large and small firms, some headquartered in St. Paul and some in Minneapolis.

Contagious Evaluations

The criterion variable is officer opinion of specific nonprofit organizations in the Twin Cities area. Selecting which of these organizations receives corporate gifts is the central business of the officers. Here, officers are compared by the extent to which they have similar opinions of the 10 nonprofit organizations given the most variable ratings by the population of officers. Sixty of the officers provided opinion data. Four of the criterion nonprofits are cultural services organizations (Twin Cities Public Television, Minnesota Public Radio, the Minnesota Orchestral Association, and Film in the Cities). The other six are health and welfare organizations (the Fairview Community Hospitals, the Harriet Tubman Women's Shelter, the Wilder Foundation, the Opportunity Workshop, the Sabathani Community Center, and St. Mary's Rehabilitation Center).

Contagion is measured by correlating each officer's opinion (Y) with the average opinion of the officer's peers and contacts. Officer opinion is correlated .22 in Figure 4.1 with the average opinion of the officer's contacts. Ties identified by the officers are vehicles for contagion via cohesion (Coh, for cohesion); $Coh = \Sigma_j\, y_j w_{ij}$, where y_j is contact j's opinion, and w_{ij} is a proportional weight measuring i's closeness to j. Following Galaskiewicz's original analysis, cohesion weight w_{ij} is $1/N$ when i and j cite each other (where N is the number of officers with whom i has reciprocal citations), and 0 otherwise. Alternative measures computed from path distances, or with weaker criteria for a tie between officers, yield similar results (Galaskiewicz & Burt, 1991).

Officer opinion is correlated .54 in Figure 4.1 with the average opinion of structural peers (SE, for structural equivalence); SE = $\Sigma_j \, y_j w_{ij}$, where w_{ij} is an equivalence weight. Two officers are structurally equivalent to the extent that they have identical relation patterns—they are directly connected to the same other contributions personnel, through these connections they reach the same other firms with which they do not have direct contact, and they are themselves directly and indirectly cited by contributions officers in the same other firms. Equivalence weight w_{ij} is based on a substitutability weight ω_{ij} that varies from zero to one measuring i's relative structural equivalence to j (detailed discussion of equivalence and substitutability weights is available elsewhere, Burt, 1982; Burt, 1987); $\omega_{ij} = \text{(i-j equivalence)}^v \, / \, [\Sigma_q \, \text{(i-q equivalence)}^v]$, where equivalence is measured with Euclidean distance.[2] Two elements in this equation describe the complexity of social structure and will be useful at the end of the chapter when we draw comparisons across the three study populations: (a) The exponent v, taken from Stevens power function in psychophysics, increases with the extent to which contagion only occurs between the most structurally equivalent people. In psychological terms, a higher value of v reduces the pressure for interpersonal comparisons. Integer values of the exponent are searched automatically by the software used to compute the equivalence weights. The value of 3.0 in Figure 4.1 for the perception exponent indicates a moderately complex social structure. (b) The self-weight, ω_{ii}, measures the extent to which officer i's pattern of relations is structurally unique within the study population. As ω_{ii} approaches its maximum value of 1.0, officer i's substitutability, ω_{ij}, with other officers j approaches zero, meaning that officer i has no structural peer in the study population. The .33 mean value of ω_{ii} in Figure 4.1 is about average. It is higher than the lobbyists in the next section, and lower than the doctors in the subsequent section. Equivalence weight w_{ij}, used to define the average opinion of officer i's structural peers, is the substitutability weight ω_{ij} adjusted up to exclude i from his social frame of reference; $w_{ij} = \omega_{ij} / (1 - \omega_{ii})$.

The correlation matrix among the three variables is given in Figure 4.1. Of the variance in manager opinion, 29% can be predicted from the average opinion of the manager's contacts and peers.

This is the white area in the variance pie chart at the top of Figure 4.1. Structural equivalence is the dominant effect (28% of the variance can be attributed to structural equivalence, versus 0.9% for cohesion). There are significant differences between the officers. They come from different industries, different firms, different roles within their firms, and different personal backgrounds. An additional 17% of the opinion variance can be predicted with variables distinguishing officers, and another 6% is gained with analysis of covariance adjustments for stronger contagion effects among certain officers. These are the two gray areas in the variance pie chart. That leaves 48% unexplained variance in officer opinion, indicated by the dark area in the variance pie chart.[3] The summary conclusion is that officer evaluations are strongly affected by social contagion, and the contagion is between structurally equivalent peers.

CONTAGION IN POLITICS

Now consider a relatively simple social structure. Heinz, Laumann, Nelson, and Salisbury (1993) describe the social system of elite lobbyists active in U.S. government policy in the areas of agriculture, energy, health, and labor during the early 1980s. Among the elite lobbyists are a few that Heinz et al. (1993, Chap. 10) describe as "notables" because of their special prominence as representatives. The 63 notables are the study population here. For our purposes, we drop the "notable" qualifier to discuss the policy representatives as simply lobbyists. Figure 4.2 is a summary of the contagion effects within this social structure.

The Social Structure of Lobbyists

Social structure is once again based on sociometric citations. Presented with a roster of the study population, each lobbyist was asked to indicate potential sources of support: "Please place a check by the names of people you know well enough to be confident that they would take the trouble to assist you briefly (and without a fee) if you requested it." The bar graph in Figure 4.2 shows closer connections between the lobbyists than between the corporate officers in the preceding section. The density of direct connections is similar

63 elite lobbyists expressing their economic ideology in evaluating policy opinions in a center-periphery political support structure of cliques (1.0 perception exponent v; .09 mean structural uniqueness ω_{ii})

     53%   contagion variance (50.1% SE, 3.3% Coh)
     21%   additional for personal differences
     5%   additional for contagion slope adjustments
     21%   residual variance

	Y	SE	Coh
Y	1.00		
SE	0.73	1.00	
Coh	0.66	0.89	1.00

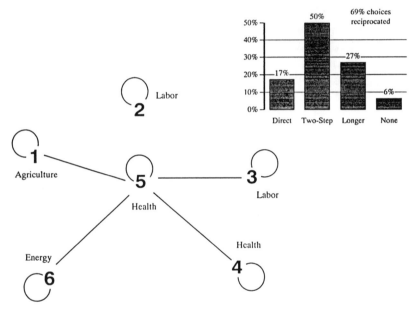

Figure 4.2. Contagion in Politics

(17%, vs. 16% in Figure 4.1), but the lobbyists are much more often friends-of-friends (50% indirect connections through one intermediary, vs. 33% in Figure 4.1), and very few pairs of lobbyists have no chain of intermediaries through whom they are connected to one another (6% of the lobbyist pairs in Figure 4.2, 34% of the officer pairs in Figure 4.1).

The high number of indirect connections through one intermediary suggests that the population has a center-periphery structure in which members are connected indirectly through shared relations with central leaders. The structure displayed in the Figure 4.2 so-ciogram is a simple star-shaped center-periphery pattern—five cliques distributed around a center position. The results are from a routine structural equivalence analysis (see Note 1). Numbers identify sets of structurally equivalent lobbyists, and arrows indicate where the den-sity of sociometric choices is above average. The generic rule in this structure is for individuals in a position to expect support from other people in the same position, as well as the central position. The one exception is Position 2, occupied by individuals who do not have direct access to the central position.

The positions are linked to policy domains. All 14 of the agricul-ture lobbyists occupy Position 1. The 15 energy lobbyists occupy Position 6. Positions 2 and 3 contain all but one of the labor lobbyists, with Position 2 containing the less influential players (less influential in the sense of not having direct access to the central position and in the sense of having an asymmetric acquaintance tie to Position 3). Positions 4 and 5 contain all but one of the health lobbyists, with Position 4 containing the less influential players (less influential in the sense of not being as widely connected to other policy domains).

The four lobbyists in Position 5 operate at the center of the population. They have support contacts in all four policy domains. They come from the health policy domain, but their interests and contacts spill over into the other domains. It is interesting to note that the four lobbyists are all lawyers who represent the interests of the Affiliated Food Producers, the American School Food Service Association, the California and Hawaii Sugar Companies, Farmland Industries, Land O'Lakes, the National Milk Producers's Federation, and the United Mine Workers. The boundary around them is nicely illustrated by considering an expansion of Position 5 to include the lobbyist most equivalent to them as a potential fifth member of the central position. That next person is another health lobbyist, the only person outside the agricultural domain who occupies Position 1. Examining measures of overall equivalence within a position, one discovers that the health lobbyist is much more equivalent to his colleagues in Position 1 than anyone in the central Position 5 (equiva-lence reliabilities of .79 vs. .49).

The four lobbyists in Position 5 are not the only intermediaries that hold the other positions together. Heinz et al. (1993) emphasize the strength of ties between lobbyists in adjacent policy areas as crucial, rather than ties through the central people (thus the "hollow core"). There are 1,711 pairs of lobbyists not in Position 5. The average path distance between these 1,711 other pairs through support contacts is 1.95 if the four Position 5 lobbyists are included in the network. The average path distance is almost unchanged (2.00) if the four are excluded from the network. In other words, the lobbyists are separated by a single intermediary whether or not the four central people in Position 5 are available to connect them.

Contagious Economic Ideology

The criterion variable is lobbyist opinion on national policy. Each lobbyist was asked to express on a scale from 1 to 5 his or her level of agreement with eight opinion items concerning government policy. The lobbyists share some beliefs. They agree that Americans should have equal access to quality medical care regardless of ability to pay. Reflecting their own positions and the interests they represent, they share a disbelief in the need to reduce income differences between occupations. We are more interested in ideas on which they disagree. The lobbyists have diverse beliefs regarding government regulation on behalf of consumers. They vary widely in their views on whether profits and power are too concentrated, and the extent to which labor unions are a benefit to the country. Still, lobbyist opinion is sufficiently correlated across items to construct a meaningful measure by averaging responses across the eight items. We have taken the average from Heinz et al. (1993), and following their analysis, we refer to the average as a measure of lobbyist "economic ideology." The measure distinguishes lobbyists on an ideological continuum ranging from extreme conservative to welfare-state liberal.

Contagion is again measured by correlating each lobbyist's ideology (Y) with the average ideology of supporters (Coh), and structural peers (SE), where Coh and SE are weighted averages computed as described earlier.[4] The perception exponent v is only 1 in this population, indicating clearer social distinctions between the lobbyists (relative to the corporate officers in the preceding section where the exponent is 3). The .09 mean substitutability weight ω_{ii} shows that the lobbyists have numerous structural peers; 91% of the average lobbyist's network position is shared with other lobbyists (vs. 67% for the average corporate officer in Figure 4.1). Therefore, it is much easier for the lobbyists to recognize with whom they should agree to bolster political support for an initiative.

The correlation matrix in Figure 4.2 shows strong evidence of contagion by cohesion and structural equivalence. The two variables combine to describe 53% of the variance in lobbyist opinion, the white area in the variance pie chart. Personal differences between the lobbyists matter about as much as they did for the corporate officers. With the stronger contagion effect, all but 21% of the variance in lobbyist ideology is explained.[5]

Structural equivalence is the stronger of the two contagion effects (50% of ideology variance can be attributed to structural equivalence, vs. 3.3% for cohesion), but it is difficult to partition the contagion variance in this population. This is the kind of social structure in which cohesion and structural equivalence make similar predictions (Burt, 1987). The lobbyists are organized in terms of nonoverlapping cliques. The people in each clique are both cohesive (have strong relations with each other) and structurally equivalent (have similarly strong relations within the clique and similarly weak relations outside the clique). The result is that a lobbyist's supporters are often structural peers, so it is difficult to distinguish evidence of structural equivalence contagion from evidence of cohesion contagion. The correlation between Coh and SE in Figure 4.2 is higher than either variable's correlation with the criterion variable (.89 vs. .73 and .66). The collinearity makes it difficult to separate cohesion from the structural equivalence effect. The most reliable conclusion is to say that social contagion has a strong effect on lobbyist economic ideology, and that cohesion and structural equivalence reinforce one another as the network conditions responsible for the contagion.

CONTAGION IN MEDICINE

Last, consider a relatively complex social structure. The study population is doctors in four Illinois cities, in the mid-1950s, deciding when to begin prescribing a new antibiotic. The cities are Bloomington, Galesburg, Peoria, and Quincy. The new antibiotic is tetracycline. These are the doctors described in Coleman, Katz, and Menzel's (1966) classic study of contagion, *Medical Innovation*. The data were also reanalyzed to compare the roles of cohesion and structural

125 internists, pediatricians and general practitioners in a complex advice and discussion structure making a decision to prescribe a new drug (9.8 mean perception exponent v; .84 mean structural uniqueness ω_{ii})

14%   contagion variance (13.6% SE, 0.1% Coh)
26%   additional for personal differences
2%   additional for contagion slope adjustments
58%   residual variance

	Y		
Y	1.00		
SE	0.35	1.00	
Coh	-.01	0.31	1.00

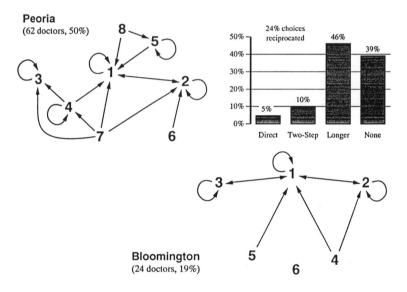

Figure 4.3. Contagion in Medicine

equivalence in the structural conditions responsible for contagion (Burt, 1987; Burt & Uchiyama, 1989). This is a well-known study, and the cohesion and structural equivalence contagion effects are described elsewhere in detail, so we can be brief. Figure 4.3 is a summary of social structure and contagion among the doctors.

The Social Structure of Doctors

Social structure is based on two kinds of sociometric citations among the doctors, advice and discussion. Doctors were asked to identify names of advisers: "When you need information or advice about questions of therapy, where do you usually turn?" They were also asked to identify discussion partners: "And who are the three or four physicians with whom you most often find yourself discussing cases or therapy in the course of an ordinary week—last week for instance?" Their responses define a (240 by 240) matrix of sociometric choices where a 1 indicates that the row doctor cited the column doctor as an adviser or discussion partner. Embedded in the large network are 125 physicians whose tetracycline prescription behavior is to be explained. These physicians are referred to as the "prescription sample." There are no citations between cities, so the large matrix can be analyzed in four sections, one for each of the four study cities.

The doctors lived in a complex social structure. The complexity is apparent from the connections between individuals, and the aggregate structure of their relations. The bar graph in Figure 4.3 shows that the doctors are not close. Only 5% of the doctor pairs are directly connected, and another 10% are connected indirectly through one intermediary. The average physician is connected either directly or indirectly with the majority of other physicians in his city; however, that connection is typically through multiple intermediaries. Many doctors are not connected at all, with 39% of the doctor pairs having no chain of intermediaries through whom they are connected. The network image portrayed is one of communities held together by strands of asymmetric professional relations through one or more intermediaries. It is correct to view the physicians in each city as connected for the most part within a single professional community. At the same time, it would be incorrect to think of them as members of cohesive cliques.

The sociograms in Figure 4.3 illustrate the structural complexity of the networks. Peoria and Bloomington are presented. Each city was subjected to a routine structural equivalence analysis (see Note 1). Numbers identify sets of structurally equivalent doctors, and arrows indicate where the density of sociometric choices is above average. Doctors are organized around central positions in each city, but the center is rarely unidimensional. Galesburg (not presented) is the least complicated, with a strong center position, an isolated clique, and a satellite position occupied by doctors who are not cited as advisers or discussion partners but claim direct access to the most central physicians. Bloomington has a strong center position (Position 1), but there are also two internally connected cliques affiliated with, but distinct from, the center (Positions 2 and 3). Quincy has two center positions. The social structure of Peoria doctors is the most complicated, with two interlocked center positions (Positions 1 and 2) and three internally cohesive cliques affiliated with the center (Positions 3, 4, and 5).

Contagious Adoptions

The criterion variable is the date by which each physician began writing prescriptions for the new antibiotic. Local pharmacy records were searched for prescriptions written by the 125 "prescription sample" doctors. The result is an "adoption date" variable ranging from 1 to 17 roughly indicating the month after tetracycline's release in which a doctor first began prescribing the new antibiotic. Sixteen doctors were nonadopters in the sense that the prescription sampling turned up prescriptions that they had written, but none of them were tetracycline prescriptions. As in the original study, we use these doctors to define a final point in tetracycline's diffusion, Category 18 on the adoption date variable.

Contagion is again measured by correlating each doctor's adoption date (Y) with the average adoption date of his advisers and discussion partners (Coh), and the average adoption date of his structural peers (SE), where Coh and SE are weighted averages computed as described earlier in this chapter.[6] The search across alternative values of the power exponent v yields different exponents for different cities, but in general reflects the complexity of these social structures. The exponent is 2 in Galesburg, which contains a single center position, 10 in the more complex social structures of Bloomington and Quincy, which contain multiple center positions, and 12 in the still more complex social structure of Peoria. The average across prescription sample doctors is the 9.8 in Figure 4.3. The near-maximum .84 mean substitutability weight ω_{ii} shows that the doctors have few structural peers—they are unique individuals; only 16% of the average doctor's network position is shared with other doctors (vs. 91% for the average lobbyist in Figure 4.2, and 67% for the average corporate officer in Figure 4.1).

The correlation matrix in Figure 4.3 shows evidence of contagion by structural equivalence, but no evidence of contagion by cohesion. The two variables combine to describe 14% of the variance in adoption dates (white area in the variance pie chart). Personal differences between the doctors matter. Five variables distinguishing personal differences among the doctors describe another 26% of the variance in adoption dates (gray areas in the variance pie chart). The doctors predisposed toward adopting the new antibiotic were professionally young, sophisticated with respect to keeping up with scientific developments in medicine, and believed that such behavior was important to being a good physician. The greater effect of contagion by structural equivalence, and the stronger effect of personal predisposition toward adoption, are the central points developed at length in Burt (1987). The conclusion here is that social contagion affected tetracycline adoption, but the contagion is entirely between structurally equivalent doctors, and it is a weaker motivation than the doctor's personal predisposition toward adoption.

CONCLUSION

Comparisons between the study populations are summarized in Figure 4.4 with data from Figures 4.1, 4.2, and 4.3. Populations are ordered on the horizontal axis by the relative strength of contagion and personal differences within the population. For example, Figure 4.3 shows that 14% of the variance in *Medical Innovation* adoption dates can be attributed to contagion, versus 26% attributed to personal background variables that predispose a doctor to early adoption. The ratio is .53, which puts the *Medical Innovation* doctors to the left of Figure 4.4. Contagion has a stronger effect on the opinions of the corporate officers (1.71 = 29%/17% from Figure 4.1), and a still stronger effect on the opinions of the lobbyists (2.52 = 53%/21% from Figure 4.2).

Our argument is that more complex social structures obscure the social frame of reference responsible for contagion. Where it is difficult to answer the question "Who is like me?"—it becomes less important for an individual to resolve differences between self and others' ideas and behaviors. Consider this claim in light of Figure 4.4.

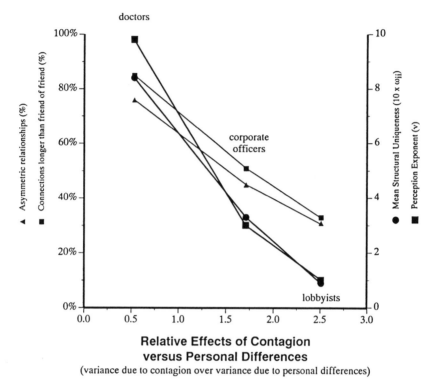

Figure 4.4 Ideas and Behaviors Are Less Contagious Where Social Structure is More Complex

The vertical axis to the left of Figure 4.4 describes the extent to which people are connected by long chains of asymmetric relationships. Asymmetric relations means that you are talking to the back of someone's head as they talk to someone else; social influence is less likely than if the exchange is reciprocal. Short chains of relations make it easier to know the boundary of the social frame around you. Figure 4.4 shows that the doctors, where contagion is weakest, tend to be connected by long chains of asymmetric relationships; 75% of their advisers and discussion partners turn to someone else for advice and discussion, 85% of their connections with colleagues require more than one intermediary. The thin lines in Figure 4.4 continue down through the corporate officers, to their minimum among the lobbyists, where contagion is strongest. The lobbyists tend to be connected by short chains of reciprocated citations; 69% of their support citations are reciprocated, and 67% of their connections with other lobbyists are direct or indirect through only one intermediary.

The vertical axis to the right of Figure 4.4 describes the extent to which people are structurally differentiated from one another. The substitutability coefficient ω_{ii} measures the extent to which a person's pattern of relations is unlike any other pattern in the study population. The more unique the pattern, the more ambiguous the social frame of reference defined by the pattern. The power function exponent v indicates the extent to which contagion is limited to people who have only the most similar patterns of relations. Figure 4.4 shows that structural differentiation is greatest among the doctors, where contagion is weakest. The patterns of advising and discussion among the doctors are so complex that the average doctor holds a unique position in social structure (.84 mean ω_{ii}). The bold lines indicating structural differentiation continue down in the graph through the corporate officers, to their minimum among the lobbyists, where contagion is strongest. The average lobbyist has an easily discerned group of colleagues with whom he or she shares a position in social structure (.09 mean ω_{ii}).

In sum, ideas and behaviors are less contagious where social structure is more complex. The more general point is that social contagion processes are contingent on the broader social structure in which they occur.

NOTES

1. By routine structural equivalence analysis we mean that (a) path distances were derived from the (61 by 61) matrix of sociometric choices and converted (frequency decay function) to measure the strength of the direct or indirect relation from each officer to each other officer, (b) Euclidean distances were computed to identify the extent to which each pair of officers were structurally equivalent in the sense of having identical relations with other officers, (c) the distances were cluster analyzed to identify sets of structurally equivalent officers, and (d) the identified sets of structurally equivalent officers were tested for the degree to which they were structurally equivalent (cf. Burt, 1982, for illustrative examples, or any network analysis textbook for the general idea).

2. As in Burt (1982, 1987), i–j equivalence is the maximum Euclidean distance of any officer from i, minus the Euclidean distance between i and j; $\max(d_{ij}) - d_{ij}$, where d_{ij} is Euclidean distance; the difference between i's and j's relations with each

other officer; $d_{ij} = [\Sigma_k(z_{ik} - z_{jk})^2 + \Sigma_k(z_{ki} - z_{kj})^2]$, here z_{ik} is the strength of i's relation to officer k. The data were reanalyzed for contagion effects using popular variations on the raw Euclidean distance measure. Euclidean distances were computed directly from the raw binary sociometric choice data (which ignores indirect relations). This reduces the contagion correlation in Figure 4.1 only slightly from .54 to .48. Euclidean distances were computed from z-score measures of relations (as in CONCOR, ignoring mean and variation differences between relation patterns). (Editor's note: CONCOR is a procedure for detecting structurally equivalent actors based on iterative correlations of the rows and columns of a sociomatrix. For more information, see Breiger, Boorman, & Arabie, 1975; Knoke & Kuklinski, 1982; Wasserman & Faust, 1994.) This reduces the equivalence contagion correlation from .54 to .34. These results do not justify a general preference for the one selected, but only show that the general one used here is well suited to this study population.

3. The partitioned variance is a heuristic. Regression coefficients computed from the correlation matrix in Figure 4.1 are .526 for structural equivalence and .041 for cohesion, with a .290 squared multiple correlation. The .290 squared multiple correlation defines the 29% in Figure 4.1, for which the independent contributions of structural equivalence (.281 = .526 × .535) and cohesion (.009 = .041 × .218) are given in parentheses. The correlations are computed across the 60 officers each expressing an opinion of 10 nonprofit organizations, for a total of 600 observations. Without defining specific qualities of the officers that might affect evaluations, we can get a sense of how much differences between them matter by regressing the 600 evaluations across dummy variables that distinguish each officer from every other. When we add 59 dummy variables distinguishing the 60 officers to the contagion prediction, the squared multiple correlation increases by .169 to .459 (thus the 17% in Figure 4.1 attributed to personal differences). When we use the dummies to capture interactions with contagion to test for slope adjustments to the aggregate contagion effect, the squared multiple correlation increases by .055 to .514 (thus the 6% in Figure 4.1 attributed to contagion slope adjustments). We cannot give a specific meaning to this additional explained variance, but we know that it has something to do with differences between the officers. In other words, we are not estimating network autocorrelation effects, nor testing contagion against personal differences. That work is reported elsewhere (Galaskiewicz & Burt, 1991). We are measuring contagion, then measuring how much personal differences matter above and beyond contagion.

4. The strong evidence of contagion by cohesion and structural equivalence between lobbyists is robust over alternative measures of cohesion and structural equivalence. In keeping with Heinz et al. (1993), Lobbyist j is a key supporter for i if i cites j for support. We tried both more extensive and more intensive measures. The more extensive measure was to include indirect connections. The proximity of j to i is the strength of the direct or indirect relationship from j to i as used to compute structural equivalence. This yields a contagion correlation slightly stronger than in Figure 4.2, but less robust in the sense that the correlation generates a slightly weaker jackknife t test (6.9 t test vs. 7.6 for the .66 correlation in Figure 4.2). The more intensive measure was to limit cohesive relations to mutually recognized relations in which lobbyists i and j cite one another (as among the corporate officers in the

previous section). Contagion through these relations is again slightly stronger than in Figure 4.2, but again less robust in the sense of generating a weaker jackknife *t* test (5.7 *t* test vs. 7.6 for the correlation in Figure 4.2). We also reanalyzed the data with alternative equivalence weights. Euclidean distances were computed directly from the raw binary sociometric choice data, which reduces the contagion correlation in Figure 4.2 only slightly from .73 to .69. Euclidean distances were computed from z-score measures of relations, which generates an aggregate contagion correlation of .71, just about identical to the .73 result in Figure 4.2.

5. Detailed analysis of the diverse background data gathered for the study led us to focus on 13 dummy variables to hold constant contagion-relevant personal differences between the lobbyists. The variables distinguish lobbyists by the policy domain in which they primarily operate (agriculture, energy, health, labor; from Laumann, Tam, & Heinz, 1992), political party (Republican, Independent, Democrat), profession (lawyer, lawyer-manager, manager), and prominence (low, average, high). Lawyers are lobbyists with law degrees working for law firms. Managers are executives and consultants without law degrees. Low-prominence lobbyists are cited for support by less than eight other lobbyists. High-prominence lobbyists are cited for support by more than 13 other lobbyists.

6. We followed the original study in using direct sociometric choices to define sources of contagion. Cohesion weight w_{ij} is one over the number of i's cited advisers and discussion partners. We get similar results with alternative measures of cohesion and alternative measures of structural equivalence (Burt, 1987; Burt & Uchiyama, 1989).

CHAPTER

5 Structural Leverage in Marketing

DAVID KRACKHARDT

The concept of networks is no stranger to the field of marketing. There is much emphasis on the quality of supplier and customer relationships as a means for improving marketing and sales positions vis à vis the competition. But the premise of much of this thinking is that one only has to pay attention to one's own relationships (to customers, suppliers, sources of capital, and so on). What the field of social networks can bring to this idea is the importance of looking at the entire constellation of relations in a system (see Galaskiewicz, Chapter 3, this volume). Thus, it is not sufficient to say that you have established quality relations with each one of your suppliers and customers. There is also decided benefit to knowing (Krackhardt, 1990, 1992) and positioning (Burt, 1992) yourself within the web of relationships among those suppliers, customers, and even competitors.

These advantages of knowing the structure and positioning within the structure are not restricted to one unit of analysis. Such structural advantages occur at the micro level (e.g., within small groups, Shaw, 1964; at the organizational level, Krackhardt & Brass, 1994; and all the way to the national industrial level, Burt, 1983). Nor are these advantages strictly the purview of organizational scientists (see Wasserman & Galaskiewicz, 1994 for a review of many fields that have benefited from network analysis). In this chapter, I would like to provide one small example of how understanding the structure of the social system in which one does business can have a decided impact on marketing strategies.

THE FREE SAMPLE PROBLEM

Consider this simple hypothetical example. Suppose that you are the marketing manager of a large domestic products firm. A new product (Theta) was just developed by your R&D group. You have found that the product sells itself—once people try it, they tend to adopt it with a reasonably high probability. Thus, you decide to market this product by sending free samples to a random sample of potential buyers. (I will refer to this randomly selected set of people as "focal persons.") Now, suppose further that there is a friendship ripple effect. That is, given that a focal person is given a free sample and then adopts Theta, he or she subsequently coaxes his or her friends into using Theta also, and each one of these friends also adopts Theta with a particular probability. With this ripple effect, we get added returns to our investment in the sense that the focal recipient of the free sample, on liking and adopting the product, has spread by word of mouth his or her support and thereby influenced these close associates to become customers also. Studying such networks makes explicit the structural process of opinion leaders and the diffusion of innovation (cf. Bass, 1969; Coleman, Katz, & Menzel, 1969; Feick & Price, 1987; Reingen & Kernan, 1986; Rogers, 1962).

The Random Sample Model

We can formalize this process as follows:[1]

α: The probability that an individual who is given a free sample of Theta will adopt Theta as a product.

β: The probability that an individual who is a friend of the another adopter (who had been given the free sample) will also adopt Theta.

F_i: The cardinal number of the set of i's friends.

The central question of interest becomes, what is the expected number of customers (people who adopt product Theta) derived from each free sample distributed? Each focal person has the probability α of becoming a customer, and each friend of the focal person has the joint probability $\alpha\beta$ of becoming a customer. Let C_i indicate the expected number of customers that will result from i being given the free sample. Then, the number of expected customers given focal person i is selected through the random sampling process is as follows:

$$C_i = \alpha + F_i\,\alpha\beta.$$

Assuming each person i has an equal probability of being selected as a focal person, then the expected number of customers resulting from a campaign of randomly distributed free samples is as follows:

$$E(C) = \frac{1}{N}\sum_{i=1}^{N}(\alpha+\alpha\beta F_i) \tag{1}$$

The Structural Leverage Model

There is nothing inherently structural about the previous model [1]. All that is necessary is to know how many friends people have. We need to know nothing about to whom they are connected or what the overall structure of friendships is to solve this problem. Suppose, however, that we alter the sampling procedure slightly in the following way: We randomly approach a set of people as before, but this time we ask them each to nominate a friend of theirs. We then give the sample to the friend they nominate instead of to the focal person.

On the surface, this appears to be an innocuous change in procedure. But the effect of this small change can be fairly dramatic, depending on the structure of friendships.

To formalize the effect, I will make one simplifying assumption: A focal person will nominate with equal probability any one of his or her friends. With this additional assumption, we can calculate the expected number of customers resulting from this modified sampling procedure—if we know the structure of the friendships. To demonstrate why knowing the structure (as opposed to simply knowing the number of friends everyone has) is important, I will proceed stepwise through an example.

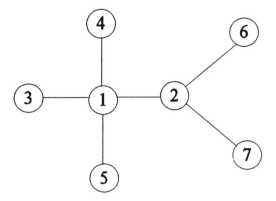

Figure 5.1. Friendship Pattern

Consider the structure of friendships provided in Figure 5.1. Suppose we were to randomly select Person 1 as the focal person. Then Person 1 would randomly select either Person 2, 3, 4, or 5 as a friend. If Person 1 selects Person 2, then drawing on the same principles derived for model [1], the expected number of customers would be α plus $3 \times \alpha\beta$ (Person 2 has three friends, including Person 1, all of whom are potential ripple-effect adopters). On the other hand, if Person 1 selects Person 3, then the expected number of customers would be only α plus $\alpha\beta$ (Person 3 has only one friend, the focal person). By extension, the expected number of customers, given that we have selected Person 1 as a focal person, is one fourth the sum of the expected number of customers we would get across each of the four friends that Person 1 might nominate.

Before we generalize this, it should be obvious that we need to know more than simply how many friends the focal person has to solve this problem. In particular, we need to know how many friends each of the focal person's friends has. I will represent the set of friends of individual i as S_i.

Calculating the effect of the leverage model is straightforward. I will use the subscript i to designate the person who was originally selected through the random sampling process. I will use the subscript j to designate a friend of i's. I will use C^L_i to indicate the expected number of customers that result from i being selected in the leverage model. That is, C^L_i is the expected number of customers

TABLE 5.1

i	Fi	Ci	C_i^L
1	4	1.7	0.95
2	3	1.4	1.1
3	1	0.8	1.7
4	1	0.8	1.7
5	1	0.8	1.7
6	1	0.8	1.4
7	1	0.8	1.4

$E(C) = 1.014$
$E(C^L) = 1.421$
Payoff = 40.1%

given that i was asked to nominate a friend, who in turn was given the sample and through a ripple effect may have influenced her friends to become customers. Then, for any given i,

$$C_i^L = \frac{1}{F_i} \sum_{j \in S_i} (\alpha + F_j \alpha \beta)$$

The expected value for the leveraging strategy as a whole is simply the expected value of these sums:

$$E(C^L) = \frac{1}{N} \sum_{i=1}^{N} \left[\frac{1}{F_i} \sum_{j \in S_i} (\alpha + F_j \alpha \beta) \right] \qquad (2)$$

HYPOTHETICAL EXAMPLE

To illustrate the effect of these two sampling strategies, I will calculate them for the structure of friends revealed in Figure 5.1. For purposes of demonstration, I will arbitrarily set $\alpha = .5$ and $\beta = .6$. Table 5.1 shows the calculations for both the randomly sampled strategy and for the structural leverage strategy. At the bottom of the table are

TABLE 5.2

β	Figure 5.1 Structure			Star Structure			Circle Structure		
	E(C)	E(C^L)	Percentage Payoff	E(C)	E(C^L)	Percentage Payoff	E(C)	E(C^L)	Percentage Payoff
.1	0.585	0.653	11.5	0.585	0.764	30.4	0.6	0.6	0
.2	0.671	0.807	20.2	0.671	1.028	53.1	0.7	0.7	0
.3	0.757	0.960	26.8	0.757	1.292	70.7	0.8	0.8	0
.4	0.842	1.114	32.2	0.842	1.557	84.7	0.9	0.9	0
.5	0.928	1.267	36.5	0.928	1.821	96.1	1.0	1.0	0
.6	1.104	1.421	40.1	1.014	2.085	105.6	1.1	1.1	0
.7	1.100	1.575	43.1	1.100	2.350	113.6	1.2	1.2	0
.8	1.185	1.728	45.7	1.185	2.614	120.4	1.3	1.3	0
.9	1.271	1.882	48.0	1.271	2.878	126.4	1.4	1.4	0

three important totals. The expected number of customers $(E(C))$ for the random sample strategy is 1.01 customers per free sample. The expected number of customers $(E(C^L))$ for the leverage strategy is 1.42. The expected payoff percentage for using the leverage rather than the random sample strategy is

$$Payoff = 100 \times \frac{E(C^L) - E(C)}{E(C)} = 40.1\%. \qquad (3)$$

That is, we can expect that, in a population characterized by the structures as represented in Figure 5.1 and probabilities of adopting Theta given by $\alpha = .5$ and $\beta = .6$, we will garner 40% more customers by using the leveraging strategy rather than the random sampling strategy to distribute free samples of Theta.

EXPLORING MODEL RESULTS

The question remains, what factors will affect this payoff ratio? That is, does this handsome return depend on α, β, or the structure?

First, in the simple model proposed here, it can be easily shown that the payoff ratio does not depend on the value given to α, as long as $\alpha > 0\$$ (the α's cancel in an expansion of [3]). The payoff does,

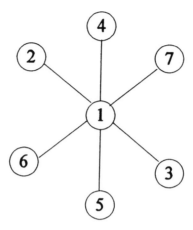

Figure 5.2a. Friendship Pattern in a Star Structure

however, depend on β and the structure of the friendships. These effects are readily evident in Table 5.2, which shows the payoff ratios for values of ß ranging from .1 to .9 and for three different structures (shown in Figure 5.2). The three structures are the one described in Figure 5.1 that we have already examined; a "star" structure, wherein friendships are highly centralized to one very popular person (Figure 5.2a); and a "circle" structure, wherein the friendships are organized in a circle (Figure 5.2b).

The first result is that higher β values increase the payoff of using the leverage structure. This is true for any structure in which there is at least some advantage for leveraging (which will be most of the time). For the Figure 5.1 structure, the payoff ranges from 11% to 48% as β increases from .1 to .9. For the highly centralized star structure, the payoff ranges from 30% to 126% as β increases from .1 to .9.

But, the more critical result is the sensitivity to the structural features of the population we are sampling. In the extreme case of no structural differentiation among (Figure 5.2b), there is no payoff at all for using a leveraging strategy. But, given any particular level of β, there are marked differences as the structure becomes more centralized. For example, at a modest β = .4, the decentralized structure provides 0% payoff for leveraging, the moderately central-ized structure provides 32% payoff for leveraging, and the highly

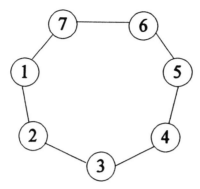

Figure 5.2b. Friendship Pattern in a Circle Structure

centralized structure provides a 85% payoff for leveraging. The key to the degree of leverage provided by a leveraging strategy is the extent to which the structure of the population from which the sample will be drawn is centralized.

DISCUSSION

The results of this introductory analysis can be summarized by the following propositions:

P1. For any given value of α and β, and for any given structure, the expected number of customers in a leveraging strategy will always be greater than or equal to the expected number of customers in a random sampling strategy.

P2. The payoff for using a leveraging strategy is independent of the probability that the individual who is given the sample will become a customer.

P3. The higher the value of β, *ceteris paribus*, the higher the payoff for using a leveraging strategy.

P4. The payoff is most sensitive to the structure of the friendship relations. The more centralized the structure, *ceteris paribus*, the higher the degree of leveraging advantage there will be for the leverage strategy.

It should be noted, however, that the door is not closed on this problem. There are several questions left unexplored here (due to space limitations). For example:

1. What are the effects of allowing the ripple effects to extend beyond just one friend? In the real world, we would expect such affects to propagate beyond just one friend (friends of friends may buy also). One could explore such effects by plotting the expected number of customers under the two models against time, in which each time period allowed for further diffusion of the product Theta through the network of friends.

2. What is the functional relationship between the payoff ratio and standard measures of network centrality? There is a large literature on network centrality (Scott, 1991) and many measures (Bonacich, 1987; Freeman, 1979; Mizruchi, Mariolis, Schwartz, & Mintz, 1986). In the examples I provided in this chapter, there is an apparent relationship between the two, although I have purposely left out of my analysis any articulate definition of what I meant by "centralized." To be fair, it is unlikely that this relationship is perfectly linear or even perfectly monotonic over all structures, depending on the particular centrality measure used. Exactly which dimension of centrality is illuminating to this problem is left to future research.

3. What happens if we make the model more complicated (and realistic)? For example, suppose that the probability that one becomes a customer is a function of the number of other friends who have already adopted Theta. Or suppose that the probability of adoption itself is a function of the rate at which one sees one's friends adopting. In combination with allowing the ripple effect to continue beyond just the immediate set of friends, this could create system dynamics that are difficult to anticipate. Exploring such dynamics could prove useful in better understanding how the structure would affect payoffs for different strategies.

4. What other strategies could be devised to take advantage of structural differentiation in the market? At a minimum, I can think of one strategy, which, when used in combination with a leverage strategy, would result in negative payoffs (i.e., one would be better off with the original simple random sample strategy). That is, suppose that we were to stratify the population such that high-status people were given a higher probability of being selected in the random sample process. In such a case, people at the center might be more likely to be sampled originally as focal persons. If we were to give the free sample to one of

their friends, and the structure was similar to Figure 5.1, then the free sample would more likely be given to someone on the periphery, resulting in fewer adoptions through friends. There is a wealth of questions to explore here, matching strategies to friendship structures.

CONCLUSION

The purpose of this chapter is not to suggest that the four summary propositions above amount to proof that the leveraging strategy is the marketer's new best friend. Rather, it is to demonstrate that the *structure* of social and influence relationships is an important and relatively unexplored area within a broad array of marketing questions and problems. Although the field of marketing has historically recognized that dyadic relationships play a significant role in an organization's success, I hope to convince the reader that focusing on isolated dyads isn't enough. Relationships are embedded in a structural context, and the shape of this context can provide critical insight into these social and marketing phenomena.

NOTE

1. For the moment, I will restrict myself to a one-step ripple effect; that is, I will only consider the effects of immediate friends of the focal person.

PART III

Theoretical Concepts of
Networks for Marketers

Networks in Socioeconomic Systems

A Critical Review

LUIS ARAUJO

GEOFFREY EASTON

The term *network* is becoming fashionable in marketing. The reasons for its increasing popularity may be sought throughout this book. In this particular chapter, we wish to place the notion of network, as it is and as it might be used in business-to-business marketing, into a rich, intellectual context so that it might profit thereby. Doing so, however, is not without its problems; marketing has long been accused of being a borrowing social science, and although the evidence for this accusation is not wholly convincing, it is clear that where it has occurred, it tends to happen in a piecemeal fashion. Concepts, models, and principles are plucked out of their original theoretical frameworks and used in an ad hoc, and often inappropriate, fashion so that their original meanings are lost. In presenting this review of 10 different schools of network thought, our aim is not to open up a happy hunting ground for "concept croppers," but rather to provide an admittedly limited sketch of the various ways in which the term network has been used in different paradigms, all of which at some level have research interests in common with marketing yet that differ in many ways.

Theory development is deeply embedded in the practices of the cognitive communities that espouse and diffuse them. Paradigms and worldviews develop and propagate as a result of the efforts of their

63

proponents to write articles in leading journals, attend conferences and give presentations, engage in intellectual discussions in different fora; in sum, it depends on enlisting and mobilizing allies, combating opponents, and building long-term, strong networks (Latour, 1987). Furthermore, paradigms are strongly conditioned by the institutional environments from which they spring. In particular, the peculiar conditions surrounding the production of knowledge, the reward structures in place, and the legitimization of what constitutes valid research themes in any particular scientific domain and country, play a key part in the production of academic knowledge (Davis, 1971; Whitley, 1995). By providing some of that background, as well as signposts to where the further background can be found, we hope to sensitize potential network researchers to the dangers of smash-and-grab conceptualizations.

It is not the case that we believe the importation of ideas is necessarily a bad practice. It is simply that the process should be considered and well-informed. One way of doing this is to attempt to discover what similarities and differences exist among the conceptualization of networks so we can feel confident that there is some commonality of thought and yet also variance to be understood and perhaps reconciled. Thus a second goal is to attempt to characterize the schools of network thought into a taxonomy to see how they might provide insights into the way the term network is, and could be, used in marketing. (For a review of interfirm networks with different objectives see Grandori & Sodda, 1995, and for an extended review of networks and economic life see Powell & Smith-Doerr, 1994.)

Although we do not argue against importation, we do not wish to promote colonization. Our third goal is to defend the term network from crude and premature attempts at operationalization, within or outside of marketing. It is clear that the term network has acquired the character of an umbrella, catch-all term under which a variety of theoretical and methodological positions in the social sciences have sought refuge. Although widely acknowledged to have sprung from social anthropology and used mainly to characterize patterns of social relations (see the review by Wellman, 1988), it has acquired the status of a metaconcept, not unlike the word "system." Its meaning can only be determined within the cognitive communities that use it, for example, sociology, management studies, economic geography.

We have argued elsewhere (Easton & Araujo, 1993) that the network metaphor is characterized by high systematicity but relatively low clarity, allowing for a measure of constructive ambiguity under which research and theorizing can proceed without excessive constraint. Nohria (1992), among others, has expressed the frustration felt by those who see this as a critical limitation: "This indiscriminate proliferation of the network concept threatens to relegate it to the status of an evocative metaphor, applied so loosely, that it ceases to mean anything" (p. 3). Others, ourselves included, would argue otherwise. Latour (1993), for example, is particularly enamored by the power of the network metaphor: "More supple than the notion of system, more historical than the notion of structure, more empirical than the notion of complexity, the idea of network is the Ariadne's thread of these interwoven stories . . . which remain more invisible than spiderwebs" (pp. 3-4). By illustrating the richness of the different perspectives that have sprung from the variety of meanings that the word evokes, we seek to convince skeptics of the dangers of premature closure. We espouse an ecological view of knowledge where the best fit requires that variety must always precede selection and retention.

In pursuit of these aims, the first section of this chapter describes a set of dimensions to help classify and compare different types of network research. The second section is devoted to a critical but brief review of 10 of the major schools of thought that employ the network concept. In the third and final section, we will explore the implications for business network research of network research from other traditions.

A CLASSIFICATION OF
NETWORK APPROACHES

The network approaches we will be examining come from the following disciplines or subdisciplines: sociology, sociology of science and technology, organization theory, social policy, innovation studies, political science, industrial marketing and purchasing, economic geography, entrepreneurship studies, and comparative studies of economic systems. Obviously, we sometimes find actors with membership of different disciplines (e.g., industrial marketing and purchasing and innovation studies) and some of the fields surveyed will reveal a large degree of dependency on approaches developed elsewhere (e.g., entrepreneurship studies). Also, we find authors employing hybrid approaches, supplementing network analysis with other theoretical approaches (e.g., resource dependency theory). Thus, the field is far from homogeneous and coherent, making our attempt at providing a classification of different approaches somewhat difficult.

The dimensions we have used to characterize the different types of network approaches include the following: (a) the basic goals of the research program (descriptive, explanatory, normative); (b) the nature of actors (individuals, groups, firms, nonprofit organizations); (d) the nature of links (what flows through links between actors: economic resources, information, texts, affect, friendship, power, and so on); (d) disciplinary background; (e) methodological orientation; (f) emphasis on structure versus process; and (g) cross-references to other network approaches. The network approaches we will attempt to map out in relation to these dimensions are (a) social networks, (b) interorganization theory, (c) actor-network theory, (d) networks of innovators, (e) network organizational forms, (f) policy networks, (g) networks in economic geography, (h) interfirm networks in comparative studies of economic organization, (i) entrepreneurship and small firm networks, and (j) industrial networks. Table 6.1 summarizes the 10 different network approaches using these 7 dimensions.

In this table we have sought to present a summary of the main dimensions characterizing each network approach before describing each approach in more detail. The first row of the table lists exemplary works of each type of network approach; we have selected a number of publications that are representative. For the next dimension along which the network approaches are compared, we have attempted to catalog what we see as the research goals or objectives of each approach and the reasons underlining the use of a network approach that we will detail in the subsequent section. Under the nature of actors and links, we have specified how each approach uses and elaborates the network metaphor by identifying the nature of the nodes and links that constitute the network. Under the disciplinary background dimension, we have sought to distinguish the background of the researchers employing a particular network approach. Whereas in some cases researchers share a similar discipli-nary background (e.g., political science), in others we find a consid-erable variety of backgrounds (e.g., entrepreneurship studies). We use the dimension of methodological orientation to discriminate between two separate methodological and theoretical approaches to the study of networks. Some researchers use the term network as an illustrative metaphor, using mainly qualitative, case-oriented meth-odologies to describe and explain network structures and processes. Others have used the term network as a tool kit of quantitative, sociometric techniques to elicit structural patterns of relationships in social and economic settings. The two approaches are by no means mutually exclusive. Some network approaches contain several exam-ples of work using both types of methodological orientations, and there are also a few examples of work combing both types of meth-odologies in the same research design.

A complementary dimension to methodological orientation is the process versus structure orientation. In some approaches, particu-larly those directly inspired by social network analysis, the concern is identifying structural patterns using quantitative data about network links. In those using qualitative and longitudinal methods, the con-cern is more with social and economic processes, and structures are regarded as the temporary and transient effects of these primary network processes. Finally, we have attempted to identify the degree of cross-reference among the different network approaches we have identified. Even though all network approaches are indebted to the same theoretical source, namely social anthropology, they have de-veloped along quite distinct and separate lines. The degree of cross-referencing is thus largely dependent on the variety of disciplinary backgrounds within any one approach and is obviously less for those approaches where researchers share the same disciplinary back-ground and work with fairly well-defined phenomena (e.g., interlock-ing directorships).

FIELDS OF NETWORK RESEARCH

We will now describe and analyze, albeit briefly, the 10 different network approaches we have identified. The discussion starts with the

TABLE 6.1 Comparison of 10 Network Approaches

Dimensions Characterizing Each Approach	Social Networks	Interorganization Theory	Actor-Network Theory
Exemplary works	Wellman and Berkowitz (1988) Alba (1982) Burt (1988) Cook and Emerson (1984)	Van de Ven and Walker (1984) Alter and Hage (1993) Provan and Milward (1995)	Callon (1986, 1987) Latour (1987, 1988, 1993) Law (1994)
Research goals	Uncover form and pattern of social relationships	Description and explanation of interorganizational relations with a view to determine best practice for network design	Description and explanation of the emergence and reproduction of sociotechnical structures
Nature of actors	Mainly individuals, but also organizations	Government agencies, nonprofit organizations	Individuals and nonhuman artifacts and materials as relational effects
Nature of links	Friendship, information, resources, power	Resources, power, service delivery	Heterogeneous associations of human and nonhuman elements
Disciplinary background	Sociology	Sociology, social policy	Sociology and history of science and technology
Methodological orientation	Sociometric techniques	Sociometric techniques, case studies	Ethnographic case studies, few sociometric-type studies
Orientation structure/process	Structure	Structure	Process
Cross references	Virtually none, some references to institutionalization theory	Social networks, interfirm networks	Virtually none

social networks approach because it is generally acknowledged to be the precursor to all other approaches and the most prolific in terms

TABLE 6.1 *Continued*

	Networks of Innovators	*Network Organizations*	*Policy Networks*
Exemplary works	Czepiel (1975, 1979) Von Hippel (1988) Håkansson (1987, 1989) DeBresson and Amesse (1991)	Miles and Snow (1986) Baker (1992) Eccles and Crane (1988) Ghoshal and Bartlett (1993)	Marin and Mayntz (1993) Jordan and Schubert (1992) Marsh and Rhodes (1992a)
Research goals	Explain the processes underlying technological innovations and the governance forms of technological transactions	Use of network metaphors and methods to explain decentralised, nonhierarchical organizational forms	Use of network metaphors to explain the patterns of interaction between government and societal groups in policy making
Nature of actors	Individuals and organizations	Individuals, groups	Organizational in the European tradition and individuals in the American tradition
Nature of links	Communication, information, resources	Communication, information, resources, power, authority	Communication, power, influence
Disciplinary background	Economics, geography, marketing	Organization studies, international business	Political science
Methodological orientation	Mainly case studies, but some sociometric techniques	Mainly case studies	Case studies
Orientation structure/process	Process	Structure	Process
Cross references	Social networks, industrial networks	Social networks	Virtually none

(continued)

of development of data analysis tools and their application to a range of social science topics.

TABLE 6.1 *Continued*

	Networks in Economic Geography	*Comparative Studies*	*Entrepreneurship Studies*
Exemplary works	Storper and Harrison (1991) Cooke and Morgan (1993) Harrison (1994) Yeung (1994)	Clegg, Redding, and Carter (1990) Redding (1990) Fruin (1992) Gerlach (1992)	Aldrich and Zimmer (1986) Larson (1992) Larson and Starr (1983) Johanisson (1988) Johanisson et al. (1994)
Research goals	Use of the network metaphor to explain the spatial dispersion of production structures and their linkages	Use of network metaphors and methods to explain market structures and organizational forms in mainly non-Western societies	Use of network metaphors and methods to explain how entrepreneurs build and sustain new organizations
Nature of actors	Organizations	Organizations, individuals, families	Individuals
Nature of links	Resources, information	Resources, information, power, authority	Communication, power, influence, resources
Disciplinary background	Economic geography, urban and regional studies	Sociology, organization studies, international business	Entrepreneurship and small business economics
Methodological orientation	Mainly case studies	Case studies, sociometric techniques	Case studies, sociometric techniques
Orientation structure/process	Structure	Structure	Structure and process
Cross references	Interfirm networks, industrial networks	Social networks mainly interlocking directorships literature	Social networks, economic geography, networks of innovators

TABLE 6.1 *Continued*

	Industrial Networks
Exemplary works	Mattsson (1985) Håkansson (1987, 1989) Axelsson and Easton (1992) Håkansson and Snehota (1995)
Research goals	Use of network metaphors and methods to explain industrial/ organizational market structures
Nature of actors	Organizations
Nature of links	Resources, information
Disciplinary background	Marketing and purchasing
Methodological orientation	Mainly case studies
Orientation structure/process	Structure and process
Cross references	Social networks, mainly social exchange theory

Social Networks

The development of the social network approach is usually attributed to social anthropology and can be regarded as a branch of structural sociology (Wellman, 1988). While tracing back the development of social network analysis to the invention of the sociogram, Alba (1982) attributes the growth of interest in social network analysis in the 1970s to the advent of powerful mathematical tools to model networks. Network analysis offered the possibility of transcending traditional statistical analysis based on random samples, which degenerated into an analysis of social structures by categories, whether individual or collective such as social class, society, or government

(Alba, 1982). Emirbayer and Goodwin (1994, p. 1414) associate the point of departure of network analysis with what they call an anticategorical imperative. Structural analysts acknowledged the existence of these categories, but believed in the primacy of the underlying social relationships that embody and transcend these social categories.

The second major point about social network analysis, stemming from the anticategorical imperative, is the rejection of all explanations of behavior that rely on culturalism, essentialism, or methodological individualism (Emirbayer & Goodwin, 1994). From a network point of view, all approaches that rely on notions of internalized norms, attributes or goals of individuals, and privilege subjective over objective factors relating to the form and pattern of social relationships, are suspect. Actors in social networks are regarded as embedded in concrete patterns of social relationships, which produce opportunities and constraints, and their behavior can only be understood in relation to these structures.

Social network analysis has been concerned with describing and explaining patterns of social relations, and developing sophisticated methods of data analysis based on either relational analysis, relying on graph theoretical techniques, or positional analysis, relying on blockmodeling techniques (see e.g., Knoke & Kuklinski, 1982 for an exposition of data analysis methods in social networks). Given the minimalist definition of a network employed by social network theorists, the tendency has been to apply the tools of network data analysis to a variety of social situations. As Mizruchi (1994) states: "Network analysis is applicable to virtually any substantive topic" (p. 330).

Alba (1982), for example, defines network as "a set of units (or nodes) of some kind and the relations of specific types that occur among them" (p. 42). He goes on to state that the units involved may be persons or collectivities such as firms and other formal organizations or even nations. The relations between units may be characterized as friendship links, coworker links in bureaucracies, awareness among members of scientific domains, or interlocking directorships.

In practice as well as in theory, the tools and methods of social network analysis have been used to study a variety of topics. Some of these studies have relied on experimental and simulation work, to determine, for example, power and centrality in exchange networks. The work carried out under the social exchange banner, first developed by Emerson (1962) and later by Cook (1977) and Cook and Emerson (1984) among others, concentrated on understanding power-dependence structures and in extending a dyadic exchange approach to the network level via the concept of connectedness. Two exchange relationships are said to be connected to the extent that exchange in one relation is contingent, in a positive or negative sense, on an exchange in the other relation (Cook & Emerson 1984, p. 3). This particular variant of social network analysis developed in parallel and influenced somewhat the industrial networks research tradition, as we attempt to show later.

Other network studies have used both primary data and published, secondary data and attempted to employ basic network concepts to organizations, interorganizational analysis, intra- and intergroup relations and even relations between industrial sectors. In intraorganizational studies, using primary data, Brass and Burkhardt (1992), Krackhardt (1992), Ibarra (1993), and Ibarra and Andrews (1993) provide recent examples of the application of network concepts, namely the importance of role centrality to patterns of social interaction within organizations.

In interorganizational studies focusing on the relations between business organizations, social network theorists have concentrated their firepower on interlocking directorships and their consequences for corporate behavior such as political or philanthropic donations. Most of these studies are specifically concerned with the concentration of economic and political power in the hands of small, heavily interlinked business elites. There is also a strong feeling here that the statement by Mizruchi (1994), quoted previously, might ring truer if it was amended to: "Network analysis will be applied to any substantive topic provided we can get our hands on useful secondary data." The literature is simply too huge to summarize here but recent examples of this type of work include Galaskiewicz and Burt (1991), Haunschild (1993), Mintz and Schwartz (1990), Mizruchi and Stearns (1994), and Stearns and Mizruchi (1993). Some of this work overlaps with other substantive approaches to organizational theory such as resource dependency, population ecology, and institutionalism.

Other studies have used network concepts to account for the diffusion of particular business practices such as "poison pills as a take-over defense (Davis, 1991), greenmail (Kosnik, 1987), golden parachutes (Wade, O'Reilly, & Chandratat, 1990), and forms of organization (Palmer, Jennings, & Zhou, 1993). Once again, there is overlap with, as well as important differences from, similar studies based on institutionalization theory. Fligstein (1990) and Fligstein and Brantley (1992), for example, argue that the existence of social relations among business elites is a poor predictor of firms' actions and that the internal distribution of power, the behavior of competitors in the same organizational field, and the positioning of firms vis à vis government legislation are better "explananda" of firms' behavior.

White (1981), Baker (1984), and Burt (1988) provide other examples of the application of social network analysis to the structure of markets and to the relationship between industrial sectors. White (1981) conceives markets as tangible cliques of producers watching each other and constructing market schedules relating volume to revenue. Burt (1988) is mainly concerned with developing measures of structural autonomy, as an outcome of a firm's relationships with its competitors, suppliers and customers, and in relating structural autonomy to profitability. Baker (1984) looks at the social networks underpinning the operation of financial markets and their impact on crowd dynamics and price volatility.

Despite the impressive progress made by social network analysis and the development of sophisticated data analysis techniques reported in journals such as *Social Networks* and the *Journal of Mathematical Sociology*, there is a strong sense in which social network analysis has evolved into a toolbox of techniques looking for substantive topics on which to flex its analytical muscles (Powell & Smith-Doerr, 1994). Three different and interrelated criticisms have been leveled at social network analysis and, by extension, at all forms of structural analysis (Emirbayer & Goodwin, 1994; Mizruchi, 1994): (a) the primacy of structure over agency, leading to an oversocialized view of behavior; (b) the primacy of structure over process, leading to a neglect of how structures are instantiated, reproduced, and changed; and (c) a tendency to conflate social structures with cultural order, leading to an unwarranted assumption of isomorphism between position in social structure and interests and belief systems, a charge that advocates of social network frequently level at categorical approaches to social sciences.

The first criticism stems from the structural analysis concern at analyzing behavior as an outcome of the social distribution of possibilities created by an unequal availability of resources (e.g., information, wealth) and the structural constraints that govern access to them (Wellman, 1988, p. 33). There is little room in this mode of explanation to account for individual or collective acts of mobilization to change the conditions of action afforded by a particular social structure. Similarly, structural forms of analysis are poorly equipped to explain how structures are created, reproduced, and transformed by the behavior of actors embedded in the social networks that are so powerful at channeling their behavior through the creation of a set of opportunities and constraints. Finally, the tendency to view behavioral norms as effects of an actor's structural location leads to the danger of conflating social and cultural structures and stands in the way of productive analysis of how the two structures are interrelated, can interpenetrate, and change each other (Emirbayer & Goodwin, 1994).

Although some of these problems are currently being addressed (see e.g., White, 1992 for a network view of agency), the tendency of social network analysis to lapse into structuralist and static modes of explanation of social behavior is still apparent. Mizruchi (1994, pp. 338-339), for example, regards network analysis as a complement as well as a substitute to other theoretical perspectives, namely, institutionalization theory. What network theory lacks in terms of theoretical power to illuminate the construction of cultural symbols in organizational fields, it can compensate by bringing network concepts to account for the success in their reproduction.

In summary, the minimalist conceptualization of networks and the development of data analysis techniques have provided the impetus for a rapid expansion of social network analysis to a number of fields. The hardening of the network concept into a method has led to a burgeoning field of studies with a high degree of integrity and a coherent set of publications, backed up by a professional society, journals, and conferences. The existence of a social network analysis school of thought can also be traced back to a few central actors (e.g., Harrison White at Harvard in the 1960s and 1970s) who have been instrumental in training new researchers, writing programmatic papers, and performing the role of ambassadors for the field. The willingness of social network researchers to publish in more applied sociology journals, open to a wider audience (such as *Administrative Science Quarterly*), and in edited volumes (such as Nohria & Eccles,

1992) has also contributed to the widespread dissemination of the output of this program of research.

In marketing there are very few direct acknowledgements of this program of research. Reingen and Kernen (1986) in consumer research, Ronchetto, Hutt, and Reingen (1989) in organizational buyer behavior, and Iacobucci and Hopkins (1992) constitute, apart from the work done under the industrial networks banner, some of the few exceptions to this rule.

Interorganization Theory

In the 1970s and 1980s, a group of researchers mainly interested in nonprofit organizations and public administration developed a network approach to interoganizational relations, which Negandhi (1980) termed interorganization theory. The origins of interorganization theory can be traced back to attempts to extend the insights of early organization theory to interorganizational relations (e.g., Aiken & Hage, 1968; Guetzkow, 1966).

Van de Ven (1976) provides a good example of an early attempt to conceptualize the nature of interorganizational relations and the avowedly prescriptive and policy-oriented overtones of this approach. The premise was that a number of social problems concerned with issues such as health or welfare were too complex to be dealt with by any one public agency and that joint agency planning and programing were necessary to cope with these problems. Interorganizational networks emerged as temporary or long-lasting associations between agencies aimed at dealing with a range of social problems. In this formulation, the nodes in the network are nonprofit organizations and public agencies, and the links are represented by resource flows typically defined as financial resources, physical facilities, client or customer referrals, and service delivery. Networks emerge thus as purposeful social systems aiming at coordinating a range of disparate resources to deliver particular types of services targeted at specific social problems. The issues that deserve attention from interorganization theory relate therefore to network design and ensuring that resources can be mobilized to provide efficient service delivery. Measures of network effectiveness and efficiency become important for public policy prescriptions. Examples of this type of research include Galaskiewicz and Shatin (1981), Provan (1984), Van de Ven and Walker (1984), and Whetten and Aldrich (1979). Provan and Milward (1995) constitutes a more recent example of this program of research and one directly concerned with comparative studies of network efficiency and effectiveness.

Increasingly interorganization theory came to use social network concepts such as network centrality and to develop its own arsenal of theoretical vocabulary. The efforts of Aldrich (1979) and Aldrich and Whetten (1981) to develop dimensions of interorganizational relations and to specify different types of interorganizational relationships (organization sets, action sets, and networks) has left a lasting imprint on all branches of network inspired theory. Simultaneously, the concern with resource flows and interdependence between organizations placed interorganization theory in close contact with resource dependency theory (Pfeffer & Salancik, 1978) and population ecology theory, through the work of Aldrich who straddled both fields. Aldrich's (1979) book, although mainly concerned with the basics of population ecology theory, includes three chapters on interorganizational relations, strategies for coping with interorganizational interdependence, and networks of economic power.

Recently, interorganization theory has become even more eclectic by drawing on the increasing body of findings on interorganization cooperation and coordination coming from a variety of disciplinary domains. Alter and Hage's (1993) spirited call for a new theory of interorganizational relations of both profit and nonprofit sectors constitutes a good example of this new trend. Authors such as Keith Provan (e.g., Provan & Gassenheimer, 1994), usually associated with interorganization theory, have recently engaged in studies of relationships between profit organizations, thus blurring the boundaries between the two fields even more.

In summary, interorganization theory, although focusing mainly on relationships between nonprofit organizations and public agencies, has made a significant rapprochement with network approaches focusing on relations between business organizations. Its concern, however, with public prescriptions and network design for effective service provision do limit somewhat the extent of this rapprochement.

Actor-Network Theory

Actor-network theory can be presented as an attempt to build on earlier insights in the sociology of science and technology, usually known as the sociology of scientific knowledge (SSK) (e.g., Pickering, 1992). The actor-network approach is generally associated with the work of Callon (1986, 1987) and Latour (1987, 1988, 1993) in France, and Law (1992a, 1994) in England. Its conceptualization of networks and its concern with process provide a useful counterpoint to the structural sociology traditions associated with most forms of network research.

Actor-network theory reverses the usual idea that networks consist of links between well-established entities. Law (1994), for example, argues that entities, whether actors, organizations, networks in the traditional sense or social relations, are the effects of, or are generated by, a heterogeneous network of materials that are both human and nonhuman in form. If we apply this logic to social or interorganizational networks, then the focus shifts from the relationships between entities to what those relationships do to help define the entities themselves.

Perhaps the most important difference between actor-network theory and other network approaches is the emphasis on process rather than structure; it is a sociology of verbs rather than nouns. The choice of what drives these network processes is also crucial. They are held to be recursive or self-generating: The social is both the medium and the outcome. Actor-network research therefore tends to look for processes of ordering that generate such effects as technologies.

In terms of agency, actor-network theory also moves beyond the simple determinism of structural sociology approaches; agency is also seen as a network effect. Although, however, actor-network theorists are concerned with power, they do not see the exercise of power as inevitable but contingent. The recursive nature of network processes require that energy is devoted to keeping the bits and pieces together—of fighting entropy. It is partly a function of the nature of the materials, for example, their stability and durability, involved in the network that allows particular agents the power to control in particular circumstances.

The term actor-network was first introduced by Callon (1986, 1987) in his description of the case of a failed project by Electricité de France (EDF) to introduce an electrical vehicle in the early 1970s. This project involved a multitude of actors and a series of heterogeneous elements whose identity and relationship to each other were problematic. In practice, the success of the project depended on the ability of the engineers of EDF to enroll the support of, and hold together, an association of social movements, political and economic interests (e.g., ministries, the Renault car company) as well as a host of inanimate elements, the technical solution to building an electrical vehicle (e.g., fuel cells, accumulators). To describe this heterogeneous association of animate and inanimate elements and the mechanisms through which these associations are established, transformed, or consolidated, Callon (1987, p. 93) introduced the term of actor-network. The purposeful association of actor and network attempts to supersede the classical sociological category of actor, a term reserved for humans and not generally associated with the notion of a network. The concept of actor-network depicts the notion that actor is an empirically based category, a heterogeneous association of human and nonhuman elements that is open to redefinition and transformation. As Callon (1987) explains, "An actor-network is simultaneously an actor whose activity is networking heterogeneous elements and a network that is able to redefine and transform what it is made of" (p. 93).

At the heart of actor-network theory is thus a determined attempt to conceive institutions, for example, organizations, the economy, science, technologies, as patterned networks of heterogeneous materials (Law, 1994). This claim is relatively novel to the extent that it regards the social world, itself, as no longer constituted by pure associations between humans and the stable background to which all explanations can eventually be relegated. Granovetter's (1985) concept of embeddedness is a good example of social reductionism; ultimately, economic relations have to be understood by reference to the social networks that underpin economic activity. Actor-network theory would reject this form of explanation and instead look for symmetrical explanations of both society and economy. Both social structures and economic relations are implicated in each others' constructions and to ascribe primacy to one or the other is unwarranted. To devolve all explanation to the realm of social networks presumes that the social realm is relatively unaffected by changes brought about by economic relations.

The networks of the social are also heterogeneous and composed of people, texts, machines, money, and a host of other intermediaries. To investigate how something is socially constructed begs the symmetrical question of how the "social" in "socially constructed" is itself the product of a construction. If the networks of the social were simply associations of people, then social order would not rest on particularly stable or durable foundations (Callon & Latour, 1981). Because the networks of the social are heterogeneous and composed of materials with different degrees of durability, society is able to recursively reproduce itself (Law, 1992a).

Lately, Callon (1992) has attempted to extend the domain of concern of actor-network theory traditionally concerned with scientific and technical domains to markets and to draw on insights from both sociology and economics. For Callon (1992, pp. 134-135) economics teaches us that relationships between actors are defined by the intermediaries that circulate between them (e.g., products, contracts, money). Sociology and structural forms of sociology, in particular, assume that an actor's identity is defined in terms of its relationships and that agency cannot be dissociated from the actor's structural position. Callon (1992) combines these two insights to state that "actors define one another in interaction—in the intermediaries they put into circulation" (p. 135). These intermediaries are defined as literary inscriptions (e.g., reports, books, documents), technical artifacts (e.g., instruments, machines, consumer products), human beings (with their embodied skills, knowledge, and know-how), and money in all its forms. These intermediaries then constitute and order the networks they describe.

In summary, actor-network theory turns some of the traditional structural sociology notions on networks on their head. The idea that society is itself the product of a heterogeneous engineering, involving both human and material elements, and that no social ordering is able to sustain itself across space and time by relying solely on human actions and words, may sound like a trivial conclusion but it has far-reaching implications for social theory. Networks are no longer simple associations between relatively stable and unproblematic entities, allowing researchers to comfortably concentrate on the nature of the links between these entities, but the entities themselves have variable content and variable geometry, to use Callon's (1992, p. 140) expression.

There is hardly any cross-referencing to other network approaches and indeed Law (1994, p. 18) is keen to stress that there is no relationship between his use of the term network and that found in standard sociological theory. It has relied mainly on detailed ethnographic studies of scientific and technological practice (for an exception see Callon, 1993) and has up to now made few forays into what Callon termed the techno-economic domain.

The approach has established a dialogue with innovation studies and the history of technology field as attested by publications such as those by Callon (1993) and Law (1992b). The impact of actor-network ideas on the study of socioeconomic life is still modest but is already visible in accounting (see, e.g., Miller & O'Leary, 1994) and organization studies (e.g., Kavanagh & Araujo, 1995; Knights, Murray, & Willmott, 1993).

Networks of Innovators

The term *network of innovators* was coined by DeBresson and Amesse (1991) following an interdisciplinary workshop in Montreal on the use of a network approach in innovation studies and the subsequent publication of a special issue of *Research Policy* dedicated to the same topic. The use of a network approach to innovation had already been pioneered by Håkansson (1987, 1989) following a number of studies focusing on buyer-supplier interaction in industrial markets. The key insight of these studies was that often buyer-supplier relationships involved a significant amount of technological transactions and exchange know-how, and that innovation was the product of a network of interacting actors (Håkansson, 1987, p. 3). Von Hippel's (1988) innovation studies had proposed a customer-active paradigm of product development in contrast to the old, manufacturer-active paradigm of new product development in industrial markets, supported with a number of empirical case studies.

An earlier string of publications in innovation studies had used the concept of information or communication networks to account for patterns of technical information transfer across firms. The diffusion of innovative products in industrial markets was explained by reference to interfirm word-of-mouth networks (Martilla, 1971). Czepiel (1975) conducted a series of studies on the diffusion of a major, discontinuous process innovation (continuous casting) in the U.S.

steel industry. The major finding of Czepiel's studies was the existence of dense, patterned, and frequently used communication networks linking technical decision makers in rival firms. These networks were found to be used both for information acquisition, validation, and verification. Czepiel (1979, p. 412) noted, however, that informal interfirm communication might be a function of four interrelated variables: (a) the similarity in production processes, (b) similarity in firm organization and division of responsibility, (c) the bases of competition in the industry, and (d) the industry's age and maturity.

Czepiel (1979, p. 413) suggests that in industries such as semiconductors, where competition is based on state of the art technology, the frequency of informal communication might be much lower, given the existence of jealously guarded trade secrets. In mature industries there is a higher likelihood that firms would have developed stable and regular communication channels, given the stability of roles they play vis à vis each other. Contrary to Czepiel's suggestions, Larsen and Rogers's (1984) study of emergent industries in Silicon Valley suggested that it is in the growth phase of an industry when technology and product design are still in a state of flux, that informal and densely patterned communication networks based on reciprocity of information exchange is at its highest. Saxenian's (1994) comparative study of Silicon Valley and Route 128 ascribes the success of Silicon Valley to these rich and dense information exchange networks that continuously cross firm boundaries and maximize the diffusion of technical know-how.

Studies by Von Hippel (1987), Carter (1989), and Schrader (1991) suggest that information is exchanged on a routine basis between rival organizations. Von Hippel (1987), for example, studied the existence of information trading of process-related know-how in the U.S. steel minimill industry—"know-how" being defined as the accumulated practical skill or expertise that allows one to do something smoothly and efficiently. When the required process know-how is not found in-house, an individual can either proceed to develop it in-house, which is costly and time consuming, or else, in the absence of publicly available information, an engineer can contact his or her peers in rival organizations who may have faced a similar problem.

The need to trade informal, proprietary know-how gives rise to contact networks among engineers with common professional interests and facing similar problems in the industry. These networks can be characterized by the content of the exchange—proprietary, process-related know-how—and also by the mode of interaction between members of the network. Reciprocity is thus the main governing rule of the interaction episodes between two professional colleagues, as far as know-how trading is concerned.

The more recent network approach to innovation studies has taken a different stance and has moved away from the focus on interpersonal information exchange networks. DeBresson and Amesse (1991, p. 366) ascribe the emergence of a network approach to innovation, to the realization that internalization of technological transactions to better guarantee appropriability of the benefits of innovation may not always be the best option. Instead, they propose that interorganizational networks may be a superior alternative to internalization for most technological transactions, in particular to develop innovations. Networks may "provide a better set of experiences, encourage learning from other sets of clients and suppliers and leave scope for various applications and experimentation, and reduce sunk investments and irreversible technical commitments" (DeBresson & Amesse, 1991, p. 368).

Innovation studies is a hybrid cognitive community populated by researchers from a variety of backgrounds employing different theoretical and methodological approaches (e.g., economists, organization theorists, economic geographers). The special issue of *Research Policy* devoted to "networks of innovators" provides a good guide to the variety of disciplinary backgrounds encompassed by this approach.

As Freeman (1991, p. 512) suggested, one of the common themes uniting researchers in this area is a dissatisfaction with market versus hierarchy dichotomy and the notion of transaction costs. Instead, other factors such as strategic behavior, appropriability of the benefits of innovation, collective learning, technological complementarity between organizations, and sociological factors such as trust, interpersonal relationships, and information exchange networks are used to explain innovation behavior.

In summary, the networks of innovators approach has been moving from a focus on social information networks carrying mainly technical information and know-how, to a focus on interorganizational relationships and innovation as a phenomenon that occurs within and across organizational boundaries. This shift of emphasis has opened up a new domain of enquiry relating to modes of governance and regimes of appropriability of innovation products and has pushed innovation studies closer to other network approaches, such as the industrial networks approach, who have long since argued the case for studying innovation and learning as the medium and product of interaction between individuals and organizations.

Network Organization Forms

Since the middle 1980s we have witnessed a plethora of publications either forecasting the emergence of network forms of organization (Miles & Snow, 1986), describing their features and extolling their virtues (Jarillo, 1988), or pointing out their limitations and dark sides (Harrison, 1994; Miles & Snow, 1992). The network organization concept is problematic because all organizations can be, and have been, treated as networks with various kinds of links joining actors (Lincoln, 1982).

A further problem with this concept is the way its proponents use it for explaining either internal processes within an organization, generally meaning the introduction of flat structures and the use of hybrid and relatively loose forms of control, and the disagreggation of the firm by outsourcing activities and establishing usually relational forms of contracting with a ring of privileged suppliers. Miles and Snow's (1992) differentiation between stable, internal, and dynamic networks is indicative of the problems plaguing the relative lack of terminological clarity prevalent in this literature. Easton and Araujo (in press) have suggested the two network organization concepts represent simply two potential responses of firms faced with a heterogeneity of demand over time. In the first instance, firms attempt to introduce a capacity for self-design and flexibility to absorb demand heterogeneity, and in the second case, firms attempt to cope with heterogeneous or volatile demand by engaging in long-term relationships with a range of suppliers and subcontractors.

Generally, the argument advanced by the proponents of the network form is an evolutionary one: As environments change, traditional organizational forms' deficiencies become increasingly exposed and new organizational forms emerge, better suited to cope with environmental demands (Miles & Snow, 1992). This evolutionary argument tends to neglect the fact that network forms of economic coordination preceded the rise of the large, bureaucratic firm and some of these arrangements have persisted to this day (Lazerson, 1995). As far as the first variant of network organizations identified earlier (flat structures with hybrid and loose forms of control), two studies deserve particular mention. Baker (1992) argues that the network organization is one way in which an organization can satisfy the classic Lawrence and Lorsch (1967) compromise between horizontal differentiation and integration. "Unlike a bureaucracy, which is a fixed set of relationships for processing all problems, a network organization molds itself to each problem" (Baker, 1992, p. 399). Network organizations, whether planned or emergent, have a high degree of integration, comprising multiple types of socially important relations across vertically, spatially, and horizontally separate formal groups within the organization. Baker studied a real estate firm that was explicitly designed as a network organization, using a variety of network analysis techniques. He found that it was moderately well integrated, given that deficiencies of integration on one dimension (e.g., the horizontal), were compensated for by mechanisms for integration through the other two dimensions. He also noted that network organizations appeared to be particularly suited to "unique customized projects, close customer and supplier involvement in the production process, and complex turbulent environments" (p. 399).

The conditions mentioned by Baker (1992) fit almost perfectly the environment studied by Eccles and Crane (1988); that is, U.S. investment banking. Eccles and Crane labeled the structures of these firms as self-designing, or network-like, and characterized them as flexible, flat, complex, and rife with conflict. Investment banks exist to mediate the flow of assets between issuers and investors, and to perform these functions they must create a set of external ties with customers and other investment banks. With the increasing portfolio of products and services and the changing pattern of relationships between clients and investment banks, matching issuers and investors requires a large number of ties between investment bank employees on either side of the market interface. Every deal pulls together a temporary team of specialists whose constitution may vary over time and is disbanded as soon as the deal is completed. Because these teams are largely self-constituted, as a function of the deals the investment bank engages in, the structures of these firms are continuously being redrawn within the broad parameters established by top management.

In the second interpretation of the network organizational form given previously, firms outsource some of their functions and reap the benefits of flexibility via the configuration of their relationships with suppliers and subcontractors. Often there is strong core versus ring differentiation in these constellations with one firm acting as the strategic hub in the network (Storper & Harrison, 1991). The managerial-oriented literature often refers to these arrangements as "value-added partnerships" (Johnston & Lawrence, 1988) or, in extreme cases "hollow corporations" (Jonas, 1986). Often-quoted examples of these types of network forms include IKEA, Benetton, and Nike (Belussi, 1992; Donaghu & Barff, 1990; Kinch, 1984).

In the field of international business, Ghoshal and Bartlett (1993) describe the structural attributes of multinational corporations using network concepts, and Hedlund (1993) uses the term heterarchy to characterize the same structures. The rationale for the use of network concepts stems from the need to address the specific characteristics of these firms. As Ghoshal and Bartlett (1993, p. 79) point out, the value chains of multinational firms are physically dispersed in environmental settings representing very different social, economic, political, and cultural milieu, and their internal structure is differentiated to respond to these local specificities. As a result of the dispersal of activities, assets, and internal differentiation, multinational firms have developed coordination and control mechanisms to respond to a variety of external demands as well as coping with internal interdependence. The multinational firm thus represents a mode of economic governance that is well removed from the traditional conceptualizations of hierarchy. The relationships between subsidiaries and between headquarters and subsidiaries are governed by a mix of incentives and control mechanisms combining price, authority, and socialization (Hennart, 1993).

In summary, the approach we have labeled "network forms of organization" suffers from many of the problems we identified previously as plaguing the "networks of innovators" approach. Here too, one tends to find the term network used for all forms of economic coordination that do not fit squarely with the rigid market-hierarchy dichotomy. In particular, organizational forms that are designed to deal with either heterogeneity of demand over time (as in the cases of real estate firms or investment banks) or a variety of environmental differences (as in the case of multinationals) and employ a variety of incentive and control mechanisms other than fiat, are lumped together under the label "network form." Similarly, vertical disintegration and outsourcing leading to the formation of relatively stable constellations of core-ring arrangements violate quite clearly the market-hierarchy dichotomy and join the broad church of network forms.

Policy Networks

The concept of networks has also found applications in political science, and has been employed mainly in describing policy-making processes in modern democracies (e.g., Jordan & Schubert, 1992; Marin & Mayntz, 1991; Marsh & Rhodes, 1992). Here again, there are divergences between the way the concept of network can be used to illuminate policy making processes. Mayntz (1993) provides an interesting and parallel account to ours on the attractiveness of a network approach to policy making:

> Organizational networks in policy formation and implementation attracted the attention of political scientists because their existence contradicted the stereotyped image of a clear state/society divide, of the state as supreme societal control center. But, as in the case of market structure, what is involved here is not only a paradigm shift. For many, the notion of "policy networks" does not so much represent a new analytical *perspective* but rather signals a real change in the structure of the polity. Instead of emanating from a central authority, be this government or the legislature, policy today is in fact *made* by a process involving a plurality of both public and private organizations." (pp. 4-5, emphasis in original)

The field of political science also appears to have mainly used the term network in a metaphorical sense rather than a sociometric sense (Van Waarden, 1992a, p. 30). Furthermore, as Hanf and O'Toole (1992, pp. 169-171) point out, there are subtle, but important nuances in how the term network is used. There are also important differences between the American and European traditions of research. The American literature has preferred the micro level of analysis, stressing the nature of social networks between key actors, whereas the European tradition has focused its attention on the structural relations between institutions (Rhodes & Marsh, 1992a, p. 7)

Some authors use the term network in a minimalist sense to draw attention to the fact that policy emerges not from an omniscient center but from the autonomous interaction of interdependent actors, both individual and collective, acting out of self-interest but coordinating their actions, pooling resources, and aligning their interests (Schneider, 1992). Others seem to push a different research agenda, by focusing on interorganizational networks as the unit of analysis and going as far as arguing that the key driving force in policy making lies in the structure of the relations between semiautonomous agencies and not in the structural or strategic characteristics of individual governments. Finally, the term network can also be used in a more normative sense to refer to the design of structures of interaction between semiautonomous agencies to promote the delivery of specific policy aims. There is, of course, a great deal of similarity between this action-oriented conceptualization of a policy network and some of the work we classified under the label interorganization theory, although there is hardly any cross-referencing between the two fields.

A policy network is thus a meso-level concept, providing a link between the micro level of analysis dealing with roles of interests and government in the context of specific policy issues and the macro level of analysis, dealing with questions related to the distribution of power within contemporary sociopolitical structures. Rhodes and Marsh (1992a) provide a simple typology of policy networks, distinguishing between policy communities and issue networks. Policy communities are characterized as having a more stable character and membership, to be dominated by professional (or expert) and economic interests, frequent interaction amongst members of the community, and a degree of consensus over basic values and policy preferences. In contrast, issue networks are characterized as involving primarily policy consultation rather than shared decision making, imperfect understanding either among interests or between interests and government bureaucracy, fluctuating interaction and varied access for members, as well as the absence of stable consensus and the presence of conflict (Rhodes & Marsh, 1992b, pp. 186-187). The concept of policy networks has been applied to a number of industry cases, namely, the chemical and telecommunication networks in Germany (Schneider, 1992), tobacco in the United Kingdom (Read, 1992), and banking in the United States and Canada (Coleman, 1991).

The field of policy networks has also close connections with studies of political economy focusing on corporatist and neo-corporatist structures (e.g., Streeck & Schmitter, 1985). In particular, the concept of policy networks is well-equipped to deal with interest intermediation in organizational fields as conveyed by intermediary organizations such as trade or business interest associations (Saxenian, 1989; Van Waarden, 1992b). Organization fields are populated by autonomous but interdependent actors, in which alignments of interests institutionalized formally through intermediary organizations and informally through issue-based coalitions and temporary cooperative structures, criss-crossing the established order of economic exchange relationships. The notions of political and collective actions to promote and defend economic interests has thus been one of the potential areas of convergence between the study of policy networks and other network approaches to socioeconomic life.

Networks in Economic Geography

In the field of economic geography, the debate about forms of economic organization has centered around the demise or otherwise of Fordist modes of production and the emergence of networks of geographically concentrated small firms, generally known as new industrial districts, as an alternative to the large hierarchical firm. Sabel and Zeitlin's (1985) historical account of the contingencies associated with emergence of mass production, and the bold forecast that new economic conditions required not the economies of scale and scope associated with large firms but the flexibility and capacity for innovation associated with small firm networks, sparked a very lively debate and much empirical work.

Small firm networks, concentrated in particular regions, with geographical proximity fostering a climate of mutual trust and socializing risk, are seen as alternatives to the large scale, big business, specialized production process, vertically integrated, Chandlerian firms that appear to have dominated Western economies for so long. Piore and Sabel (1984) implicitly argued that Fordism was dead and that a post-Fordist, flexible specialization era was dawning. It is perhaps worthwhile to point out that such a characterization is probably overdrawn (e.g., Sayer & Walker, 1991, p. 196) and that one should beware the polemics attached to much of what is written on this subject.

The argument of Piore and Sabel (1984) parallels some of the work classified under network forms of organization. A number of different arguments are conflated but the underlying rationale appears to be concerned with size and complexity. Large complex organizations cannot be understood and managed and therefore cannot change to meet new circumstances. Firms are composed of a core of intrinsic and idiosyncratic capabilities and a set of ancillary capabilities that can be supplied internally more cheaply than they can be acquired through market transactions. But, as Langlois and Robertson (1995) emphasize, as time passes and other firms have the chance to learn, the temptation to outsource or discontinue activities that rely on capabilities that have been replicated at a lower cost by other firms may prove too strong. The boundaries of the firm contract accordingly and its dependence on outside sources increases. Sabel (1991, p. 25) labels these structures metacorporations or Moebius strip organizations. The term metacorporation is used because they are more of a federation of loosely coupled units than a single organizational entity. Moebius strip organizations is used as a metaphor to suggest the difficulty of drawing boundaries around them and distinguishing their insides from their outsides.

Part of the appeal of the notion of new industrial districts is that they appear not to be confined to one institutional context, with some authors claiming that their proliferation is by no means confined to Western economies (Park & Markusen, 1995). With the rise of Fordism it was assumed that corporations were the vector for industrial production and given that their plants could be located anywhere, industrial districts would cease to play a role in industrialized economies. After the war, however, there emerged in a number of different countries (the United States, Italy, Germany, France, and Japan) at different periods similar geographically concentrated industries often, but not always, based on new technology (e.g., Storper & Harrison, 1991). These new industrial districts appeared to represent a general phenomena and one that is related to both size of firm and flexibility.

As Sabel (1989) makes clear, however, there are as many differences as similarities among these regions.

A description of the classic New Industrial District is given by Capecchi (1989) and describes the industrial system in the Emilia-Romagna area in northern Italy from the 1950s to the 1970s. It comprised a large number of small, geographically concentrated firms, small-batch producers with flexible and skilled workforces cooperating closely with their customers. The roles that individual firms took in the system were not clear-cut and there was a mixture of competition and cooperation. Such systems were inherently flexible and met the needs of markets that were both fragmented and changing rapidly. Industrial districts provide an alternative to the major corporation trading on economies of scope instead of economies of scale, and flexibility and innovation instead of standardization and low costs. It should be noted that implicit in this view is the notion that flexibility lies in the network of relationships between firms and their ability to change configurations in response to demand heterogeneity over time rather than in the structure or manufacturing flexibility of individual firms.

There has been also a backlash of counterarguments about both the demise of Fordism and the importance of flexible specialization and new industrial districts. Sabel (1989), for example, points out that large firms equipped with flexible manufacturing systems are offering small firms in the new industrial districts intense competition. It is also clear that the social and political contexts that supported the emergence of this form of industrial system have changed and with it some of the underpinning. The phenomenon of the globalization of economic activity has, according to some (Amin & Thrift, 1992), relegated new industrial districts to the role of a node in a global network of multinational production structures. Harrison (1994) has coined the expression "concentration without centralization" to express his conviction that big firms, although hollowing out, remain firmly in control of the decentralized networks that have supplanted hierarchical structures. Still, other commentators (Best, 1990; Lazerson, 1995) point out that in industries in which there are few throughput efficiencies and limited economies of scale as well as supportive institutional frameworks, decentralized networks of producers may be an extremely efficient mode of economic coordination to respond to heterogeneity of demand and continuous changes in consumer tastes.

In the wake of these debates, a few proposals on network approaches to economic geography have emerged. The Groupe Européen de Recherche sur les Milieux Innovateurs (GREMI) has used the term innovation network in much the same way as we identified in the networks of innovators section (see Camagni, 1991). Cooke and Morgan (1993) use the term network paradigm and qualify it "not so much as a theory as a potentially rich analytical framework for understanding new trends in corporate and spatial development. The fact that it is not beholden to a single theoretical position is clear from the way in which a number of theorists have used the term 'network' to explain new departures in corporate and spatial development" (pp. 543-544). Cooke and Morgan go on to use the terms network and networking at the intra- and interfirm level as well as at the interregional level.

Yeung (1994) presents a more positive and explicit exposition of a network approach to economic geography by contrasting it with a post-Fordist or flexible specialization position and a regulation school stance. Yeung's (1994, p. 462) agenda and theoretical position is stated in terms of using network analysis as the vehicle for resurrecting the firm as the focal unit of the capitalist organization of production, while allowing for a culturally sensitive analysis of the institutional context in which firms operate and in particular their relationships with other economic and political actors. What is perhaps ironic about Yeung's characterization is that although other approaches have used the concept of network to escape from firm-centered analysis, Yeung invites economic geographers to use network analysis as a means to escape from the macro-level arguments of both the post-Fordist and regulation schools of thought.

Yeung (1994) also berates the ambiguous use of the network metaphor but then proceeds to use the term as "the *only* means through which business activities are coordinated and integrated along the production chain" (p. 477, emphasis in original). As such, networks are a higher level concept than either market or hierarchy, and both market and hierarchy should be seen as variants of networks. More interestingly, Yeung proposes a similar typology of network relations to Cooke's and Morgan's (1993) focusing on intrafirm, interfirm, and extrafirm networks. The last category encompasses relationships between firms and political and social institutions, a key topic in the policy networks literature. Finally, Murdoch (1995), following a parallel line to Yeung, has proposed an actor-network approach to the study of change in economic systems as a superior alternative to both flexible specialization and regulation school arguments.

In summary, an incipient network approach to microeconomic phenomena seems to be taking shape in economic geography as a result of some dissatisfaction with broader, macro approaches as represented by the flexible specialization and regulation schools of thought. Ironically, a network approach seems to be emerging as a meso-level compromise to escape from the abstractness of macro-level frameworks and the theoretical barrenness of firm-centered perspectives. In following this trajectory, economic geography seems to be meeting most other network approaches, traveling in an opposite direction.

Comparative Studies of Economic Systems

Over the last decade, propelled by the economic success of East Asian economies, a number of comparative studies have focused on the differences between the Western and the East Asian model of economic organization. Here too, concepts such as market or hierarchy have been found wanting and authors have often delved deeply into the institutional background of these economies and societies to explain patterns of business organization and economic life (e.g., Hamilton & Biggart, 1988). Biggart and Hamilton (1992) and Hamilton (1994) provide excellent summaries of the institutional foundation of firms and markets in Western and East Asian economies and the limits of explanations based on neo-classical economic models. In particular, Hamilton (1994) stresses the historical emergence of notions of individual autonomy and the firm as an autonomous legal entity in the Western world and the contrasting patterns of development in East Asia. The differences are neatly encapsulated in the phrase: "whereas in the West laws regulate the actions of people, norms in Asia regulate the relations among roles" (Hamilton 1994, p. 198).

Comparative studies have focused on the areas of enterprise systems and business groups, management and manufacturing practices, and the background, institutional contexts of societies, and cultures. Other more detailed studies have focused on more specific domains such as labor relations or product development and will not be mentioned here. Under the first heading, the study of Japanese firms and business groups deserves particular mention. Imai and Itami (1984) conclude that although modes of economic organization in the United States and Japan can ultimately be seen as interpenetration between organization and market-based principles, the interpenetration patterns differ markedly between the two countries as a result of institutional, economic, and societal differences. Aoki (1990) and Aoki and Dore (1994) pursue the same research agenda in attempting to build an economic model of the Japanese firm. But for the most part, authors have been concerned with understanding the nature of linkages between business groupings in East Asian economies and the nature of interfirm linkages in production systems. Gerlach (1992), Gerlach and Lincoln (1992); Imai (1992); Lincoln, Gerlach, and Takahashi (1992); and Orrù, Hamilton, and Suzuki (1989) studied in different ways the structure of Japanese business networks using different concepts of network and research methods. Whereas authors such as Imai (1992, pp. 199-200) use the term network in a relatively loose sense, others such as Gerlach (1992) use the term network in both a metaphorical and sociometric sense and make use of blockmodeling techniques to capture the complex pattern of linkages between Japanese firms.

Fruin (1992) provides another excellent example of a historical study of the development of the Japanese enterprise system and highlights the role of interfirm networks in this process. In Fruin's (1992) view, the evolution of the Japanese enterprise system can be understood by reference to the interaction between focal factories, firms, and interfirm networks:

> Competitive strategies and cooperative structures, that is the certainty of permeable boundaries between factory, firm, and network, represent a new and convincing model of interorganizational action, one that differs from prevailing industrial policy explanations for Japan's economic success and one that offers an example of organizational correspondence, reciprocity, and resonance in the midst of change. The strategic consequence is to move whole sets and subsets of interrelated firms in patterns of coalition and network coordination that maximize firm-specific competencies while building network-specific competitiveness and interdependence. (p. 320)

Although some authors stress the unique features of Japanese society and culture as the bedrock on which modes of economic organization rest (e.g., Kumon, 1992, describes Japan as a network society), others would contend that there is nothing unique in the Japanese model of economic organization, stressing instead the role of specific historical contingencies after World War II as explananda for its evolution (Nishiguchi, 1994; Smitka, 1991). Other studies have focused on the transfer of Japanese management practice to their subsidiaries abroad, and the impact of Japanese implants on supplier structures in different countries.

Womack, Jones, and Roos (1990), in a comparative study of the world auto industry, examined the concept of lean production and the way Japanese firms had carved a significant advantage over their American and European counterparts. Cusumano and Takeishi (1991) compared the performance of Japanese and Japanese owned U.S. auto plants, and Kenney and Florida (1993) focused on the performance of Japanese implants and the transfer of Japanese business practices to the United States. Oliver and Wilkinson (1988) studied the impact of the transfer of Japanese management practices to Britain, and Sako (1992) compared interfirm relations in Japan and Britain and concluded that relational forms of contracting are far more prevalent in Japan than Britain.

The same lines of enquiry have been extended to other East Asian business systems and comparisons have been drawn in relation to both Western and Japanese business systems. Hamilton and Biggart (1988), Hamilton, Zeile, and Kim (1990), Orrù et al. (1989), Redding and Whitley (1990), and Whitley (1990) pursue in different ways comparisons between Japan, South Korea, Taiwan, and Hong Kong business systems and their network structures. Tam (1990) contrasts the development patterns of Japanese and Chinese, Hong Kong firms, and Redding (1990) studies the Chinese family firms in Pacific Asia. Like Kumon (1992), Redding stresses the embeddedness of economic activity in social networks and the relatively weak status of firms in these strong social networks.

In the Western world too, institutional differences between different business systems and modes of economic coordination have been receiving increasing attention. Porter (1990), pursuing a midcourse between an industrial organization and a strategic orientation, examines different paths to national competitive advantage and concludes that the role of geographical clusters, networks of tight interdependencies between producers and customers coupled with strong rivalry between producers, played a key role in the competitiveness of a nation. Whitley (1992); Hollingsworth, Schmitter, and Streeck (1994); and Kogut (1993) constitute recent examples of another type of study, pursuing a comparative, sector-oriented institutional agenda.

In summary, the area we have labeled comparative studies supplies us with countless examples of applications of network ideas to socioeconomic life. In examining other business systems, in particular East Asian systems, different authors seem to struggle with traditional notions of market and firm, and often resort to cultural and institutional factors to account for otherwise unexplainable economic phenomena. The need to examine the differences between these economic systems and our own has had the added benefit of highlighting the historical genesis and evolution of economic forms we have long taken for granted, such as the autonomous, legal entity we call the firm. In Chinese family businesses, for example, the firm seems to be rather submerged within a societal structure that privileges roles in social networks rather than autonomous individuals, whose social status and work role are linked in different ways (Redding, 1990). The key insight from comparative studies is that, reinforcing Granovetter's (1985) embeddedness argument, economic life is inextricably bound with a society's culture and institutions, and that sharp differences exist from one society to another. Notions such as market or hierarchy also vary from society to society and in particular, the nature of interfirm relationships and networks is a key ingredient in explaining patterns of business organization in some economic systems.

Finally, we should also point out that there is a considerable degree of overlap between some of the studies quoted here and works we referred to under other headings. Lincoln (Gerlach & Lincoln, 1992; Lincoln et al., 1992), for example, has pursued a research agenda using sociometric notions of networks and applied them to both Japanese and American business groupings. Some theorists quoted under the policy networks heading, in particular Streeck and Schmitter who have studied neo-corporatist regimes, have appeared as coeditors of a volume on comparative studies (Hollingsworth et al., 1994).

Networks in Entrepreneurship Studies

In entrepreneurship studies the use of the term network shares a common ancestry with many of the other perspectives reviewed in this chapter. In particular, entrepreneurship studies took an important turn when the focus shifted from the analysis of sociopsychological characteristics of entrepreneurs to the social and institutional context in which entrepreneurship is embedded (Aldrich & Zimmer, 1986; Birley, 1985). Entrepreneurship represents thus an interesting phenomena to examine from a network perspective. On one hand, entrepreneurs are generally associated with independence and innovation, breaking existing modes of organizing and production of goods and services. On the other hand, entrepreneurship seems to emerge at the junctions of social and professional information networks that supply would-be entrepreneurs with ideas, exchange opportunities and access to valued resources—for example, finance, potential customers, and collaborators (Baba & Imai, 1993). Or, as Sverrisson (1994, p. 412) notes, an entrepreneurial position is a position in which an array of different types of links, connecting to a variety of different networks, is actively focused. In addition, entrepreneurship can be seen as meaning the creation of new firms or internal corporate ventures inside existing firms. The balance between agency and structure, between independence and interdependence in structured contexts can be seen to be at the hub of the entrepreneurship phenomenon.

Most of the research on networks in entrepreneurship studies has used the term in a variety of senses. Some authors see entrepreneurial networks as mainly social in character, stressing the embedded and processual character of entrepreneurial activity. Others attempt to distinguish between different types of networks (e.g., professional, social, commercial) and highlight the interaction between these different networks in entrepreneurial settings. Entrepreneurs often mobilize different networks (e.g., business contacts, family, friends) for resources (e.g., information, capital, other business contacts) to translate their visions and business plans into reality. The use of the same networks for a variety of different purposes and the heterogeneous engineering of these links in support of an entrepreneurial idea seems to be an important characteristic of this phenomenon (Johanisson, Alexanderson, Nowicki, & Senneseth, 1994).

Others use an actor-network approach, combining social and technical networks, for the study of entrepreneurship (Sverrisson, 1994). Another set of studies has focused on the growth processes of start-up, entrepreneurially driven firms and how they use network forms to gain access to valued resources and to establish stable exchange structures based on trust, reputation, and reciprocity (Larson, 1992; Lorenzoni & Ornati, 1988). Larson and Starr (1993) present a useful network model of organization formation based on studies of entrepreneurial firms that constitutes a counterpoint to studies that show how hierarchies evolve into network forms.

In terms of research methods, networks approaches to entrepreneurship have used both qualitative and quantitative, sociometric methods. Studies such as Larson (1992) have relied on case methodology while Johanisson et al. (1994) represents a good example of a comparative, sociometric study of different entrepreneurial settings. Johanisson (1994) makes a cogent argument for expanding the study of entrepreneurial networks using both a qualitative, case-based approach and a quantitative, sociometric methodology.

In summary, network approaches to the study of entrepreneurship have flowered over the last 10 years as a reaction against atomistic and undersocialized views of the entrepreneurial process. The use of the term network is still open to debate as different authors often use the term to refer simply to the social networks of entrepreneurs whereas others insist the act of entrepreneurship consists precisely of the ability to mobilize a heterogeneous assortment of network linkages in support of a project, vision, or business idea.

The links of entrepreneurship studies to other approaches reviewed here should also be noted. The work of Aldrich and associates has strong links to social network analysis, interorganization theory, and population ecology. Johanisson's approach has some interesting resonances with similar conceptualizations of entrepreneurship in industrial networks (e.g., Snehota, 1993). Sverisson (1994) makes explicit use of actor-network theory and Larson's (1992) study fits into the mold of network approaches to the study of organizations. Finally, there are many points of convergence between network approaches to entrepreneurship and economic geography as noted in Malecki's (1994) review. Studies such as Saxenian's (1994) comparison between Route 128 and Silicon Valley focus on entrepreneurship and innovation, and the geographical and institutional context of these phenomena.

Industrial Networks

The industrial networks approach to industrial systems represents a different tradition of research from most of the ones surveyed in this review. First, although there are important cross-references to other network approaches, particularly social exchange theory, the genesis of this approach lies in empirical studies of dyadic relationships in industrial markets, internationalization, and distribution channels. Second, although it can be constructed as a network approach to industrial marketing and purchasing, its scope has broadened to encompass all forms of interdependencies and relationships in organizational markets. In particular, as noted previously, the industrial network approach to innovation and technology transcends the relatively narrow disciplinary boundaries of both marketing and purchasing. Third, it has been developed in parallel with, rather than in response to, other approaches such as transaction cost economics, relational contracting, and interorganization theory. As such, its intellectual trajectory has been somewhat autonomous and less dependent on some of the existing trends that we hold largely accountable for the popularity of network approaches. Finally, its primary proponents have mainly been Swedish researchers and as readily acknowledged by some of them (Johanson & Mattsson, 1994, p. 336), the specific conditions affecting the production of academic knowledge in Sweden and the empirical domains constitutive of the Swedish business systems have played a major role in the development of the industrial networks approach. Such conditions have also facilitated the gradual development of a novel approach, without a clear disciplinary home and with its descriptive and explanatory rather than a prescriptive, managerial focus. These conditions are absent from other management academic settings, notably the academic marketing scene in the United States, with its strict insistence on clearly demarcated disciplinary boundaries, the application of statistical and quantitative methods, and the pressure to move rapidly from the realm of explanation to managerial prescription, as acknowledged by Wilson (1994).

As we indicated previously, the genesis of the network approach lies in the more recent past, in the publications dealing with buyer-supplier relationships in industrial markets and classified under the interaction approach (Håkansson, 1982; Turnbull & Valla, 1986). The interaction approach dealt in relatively fine detail with the development and institutionalization of economic exchange relationships between industrial companies and departed quite radically from the discrete, transactional focus prevalent in the scant industrial marketing and purchasing literature. In particular, the interaction approach demonstrated the existence of complex and multilevel patterns of exchange surrounding each transaction episode in a buyer-supplier relationship. Furthermore, the embeddedness of transaction episodes in a history of prior transaction episodes created a relationship atmosphere, a set of local rules and norms characterized by variables such as conflict, cooperation, power, and dependence that affected and were affected by each transaction episode (Håkansson, 1982).

The provenance of the network approach can thus be primarily associated with the study of dyadic relationships in industrial markets (Easton, 1992). The other major influence has been social exchange theory. Like the industrial networks approach, social exchange theory has aimed to explain the emergence of various forms of social structures, departing from a clear conceptualization of the dyadic exchange relationships. The central plank on which a network approach is built in social exchange theory is that of connectedness of exchange relationships. The concept of connectedness allows us to move away from dyadic analysis and understand the impact of indirect relationships and systemwide effects on individual relationships (Anderson, Håkansson, & Johanson, 1994; Easton, 1992). Håkansson and Snehota (1995) attribute the existence of a network to connectedness effects: "Generalized connectedness of business relationships implies the existence of an aggregated structure, a form of organization we have chosen to qualify as a network" (p. 19).

The network structure thus appears as represented in microinteraction episodes through the enactment of the constraints and opportunities each actor faces as a result of the sum total of relationships she or he is engaged in. At the same time, the network structure is continuously being reproduced or changed through interaction episodes between situated actors. As Håkansson (1987) states: "The network is the framework within which the interaction takes place but is also the result of the interaction. Thus it is affected by the exchanges between the actors" (p. 210). Networks are seen as interacted as well as enacted environments (Håkansson & Snehota, 1989).

The notion of connectedness of business relationships also implies that dynamic processes are at the heart of the industrial networks approach. As Axelsson and Easton (1992) state, "It is only with change that network properties like connectedness and indirect relationships are manifest" (p. 85). Thus a great deal of empirical work under the industrial networks tradition has been concerned with change, particularly technological change (Håkansson, 1987, 1989; Lundgren, 1995).

Although the term network has been used in a variety of senses (see the review by Easton, 1992), recent work has tended to consolidate the approach around the actors-activities-resources model (Håkansson & Johanson, 1992). As we argued earlier (Easton & Araujo, 1992), this model is framed at a high level of generality and its complexity derives from the conceptual interdependence· and interaction between its constituent elements. Recently, Håkansson and Snehota (1995) have attempted to develop the model by specifying the evolution of networks as a result of the dynamic interplay between actor bonds, activity links, and resource ties. This latest work also marks a willingness to move from model building explanations to the managerial implications of a network approach (e.g., Håkansson & Snehota, 1995, Chap. 8).

In terms of research methods, the industrial networks approach has favored qualitative, case-based methodologies, although there are examples of studies combining sociometric with qualitative methods (e.g., Lundgren, 1995). Easton (1995a, 1995b) has examined in detail the set of assumptions governing research in industrial networks and has mounted an argument in favor of a realistic epistemology and case-based methodologies to capture the interdependence and dynamic aspects of industrial networks. For a recent example of the application of this methodological approach see Li's (1995) study of the dynamics of export channels between the United Kingdom and China.

In summary, the industrial networks approach shares some of the antecedents and concerns of other network approaches reviewed here but presents some unique features too. The genesis and evolution of this approach has more to do with the extension of dyadic studies to a systemic level of analysis through the use of the concept of connectedness than with a dissatisfaction with the traditional market-hierarchy approach. The industrial networks tradition has some points of convergence with transaction cost economics but differs quite radically from this tradition in many others (Johanson & Mattsson, 1987). Last, the industrial networks approach has been concerned with process and change as much as with structures, and has tended to adopt a view of network structures as instantiated in the sets of constraints and opportunities enacted in individual interaction episodes.

As far as impact is concerned, we should note that although the industrial networks approach is having a degree of impact on marketing (e.g., Anderson et al., 1994), Håkansson's innovation studies have had a lasting impact on all those studying this phenomenon regardless of their disciplinary background. As we noted in the networks of innovators section, these studies have largely helped to shift the focus from social information networks in innovation to the study of innovation as an interorganizational phenomenon.

IMPLICATIONS FOR NETWORK
RESEARCH IN BUSINESS MARKETS

The main goal of this review has been to contextualize the notion of network as it might be used in describing marketing activities between organizations. We have presented a mapping of 10 fields of study in which the notion of network is being used in terms of a number of key dimensions. These dimensions can be divided into two broad groups. The first group describes the content of the research fields and includes the research goals, the nature of the network links and actors, and the orientation toward structure or process. The second group has to do with research process and comprises the methodological orientation, disciplinary background, and reference to other research fields.

In terms of content, a business network marketing paradigm would have to be concerned with the research goal of explaining how business-to-business markets work. It would have to concentrate on businesses as actors, and links as exchanges of resources. It would be preferable if it espoused a process orientation given that markets are, by definition, dynamic. In terms of research process it should adopt an eclectic set of methodological orientations, be grounded centrally in the discipline of marketing, and make extensive reference to other research fields. Of the 10 candidates discussed in this chapter, only one comes anywhere close to meeting these criteria, the industrial networks approach. We do not claim that the industrial networks approach is the only way to model network phenomena in business markets. We do not even claim that it is a monolithic or even particularly coherent paradigm. It can, however, provide a testing ground on which to explore how other ways of conceptualizing and researching networks can be used to enrich research in our field, keeping in mind all the provisos set out in the introduction to this chapter.

We begin with the content of the network literatures reviewed, further refine the analysis by using links, actors, and structure and process as finer gradations to help in the process of understanding. In terms of research process, we would wish to consider the dialectic between what might be called the analytical and metaphorical methodologies. It should be pointed out, however, that not all of the network fields we have reviewed will have implications for business network research in all the categories we have defined.

In industrial networks, links are defined as economic exchange relationships. In terms of deepening our understanding of such relationships we might wish to borrow from interorganization theory in which the resources may or may not be primarily economic, and exchange may not be the sole form of interaction. In other words, we should recognize that market exchanges may not be the only form of relationships between organizations that are buying from and selling to one another. Similarly, the work on innovator, entrepreneurship, and regional networks points to the conclusion that although market exchanges are involved, they are mediated by strong social ties that will not only influence particular exchange relationships but may involve a different network structure that overlays and constrains or enables the business networks. Comparative network studies extend this idea to include the likelihood that such social networks will differ in structure and process as between countries and will be especially important where the links are themselves cross-cultural. Although the policy network literature is largely concerned with political institutions, it has implications for business network research in that the locus and exercise of power through networks represents a neglected feature of research in this field.

The network organization literature prompts us to consider the nature of exchange in a more fundamental fashion. If the forms of economic organization were conceived of as forming a continuum from hierarchy to market through networks (a view that would be strongly rejected by those working within the industrial networks paradigm), then network organizations could be seen as occupying a position between hierarchy and networks. In that sense, they offer an opportunity to study the form of links within yet another hybrid form, one in which hierarchy breaks down into markets as opposed to the industrial network model, which might be characterized as assuming that networks occur where markets begin to form hierarchies. On a radically different note, actor-network theory reminds us of the important role that the material plays in exchanges and networks, and asks us to consider not only the impact of that which is exchanged (perishable vs. nonperishable commodities) but also the way in which all the material aspects of exchange (invoices, reports, electronic messages) influence the process.

Continuing with network actors, we argue that in this case two different development paths are apparent, deepening and broadening. Deepening refers to new ways of conceptualizing business networks. Broadening describes the processes of extending the notion of business networks to cover other closely related phenomena, as well as placing business networks in more carefully researched social, political, and economic contexts. In business networks we should apparently identify business firms as the actors. The concept of a network organization, however, might lead us to the conclusion that the level of actor aggregation is problematic. Should it be the individual (entrepreneurship studies), the department (innovation studies), the organization (interorganization theory), the net (regional networks studies), or the network (comparative network studies)? The answer would surely depend on the research question, but the identification of actor-with-firm should not be taken for granted. As usual actor-network theory offers an even more radical approach to actor definition. In this paradigm, actors are the nexus of a whole series of material and social relationships and are themselves understood by their effects. In this sense actor-network theory stands network thinking on its head by placing emphasis on actors as relationships rather than actors' relationships. This view also questions the basis for agency as inherent in human actors and offers some interesting ways of resolving notions such as network position.

Broadening our view of actors involves thinking about both the kinds of networks we should study and the other actors we need to understand if we are to make sense of focal business networks. In the first category one might include the obvious nonprofit and institutional sectors as implied by the inclusion of interorganization theory and policy networks in this review. Put another way, would we progress more quickly by studying organizational networks, as opposed to business networks, by virtue of having more contrasting situations to study and by tapping into research in this closely related field? An intermediate category might include the study of actors such as entrepreneurs and networks of actors involved in innovation. In both cases we might argue that they involve issue-based networks, that is networks that occur to resolve particular issues, for example, setting up a new venture, or the innovation processes involved in the creation and adoption of a new product or service. Business networks exist in a context comprising other actors and their relationships with each other and with actors in the focal business networks. These comprise, once again, a whole variety of nonprofit and institutional actors (interorganization theory and policy networks). The structures and processes of these networks are being studied, for example, in regional and comparative network studies, and their results and concepts should surely help establish a broader view of what business networks comprise.

The structure or process orientation differs markedly between the network fields of study we have reviewed. It seems clear, however, that there is a strong structural imperative to network research whether it be analytical or metaphoric in flavor. The power of networks lies at least partly in their ability to characterize conceptual spaces and to do so in a striking visual or mathematical, yet static, way. It is difficult to defend a purely structuralist approach, however, particularly in the field of business networks. Not only is change endemic in these markets, but the constant need by organizations to access and replenish resources through exchange and to maintain their structures against entropic drift suggests that any perspective that does not attempt to model process is doomed to failure. Moreover, the most appealing and radical fields of study are precisely those in which a process orientation is most obvious. This is not to argue that structure should be ignored. Rather, we would prefer to see a situation where the two elements coexist within a theory of network process with neither dominating.

We turn now to the research process. The key issue here is best captured by the analytical versus metaphorical dichotomy. The social networks analysis paradigm provides the best, although not only, example of the former category. Almost all other network research reviewed here is metaphorical to a greater or lesser extent. Social network analysis is best described as a set of mathematical, largely matrix-based techniques, which can be, and have been, used to describe a whole variety of network phenomena. The limitations of social network analysis for business networks are twofold. It is apparent that the social concepts employed (e.g., centrality) spring from the techniques rather than vice versa, although there is evidence that that is changing (see Nohria & Eccles, 1992). This is a grave constraint on theory development. The second limitation is the limited access to relevant data. Large and complete data sets of nodes (business firms) and their links (exchanges, exchange relationships, communications, ownership ties, and so on) are required but are rarely available via secondary sources. Primary data collection is likely to be prohibitively expensive and time consuming, even assuming access to confidential data (e.g., lists of customers) is possible. The existence of these problems explains the rather esoteric data sets to which network analysis has been applied, most notably interlocking directorships. The alternative methodologies are largely case based or qualitative, which at least have the potential to tease out network processes but cannot handle large data sets, are time consuming, unacceptable to positivists, and can be faulted on their ability to allow generalization (but see Easton, 1995b). Clearly the research questions should dictate methodology but economic and access constraints cannot be ignored, and there is always a temptation to work along the fault lines of the research phenomena, looking for the easy and convenient rather than most appropriate route (Easton, 1995a).

The second dimension of the research process is that of disciplinary background. It is hardly surprising, given the popularity of social networks analysis and its genesis, that sociology appears as the most frequent source of network research literature. An equally interesting finding, however, is that all other social science disciplines, and some non-social science disciplines, can (or could) be represented as having a body of researchers interested in network phenomena. If network researchers in business-to-business marketing are looking for a justification for their interest they need look no further. We hope and believe that the current fashion for network research is more than just that.

The final comparative dimension is that of cross-referencing of research. In some cases there is none—in others, limited reference to, perhaps, work in one other discipline. This observation takes us full cycle back to the introduction. It would be easy to suggest that all network researchers (indeed all researchers) should read relevant literature in other disciplines. There are obvious barriers to this process—time, expertise, relevance, credibility, misapprehension, and so on. The benefits are not always obvious. As we stated earlier, it is not always easy, desirable, or even possible to transfer directly understanding in the form of concepts, research findings, or theory from one paradigm to another. The process of diffusion should perhaps be more subtle than that. It ought to proceed from a greater understanding of the world in general by the individual researcher, which is then translated into better research in his or her field. We hope that in this chapter we have gone some way to helping this process along for researchers of business networks.

Strategic Alliances in a Network Perspective

HÅKAN HÅKANSSON

D. DEO SHARMA

How to cope with strategic alliances is a widely discussed issue in the current business literature. Researchers from different fields such as marketing, strategy, international business, and industrial organization are paying increasing attention to strategic alliances. A reflection of this trend is an increasing number of publications dealing with strategic alliances. Most of these studies have been based more or less explicitly on approaches connected to classical market theory, especially the transaction cost theory (e.g., Coase, 1938; Williamson, 1975, 1985). In recent years, on the other hand, an alternative approach, the network approach, to study market behavior has developed. An issue of interest is, then, how these two approaches differ in their way of analyzing strategic alliances. In what respects do they differ and resemble each other, respectively? The purpose of this chapter is to elucidate the similarities and differences between the two approaches with respect to strategic alliances.

STRATEGIC ALLIANCES FROM A MARKET VIEW

Strategic alliances are defined in a variety of manners. Faulkner (1995) defines a strategic alliance as a "cooperative arrangement between organizations in which the partners make substantial investments in developing a long-term collaborative effort and common orientation" (p. 189). Parkhe (1991) defines strategic alliances as a "relatively enduring interfirm cooperative involving flows and linkages that utilize resources and/or governance structures from autonomous organizations, for the joint accomplishment of individual goals linked to the corporate mission of each sponsoring firm" (p. 581).

Both definitions refer to external relationships between two firms, which, in principle, are independent with prespecified goals. Strategic alliances are seen as different from the normal buyer-seller relationships, but they are also different from full acquisitions and mergers. The term *strategic* indicates that the alliances are formed to improve the future position of the firms. Alliances that concern either the present or the immediate future are not seen as strategic. Strategic alliances should have very clear and prespecified long-term goals or ends.

The empirical base for the research on strategic alliances from this view has come from diverse sources, and the analyzed relationships are frequently pictured as nonmarket relationships that lie in between markets and hierarchies (Nielsen, 1988). There are exceptions. Hamel (1991) in his research concludes that a strategic alliance "is viewed not as an alternative to market-based transactions or full ownership, but as an alternative to other modes of skill acquisition" (p. 99).

Much research has been focused on the motivational aspects of strategic alliances, namely, forming strategic alliances to acquire skills (Hamel, 1991), strategic alliances between competitors (Burgers, Hill, & Kim, 1993), and strategic alliances in purchasing (Centry, 1993). Less attention has been given to the dynamic and developmental process aspects (Thomas & Trevino, 1993). Strategic alliances are formed with either the competitors (competitive alliance) or with noncompetitors (collaborative strategic alliances).

STRUCTURAL CHARACTERISTICS

Instrumentality and Rationality

Both the aforementioned definitions emphasize the instrumental and rational aspects of strategic alliances. Firms enter into strategic alliances with their purpose being to achieve some well-specified goals. These goals are articulated in advance. Strategic alliances are characterized by the following three characteristics: (a) partners have well-specified goals, (b) each partner makes a search for an appropriate counterpart to enter into a strategic alliance. This search is objective in the sense that only the future matters. The history of the cooperating partners and their other existing exchange relationships with other firms are not considered, and (c) firms enter into a negotiation process with the counterpart firm to formulate the strategic alliance.

The existing literature identifies a number of different reasons for firms to enter into strategic alliances. A common reason often identified is that the partners want to get access to critical external resources (Aiken & Hage, 1968). As an example, Kanter (1989) states that strategic alliances allow "getting the benefits of what another organization offers without the risks and responsibility of owning it" (p. 7). Other reasons for getting into a strategic alliance could be rapid technical changes in an industry (Hamel, 1991), financial difficulties, reducing risks, and to rapidly enter markets (Lei & Slocum, 1991). Given these differences, alliances can be characterized in terms of collaborative versus competitive goals, and internalization of partners' skills versus access to these skills externally.

Rationality is also an obvious factor to consider when the choice of the counterpart firm is analyzed. The partner is (or should be) carefully selected, and a governance structure developed to check opportunism. Selecting a right alliance partner is a basic issue. By the right alliance partner is implied that the cooperating firms should be matched strategically and culturally. Strategic matching means that the assets and the skills of the partners are complementary so that by entering into a strategic alliance the partners enjoy the fruits of synergy. An optimal alliance is one in which the assets, skills, and the culture of the partners are complementary. Hamel (1991) argues that companies with a clearly stated objective to acquire skills and know-how from the partner are indeed more successful in doing so. The alliances that viewed alliances as a substitute for learning did not produce much of a learning effect. Rather, in the successful alliances, "learning took place by design rather than by default" (p. 92). Trial and error must be avoided.

Continuity

A typical strategic alliance is a long-term continuous relationship. The definition of "long-term" varies. Continuity in strategic alliances is achieved primarily through a formal and legally enforceable agreement, which specifies a termination point in the alliance. Within this time period, partners in the strategic alliance are supposed to achieve their goals. Telser (1980), however, argues that the more uncertain the termination point of the agreement, the more self-enforcing the alliance. This situation does not demand that strategic alliances continue forever, but simply that the termination point is uncertain. In this respect it is important to remember that the strategic alliances are means to an end. Consequently, it is expected that the decision makers will terminate the alliance once the stated or perceived aims are achieved.

Typically in this analysis, the past relationship between the alliance partners is not included or seen as relevant. Each strategic alliance is a separate entity, unrelated to the other exchange relationships between the partners or to those with other partners. The alliance is begun through the two parties doing their homework and then combining their suitable resources in the alliance.

The issue of continuity in the strategic alliance is taken up indirectly in this literature by assigning the future pay-off pattern an important part in explaining the persistence in strategic alliances. As Parkhe (1993) states, "the driving force behind alliance formation is each participant's assignment of a net positive value to expected alliance outcome" (p. 797). In the literature since 1990, the dynamic aspects have come more to the surface, a point we discuss in more detail in the process section.

Complexity and Informality

The literature on strategic alliances prior to 1990 focused its attention on two aspects, namely, form and structure. These properties of alliances determined the exchange between the partners. This literature, based mainly on the transaction costs approach, emphasizes the legally enforceable contracts to contain opportunism and cheating.

Earlier we discussed the motivational aspects of strategic alliances. The partners are independent but they expect to make gains by joining into an alliance. Strategic alliances are formed because "each needs the other to advance their individual interests" (Gray, 1989, p. 7). These needs, however, can evolve into opportunism. Parkhe (1993) states, "these needs intersect with behavioral uncertainty to create vulnerability to opportunism" (Parkhe, 1993, p. 798). Thus, an important managerial task is to create mechanisms to oppose and suppress opportunism in strategic alliances. Doing so is important because both partners invest resources and stake their future in the alliance. Here dynamic factors are seen as a problem. It has been stated that initial conditions may change and therefore these "dynamic changes in the internal and external environments of firms may alter the initial payoff conditions and contribute to the improvement or deterioration of the structural viability of cooperative relationships" (Parkhe, 1993, p. 799). Hence, legal contracts are important.

Due to the emphasis on opportunism and cheating, conflicts and efforts to contain conflicts have received much emphasis in the literature. One way to resolve conflicts is through legally enforceable contracts. Conflicts are seen as a threat to the satisfactory functioning of the alliance, thereby threatening the possibilities for the partners to achieve their goals. At the same time, conflicts can evolve from the fact that partners have different and opposing goals—the strategic alliances are often seen as a zero-sum game.

The recent literature has integrated the game theory approach with the transaction costs approach. Aspects such as informality and reciprocity between the alliance partners and the commitment made by the partners have entered the literature. An increasing number of researchers emphasize the prospects of future cooperation and payoffs as mechanisms to govern strategic alliances. Parkhe (1993), borrowing from Telser (1980), sees strategic alliances in which "each firm compares the immediate gains from cheating with the possible sacrifice of future gains that may result from violating an agreement." The partners are thought to be behaving in a rational manner, so they are guided with the future expectation of returns and reciprocity. The reciprocity is not necessarily balanced. However, "the magnitude of the difference among the payoffs within a given class of game can be an important determinant of cooperation" (Parkhe, 1993, p. 800). Similarly, it is argued that "the thicker the nexus between current moves and future consequences, [the greater the coopera- tion] because forward-looking expectations of gains hold in check proclivity toward agreement violations" (Parkhe, 1993, p. 800).

One view is that open-ended strategic alliances are optimal (Roehl & Truitt, 1987), but this is a minority view. The majority of the researchers recommend rather foolproof alliances in which the part- ners agree on the goals and the procedures to govern the strategic alliance in advance. Well-established procedures for resolving dis- putes and conflicts, and procedures to ease divorce between the partners are also recommended. An increasing number of researchers have recognized that evolving a foolproof, legally enforceable gov- ernance structure is hardly possible. This issue has brought the process of how to design an alliance into focus.

PROCESS CHARACTERISTICS

Cooperation, Conflict, and Adaptation

In general there has been very little interest among researchers regarding process characteristics. Process was seen as more or less given by structural conditions, and was necessary only to get the structural dimensions formulated into a legal alliance. Process was thought to follow rational criteria. For example, in the choice of partners, rationality implies identifying optimal criteria for partner selection, searching and scanning for potential partners, assessing partners' cultural and strategic complementarity, and negotiating, deciding on, and formulating the nature of the strategic alliance. Next, resources that have been contributed are handled, and returns from the alliance allocated. The gradual process of relationship building has not been receiving much attention in this literature.

A majority of the researchers recommend formal and well-estab- lished procedures for resolving conflicts, and procedures to ease divorce between the partners. Formal procedures force partners to stick to the terms and conditions of the legal agreement. It is increas- ingly being recognized that because of the bounded rationality of the human brain, the future is unknown and evolving a foolproof, legally enforceable governance structure is hardly possible. It is important for trust and commitment to evolve between the alliance partners

(Granovetter, 1985; Killing, 1988; Parkhe, 1991, 1993). Hamel (1991) stressed a similar point. Niederkofler (1991) stated that trust increases the partners' tolerance for each other's behavior and helps to avoid conflicts. Trust between alliance partners allows for an informal resolution of conflicts. Informal measures to resolve conflicts allow the partners to adapt to the needs and capabilities of the counterpart firms. Adaptations are important in coping with future contingencies. Gaining power is important and less emphasis is given to social interaction between the partners.

These developments indicate that once a strategic alliance is formed, some dynamic changes are expected to occur. The goals of the partners change, the environment surrounding the strategic alliance is changing and may alter the initial payoff conditions and contribute to the improvement or deterioration of the "structural viability of cooperative relationships" (Parkhe, 1993, p. 799). Therefore, it is important that an appropriate governance structure evolve.

OUTCOME

The outcome and success of strategic alliances is discussed in terms of longevity and satisfaction (Beamish, 1984; Gomes-Cassers, 1987). Longevity, or the duration of the strategic alliance, is used as a measure of success in strategic alliances (Harrigan, 1988; Lewis, 1990). Satisfaction is usually derived and measured along several dimensions, namely, profit and market share. Satisfaction is determined by the congruence between the goals for entering into the strategic alliance compared with what the partners actually achieve (Geribger & Herbert, 1991).

The two measures are related. The longer the alliance persists, the more successful was the alliance. Satisfaction is discussed in terms of success and failure in achieving the prespecified goals of the alliance partners. The outcome of the strategic alliance and the extent to which the respective partners achieve their goals is explained with the help of the bargaining and bargaining power of the respective alliance partners. Hamel (1991) thus concludes, "depending on its bargaining power, a partner will gain a greater or lesser share of the fruits of joint effort" (p. 100). A similar view is expressed by Moxon, Roehl, and Truitt (1988). Hamel (1991) discards longevity as a

TABLE 7.1 Network Versus Traditional Views of Strategic Alliances

	Early Literature	*Recent Literature*	*Network*
Purpose	—Quasi internalization means to an end well-defined in advance	—De facto internalization means to an end well-defined in advance	—De facto internalization means to an end not well-defined in advance
Underlying process	—Value creation	—Value creation and value appropriation	—Value creation and value appropriation
Success factor	—Structure and the legal shape	—Legal shape important, nature of the exchange, development of trust and adaptation between the parties	—Nature of the exchange, developing trust and commitment; legal shape less important; informal processes important
Complexity	—Simple and legal based	—Complex and informal	—Complex and informal
Division of labor and benefit	—Clear and sharp	—Blurred and changing	—Blurred and changing
Time duration	—Well-defined	—Well-defined	—Less well-defined
Level of analysis	—Two firms, past not considered	—Two firms, past not considered	—Whole network, past very important
Example	—Harrigan (1988), Tyebjee (1988)	—Hamel (1991)	—

measure of success. Rather, the success of strategic alliances is considered in terms of collaborative exchange based on macro bargaining. Table 7.1 summarizes the major points made in this discussion.

THE NETWORK VIEW

Companies in a Network Structure

In a network structure, every actor (company) has a set of relationships with different counterparts (customers, suppliers, complementary producers, and competitors). The relationships in this set can vary with regard to being long term, resource demanding, and so on. Some of these relationships fit nicely into the previously stated definitions of strategic alliances.

Here we can see, however, the first major difference. Because cooperation is expected to be more or less the rule in a network, it will not at all be seen as so special as in the "market" view of strategic alliances. A consequence is that it will be much more difficult to distinguish between strategic alliances and "normal" alliances. There will be many more examples of relationships from which to choose! The approach basically suggests that the whole question could be turned upside down. In a network approach, it might be a more strategic decision for a company to determine those others with which it ought not to work closely!

Among the existing relationships there are, however, certainly some that can be seen as more strategic than others. They can be, for example, very critical if a certain situation emerges or they can be more important over a longer time period. Those being critical (strategic) in a specific situation are probably impossible to characterize in any general way, because their importance is clearly determined by the situation. That is, some specific feature in the situation is what makes a certain counterpart become so critical. Consequently, the discussion here will be limited to those alliances that are expected to be more important over a longer time period.

In the first section, we will discuss the strategic alliances from three points of view. We will start with the process and discuss how the alliances are expected to come into being given a network approach. We will then analyze the structure, or the alliance as a part of a structure, and finally we will turn to the expected results.

Processual Aspects

The typical business relationship in a network evolves in an organic way. It is formed step-by-step through an interaction process (Håkansson, 1989; Håkansson & Snehota, 1995). Some important features of, or ingredients in, this organic process are social exchange, adaptations, and institutionalization. Social exchange means that trust and commitment is built up over time in accordance with the description given by Blau (1964):

> Typically, . . . social exchange relations evolve in a slow process, starting with minor transactions in which little trust is required because little risk is involved and in which both partners can prove their trustworthiness, enabling them to expand their relations and engage in major transactions. (p. 454)

The interaction process leading to a relationship is in this way a trial and error process. Furthermore, it is a process where the next act is always dependent on the earlier ones and where the act also will be seen as a reaction to earlier actions. It is not a series of separate actions but parts in a continuous process framed by the actors involved. The dynamic aspects are obvious. What can be achieved is more related to what is happening during the process than to predetermined goals or ambitions. Each of the two counterparts in an interaction process can throw in whatever type of problem and opportunity they have internally, or in relation to other parties. The process can thus become very much embedded into other processes. Two important consequences can be identified. First, these connections can have a strategic importance because they can be used to influence others. The more connections that exist, the larger these possibilities will be, and the more the relationship will be central to the context, thereby having a strategic content. Second, the embedded character of the process can make it difficult to identify the boundaries of the process itself. It will be interwoven with other processes and there will be different types of interconnections between them.

Adaptation is the second ingredient. An adaptation means that one or both of the involved actors change one parameter—it can be in technology (process or product), in administration, or in some other aspect—to function better in relation to the counterpart. These adaptations are partly done in a conscious way in which different consequences have been evaluated, but partly also to solve upcoming problems in the interaction process. Adaptation might be done locally in these cases meaning that there will be only a few persons informed about them. Such adaptations will be revealed first when someone is trying to change the relationship, for example, change the counterpart firm. Adaptations of both types clearly have strategic importance. They can be important change elements (innovations), such as when a new product is developed together with a customer, or they can be an upholding factor giving the company a certain amount of time in a crisis situation.

The third ingredient in the interaction process is institutionalization. When several persons from each side have contacts over a longer time period, the relationship will become institutionalized; that is, there will develop routines and sentiments giving the two counterparts a feeling of belonging together. Other parties will also see them as belonging together, or "married," thereby seeing them as related long term. A consequence of this is that the relationship will be perceived as strategic by others despite what the parties' ambitions are in relation to each other.

Structural Aspects

One important difference to the market view is that in the network case there is a certain specific structure in which the relationship is a part. The relationship is not a special dyad within a market sea of independent actors, but an element related to similar elements in a certain structure. Obviously, the relationship will have quite different functions given its role within this structure. The analysis of the structural aspects will thus be much more extensive than in the market case. From the description of the interaction process, it is possible to identify three different types of contents in the relationships that are important from a structural point of view (Håkansson & Snehota, 1995). First, we explore how a relationship can relate resources on the two sides to each other. Through the relationship, the knowledge of the resources and their features is confronted and can be adapted in different ways. Second, a relationship can be a means to link activities performed by the two parties. The activities can be coordinated through the relationship both in terms of design and time. Third, through the development of a relationship the parties will change their perception of each other, as well as how they are perceived by others. Each of these three structural aspects will now be discussed in greater detail.

Tying Resources

Resources of the two counterparts can become related to each other through the interaction process. A relationship can, in this way, be a part or an element in each of the two companies' resource collections. To assess the importance of a certain relationship in this dimension we can use three criteria: (a) the share of total resources the relationship accounts for (volume of total costs), (b) the importance of the relationship for the technical function in the production process or product, and (c) the number of alternative sources with which a corresponding relationship can be developed. In the situation in which volume is large, even a very small deviation can be important from an economic point of view in terms of how the resource is handled, how it is related to other resources, and so on. Consequently, it can be strategic to have a counterpart firm who is prepared to change even small details. This counterpart must have a feel for how important the resource is for the focal company. A special problem arises when the volume is important for one party but not for the other.

When the resource is strategic from a technical point of view, there are thousands of technical developmental opportunities that must be considered over time. The value of these opportunities is generally very much influenced by how they can be combined with other developments, that is, that they become part of the total resource constellation. To get that kind of priority it might be valuable with a "strategic alliance"—or it can be the only way to get such special treatment.

The third aspect of tied resources regards the number of possible counterparts. When there are few alternative firms with which to form a strategic alliance, it becomes particularly important to be a high priority by at least one of the alternatives.

The conclusion is that when these dimensions have certain values (large volumes, high technical importance, few alternatives) there are obvious reasons for a company to develop one specific relationship in such a way that it can be regarded as more strategic than others. The higher priority can be given in terms of the company being more alert to signals from the counterpart, or more conscious about its importance, or attempting to build the relationship closer into the network (connect it more with other relationships).

Linking Activities

An activity performed by external actors can be critical for a focal company if its performance influences the performance of the firm's own activities. Such an activity can be situated before or after, or parallel to, the firm's own activities.

Activities done before or after can be dependent in technical terms, in timing, or from an administrative point of view. These dependencies can be extensive because, for example, technical parameters given to a product in one production stage are often critical for the performance of the next production stage. Timing is a factor that has merited much attention during the last decade due to the interest in the concept of just-in-time delivery systems. The dependency can also be more indirect, however, such as when the focal company is valued because a counterpart (supplier or buyer) can combine it with some other relationships with some special positive effects.

In the parallel cases, there is always the question of indirect dependency; dependencies between activities in the focal company with activities performed by complementary or competing actors. The linking of activities gives possibilities to rationalizations over several production stages and in relation to different directions. The links are means to materialize production dependencies without getting into the full integration. Some of these links can be so critical from a productivity point of view that the corresponding relationship must be considered strategic.

Bonding Actors

A relationship means that two actors are bound together. They will become known to each other; that is, they will get very clear identities in relation to each other. Their being bound also affects how they are seen by others. This can also be strategic; it can be that the other actor has close contacts with other actors who can be important to the focal company in different ways. Alternatively, the relationship can provide special contacts with influential actors (legal or others), or it can be more general contacts with a large number of actors within the network. In the latter case, the relationship can give a certain general identity to the focal company, clearly strategic for the focal company.

Results of Strategic Alliances

Discussing the results of strategic relationships gives us a reason to look once again at what can comprise a strategic relationship in a network setting. In a world in which a company has a whole set of relationships to counterpart firms, there is hardly any specific relationship feature that will characterize strategic ones. Thus, we can only use quantitative aspects of the relationships (length of time, volume, and so on) to some degree to identify the strategic ones. In combination, we have to use the qualitative dimensions of the relationships. A relationship can be more or less important as a determinant for actions in different dimensions. A strategic relationship can be one that is influencing the characteristics of other relationships, or for which specific demands are prioritized.

Consequently, there are several characteristics of the results that are unique to a network approach. They can be summarized in the following points:

Results of strategic alliances can be rather unexpected because they will be the result of the process more than of the ambitions at the moment the relationship began (i.e., a dynamic aspect);

Results can be difficult to identify because the development process of a single relationship is embedded, and consequences can appear quite far from the origin, that is, in other relationships (i.e., a limitation aspect); and

Results can appear in a number of different dimensions (i.e., a multidimensional aspect).

DISCUSSION

The presentation of the two approaches to strategic alliances shows a number of distinct differences but also some interesting similarities. Especially when the approaches are used for the description of the phenomenon itself, there are clear similarities. They clearly differ, however, in regard to explanations or normative advice. We will concentrate the discussion on three points: first, the unit of analysis; second, the value created by an alliance; and third, the governance form.

The Unit of Analysis

An important difference between the two approaches lies in the unit of analysis. The unit of analysis in the traditional market literature is the dyadic relationship between the alliance partners. No importance to the remaining exchange relationships of the alliance partners is given. It is assumed that the alliance partners are free to choose, that the other connections and exchange relationships of these firms are neither problematic nor an asset in relation to the alliance. Each strategic alliance is viewed in isolation from the rest of the exchanges by the involved firms. One advantage is that each relationship is defined by very clear boundaries; it becomes easy to describe and assess. But at the same time, this assumption also determines what type of explanatory variables will be used. Consequently, it will be the ambitions and the characteristics of the partners that will be viewed as the most important influencing variables. As a unit of analysis, the dyad is, furthermore, generally seen as having a certain fixed content over time. Little interest is devoted to its development or to dynamic consequences.

The network approach, on the other hand, stresses the interdependence between relationships. Any relationship has to be analyzed in relation to the whole set of relationships in which each of the partners are engaged. One obvious problem is the identification of the features of such relationships because it is impossible to identify the boundaries. Still, it is possible, at least according to those advocating a network approach, to identify characteristics that should cover the connectedness of the relationship. One important consequence is a focus on the developmental process—strategic alliances evolve as a result more of what is happening than from the firms' initial ambitions.

Value and Value Creation

The traditional market literature discusses the value of a strategic alliance in relation to the existing ambitions and resources of the partners. Later research within this tradition, however, has moved more toward the issue of value generation and value distribution between the alliance partners. The network literature emphasizes that strategic alliances are like any other exchange relationship in that the results of a value creation process are based on a fair and balanced division of both labor and benefits. The value is created by frequent interaction between people on various levels in the alliance partner firms. In this manner, in the network view, a strategic alliance takes on an independent life after a period of time and develops into an "independent" organization. The term independent here implies that the strategic alliance develops its own context in terms of connections to internal resources and activities within the two counterpart firms, as well as to other exchange relationships. These other relationships can be a source to mobilize resources or a base from which to rationalize activities. Over time, strategic alliances emerge as semi-independent structures and entities with connected actors, resources, and activities. Alliances acquire their own legitimacy and value and an independent right to survive. Therefore, a strategic alliance is not only a rational purposive means, but it will also take on its own development. It will ensure its survival, and to maintain its legitimacy, an alliance will alter the goals and missions to suit the needs of its different exchange partners in the network. In exchange, the network will ensure the supply resources for the strategic alliance to carry out activities. Formally, the alliance may continue to exist as before, but in reality it will function more or less independently of its parent organizations.

This network view is different from the traditional literature, which considers strategic alliances as discrete, time-bound, rational structures developed with the purpose of executing a prespecified task. In this view, once the task is executed and the mission is achieved, the strategic alliance is dismantled. Then, strategic alliances cannot have an independent life, value, or legitimacy of their own. Alliances are thought to exist as long as the respective parent organizations want the strategic alliance to continue, and as along as they are willing to supply resources to the strategic alliance. Basically, strategic alliances are not considered or expected to have their own identity.

Governance Form

A major difference between the two approaches lies in their emphasis on the governance structure in strategic alliances. On this issue, the traditional approach places more emphasis on the importance of the structural aspects than does the network approach. The traditional approach puts emphasis on developing an appropriate legal structure to define the contributions by the alliance partners, a division of labor between the alliance partners, and a division of benefits between the partners. Thus, the value of the legal contract is emphasized. The network approach emphasizes the limitations of any legal structure in governing strategic alliances. These limitations are due to the cognitive limitations of the human brain, but also the inability to control the environment, which keeps changing. Thus, the network approach is concerned with the issue of developing extensive relationships, where there is a free exchange of views, problems, and prospects between the alliance partners, and a development of an appropriate process to relate and coordinate activities and resources with the counterpart firm.

The traditional literature on strategic alliances, based on the transaction costs approach by Williamson (1975, 1985), emphasized opportunism and cheating. The value of legally enforceable contracts is emphasized. Thus, a water-tight, legal contract is required in which the partners agree in advance on goals and procedures to govern the strategic alliance. Well-established procedures for resolving disputes and conflicts, and procedures to ease divorce between the partners, are recommended. The recent literature integrates the game theory approach with the transaction costs approach. Thus, terms such as reciprocity, fairness, trust, equity between the alliance partners, and commitment made by the partners have entered the literature (Parkhe, 1993; Tesler, 1980). Reciprocity and future gains are important in governing strategic alliances. Alliance partners behave in a rational manner and they are guided with the future expectation of returns and reciprocity. In this, strategic alliances as described by the traditional approach and the network approach are rather similar; both emphasize the importance of future gains for the alliance partners. These researchers recognize that evolving a foolproof, legally enforceable governance structure is hardly feasible. It is recognized that because of the bounded rationality of the human brain, and the fact that the future is unknown, drafting water-tight, legal agreements is hardly feasible. It is important for trust and commitment to evolve between the alliance partners (Granovetter, 1985; Killing, 1988; Parkhe, 1991, 1993).

CHAPTER

Managed Networks

Creating Strategic Advantage

ALEXANDRA J. CAMPBELL
DAVID T. WILSON

How can firms build a competitive advantage that is difficult to copy? Recent strategic thinking (Pralahad & Hamel, 1990) views positional and performance superiority as a consequence of relative superiority in the resources that a business deploys. In turn, these resources are the result of past investments made to enhance the firm's competitive position. Resources, comprising integrated combinations of assets and capabilities (Day, 1994), have traditionally been thought to reside primarily within the firm. There is increasing empirical evidence, however, that suggests that superior resources can also emerge from the synergy resulting from the coordination of independent firms in a series of value-adding partnerships. Wal-Mart's cross-docking logistics system, which enables the transfer of inventory from suppliers to stores in less than 48 hours (Stalk, Evans, & Schuman, 1992) is the result of close linkages that harmonize the skills and knowledge of diverse sets of suppliers. Capabilities and interorganizational processes are closely entwined, because it is the firm's capability that enables the activities in a business process to be carried out by independent firms operating autonomously.

In an expanding global economy, firms are finding it increasingly difficult to remain autonomous if they want to stay competitive. Although many industry structures are now defined by networks of

125

relationships in which firms are increasingly interdependent, few networks reinforce a firm's long-term competitive advantages—even fewer develop into a system of relationships that create a sustainable advantage. One reason for this is that most managers still view their firms as discrete entities and believe that advantage can be gained through adversarial behavior or through forward or backward integration. At best, managerial attention is focused on identifying individual dyadic alliances, which create strategic advantage. Firms integrate their buyer-seller relationships or form strategic alliances with a partner to develop new products or markets. Such relationships are often piecemeal and unconnected to the rest of the firm's core capabilities. Yet there is a clear evolution toward entirely new forms of organization for conducting business affairs. The traditional distinction between firms and markets, between the company and its external environment, has disappeared (Badaracco, 1991). The value-creation abilities of interconnected dyadic relationships can be seen in industries as diverse as furniture, automotive parts, and retailing. IKEA, for example, is able to provide consistent quality at the best price through a standardized business system that minimizes the cost and difficulty the customer faces in acquiring furniture. IKEA's strategy of operational excellence is achieved through a series of interconnected partnerships with furniture manufacturers that optimize their business processes across organizational boundaries.

The emergence of cooperation between firms in interconnected relationships has been given various names including "the virtual corporation" (Byrne, Brandt, & Port, 1993), "value-adding partnerships" (Johnston & Lawrence, 1988), and "strategic networks" (Jarillo, 1993). In practice, many value-creating networks emerge slowly over time in a naturalistic way. The importance, however, of seeking new advantages in markets while slowing the erosion of present advantages will increasingly require that firms look beyond their organizational boundaries for value-creation opportunities. For firms like Corning and IBM that are redefining themselves as networks of strategic alliances, the key activities in the core organization have to do with strategy, coordination, and relationship management (Grant, 1991; Webster, 1992). We believe that value-creating networks represent the next logical step as firms move from long-term dyadic relationships to a broader systems perspective.

In this chapter we explore the choices of firms to strategically combine the resources of several independent enterprises into a linked set of long-term relationships. We define a value-creating network as a series of dyadic and triadic relationships that have been designed to generate customer value and build sustainable competitive advantage to the creator and manager. What makes value-creating networks of interest to scholars is their purposeful nature. Network creators, or network captains, use the core capabilities of the other network members to create value for the final customer, and thereby build a competitive advantage for themselves.

The purpose of this chapter is to offer guidance, derived from available theory and "best practices" from successful firms, on how firms turn individual relationships into a value-creating network. Our focus is on how network advantages can be created and sustained. We briefly review current network thinking and explore the motivation for the formation of value-creating networks by a network captain.

PERSPECTIVES ON
NETWORK ADVANTAGE

The business network approach enriches a dyadic perspective by contributing the knowledge that focal relationships cannot be managed in isolation from the other relationships a firm has, and represents a conduit to other relationships through which resources may be accessed (Easton, 1992). Network theories suggest that a specific firm's behavior is primarily controlled by its relationships with other firms rather than by internal firm factors or external factors such as markets for supply and demand. The behavior of the whole network, in turn, is controlled by its specific pattern of interrelated firms.

The conceptual development of industrial networks is rooted in both a behavioral theory of firm decision making (Cyert & March, 1963) whereby organizational goals are the result of a social bargaining process based on existing coalitions of organizational participants, and in a resource dependence perspective (Heide, 1994; Pfeffer & Salancik, 1978) in which organizations are always subject to external control given that they must inevitably acquire resources by interacting with their social environment. These conceptual roots can be seen in the varying ways industrial networks have been described in different studies.

Because there is always some path of relationships that connect any two firms, Mattsson (1987) proposes that, at a macro level, we can regard the industrial system as a "giant and extremely complex network." This perspective on networks emphasizes the naturally emergent component of network relationships, which evolve slowly over time. For obvious analytical reasons, researchers adopting this view subdivide the total network according to criteria such as the interdependence between positions due to industrial activity chains, geographic proximities, and the like.

Other perspectives on networks seek to define the micro subprocesses that occur within this broad industrial network. Easton (1992) identifies three broad definitional groupings. One set of definitions (e.g., Håkansson, 1989; Van de Ven & Ferry, 1980) describes a network as the total pattern of relationships within a group of organizations; firms recognize that the best way to achieve common goals is to coordinate the business system in an adaptive fashion. A second set of definitions focuses on the bonds or social relationships that link loosely connected organizations (Aldrich, 1979; Lundgren, 1995). A third definition focuses on the exchange dimension in two or more connected relationships (Anderson, Håkansson, & Johansson, 1994; Cook & Emerson, 1978). Each of these definitions implies a different level of analysis and has different implications for the advantages accruing from networks.

As can be seen from these perspectives, the term *network* in itself is an amorphous concept that takes its form from the context in which it is applied. This is due not only to the network extending farther away from the actor, but also to the basic invisibility of network relationships and connections. Descriptive networks are in some respects without boundaries for it is arbitrary to say where the network begins or ends. When networks are used by researchers to describe the broad net of all direct and indirect interconnections between firms, the network setting extends without limits through connected relationships, making any business network boundary arbitrary (Anderson, Håkansson, & Johansson, 1994; Mattsson, 1988; Wilson, 1995). What these definitions gain in generality as an overriding classifying mechanism for industries, however, they lose in managerial relevance. We believe that in many networks described by academics, the network members themselves do not recognize or identify their network position. Most managers have well-developed mental models of their competitive position that shape the information they seek and the lessons they extract (Day & Nedungadi, 1994). These mental models affect the extent to which managers are likely

| | Emphasis on Joint Creation | |
Importance of	Low	High
Structural	Low	Social Networks	Value-Creating Networks
Autonomy	High	Market-Based Transaction	Vertical Integration

Figure 8.1. Managerial Representations About the Importance of Networks

to conceptualize themselves as part of a network. In our view, these conceptualizations extend only to dyadic or triadic relationships— managers have no sense of being part of a larger entity.

For our purposes, a business network is defined as a set of two or more connected business relationships in which exchange in one relationship is contingent on exchange (or nonexchange) in another (Anderson, Håkansson, & Johansson, 1994). This view of networks highlights their governance aspects in coordinating economic exchange. Figure 8.1 illustrates two dimensions along which managerial representations of networks can vary. The first dimension describes whether managers emphasize their own internal value-creation capabilities and performance, or look to external linkages to reinforce their own internal capabilities. Although joint value creation can lead to superior profits, firms that achieve superior value creation through tightly coordinated sets of relationships do so at the expense of autonomy. The second dimension in Figure 8.1 describes the importance to the firm of preserving its structural autonomy within its set of relationships.

The combination of these two dimensions yields four types of representations. Each reflects the influence of networks on a firm's choice of strategy in how it creates a competitive advantage.

Social Networks

Networks have been defined as a social system of interconnected relationships (Lundgren, 1995). Organizations recognize the value of having relationships in which individuals are spontaneously motivated to go beyond prescribed roles and perform above and beyond the call of duty. The social embeddedness of economic exchange (Granovetter, 1985) implies that individuals may have an affective attachment to each other for its own sake. In a socially developed network, firms act for the benefit of each other because of the loyalty and involvement developed through friendship and strong personal ties. This affective commitment has been called psychological attachment, identification, affiliation, and value congruence (Allen & Meyer, 1990; O'Reilly & Chatman, 1986). Socially developed networks provide the basis for parties to develop confidence in the stability of their relationships. Although such networks constitute social capital (Burt, 1992), which provides resource contacts, they do not necessarily lead to future-oriented relationship investment. Because these networks develop along personal rather than industry lines, they may transcend industry boundaries, thereby limiting the opportunities for joint value creation.

Market-Based Transactions

Firms that have a low emphasis on joint value creation and attach high importance in maintaining their own autonomy pay little attention to the network of relationships in which they are embedded. Although it is possible for firms to conduct repeated transactions over time with the same buyers and suppliers, these relationships are conducted in a transactional mode with a high emphasis placed on price competitiveness. These firms have an inward perspective that depends on the market mechanism to regulate their relationships with outside firms.

Vertical Integration

Firms that recognize the potential for joint value creation but attach considerable importance to preserving their own independence are likely to vertically integrate to maintain control of the value-creation process. Vertical integration represents a traditional approach to capturing value by acquiring increased control and margin within the value chain. At one time, the Ford Motor Company Rouge River plant was highly integrated with its own steel mill that produced steel for the factory. This level of integration has fallen from favor as the Japanese automobile manufacturers showed that a firm can be very successful with a low level of integration. Toyota, for example, manufactures 20% of the value of their automobiles, whereas

Ford and GM manufacture 50% and 70%, respectively. Integration has lost its cachet as a strategy for value capture and creation.

Value-Creating Networks

Value-creating networks describe the purposeful cooperation between independent firms along a value-added chain to create strategic advantage for the entire group. Firms with this orientation recognize the potential for synergy in developing capabilities that reinforce rather than minimize their dependence on outside firms. The key concept that drives value-creating networks is the delivery of superior customer value. The traditional ways of adding value by integration or pushing suppliers for concessions are not as effective as before, which is prompting firms to move toward long-term relationships with suppliers. Kalawani and Narayandas (1995) found that suppliers in long-term relationships achieved inventory savings, better cost control, and lowering of selling, general, and administrative costs. They suggest that these cost reductions stemmed from lower customer turnover, higher customer satisfaction leading to lower service costs, and higher effectiveness of selling expenditures. The natural extension of these cost advantages is to push them further up or down the value chain to create a network.

Our focus is on long-term purposeful arrangements among independent firms that allow those firms to gain or sustain competitive advantage vis à vis their competitors outside the network (Jarillo, 1993). This orientation implies that firms recognize and define the boundaries of their network to encompass only the direct linkages that help them capture value.

The essence of sustainable profitability for any given economic activity is that it can be performed in a unique way (i.e., that the company performing it cannot be replaced by another company that does the same thing). If networks of interconnected relationships possess advantages beyond the sum of their individual dyadic relationships, they must be able to consistently offer superior value to a distinct customer segment. The total costs incurred in delivering value to the final consumer can be divided into two main categories: the activities necessary to manufacture products or perform services, and the costs incurred in coordinating those activities. How networks can be used to optimize activity costs and minimize coordination costs is discussed next. The rewards from competitive advantages acquired through other means are customer loyalty, market share dominance, and superior profitability (Day, in press).

ENHANCING CUSTOMER VALUE
THROUGH VALUE-ADDING NETWORKS

Value is created through offering superior attributes at a price that is fair or better than fair for the market offering. Customer value can be conceptualized as the relationship between the firm's market offering and the price paid for it. Anderson, Jain, and Chitangunta (1993) define value as

> the perceived worth in monetary units of the set of economic, technical, service and social benefits received by a customer in exchange for the price paid for a product offering, taking into consideration the available alternative suppliers' offerings and prices. (p. 5)

Market offerings can therefore be described in terms of attributes that have different importance levels to the consumer. Customer value can be increased by providing more of the high importance attributes at the same price, or the same attribute bundle at a lower price. The customer chooses between the value packages offered by the firms in the market to select the best value within a category. The market sets the competitive price level, so firms strive to provide a value package that holds or increases their share of market and provides a profit that is greater than or meets the industry average.

Traditionally, value in buying was created through an adversarial competitive process in which the buyer plays sellers against each other. Although these relationships could be stable, the rule of thumb was that three suppliers were needed to ensure competitive pricing and a back-up source of supply. More recently, competitive pressures have led to the emergence of single sourcing within the context of long-term committed relationships. With the need for increased quality and just-in-time (JIT) delivery, buyers found it too difficult to manage multiple sources of supply and meet the JIT and quality goals of their firms. The next logical step was to create value by drawing on the unique resources of partners and combining them in a synergistic way to improve product or service performance, or to lower the cost of providing the offering. Many of the early value-creating networks emerged from the dyadic and triadic relationships that firms need to conduct business. These networks were probably not purposely defined a priori, but developed slowly as the key firm built relationships with other firms in the supply chain. As managers pursued goals of creating both customer value and a defensible competitive position, the key firm increased its coordinating activities between various partners until the network, or set of dyadic and triadic relationships they had created, gave them a unique and defensible competitive advantage. Network management then becomes a strategic activity whereby the key firm begins to actively manage the network and develop a value-creating network strategy.

Value-creating networks are, by their very nature, managed relationships. We contend that the next phase in the quest to create value will be the emergence of directed networks that are created and managed to produce unique value. Recent studies of market leaders have revealed three strategies by which firms can consistently offer superior value to a distinct customer segment: operational excellence, customer responsiveness, and performance superiority (Treacy & Wiersema, 1995). Each of these value strategies can be accomplished through networks of relationships.

Operational excellence means the provision of consistent quality at the best price, through a standardized business system that minimizes the cost and difficulty the customer faces in acquiring the product. The Bombay Company, a retailer of quality self-assembled furniture sold in high-traffic locations in upscale malls, has developed a competitive advantage through building a network of designers, manufacturers, and shipping firms that is hard for a competitor to replicate. Value from the customer's perspective is handsome, well-designed furniture at reasonable prices. The Bombay Company achieves this by having designers who create designs that are not only aesthetically pleasing but are easy to manufacture and can be easily assembled by the consumer. Designers work with the Bombay Company and suppliers to produce a design that meets styling criteria but is easy to manufacture. Sometimes a simple change of the curve in a design can make a major difference in the time it takes to cut the curve in the wood. The furniture is also designed to minimize the knocked-down size of the carton to maximize the number of units per container, and thereby lower the per unit shipping cost. The Bombay Company has developed relationships with shipping firms to send partially filled containers from one manufacturer to another to fully load the container and minimize shipping costs. In this way, the core capabilities and resources of a series of independent firms are combined within a network of relationships. Triadic and dyadic relationships are managed to provide a high-quality product that delivers on the important attributes and cuts costs at all levels. Even the consumer is a partner to the network by performing the assembly task. The result is a good margin to the firm and an attractive product at a significant savings over traditional furniture outlets.

Customer responsiveness strategies put the emphasis on the careful tailoring and adaptation of their products and services to increasingly precise requirements. There is a strong orientation to addressing the distinct needs of individual customers or micro segments, to nurture long-term relationships with customers. Calyx and Corolla has been able to successfully establish a network to provide fast delivery of fresh flowers to working women. The founder, Ruth Owades (*Working Woman,* 1991) described her vision as follows: "I envisioned a table with three legs—Calyx and Corolla was one of them. The second was the best flower growers available, and the third was Federal Express, the number one air carrier." This a priori vision defined the network of triadic relationships that needed to be in place to deliver value to the customer. Working from this vision, Calyx and Corolla trained 30 growers who had traditionally packed 500 to 1000 stems in large cartons and shipped them to distributors and retailers to "carefully pack 11 perfect stems in special cartons, packed according to stringent aesthetic specifications and to include a neatly hand-written gift card" (*Working Woman,* 1991). They also worked with Federal Express to ensure that flower deliveries were made in person and flowers were not left on doorsteps to freeze.

The role of Calyx and Corolla in developing this value-creating network illustrates the functions of a network captain. The network captain forges relationships with key firms and manages their interactions to deliver the value to the end user. Although many firms may be loosely connected to the network, the primary value is determined by a smaller number of key players. For example, Calyx and Corolla buys 80% of its flowers from 8 of the 30 growers in its network. The other 22 growers are less central to the network's value-creating capabilities.

The third value-creating strategy is performance superiority attained by continuous, fast-paced innovation that yields a steady flow of leading-edge products. From a network perspective, innovation comprises three aspects: knowledge development, resource mobilization, and resource coordination (Håkansson, 1987; see also Leonard-Burton, 1992). Emerging networks in the global telecommunications industry illustrate how firms are attempting to combine these three elements to provide additional value-added services. The alliances between Disney, Bell South, Southwestern Bell, and Ameritech to carry the Disney cable movie channel is an example of firms at different stages of the value chain coordinating their efforts to push the state of the art of the technology. The World Partners venture is an example of firms achieving performance superiority by enhancing a customer's uses or applications. The World Partners venture has been formed by a number of different companies using different platforms: AT&T, Kokusai Denshi Denwa, PTT (Switzerland), Telefonica (Spain), KPN (Netherlands), and Telia (Sweden). Its purpose is to provide global service capable of supporting voice, data, and video applications for multinational customers.

Whereas the emphasis of operational excellence, customer responsiveness, and performance superiority strategies differ, each excels at meeting the needs of one segment, while offering acceptable performance on the attributes. These examples demonstrate that the process of simultaneously lowering costs while raising performance can be effectively executed by a network of interconnected, independent firms. How this network is created is discussed next.

CREATING THE VALUE NETWORK

Although value networks are not necessarily created in a linear fashion, Figure 8.2 proposes that the network development process can be characterized by a cycle of actions that define its competitive advantage. Value networks are created by individual entrepreneurs or entrepreneurs who have a vision about how customer value can be enhanced. This value concept is based on accessing the core capabilities

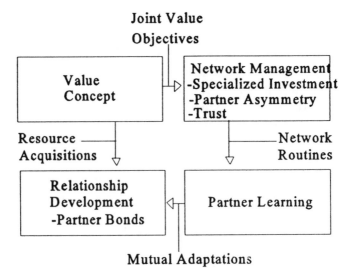

Figure 8.2. The Value-Creating Network Development Process

of external firms through vertical linkages and relies on effective network management to coordinate the skills and resources of independent firms. The sustainability of the network is based on partner learning, which is used to acquire superior assets and distinctive capabilities and leads to the development of better partnership relationships.

Value Concept

The network captain develops a value concept that defines a target market and a product or service offering at a price point that will provide clear value to the target. The value concept is based on extending the boundaries of the organization to encompass the efforts of different autonomous firms. The value concept of Ruth Owades, that fresher flowers would be highly valued by upper-income women, included the vision that flowers could be delivered fresher by being sold directly from the grower through a catalog rather than through traditional channels. Sam Walton's belief that Procter & Gamble, his largest supplier, and Wal-Mart, P&G's largest customer, could create more value for the customer by working closely together is another example. These value concepts initiate action to access the resources necessary to deliver the value concept.

Value concepts are most effective in business systems that call simultaneously for close coordination and the maintenance of independent firms. Jarillo (1993) outlines four characteristics of a business system that favors the development of strategic networks. First, at least some critical activities have advantages if carried out in a de-integrated way, due to widely differing optimal scales, differences in barriers to entry and competitive advantages, or an entrepreneurial impetus for innovation stemming from relatively small business units. Second, specialized investment results in higher efficiency. These investments may be hard, such as capital investments, or soft, such as people and time. Third, speed of responsiveness is important, and leaving coordination to arm's length market mechanisms is inefficient or inflexible. Finally, innovation demands understanding the whole system. Based on this reasoning, we propose that value concepts that lead to the formation of a value-creating network are more likely to occur in a business system characterized by complex, multistage processes.

Relationship Development

Gaps between the value concept and the resources necessary to execute the value concept help define the characteristics of ideal partners and the core capabilities they will contribute to the network. The actual creation of a network begins with selling the concept and developing relationships with and between key firms. The network manager works with the key partners to integrate their activities. Although the total network may range from a triad to a complex network of firms depending on the scope required by the value concept, we believe that value-creating networks start with several strong primary relationships characterized by strong partner bonds.

Relationships within the network have to be clearly denser and deeper than relationships outside the network. What is critical is the integration of independent firms through strong committed relationships allowing the network to minimize the costs of the system. The network captain or manager creates the primary relationships and may participate in developing the secondary relationships. Partner bonds reflect the tightness or looseness of the coupling between partners. Bonds have economic, social, technical, logistical, administrative, informational, legal, and time-based dimensions (Mattsson, 1984), which make them difficult to dissolve at will. The strength of these bonds, however, is difficult to measure because the relationship between partnership longevity and bond strength is not a simple one. Even strongly bonded partners will dissolve relationships if external forces are powerful enough, and weakly bonded partners may continue relationships in benign and unchanging competitive conditions.

Relationships form the context in which transactions take place. They comprise the processes through which firms adjust products, production, and routines, and imply a long-term orientation (vs. interactions that comprise the day-to-day exchange and adaptation processes). Relationships also offer access to third parties that may have resources or information that are either valuable or essential to survival. The picture of relationships provided by the network approach emphasizes cooperation, complementarity, and coordination. To understand how networks create value, it is necessary to understand both the relationships between the member firms and their relative positions.

Network Management

Although a value creating network shares many characteristics typical of other types of networks, its main differentiating factor is the joint value objectives shared by network members. The underlying motivation for network members to organize and integrate activities is to create competitive advantage for the network as a whole. It is not an altruistic motivation. The network captain reaps significant rewards for its entrepreneurial efforts; however, all members must believe there will be more to share by cooperating than by remaining autonomous. The motivation to join and to stay in the network is the belief that by working with others, a firm will be more productive and at least part of that productivity will be passed along to the firm.

Joint value objectives are important in fostering the commitment necessary for any long-term relationship. To create value, a network has to be both efficient compared to other ways of coordinating economic activities (such as vertical integration or market relationships) and effective. Wilson and Moller (1991) provide a discussion of the range of variables that have been used to describe and model relationships between firms, including dependence, trust, power, communication, expectations, perceived competence, and ease of relationship termination. Although most of these variables are relevant, specialized investments, partner asymmetry, and trust are particularly important in determining the effectiveness of a value-creating network. Each of these reinforces the core capabilities of the network as a whole.

Empirical research has demonstrated that committed partners are willing to invest in valuable assets specific to an exchange, demonstrating that they can be relied on to perform essential functions in the future (Anderson & Weitz, 1992). The role of specialized investment in a value-creating network is to add as much value as possible to the system—specialized investments give consistency to the network. Specialized investment is particularly important in a value-creating network because without it, the network is no more than a collection of suppliers and buyers without any particular competitive advantage being gained by the network itself. Any resource committed above and beyond that required to execute the current exchange may be regarded as an investment. Cooperation within a network of relationships does not subvert the competitive goals of the individual firms. Instead, the network brings new modes of competition. Firms compete over their share of the value-creation ability residing in the network. Although the level of specialized investment committed to the network by its members may vary, the more successful a company becomes at adding value, the stronger its position within the network becomes.

The second defining characteristic of network management is partner asymmetries. Network relationships can be regarded as a hierarchy: At the base there are major partners with a strong commitment to each other. These relationships are supplemented by minor second-tier alliances. Finally, there are niche arrangements developed for a focused purpose. This hierarchy is based on each partner's contribution to the total value-creating abilities of the network.

A firm's position within a set of relationships represents the role that an organization has with respect to other organizations to which it is related (directly or indirectly). Håkansson and Johannson (1992) describe a related concept, strategic identity, which refers to the views about the firm's role and position in relation to other firms in the industrial network. Partner asymmetries necessitate a network captain to control the network's resources, activities or both. Network captains exert control over the resources and knowledge embedded in the network. Dominance in the network's value-creation activities may be achieved through control of marketing (firms that are closer to the customer can provide market direction to the rest of the network) or by controlling of resources that support value-creating customer attributes. For example, some industry experts suggest that telecommunication networks will not be dominated by the telecommunications and audio-visual companies but by the software firms who develop the national and international information infrastructure.

The third defining characteristic of value-creating networks is trust. Trust is at the core of network management because it is the mechanism that lowers transaction costs, thus making the network economically viable. Jarillo (1993) argues that a network is effective when the gain resulting from the network's competitive advantage is shared in a way that all participants feel to be fair. The network has to distribute gains in a way that fosters loyalty, for without this loyalty there is no network. The network captain may need to assume some of the risk involved in the relationships to protect smaller, highly specialized firms from economic downturns.

The strategy pursued by the network captain is to manage the network in a way that facilitates the creation of value. The three characteristics of specialized investment, partner asymmetries, and trust promote integrative relationships in which independent firms cooperate and coordinate activities to minimize network cost and maximize the network's ability to provide significantly greater customer value than alternative arrangements.

Partner Learning

Partner learning is critical and defines the network's ultimate success. Partner learning embodies a lot of tacit knowledge that is based on firms working together and is accumulated through experience and refined by practice. Similar to the notion of organizational routines proposed by Nelson and Winter (1982), this embedded knowledge represents "network routines," which define the operational activities of the network and its way of doing business. For example, many Federal Express delivery employees learned not to leave flowers on cold days because frozen flowers are not part of the value concept on which the Calyx and Corolla network is built. The creation of embedded knowledge makes it difficult for competitors to easily copy the network. A rival trying to acquire this knowledge would have to replicate much of this learning process.

Value is added to the network by learning and diffusion of that learning through adaptation. Continuous learning aimed at searching for ways to lower cuts or improve performance becomes a distinctive capability that protects the network from competitive imitation. This learning promotes mutual adaptation to enhance network value. The better adapted to each other's working ways the members of a network become, the more efficient coordination becomes, thus paving the way for more and more adaptation. In this sense, the whole system is self-reinforcing.

Value-creating networks gain an advantage over individual dyadic relationships because of their ability to erect barriers to imitation. Mutual adaptation creates causal ambiguity and duplicability barriers that permit the network's competitive advantages to persist despite attempts by other firms to copy the network. Causal ambiguity occurs when it is unclear to the competition how the source of advantage works. When network relationships are characterized by a mutually adaptive pattern of coordination among firms, it is likely that a rival will not be able to grasp the functioning of the entire system. Even if competitors understood the advantage, they still may not be able duplicate it. Duplicability difficulties arise in value-adding networks because the assets of the network members are specifically committed to the activities in the network and cannot be used elsewhere. Investment specialization reduces the number of partners available for competing networks.

SUMMARY: THE FUTURE FOR
VALUE-CREATING NETWORKS

We have argued that a system of relationships can compete to deliver value thereby creating a competitive advantage for its members. This chapter complements the growing recognition in the marketing literature (e.g., Anderson, Håkansson, & Johansson, 1994), that to understand any particular firm's strategy and decisions, it is necessary to look at the network of relationships within which the firm is embedded. In this chapter, we have examined how firms create sustainable competitive advantages by adopting a strategy of managed networks. The distinguishing features of these value-creating networks are the a priori value vision and the use of integrative relationships to accomplish the goals of the network. Webster (1992) calls for an expanded view of the marketing function within the firm, which specifically addresses the role of marketing in firms that go to market through multiple partnerships. We have proposed a descriptive model of the value-creating network development process as a first step to understanding this important and interesting new strategy.

Although value-creating networks can evolve over time, empirical evidence suggests that to be sustainable, a network captain must take control of the network and manage its value-creating capabilities in a way that creates synergy between the key players. We propose that a value-creating network is devised a priori with the purpose of creating value for customers by integrating the resources and activities of independent firms through a cooperative set of interlocking relationships. Based on our analysis, value-creating networks have a number of distinguishing characteristics: purposeful linkages, focal dyadic or triadic relationships, a network captain good at establishing and maintaining relationships, a hierarchy of relationships, and a combined bundle of attributes that provides significantly greater customer value than alternative arrangements. These characteristics could constitute a test to determine whether a network is truly value creating.

Clearly there remain a number of unanswered questions about value-creating networks. We need to understand how competitive value is maintained within the network. For example, can managers isolate embedded knowledge to maintain the network's value? Another interesting avenue for future research is whether the value-creation abilities of a network can be assessed a priori or only post hoc.

Our analysis suggests that it is the distinctive capabilities within the network that create value for the final customer: trust and cooperation are not enough. Changing the unit of analysis from the firm to a series of interconnected firms may change the way researchers can apply existing theories about distinctive capabilities and resources. We need to identify the value-creation abilities of networks and determine what capabilities are required to develop purposeful value-creating networks. The ability of the network captain to manage relationships in the network is a critical core capability that is not widely available. Similarly, being a good network member is essential to network growth and will determine the success of the network.

Managed networks are an important and interesting topic for business scholars. We believe that the capability to develop and sustain managed networks will become increasingly important for long-run competitive success as the competition between clearly defined value-producing networks accelerates. Firm experiences with strategic alliances and other longer-term cooperative dyadic relationships have demonstrated that initial attempts with any new organizational form often result in failure. As scholars, we may be able to add value to business through an increase in knowledge about how these networks are created and sustained.

9

Relationship Strategy, Investments, and Decision Making

DAVID FORD
RAYMOND McDOWELL
CYRIL TOMKINS

This chapter arises from continuing research into the nature of intercompany relationships in business markets. A particular concern that forms a background to the research is that despite something like 20 years of research into buyer-seller relationships, managerial practice does not in many cases seem to have advanced significantly. Because of this concern, our research is currently directed toward an examination of managerial decision making in relationships, the influences on that decision making, and the limitations to the idea of strategy in business market relationships. This chapter presents some ideas on these issues and relates them to some of our developing empirical work. The overall aim of the research is to provide a contribution to managerial understanding of the nature of business relationships and to assist in the structuring of decision making within them. This chapter outlines some of the ways in which that contribution to decision making can be made.

AUTHORS' NOTE: This chapter is one of the outputs from a major research project that is investigating how companies can develop a strategic approach toward the network of intercompany relationships of which they form part. The authors would like to acknowledge the financial support of the Economic and Social Research Council for the work undertaken in this project.

THE NATURE OF RELATIONSHIP DECISIONS

Intercompany relationships involve a variety of decisions for the participants. Examples include the decision of a supermarket chain to abandon a relationship by delisting a supplier, or a manufacturer's decision to raise its commitment to a customer by increasing its level of sales support. A supplier may decide to develop a new product to suit a customer's requirements, or it may alter its production schedule to match that of a client, or simply increase its price to that customer. These decisions by a supplier, as well as those made by its customer, may have an immediate effect, so that a price increase will simultaneously increase the revenue of one party and the costs of the other. The decisions may also affect the nature of the relationship between the two companies in the longer term; perhaps the price increase may generate resentment in the customer and this will affect its willingness to buy from that supplier in the future. Additionally, a decision by a company within a single relationship may also affect other relationships in that company's portfolio. For example, the price increase to one customer may lead others to change suppliers if they anticipate a price increase to themselves. Finally, this single decision may also affect the wider network within which the relationship exists. The price increase may have been introduced by a price leader in the network and this may trigger a more general round of price increases. Of course, both parties in a relationship are simultaneously making decisions that have both immediate effects on their partners, and longer term effects on the relationship they share. The two parties are also subject to influences from the actions of other companies with which they interact, and from the actions of companies elsewhere in the network with which they have no direct contact.

The decisions that companies make will be affected by many factors. First, relationship decisions will reflect the individual and collective experience both inside the relationship and elsewhere of those involved. Decisions will also be influenced by the core beliefs and aspirations of the participants as well as the interactions that occur within the relationship. Decisions will also be affected by the decision makers' perceptions of the likely effects of their decisions and the utility value to the participants of those effects and of the relationship itself. In this manner, relationship decisions have an implied risk and return trade-off.

All of these issues make it clear that an analysis of relationship decision making is inherently complex and attempts to assist managers in improving their relationship decision making; relationship strategies must take into account this reality. This complexity also means that the manager must be wary of simplistic techniques of how to design relationships, let alone how to design networks, and they must understand the limits and subtleties of strategizing in networks. These challenges lead to the basis of our current research, which is the belief that the key to improved relationship decision making must be through helping managers to coalesce, structure, and evaluate their relationship experience and the observed effects of their decision making. This process can lead to increased awareness on the part of relationship managers of the decision process that they adopt, the sorts of trade-offs that they make as a matter of course, and the potential multilevel effects of their decisions.

CONCEPTUAL BASIS

The conceptual basis for our analysis of relationship decision making is the interaction approach to business-to-business marketing (as in the Industrial Marketing and Purchasing Group [IMP]; see e.g., Ford, 1990; Håkansson, 1982). This approach suggests that business marketing cannot realistically be seen as a process in which the seller acts to influence the buyer, who in turn may or may not react. Instead, it is more accurately seen as a process of interaction by two active parties. Also, business sales and purchases do not exist as individual events and hence cannot be fully understood if each one is examined in isolation. Instead, each interaction between companies, whether for product, service, financial, social, or information exchange is an episode within the relationship between the companies. This relationship may be close or distant, complex or simple, and each episode within it is affected by the relationship and in turn may affect the relationship itself. The relationship between the companies consists of learned rules and behaviors that provide the atmosphere within which interaction takes place. Individuals will approach each episode on the basis of their experience within the relationship and elsewhere and on the basis of the values that they hold, both in general and in regard to the particular relationship.

For the majority of companies in business markets, a small number of suppliers and customers tend to be responsible for large volumes of their purchases or sales. In these cases, relationships tend to be close, complex, and long term. These relationships evolve over time and this evolution is often described as a series of stages characterized by increased mutual adaptation, reduced distance between the companies, and increased commitment (Ford, 1989). These descriptions of relationship evolution in terms of stages run the risk, however, of being overly deterministic, implying the inevitability of a process that may not mirror either the complexity or the unpredictability of relationship change.

Companies in business markets will have a number of relationships with more or less significant suppliers, customers, and other partners. These relationships will be surrounded by many more relationships including some of those companies with which they interact and some with which they have no contact. Despite this, these third-party relationships will indirectly affect, and be affected by, the company's own interactions, and together they constitute the network of which the company forms part. This is the manifestation of what Håkansson and Snehota (1995) call the connectedness of the business relations of a company. An example of such a network is illustrated in diagrammatic form in Figure 9.1.

Relationships as Investments

Generally speaking in business, managers are interested in a financial index of how much return has been received from an undertaking, bearing in mind the risks associated with it and the investment that has been made. If a company wishes to improve its relationship with a partner or partners to achieve future benefit, then it is likely to involve a commitment of resources, whether expressed in terms of managerial or salesforce time, product or service development, process, financial or administrative adaptation. This commitment is not trivial and is not reversible without considerable loss. (Williamson, 1981, refers to these in a slightly different context as transaction-specific investments.) For this reason, buyer-seller relationships can be regarded as investments. Yet an examination of the accounting and financial literatures shows few works that examine the investment issues surrounding relationship decision making. There is, for exam-

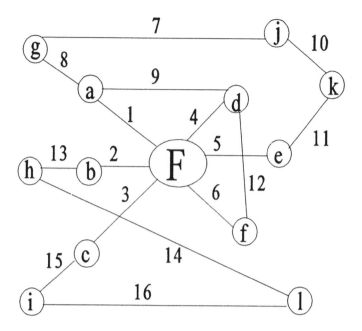

Figure 9.1. Network of Relationships Surrounding a Focal Company (F)

ple, no mention of the issue in a couple of the more up-to-date texts in advanced management accounting (e.g., Brealey & Myers, 1991; Kaplan & Atkinson, 1989), although Carr, Tomkins, and Bayliss (1994) have recently completed a study demonstrating how intercompany relations drive investment decisions in both the U.K. and German auto-components industry. One of the few other recognitions of this state of affairs within advanced management accounting can be seen in Hagg (1992), who discusses the issue of activities that are undertaken by more than one company and suggests that investment involved in these activities is a research question that has yet to be addressed.

It may seem strange that relationships have not been widely considered in investment terms. Relationships demand cost commitments, which over time are expected to generate sufficient cash flows to make the investment financially worthwhile, particularly when commitment to some relationships inevitably implies exclusion of other possibilities. To consider relationships in any other terms fails to appreciate their potential as a means to generate profits. Hedaa (1995) points out that the overriding conception of relationships as costs may have a lot to do with how managers treat relationships—after all, prudent managers cut costs when they can. He believes that a mental realignment needs to take place wherein managers come to view relationships as potentially long-lived assets. Because an organization's relationships are assets that enable it to exploit the resources it has, they provide an alternative index of valuation for the company as a whole. Ford (1994) has pointed out that the essence of relationship strategy is that it "involves the process of exploiting the company's technologies in its relationships so as to maximize the return on the company's technological investment" (p. 9). We will return shortly to this view when we consider further the nature of relationship strategy.

The Issue of Measurement

The argument for viewing relationships as investments seems therefore to be compelling. As soon as one accepts such a view, however, and one looks to the investment appraisal literature for guidance, one is faced with real difficulties. Which investment appraisal technique should be used to determine the worth of a relationship investment opportunity? There are a variety of approaches to determining the potential acceptability of an investment option. The most generally accepted approach is to calculate the net present value (NPV) of the investment, based on the set of cash flows associated with it. For a relationship, this would involve attempting to determine the various in-flows (revenue) and out-flows (costs or opportunities forgone) associated with the relationship over time. The costs and benefits would, in essence, derive from relationship factors that one would aggregate. Furthermore, the calculations would have to be discounted by a factor equivalent to the cost of capital for the relationship to compensate for the time-dependent value of money and risk. Given measurement of the numbers, this would be easy to accomplish. There are, however, major problems associated with this approach.

The first problem is that the NPV calculation is regarded as being particularly important because it establishes the basic financial viability of an investment. As with any tool, however, it is only useful when used correctly and with some thought. Hayes and Abernathy (1980) have shown that some manufacturing breakthroughs, such as computer integrated manufacture or flexible manufacturing systems, would fail the NPV test because of the emphasis on short-term financial results and the fact that issues that are difficult to quantify are ignored. This is not a criticism of the NPV technique per se, but of how it is sometimes used. The real problem in these situations, which is paralleled in relationship investments, is the adequate iden- tification of cash flows and of a time horizon that is appropriate to the investment project. Shank (in press) stresses that all investment decisions need to be considered in strategic terms before any NPV calculation is undertaken and contends that judgmental issues relat- ing to strategy almost always play a far more important role than conventional NPV frameworks allow.

Another dimension of this problem is more operational and cen- ters on the task of identifying relevant flows between the companies. Even if relationships are considered to be only short-term, two-party transactions, the problem of identifying the flow of benefits and costs is considerable. This is inevitably burdensome because all contacts between the relationship parties need to be considered in cost-benefit terms—the return achieved for all efforts expended. Even those companies that create accounts for all customers or suppliers, and that make a point of recording the capital investment activities in which they have engaged with these parties, will find it difficult to ascertain all this cost-benefit information. This problem is further compounded because it involves consolidating all the accounting infor- mation pertaining to an exchange partner, regardless of the specific product bought or sold, at all times of the relationship history.

This view is strongly supported by Hagg (1992), who doubts that current accounting practice can easily enable relationships to be examined:

> Finally, another complicating dimension should be mentioned where accounting has little to say as yet [and that is] a market investment in a buyer-seller relationship. . . . Existing accounting systems probably im- pede the company's perception of these interrelations. It is a challenge to explore the possibilities of developing capital budgeting methods and information/accounting systems which would consider seller-buyer relationship characteristics. (p. 207)

Some organizations, such as those in the construction industry, are able to base their accounting on independent projects (with pricing mechanisms designed to incorporate company overhead and other indirect costs) and consequently have strong visibility within individual projects of costs and revenues. For most companies, however, it is not common practice to maintain accounting records of the costs and returns of all interactions with specific companies. Given that such interactions and cost-incurring activities will frequently cut across individual projects over a period of years, maintenance of such records would be a necessity for determining overall the financial value of the business-to-business relationship. Even if this level of visibility of commercial dealings with other organizations could be achieved, the nature of exchange relationships is such that noncommercial variables, such as pattern of social exchange, levels of trust and commitment, and others, have very important roles to play. Although a company may well appreciate the role that some of these variables play, its accounting system will certainly not reflect this.

This historical recording problem is nothing, however, compared to the difficulties in making estimates of the likely future value of a particular action in a relationship, or the value of the relationship itself. The notion of a relationship is generally, but not always, based on an expectation of continuity. The anticipated future cash flows of a relationship are quite unknown, however, beyond the expectation that they ought to be greater than the required investment in it. Moreover, the incremental benefits and costs to be evaluated also relate to the effect a change in a relationship has on the whole network of relations, and one must seek to isolate these incremental flows from the firm's total flows. Thus, it soon becomes apparent that the direct estimation of the financial value of the relationship is impossible.[1]

The limitations of conventional financial analysis as outlined here make it difficult to propose that relationship decisions should be made on the strength of a direct financial analysis. It is not possible to identify all the components to relationship decisions directly in financial terms. It is, after all, perhaps not so surprising that accounting capital budgeting texts have not addressed the issue of investing in relationships. Our state of knowledge is such that, despite the call of Hagg (1992), there is not likely to be much mileage gained from directly encouraging managers to relate their problem of relationship decision making to conventional capital budgeting models.

This state of affairs has led us to the conclusion that the most appropriate research focus at this stage is to try to understand how managers do identify and evaluate the benefits to be derived from their actions within relationships. We need to build a more solid foundation for understanding the nature of decision making in existing relationships and the surrogates that managers use for the implicit and underlying financial benefits and costs inherent in the relationship. This knowledge may lead back, eventually, to a better understanding of how managers can address investment decisions on relationships and integrate them with the capital budgeting model, but the lead time is likely to be long.

RELATIONSHIP STRATEGY

The Nature of Strategy

We have already noted that the inherent complexity of intercompany relationships and networks means that it is unrealistic to imagine that they can be wholly "designed" by any one party, still less that the evolution of a relationship can solely be the result of conscious, one-sided plans. The state of a relationship at any one time is the result of the actions of many individuals in both companies and elsewhere, based on their respective motivations and the interactions between them. Nevertheless, despite this complexity managers do have to make decisions within relationships, and some of them do try to develop a strategic approach. To be effective, this decision making must be based on an analysis of their experience of what has happened within their company's relationships. The importance of this experiential analysis has recently been expressed by Håkansson and Snehota (1995):

> Purpose-directed behavior . . . calls for the adoption of behavioral rules that do not necessarily derive from a cognitive elaboration of the specific situation as it is met, but rather from an individual elaboration of past experience. (p. 49)

There is scope for the company to coalesce its relationship experiences as a knowledge base for future decision making. Thus, the development of relationship strategies can be viewed as the process of acquiring and exercising this wisdom through interacting with another party. This view of a relationship strategy is closer to Mintzberg's (1991) general view of strategy as a perspective, rather than as the exercise of strategy as a plan. This view of strategy also ties in with our research focus on methods of describing and evaluating existing relationships, where the notion of satisfaction with the relationship is ongoing and the possibility of modifying relationship decisions is ever present. Also, this experiential approach to strategy development may encourage managers to an understanding of those wider factors that they must bear in mind and may seek to change. Without an awareness of both the longer term and the wider network issues involved in a relationship decision, there is a danger that managers will restrict themselves solely to a short-term approach and to existing ways of thinking. Such a restricted approach can also mean that the company may be unaware of the dangers arising from the actions of other companies elsewhere in the network or the opportunities for improving its overall network position. In this way, our view of the issues facing managers in seeking to strategize leans heavily on the ideas developed by Nonaka and Takeuchi (1995) that "organizational learning is an adaptive change process that is influenced by past experience, focused on developing or modifying routines, and supported by organizational memory" (p. 45).

Company Interdependence

The starting point for understanding the development of a relationship strategy is the interdependence of companies. This interdependence takes many forms. Perhaps the most obvious is the need for a supplier to generate revenue by making sales to customers to ensure its continuing existence and development. Correspondingly, a customer company will need to use the knowledge and abilities of its suppliers. This knowledge is delivered in the form of products or services, although the knowledge itself is retained by the supplier. A company may also be dependent on others because it wishes to acquire some of their knowledge for itself, perhaps directly through a licensing deal. Alternatively, it may seek to develop its own knowledge less directly, through interaction with the other company as part of a joint venture based on their respective abilities.

Resources

The interdependence that exists between companies is based on their respective resources. Companies interact with each other and develop relationships to exploit and enhance their own resources and to use those of others. To do this a company will seek those companies that require the use of their resources and that have the resources that the company itself values. The resources possessed by any company are passive and their value is that which is perceived by an interacting partner. It is useful to divide these resources into three categories.

First, financial resources obviously affect the company's ability to acquire new resources, or to use the resources of others. Second, a company's network positional resources consist of its portfolio of relationships and the reputation, rights, and limitations on behavior and obligations it has acquired over time. For example, one aspect of a company's position that could be a valuable resource would be its reputation in a large consumer market, as would be the case with a major retail store chain. Such a chain would probably believe that its position gave it the right to be consulted by a manufacturer that was planning to change its product range, distribution, or pricing structure. At the same time, the chain would perhaps feel that its position meant that it was obliged to operate to the highest standards of safety and employee welfare, and it would feel that it could not get away with the sort of practices carried out by lesser companies. A manufacturer's brand is a measure of reputation in the network and hence constitutes a positional resource. For example, a manufacturer of vehicle components may win orders from small vehicle assemblers based on its brand strength, acquired as a supplier to a major and well-regarded assembler. The corresponding position for the major assembler would be as an important reference customer for its suppliers. The value of its seal of approval to suppliers could mean that it was able to develop further relationships elsewhere in the network on favorable terms. In contrast, a company's wish to preserve its position in a particular relationship may restrict its ability to take advantage of a situation elsewhere in the network. For example, a company that enjoyed a position as an industry leader may feel inhibited in raising its prices to take advantage of a situation of short-term product shortage. In sum, network position is a company resource that is developed through interaction with others in the network. For example, reputation is built by performance over time and it can be lost through a particular interaction. In this way, a firm's network position is a dynamic and evolving characteristic.

The third category of resources is that of technology. Technological resources exist in many forms, and for the purposes of analyzing network position, they can usefully be separated into three areas: (a) Product technology consists of the ability to design products or services. This technology includes the ability to design microcircuitry, develop a new drug, or create the service package for business class on an airline; (b) process technologies comprise the ability to manufacture or produce these products or services. These abilities range from those needed in assembling new cars to the skills necessary to ensure consistency of crispness in the French fries in a fast-food restaurant; and (c) marketing technologies consist of the ability to analyze the requirements of others and to relate the company's resources to that other organization for mutual advantage. It includes skills in managing relationships themselves, whether as a buyer or a purchaser. It also includes the skills of logistics and distribution to transfer goods and services produced on the basis of the two companies' technologies.

These technologies are all learned abilities that can be applied in a variety of ways. They can be used to provide an offering of a product or service, such as when a company operates a chain of restaurants itself. Or they can be transferred whole to others for the others' use, such as when that same company franchises others to use its abilities. Technologies are the basis of all companies' existence and are not something confined to so-called high-technology companies. In themselves, the technologies have no value. They exist only as potential and are valuable only if they are worth something to another company. This value to others is transmitted through the process of interaction between the companies.

A company's pattern of interaction with others, based on the technologies of all parties, effectively defines the company's network position, and, indeed, the nature of the company itself. Interaction in business markets involves the technologies of both companies. For example, a company may buy components from another, which are based on the seller's basic design, modified by the buyer to match its products (i.e., using both parties' product technology). The product may have been manufactured by the seller based on its own process technologies and the whole relationship could have been initiated and managed by the buyer, using its market technology. In turn, the buyer will use the components in its production (based on its own process skills) and use other elements of its technology to sell them to a number of resellers, who will in turn use their market skills to reach a wider market.

Technology Bundles

In the case of conventional product or service exchange, interaction between companies can take place on the basis of one or, more usually, a number of technologies of the supplier. For that technology to be effective, it will have to be combined with one or more of the technologies of the buyer to transfer and transform an offering for a buyer elsewhere in the network. We refer to this combination of the technologies of different companies in the network that delivers a final offering as the "technology bundle." This bundle may be the result of a number of uncoordinated interactions between companies. Alternatively, it may arise largely through the controlling or negotiating activities of a single company. Skill in assembling a bundle is itself an important technological resource. For example, prime contracting agents typically display an ability to put together the skills of others (e.g., subcontractors) with their own skills to offer a package to customers. Similarly, some retailers will manage the skills of a number of raw material, component suppliers and assemblers to build an offering for their customer base. Well-known examples of this include IKEA, Benetton, and Marks & Spencer. These companies face the same critical resource decisions as all others: (a) which technologies they should retain or acquire for themselves; (b) which of these technologies they should use themselves and which they should transfer to others, either as part of the process of acquiring the products they need or as a license deal; and (c) which technologies they should rely on suppliers for. The companies must trade-off the long-term costs and competitive advantages of acquiring or maintaining particular technologies against the comparative price and quality of the technologies available in their product suppliers.

The technological skills that a company perceives in an exchange partner are undoubtedly a source of value to it. That value is not intrinsic to the technologies themselves, but derives from their use. This emphasizes how important it is for a company to discover exactly what it is about their resources that a company actually values. For example, a prime contractor developing a new avionics system may seek to use the software design (product technology) and implementation skills (process and market technologies) of a subcontractor. It may well be, however, that these design skills are based on a product technology that is widely available to many companies. Thus, the prime contractor will only differentiate between alternative suppliers on the basis of its ability to deliver software to a specification that is technically undemanding, but that is tailored to the prime contractor's precise requirements and that is delivered on time.

Managing the Diversity of
a Portfolio of Relationships

Any one company in a network will have a variety of relationships each with different characteristics. These characteristics will depend on both the resources that each party possesses and their respective motivations. For example, a relationship based on the purchase of a component to the buyer's design (product technology resource), often known as "make to print," is likely to be different from that which centers on a component based on a supplier's proprietary product technology. Similarly, the relationship between a franchisee and a franchiser (where product, process, and market technologies are provided by the franchiser) is likely to be different from that between a major retailer and a manufacturer that supplies garments to its specification. Such a relationship will also be different from that between joint-venture partners in a new technology development relationship. A company's relationship with its main bank is also likely to be different from that which it has with a financial or other professional adviser. Finally, of course, relationships with large suppliers or customers will differ from those with small ones.

The motivations of the participants in a relationship, whether as individuals or collectivities are, of course, complex. These motivations will effectively categorize the company's portfolio of relationships and condition the decision making in each of them—a topic to which we turn shortly. The categorizing of relationships, and consequently the decision criteria that are applied, is likely to be implicit in many cases and the task of making these criteria explicit is a major ingredient in the process of making a more strategic approach to relationships for many companies.

An example of an explicit categorization that has proven useful in helping companies develop their own, more strategic view of relationships is illustrated in Figure 9.2. This figure illustrates the portfolio of customer relationships of a hypothetical company. A similar diagram could also be constructed for its supplier portfolio, or indeed any other subset of its total relationships. This portfolio consists of 10 significant relationships and an 11th group of relationships that together are significant, but individually are small (the "Tiddlers") and that require particular management skills. The first two relationships ("Cash Cows" or "Bottomless Pits") illustrate the frequent situation in which a company may have a few major customers that are large generators of cash and fillers of capacity, but that conversely may represent a major drain on the company's account management, product, and production resources and may not be profitable.[2] Relationship number three ("Today's Profit") represents the situation of a customer that is currently a source of both revenue and profit. It is an important managerial issue to consider whether that relationship can sustain its performance, for whatever reason, or whether it needs to be distinguished from Relationship 4 ("Tomorrow's Profit"), which may currently be at the development stage and hence cash-negative, but have the potential for future profit. Relationships 5 and 6 are those that require the company to meet "New Market Requirements," such as enhanced customer service. These requirements are likely to involve additional costs or resource investment in the company's market technology. In this manner, they are similar to Relationships 7 and 8, which have "New Technical Requirements," involving investment in product or process technologies. The issue facing managers in these relationships is that of choosing which relationships to invest in and limitation of the overall level of costs—it may well be that the company can sustain four of these development relationships, but not eight. Relationship 9 is inert ("Old Man"). This is a relationship that is nominally active, perhaps with sales calls still continuing, but has no potential for growth in its current form. Managers, from both sides, therefore face the task of reevaluating this relationship and either developing or discontinuing it. Finally, Relationship 10 is a "Fall Guy." This is a relationship that the company

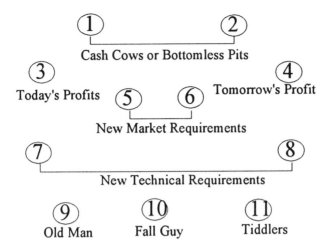

Figure 9.2. Categorization of Relationships in a Portfolio

seeks to exploit for short-term advantage at the cost of the partner. For example, it may be a distributor in a major market that the company is using until such time as it has found out about and established relationships with its customers when it will go direct. Explicitness in examining relationship strategy is perhaps an important basis for relationship ethics!

Regardless of the diversity of relationships in a company's portfolio, in all cases the value of a relationship perceived by a company, and its motivations in it, is invested in the terms it uses to characterize it and in its behavior within it. Examining this characterization and behavior opens up the prospect of understanding the participants' valuation of different relationships and decision making between different options. We now turn to such decision making.

RELATIONSHIP DECISION MAKING

Intercompany relationships are often complex, so it is simplistic to suggest that they can or should develop along a single continuum between "distant" and "close," "good" and "bad." All intercompany relationships simultaneously exhibit conflict and cooperation, with guile and self-seeking. For example, the relationship between a distributor and its customer may be described superficially as being one in which the distributor achieves success by satisfying the customer's requirements. The distributor may, however, try to manipulate the customer's behavior so that it changes its consumption habits or becomes more dependent on it. On the other hand, the customer may wish the distributor to act merely as a supplier for those low-volume items that it does not wish to stock itself, while it seeks to do deals with manufacturers elsewhere in the network for the direct supply of high-volume lines. Thus, it seeks to reduce its costs and avoid dependence on this particular distributor.

This complexity means that an understanding of relationship decision making requires analysis of a number of areas, whether that analysis is carried out by a researcher or a participant manager. These areas of analysis are as follows: (a) the state of the relationship at any point in time, (b) the experience of the participants, (c) the effects that are expected from a decision, (d) the personal belief systems of the participants, and (e) the value that participants put on the potential effects of different decisions.

Relationship State

Relationship decision making is part of the pattern of continuing interaction between the two companies. Each company's decisions will be affected by these interactions as well as by those with other companies elsewhere in the network. All these interactions and decisions take place within the context of their relationship at that point in time and an understanding of this decision making requires an examination of this context. We describe the context as the "state" of the relationship. The state of a relationship can be described by two measures. The first is its "overt state," which includes such factors as the volume and nature of trade between the companies involved, the resources that each brings to the relationship, the perceived importance to the parties of the relationship within their wider portfolio of relationships and the network that surrounds them, as well as the participants' position in that wider network. Second, the state of a relationship can also be described by the "atmosphere" that exists between the two parties (Hallen, 1986). Atmosphere comprises such factors as the extent and areas of conflict or cooperation existing between the companies, their knowledge of each other, and the norms of conduct and expectations that have developed between the companies. Another way of describing the atmosphere of a relationship, that has proven useful for managerial assessment, has been provided by Ford (1982), using the concepts of width, depth, and closeness. The width of a relationship is a measure of the range of activities that it comprises, whether it is a narrow relationship consisting simply of the sale and purchase of a standard product, or a wider relationship consisting of a range of activities, such as the development of a product specifically for the client, dedicated production, extensive social contacts, and so on. The depth of a relationship is a measure of which of those activities are done together. Rather like an interpersonal relationship, a deep intercompany relationship would be one in which many things were done together— products were developed jointly, price changes were jointly discussed on the basis of transparent costing (open books), and the customer's uses of the product in its markets were jointly decided. Closeness is a term that has been used widely in the literature on buyer-seller relationships and internationalization (Ford, 1980). It refers to the extent of mutual understanding and predictability of behavior that exists between the two parties.

Experience

The decisions of the participants in a relationship will also be affected by what they have learned from their previous experiences in that relationship and elsewhere. This experience will influence their views of what the immediate outcomes are likely to be of particular actions, as well as their longer term effects on the relationship as a whole and the network that surrounds it. The buyers in a fashion chain we have been researching provide an extreme example of the effects of individual experience. In this particular case, the buyers' supplier relationships were strongly personal and would be contained in what was referred to as their "little black book" of contacts. When a buyer in the fashion industry changes the company for which he or she works, the importance of maintaining his or her existing relationships is such that the new store's portfolio of relationships rapidly changes to reflect the buyer's previous experience elsewhere. More commonly, corporate experience of a particular customer or supplier would be transferred to each new participant

TABLE 9.1 Relationship Effects and the Nature of Value to the Participants

	Level 1	Level 2	Level 3	Level 4
Level of effect	In the relationship	On the relationship	On the relationship portfolio	Within the network
Nature of value	Immediate return	Return in terms of change to the state of the relationship	Return in terms of change in the total relationship portfolio	Return in terms of change in the network

in the relationship in the form of informal warnings and guidelines. Needless to say, these affect interaction between the participants.

Relationship Effects

Participants' view of the state of their relationship and their experience of previous interactions both in the relationship and elsewhere will influence their predictions of the likely effects of different relationship decisions, and the responses to them of others in the relationship or the wider network. These predictions of likely effects will be a major influence on the decisions that are made. Even with the benefit of experience, however, the effects of any decision within a relationship can be imperfectly predicted at the time at which it is made. The effects of relationship decisions can also be complicated, but they can be structured usefully by examining them in terms of four levels. These four levels of effect are illustrated in Table 9.1 from the perspective of a single participant.

Level 1: Effects In the Relationship

Any action by a relationship participant will have a number of direct effects *in* that relationship. For example, a decision by a customer to source a particular component from a single supplier will reduce the number of orders it places and reduce the workload of its purchasing staff. The decision may also reduce the need for inward inspection and simplify the company's assembly processes and hence reduce its costs. It may also mean that the company will increase the number of units that it buys from its preferred supplier, which will further produce corresponding changes in the supplier's organization. These consequences of the company's decision are likely to be apparent relatively quickly and are easily identified and attributable to the company's decision. The perceived value to the participants of these effects, both positive and negative, relate to the transactions that will unfold as a consequence of the decision. For example, it may be that the customer's main motivation in the single-sourcing decision was to streamline its production and that if this effect occurs then it will be valued highly. Conversely, the effect of reducing the workload on its buyers is not valued because it will not be able to dispense with any of them. The preferred supplier that has also been subject to the effects of the decision may value the reduced logistics costs of supplying a larger volume to a single customer, but it may not value the higher levels of contacts, questions, and checking that immediately ensue.

Level 2: Effects On the Relationship

The initial decision to sole source a product will also have effects *on* the relationship between the companies, which may be less easily identifiable at the time of the initial decision than its Level 1 effects. For example, the decision to sole source may have the direct effect of increasing the mutual dependence of the two companies and paradoxically, this increased dependence may reduce the trust that previously existed. The initial decision may also lead less directly to an increase in the resources in one or more of them. For example, the supplier company's increased attention to this important relationship may lead it to change its production methods and so to enhance its process technology resources. Consideration of future effects of a decision on a relationship represents a classic issue in buyer-seller relationships. For example, a supplier may have the opportunity to achieve a short-term gain by increasing its price to a customer in a time of product shortage. It may well decide, however, to forego the positive effects of the price increase in the relationship because of its concerns about the possible negative effects on the relationship of a lessening of trust between the companies. Of course, many situations are less straightforward than that of a simple price decision. For example, a company may seek to achieve more subtle changes to a relationship over time by a series of decisions made over relatively detailed issues. The firm may be concerned that a long-term supplier is taking it for granted and so it will seek to make the relationship less close by being less predictable in both its ordering pattern and its more personal interactions (Ford, Håkansson, & Johanson, 1986).

More generally, a company may make a decision narrowly to achieve an effect in a relationship and may be oblivious to or uncaring about any longer term effects of that decision on the relationship. Alternatively, it may make a decision on the basis of some explicit or implicit view of the current state of a relationship and of the state it would like to achieve at some stage in the future. Thus, it may seek to achieve a Level 2 effect, which changes the state of that relationship.

Level 3: Effects On a Portfolio

In addition to a decision having a future effect on that relationship, it may also have effects on other relationships in the company's portfolio. Just as in the case of Level 2 effects, these wider effects can be both direct and indirect, conscious and unconscious. For example, when a customer engages in a single sourcing deal for a particular product with a supplier, this action will have the direct and conscious effect that it will not buy that product from other suppliers in its portfolio. The decision may also have the indirect effect that other suppliers of other products believe that this is part of a more general policy. Sending this message could have been the conscious intent of the original decision with one supplier. Some of these other suppliers may seek similar sole-supply arrangements, while others may believe that they are unlikely to be considered as single suppliers and so will reduce their commitment to this customer.

Level 4: Effects On a Network

A decision within a relationship may also have effects on the wider network. Some of these effects may take a considerable time to become apparent. For example, if a supplier makes the decision to develop a new technology for application in a particular relationship, this new technology may subsequently become the standard throughout the network. The technique developed by a major retailer for matching color between different rolls of fabric bought by its clothing suppliers has now become the standard, not only throughout the clothing industry but also in other companies where color matching is important such as those producing curtains and carpets for use in areas as vast as airports and hospitals. Such standardization could generate positive value to the initiator in terms of royalty revenue or may indeed be a prerequisite for the success of its own products in a market. Similarly, a decision by a major customer to buy from a large supplier could be emulated by others in the industry and hence radically alter the pattern of supply and competitive activity within a network. Other network effects are more immediate, such as when a relationship decision by one party can affect the other parties' relationships with companies elsewhere in the network. For example, in the U.K. retail circles, when a company becomes a supplier to Marks & Spencer, it is tacitly accepted that the supplier's customer portfolio will revolve around this single customer relationship. This situation is likely to lead to a major change in that supplier's relations with its own suppliers and with other customers elsewhere in the network.

Managers' Views of the
Different Levels of Effects

Of course, we do not suggest that participant managers *do* take all of these potential levels of effects into account in all their decision making. Our research has shown that managers are able to think clearly about the Level 1 effects of their decisions *in* the relationship, as well as those of their partners. They are often much less clear in thinking about the Level 2 effects of decisions *on* the relationship. In fact, managers who are concerned about the higher level effects of their decisions will frequently articulate those effects at Level 1. For example, a business buyer may say that it would not give an order to a particular supplier because the price was too high, when in fact the buyer may wish to "teach the supplier a lesson," because it had become somewhat lazy and inattentive as a relationship partner (Level 2). Or, it may be that the order was being diverted from that supplier, because it was becoming too dominant and the customer was concerned to maintain the competitive position of another supplier (Level 3). Despite its complexity and the methodological challenges it represents, we believe that the separation into different levels is a prerequisite for an outsider to analyze relationship decision making. We would also suggest that managerial decision making within relationships would be enhanced if it took place with a more explicit consideration of the different levels of effects of those decisions, and it is a major aim of this research to assist managers in that process.

Personal and Corporate Belief Systems

Relationship decisions are also affected by the personal and corporate belief systems of the participants. These beliefs encompass the nature of the participants' roles in their jobs and in society, and the values to which they adhere. The beliefs can be differentiated from, but they underpin the specific values that an individual would apply to the effects of a particular decision, to which we will return shortly. An example of these belief systems is provided by Johnson and Johnson, which has always prided itself on a particular corporate ethos, valuing societal benefit over narrower corporate profit. This value priority has shown through in the company's reputation with consumers and some years ago it enabled the company to successfully withstand the potentially catastrophic effects of the sabotage of its analgesic brand, Tylenol. Part of the company's ethos had been to expand organically, rather than by acquisition. The company has more recently, however, embarked on a number of acquisitions and it has not always been able to immediately instill its corporate belief system into some of the individuals in the acquired companies, as illustrated in some of their relationship decisions.

Personal and corporate belief systems are idiosyncratic; they are complex and multidimensional, and often conflicting dimensions can affect interactions in any one relationship. For the purposes of understanding relationship decision making, we must be concerned both with those beliefs that are stated at either the corporate or individual level, and those that are unstated, but that show through and are observable in participant behavior. An important but often unstated aspect of these unstated belief systems is the participants' attitude toward risk.

The impact of individual belief systems can again be illustrated by reference to our research into the relationship strategies by a retailer of women's clothing. When discussing their relationships with suppliers, it became clear that the retail buyers' beliefs about themselves were expressed largely in terms of *fashion*. Thus, they were overwhelmingly concerned in their work with the concept of their "handwriting" or definition of their fashion statement, both as individuals and as a store. At the individual level, this handwriting and the supplier relationships with which it was associated were transferred with them when they changed jobs between different garment retailers. Because of the primacy of this fashion value, the buyers made decisions within relationships that often meant that they had to accept inadequacies in product quality and delivery scheduling, which would have been unthinkable in most manufacturing companies. These problems of quality and delivery then had to be *coped with* in the relationship by various mechanisms of pricing and control, such as mark downs in price for late delivery or product inadequacy. Furthermore, because of the primacy of fashion in their self-image, the buyers had a very restricted view of commitment to suppliers. If a supplier failed, either because of the failure of a design to sell well or because of quality or delivery problems, then that would affect subsequent business, rather than act as the trigger for joint efforts at supplier improvement.

In contrast, interviews in the auto industry indicated that many buyers made relationship decisions based more on their values in their perceived primary role as providers of relatively standardized material that ensured continuity of production. The effects they sought in their relationship decision making were thus expressed in terms of production reliability and consistency. In contrast, project buyers in the aerospace industry had belief systems that centered on their role in developing and integrating the various technologies of their suppliers.

The Value of Relationship Effects

We have seen that a number of factors—the experience of the participants, the state of the relationship, the possible effects of a decision, and the value structure of the participant—will all affect decision making in a relationship. The final and perhaps most important factor in analyzing relationship decision making, to which we now turn, is the value that a participant sees in the possible outcomes from any decision. It is clear that the value of specific decisions to a participant (either directly to the decision maker, or to someone else subject to the decision) can be seen in terms of the effect of the decision on the relationship in which it is made, and on the wider network as well as in terms of its immediate outcome in the relationship. All decisions will be made, however, on the basis not only of the likely effects at these four levels, as perceived by the person involved, but on the basis of what each manager thinks to be important or personally values most. What is valued most may be witnessed, for example, in the trade-off between immediate outcomes of a decision in the relationship and the relationship's future; the trade-off between that relationship's future and a change in the network position, as well as the trade-off between different ways of receiving value at each level, such as improving technological resources as opposed to generating cash, or achieving a more certain, but lower reward or a speculative jackpot.

There is likely to be considerable diversity in the ways in which different individuals and functions in the same company and in different companies in a relationship perceive, describe, and assess any action in that relationship. Even the terminology that one company uses to describe its relationships may be substantially different from another's. For managers, it means that the development of a strategic approach to their relationships requires them to appreciate not only the different levels of effect of their decisions, their own values and the value to them of different effects, but also the corresponding factors for the other parties. The researcher studying relationship decision making faces the considerable task of carrying out a relationship analysis that is company-centered and based on the stated, observed, and inferred relationship imperatives for the organization, and using the company's descriptive framework as the basis for discussion.

Previous Research Into
Value in Relationships

The emphasis in much relationship research, as reflected in Ford (1990) for instance, has tended toward describing what may be valuable within a relationship in terms of a variety of global dimensions, such as the level of interdependence, degree of trust, amount of commitment, and duration of relationship, among others. That is, studies have sought to describe what a relationship is composed of. These constituents are generally not measured in such ways that the consequences of specific decisions can be described in meaningful terms with respect to them. In this sense studies have tended to be descriptive rather than focusing on the evaluation of the constituents as a basis for decision making. This lack of attention to evaluative components of relationship decision making has had the consequence that there has been little attention in research to concepts of value definition that individual companies could interpret easily and apply, particularly the absence of quantification of relationship constituents at more than a binary level, that is, the presence or absence of a factor. There have, however, been some exceptions to this general treatment of value in business-to-business exchanges. Krapfel, Salmond, and Spekman (1991) have attempted to define relationships in such a way as to devise categories that differentially formulate strategy. They characterize relationship value as a function of the criticality and quality of the goods exchanged, replaceability of the seller, and the cost savings resulting from the buyer's practices and procedures. Their treatment, however, also considers relationship values in dichotomous terms (i.e., high and low). This may be satisfactory for the purposes of arriving at a conceptual device such as a "relationship mapping model" (characterizing relationships as partner, friend, acquaintance, or rival), which trades off value with common interest, but it does not enable an organization to easily determine the point at which an acquaintance becomes a rival, a friend becomes a partner, or an acquaintance becomes a partner, or indeed what is necessary to achieve such a state, should it be desired. This ability is extremely important for a company to be able to strategically manage its exchange relationships. The particular metaphoric categories for business relationships that Krapfel et al. (1991) use may also be questionable in themselves because they revolve around relationship images that are extrafamilial, whereas the success of the "open kimono" approach to business-to-business relationships in Japan owes more to the paternalistic nature of the buying partner (Sako, 1992); suppliers become part of the family.

Anderson, Jain, and Chintagunta (1993) have provided a comprehensive consideration of the methods used by marketers to assess the value that their customers receive. They define value in business markets as the "perceived worth in monetary units of the set of

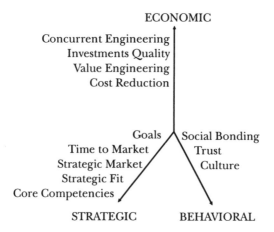

Figure 9.3. The Expanding Dimensions of Relationship Value

SOURCE: From Wilson and Jantrania (1994). © Department of Marketing, Faculty of Business and Economics, Monash University, Melbourne, Australia. Used with permission.

economic, technical, service and social benefits received by a customer firm in exchange for the price paid for a product offering, taking into consideration the available alternative suppliers' offerings and prices" (p. 5). The treatment of value in this way certainly seems appropriate for assessing the economic value in use of a single product to the recipient of the value, but it does not help in understanding the value accruing to both participants in a relationship over time and across a range of exchanged goods or services. In contrast, the conceptualization provided by Wilson and Jantrania (1994) examines value to both parties along three dimensions: economic, behavioral, and strategic (Figure 9.3). They outline the difficulties associated with the observation and measurement of these dimensions in all but the simplest of cases and certainly, they have difficulty in being circumscriptive on all but the narrowly defined economic level. Furthermore, their measurement of economic value is product based rather than relationship focused; for example, value-in-use of a biocide chemical rather than the value associated with industrial exchange relations with the chemical supplier.

These studies are laudable in their concern for objective measures of value and attempts at circumscription. A major problem, however, is that in terms of the levels of effects that we have described, these studies are predominantly focused on Level 1 (i.e., "In the Relationship"). The studies acknowledge no apparent role for effects at the other levels. As a consequence, they ignore the apparently subjective (possibly even arbitrary) nature of relationship decisions.

Using the levels of effects as a basis for consideration does enable some objective measurement to be made at lower levels, very much in line with the emphasis placed on the economic dimension by Wilson and Jantrania (1994). For instance, it is possible at this level to conduct the sort of analysis that Turnbull and Zolkiewski (1995) have undertaken to determine the total (real) costs of supporting one's portfolio of customers. Cost-to-serve data of this sort provides a baseline for Level 1 effects from which it is possible to consider higher level effects. These more objective measures may be supplemented by more subjective measurement at the higher levels. In the absence of circumscription, it is more important to provide help in understanding the relationship and the possible consequences of action. Because the actions may involve investments of time and money, financial directors may not be satisfied with such an approach, but it may be the best that is available. The work of Cousins (1994), using a multicriteria decision-making approach (in an analytic hierarchy process) is an example of an attempt to use consensus measures as the basis for dealing within relationships. Although stemming from a preoccupation with supplier assessment, the approach has yielded idealized models of suppliers, which cross-functional groups in organizations could use as the basis for making sourcing decisions. Studies such as this provide a possible methodological basis for analyzing how value affects relationship decisions. Further development of this approach requires incorporation of an increased understanding of the nature of intercompany relationships and network phenomena, the basis of relationship decision making and the perceptions of participants in the relationship.

A CONTINUING RESEARCH DIRECTION

So far we have outlined some aspects of the nature of relationship strategy and of decision making within intercompany relationships. In doing so, we have emphasized both the complexity of the issues involved and the difficulty of applying the more conventional techniques of investment appraisal to relationship investment decisions.

Despite these complexities and difficulties, managers do make both tactical and strategic decisions, and our continuing research aims to better understand this process as a precursor to improving the decision-making activity itself. Our current approach to this research builds on earlier IMP studies. We use the IMP research instruments to identify a company's network of important relationships and to obtain the perceptions of both parties in each of the company's significant relationships of the state of that relationship, the experience and resources that they bring to it, and where it fits into their respective portfolio and network position.

Following from this, we are currently developing and using further questionnaires to try to understand what it is that drives both individuals and companies in their dealings with each other. Questions about these drivers must encompass the belief systems of the relationship participants and the value that they assign to the different effects of their relationship decisions, the response of partners, and the overall state of relationship that they would like to achieve. Of course, the relationship and network situation facing each participant on each side of the relationship is unique. If, however, we are to develop an understanding of the nature of relationship decision making, it will be necessary to search for whatever commonalities in approach exist in different situations and to develop a taxonomy of relationship decision approaches and concerns. Based on our initial research, we now present such a taxonomy with two caveats. First, these drivers are not mutually exclusive and a participant could manifest more than one at different times or in different circumstances. Second, the taxonomy at this time is still largely a conceptualization and not the result of detailed fieldwork.

A Preliminary Taxonomy of Relationship Drivers

1. The Revenue/Cost Driver. In this situation the participants are driven by short-term, financially oriented concerns, that is, with their Level 1 effects. Examples include a buyer concerned with reducing costs by lowering price paid, or a seller concerned with increasing price or generating additional sales. In this way, the participants seek to achieve value through the existing exchange goods and services mix, without engaging in adaptations as a means of adding extra value.

2. *The Added-Value Driver.* The concerns in this driver may also be financial, but the means to achieve this desired end involve adding extra value via the exchange. Thus a buyer in a relationship may choose to pay more for a component made using a different process, or purchase a different component (at extra cost) in order to improve product reliability or performance, and ultimately increase sales volume or reduce product support costs. In this case the driver is based on an end-customer focus. Similarly, a seller in a relationship may make decisions driven by a motivation to add value to the buyer as a way of generating additional revenue immediately (Level 1).

3. *The "Obeying Orders" Driver.* This driver refers to the situation in which an individual's approach to relationship decisions is based on instructions from above or standard procedures, rather than on an evaluation of the state of a relationship or any relationship-specific variables. The instructions from above may be based on conscious strategic decisions on how to operate in relationships in general or they may be based on tradition or arbitrary rules, but these instructions are interpreted and acted on at the lower levels without individual question.

4. *The Relationship Driver.* In this driver, the overriding interest revolves directly around the relationship partner. Decisions are made to achieve changes in the state of the relationship (Level 2), rather than for their Level 1 effects. Examples of this driver would include making decisions with the intended effect of building up a relationship because it has future potential benefits; making decisions aimed at punishing a partner as a means of exerting control or to demonstrate that the balance of power resides with the company; making decisions intended to "keep a partner honest" by publicly demonstrating that the dependence is not as great as it believes (by, for instance, awarding a contract to another supplier on a particular occasion). The time frame of the effects sought by these decisions may be quite expanded, although the benefits of actions that have a relationship element as their core may also be realized in the short term. For example, switching from one supplier to another for a single contract may well have the immediate effect of bringing a rogue supplier to heel (a Level 3 effect). The relationship driver,

however, more generally involves incurring costs in the short term to achieve benefits in the long term.

5. The Teaching and Learning Driver. This driver is apparent when a relationship provides a vehicle for corporate learning and thus a way of enhancing the company's resources, whether by improving its procedures, technological knowledge, or technologies (product, process, or market). This driver also encompasses teaching, as in the situation where a company is keen to teach its partners so as to enhance their resources for its benefit. Examples include a marketing company providing training in the use of its product, or a retailer educating its suppliers in quality control techniques. By its nature, this driver is likely to be oriented toward the long term, to a time when the company has attained the knowledge for itself or has conveyed the knowledge sufficiently to its partner such that it can benefit.

6. The Network Driver. Decisions within this driver are truly strategic. The overriding interest is on the consequences for the company of actions elsewhere in the network and how these will affect the company's relationships. This driver leads to decisions that take into account these external phenomena or that seek to change the wider network, or the company's position in the network for corporate advantage. An example may help to illustrate the importance of being driven by concerns about what is or could happen elsewhere in the network. This example also illustrates the difficulties that companies face in taking network considerations into their decision making. Lucas, the major U.K. automotive and aerospace components company, had a strong joint-development relationship for fuel-injection equipment with the U.K. car maker, Rover, which was its major customer. Its dependence on one customer has made it very vulnerable to the effects of the takeover of Rover by BMW, which already has its own close relationship, elsewhere in the network, with Bosch for development of future fuel-injection equipment.

We are sure that this taxonomy is incomplete. Nevertheless, we regard the development of a categorization of the different drivers of relationship decision making as an important first stage in the process of helping managers examine their own decisions and the implicit and explicit motivations on which they are based. This self-examination can then form the basis for a better ordered and more strategic approach to that decision making.

CONCLUSION

This chapter has explored some of the issues associated with studying the concept of value in the area of intercompany relationships. We have emphasized that such a study needs to be undertaken in the context of the overall network of which those relationships form part. This means that an understanding of the real and perceived value of the effects of relationship activity requires analysis at a number of levels, ranging from their immediate effect in terms of such outcomes as an increase in sales or in price paid, through the effects of decisions on the future state of both relationship and on others and on the wider network of companies.

Despite the apparent relevance of considering relationship decisions as investments, this chapter has concluded that attempts to examine relationship decision making in standard investment appraisal terms are highly problematic. This is true for no other reason than the difficulty of identifying all the past and future flows necessary to undertake a financial appraisal. Given this present state of knowledge, we conclude that a more productive approach is based on an exploration of the decision preferences that company representatives make when considering options associated with their relationships.

Our initial approach to this research was based on a frustration with the limited effect on managerial decision making of the research over recent years. It is not our intention to construct a further conceptual framework for its own sake. Instead, we are seeking to examine relationships in a way that is meaningful to managers and that addresses their problems. We believe that managers do approach their relationship decisions on the basis of a set of values, and these are more likely to be implicit than explicit. We also believe that they seek to examine the likely outcomes of their relationship decisions and those of their partners, and that they would like to bring both long- and short-term considerations into their deliberations as well as seeing each decision in its wider context. They are also conscious of the risks involved in these and other decisions. Although we continue to research decision making within buyer-supplier relations, our conclusion so far is that our best way of contributing to a more strategic approach to relationship decision making is to help managers examine the basis of their current decision making and how this relates both to its outcomes and to their expressed and apparent value structures and risk preferences. We believe that this examination will enable them to have a clearer view of their own experience, the effects of their decisions, and the aims they are seeking to pursue.

NOTES

1. Throughout this discussion we are concerned with relationships in the context of business-to-business markets in which each relationship is individually significant (although not necessarily of overwhelming importance) to the two parties. What has become known as the "relationship marketing" literature in the consumer marketing context does examine the likely revenues and profit streams from whole markets or segments (Payne & Rickard, 1993). In this case the researcher is concerned with comparison of the costs of acquiring new clients relative to the subsequent revenue streams generated from them. The differences between the two contexts are that the consumer marketing researchers are able to generalize from past experience of aggregate behavior, and the pattern of interaction between the parties is both simpler and less subject to variation. Of course, some business-to-business situations approximate this situation, such as those between an industrial distributor and its many thousands of customers.

2. Turnbull and Topcu (1994) have analyzed the common, but often unrecognized situation, in which there is wide variation between relationship profitability within a portfolio.

PART IV

Dynamic Networks
and Market Structure

10

Drifting Closer and Drifting Away in Networks

Gradual Changes in Interdependencies of Networks

SUSANNE HERTZ

In an industrial network there is a constant process of change. Closeness and distance between firms are continuously shifting. Firms are connected to other firms in different ways. Every firm has its own specific context of firms to which they are related. Processes of change can be either of a slower and gradual character or swifter and more radical. The gradual changes, which seem to be endogenous to the network, are more common and less visible. The fact that they are common and less visible, however, makes it even more important to know about them and how they interact with other changes in the total network.

For the industrial system to perform in an effective way, there are different governance structures involving a number of directly or indirectly connected firms. Firms that are part of the same governance structure show a high interdependency. These firms of higher interdependency form clusters or smaller groups of related firms in the total network. Even though each firm forms its own cluster of interrelated companies, some large firms and their clusters dominate over others in the total network.

This chapter focuses on gradual changes going on between such large dominating clusters of companies within the total network and the effects for the network. The clusters are said to be *drifting closer or away* from each other.

179

Drifts closer or away between these clusters are seen as systematic changes in priorities in existing relationships as well as changes in the indirect relationships, and their purposes can be either strategic or just a result of solving temporary problems. Hertz (1993) noted that drifting closer or away are ways to reduce uncertainty and to prepare for larger commitments such as future strategic alliances, merger, or acquisitions. Therefore these gradual changes might be important indicators of other more radical changes developing in the network. Very seldom are acquisitions or large international alliances formed without a history of cooperation between at least one or both of the organizations (Hertz, 1993); instead, these more radical changes have often been forgone by the slow process of drifting closer over time.

In certain periods of time, under more or less dynamic circumstances, certain structures of clusters seem to be more viable than others. When clusters in the total network are highly integrated the effects of a change tend to be larger. On the other hand, when there are more loosely integrated clusters the effects are smaller. Over time, internationalization of firms and international competition have caused an increased interdependency in the total network. Thus, integration within clusters has increased, and so the reactions and effects of drifting closer and away are causing further changes in the network. The purpose of this study is to discuss the importance of drifting closer and away between clusters in the large international network in general for a focal organization and cluster, and as indicators of more radical, resultant changes.

NETWORK CHANGES

An industrial network of organizations might be analyzed from three different perspectives, that is, the single organization, the relationship between organizations, and the total network. Similarly, internationalization in networks is based on changes in single organizations, relationships among them, and the total network.

In the network approach, coordination or integration between organizations and their production system is the basis for the formation of and changes in relationships. Integration is a process of coordination with the specific purpose of creating a whole. Within these *exchange relationships* the organizations develop. Changes in integration are vital when studying dynamics from a network perspective. Over time, trust and resource commitments lead to an increased interdependence and long-term relations. Johanson and Mattsson (1987), in their discussion on international integration, claim that not only is integration more important for a highly internationalized company but integration increases in importance when the market is highly internationalized.

Furthermore, in the total network there are clusters or *nets* of interrelated organizations showing greater interdependence between each other than to other parts of the network. Changes of single, dyadic relationships are seen as changes on the micro level, while changes of nets take place at the macro level. Change at the relationship level is a prerequisite for change in nets. Therefore, changes in relationships and clusters or nets are combined, and following the reasoning just discussed, both are discussed in terms of changes in degree of coordination and integration.

RELATIONSHIP CHANGES AND LIFE CYCLE

The relationship is the cornerstone of the network approach. The establishment of new relationships and changes in existing ones together influence the position of the company in the network. The network position is considered here not only as a matter of exchange relationships and the identities of the counterparts in the network (Di Maggio, 1986), but also a function in the industrial system (Johanson & Mattsson, 1988, 1992).

The position of a company in a net will therefore be influenced by changes in its relationships, which in turn reflect changes in integration between companies. It is important to clarify, however, that integration in this chapter is used in a wider sense and is not limited to the legal or economic dimension of a relationship; that is, formal agreement, ownership, and so on, but also includes social, flow of activities, and control or power aspects of integration. Legal integration in terms of ownership is only one extreme of the legal aspects. These dimensions interact in the relationship (Mattsson, 1969; see also Heide & Miner, 1990).

The changes at the relationship level involve single dyadic relationships, while changes at the small network level concern changes in several relations (more than two). In the study by Hertz (1993) on patterns of internationalization using the network approach, it was shown how single relationships developed in a typical life cycle pattern over time. This relationship life cycle involved five different phases: establishment of a new relationship, closer cooperation within the relationship, enlargement of the commitment, looser cooperation, and finally cessation of the relationship. The first three are phases of increasing integration and the last two are of decreasing integration in the relationship.

A similar life cycle involving phases of establishment, expansion, and dissolution has been noted by several other researchers (Dwyer, Schurr, & Oh, 1987; Gadde & Mattsson, 1987; Liljegren, 1988). Furthermore, Liljegren (1988) found in a large longitudinal empirical study of the development of a relationship that changes did not always go into a phase of cessation but instead could be reconsidered and restarted in the stage of looser cooperation leading to closer cooperation. In the empirical studies of Hertz (1993), Liljegren (1988), and Gadde and Mattsson (1987), negative changes in an existing relationship seem to be less clear and therefore more difficult to follow. In most cases, there was a fading out rather than an abrupt switch from high to no involvement. Gadde and Mattsson (1987) found that very seldom was there a direct change from a single supplier to a new single supplier. Instead, the new suppliers were taking on more and more activities over time and the old relationship lessened until there was a cessation. These gradual changes in priorities are less visible and difficult to measure. Changes in a direct relationship, however, often are dependent on changes in other direct relationships related to the same company, so adding another direct relationship will probably have an effect on priorities and visibility. The change from being an exclusive partner to one of two partners will of course change the situation and influence the relationship with the customer, for example.

When we discuss an exchange relationship, we focus on interrelationships. A certain frequency, intensity, and stability have to be present before it will be defined as an interactive relationship. There are, however, other types of relations that cannot fulfill these conditions, such as one-way, passive, infrequent, temporary relations, or all of these. These relations might be the forerunners of the establishment of a relationship, in that they are not yet defined as exchange relationships, but are either still indirect relationships in the total network, or on their way to being established as direct or indirect relationships.

Dwyer et al. (1987) included in their relationship life cycle a searching and exploitation of relationships seen to be parts of the establishment of a relationship. Some of these relationships, however, might never become established. To what extent will it still be registered in the relationship life cycle? They also compare the relational exchange to that of a discrete transaction; that is, characterized by short duration, distinct bargaining, minimal personal relationships, no joint efforts, and so on. There seems to be a grey zone in the development from discrete transactions to relationships, which is of importance for the development. Furthermore, as Dwyer et al. (1987) stated, "There are bilateral costs and benefits of a relational exchange. Therefore a durable association is not always desirable" (p. 25).

Anderson and Weitz (1987) found significant positive effects on the continuity of a business relationship to be the result of the stake of the organizations, the trust, the level of communication, and the age of the relationship. These things do not come to be by themselves but have to be gained over time. A way to gain trust, a higher level of communication, and so on, would be to develop gradually from a very low level of commitment, such as drifting, involving also changes in infrequent, temporary, and passive relationships.

The effects of changes in indirect relationships will differ depending on whether the relationships are *positively or negatively connected*, which reflects the degree of complementarity and competition between relationships. Relationships are positively connected to the extent that exchange in one relationship increases the likelihood of exchange in another relationship, and negatively connected when the likelihood decreases exchange in another relationship (Cook, 1982; Emerson & Cook, 1978).

Thus far we have only discussed the changes happening in the dyadic relationship. Underlying the life cycle of the relationship, however, there may be not only changes in a focal relationship but also effects from changes in other relations in the network. Gadde and Mattsson (1987) argued that not only direct but also indirect relationships have to be taken into account to understand changes occurring within a relationship. Furthermore, the fact that the impact of indirect relationships increases with growing international interdependencies is an important reason for studying a wider context of organizations to understand the changes going on.

NET CHANGES

When does a cluster or net of organizations exist? How many organizations have to be involved? Where should the boundaries for the net be set?

Quantitative network analysts discuss these questions in terms of distances, number of paths, and so forth in the network, which then is the base for identification of cliques and clusters (cf. Knoke & Kuklinski, 1982). This analysis requires that there exists an overview of the total international network of organizations in which such clusters can be identified. Such overviews do not exist for many industries, including the international freight industry. Because we lack the necessary overview of the total network, the net discussed here is limited to that of a focal company and its direct and indirect relationships of higher interdependence.

A direct relation is defined in network terms (Easton, 1992; Håkansson, 1987; Laage-Hellmann, 1989; Mattsson, 1986) as an organization with which the focal company has an economic exchange. An indirect relation is defined here as all other relations in a network. In this study, the direct relations are those between the parent company and its subsidiaries, and relations between subsidiaries and any firm other than the parent company are defined as indirect relations.

Changes at the relationship level and the net level interact. Several relationship (more than two) changes taken together, however, are assumed to be needed to show a change at the net level. A single change influencing only a dyad will usually have a minimal marginal effect to be accounted for at the net level. Changes may take place gradually over time or almost simultaneously, depending on types of events.

What are the possible changes taking place at the net level? The basic changes seem to concern either changing the size of the net or

		Type of Change	
		Gradual	Radical
Integration	Decrease	Drifting Away	Splitting a Net
	Increase	Drifting Closer	Joining of Nets

Figure 10.1. Changes Between Nets

the cooperation between and within the relationships of the network. This can be seen and described in different ways. Håkansson and Lundgren (1995) mentioned coalescence and dissemination as the two dominating change processes. Mattsson (1987) discusses change in terms of expansion and contraction of the size of the network. Cook (1982) talks about power balancing using extension and consolidation of the net as examples of the changing power of a net. Astley (1985) discusses closure of a network, which means increasing integration within a net.

Even though we will focus on coordination or integration *between nets*, there are always changes going on *within nets* at the same time in terms of increasing or decreasing integration. The nets are seen here from a focal company's network perspective. For the change processes at the net level to lead to a visible change at the net level we assume that the changes must occur in more than two relationships.

Consider Figure 10.1, which depicts classes of changes between nets. An interpretation of the categories follows. Even though each of the changes will be defined and presented, we shall here only go deeper into the changes of drifting closer and away.

Joining of nets means that a large and major part of two nets are changed through joining two nets. Joining takes place through an establishment of a number of new direct relationships between the two networks. A typical incident would be the formation of a strategic alliance in which a number of organizations are cooperating between the nets. Another example might be acquiring a large international company with many subsidiaries and agents that would lead to many new direct and indirect relations with the existing network. These are radical changes for the core companies of the net. An important part of the change when it starts it is not a gradual change. A number of changes between the two nets are designed to take place within a short period of time.

Splitting a net means leaving a number of direct relations within a very short period of time. An example of splitting is when a large group of companies in an integrated net leaves almost at the same time. Another example would be breaking a former strategic alliance such as the Volvo and Renault case. There are a large number of organizations (suppliers, distributors, their own subsidiaries, and so on) involved with Volvo and Renault groups that now have to leave their former direct relationships as a result of the split.

Drifting closer and drifting away are forms of development of existing relationships between organizations belonging to different nets that over time are moving closer or further away from each other. There is a change in the relationships one by one over a period of time. It is based on a change in priorities in certain of the existing direct and indirect relationships that will lead to integration between two nets. This change of priority can be expressed in terms of change in attitudes, roles, and efficiencies. Drifting is a very common change that in comparison to joining and splitting of nets includes changes also in indirect relationships. Drifting means that through an increase or decrease in integration in relation to specific organization(s) a number of organizations of another net will move closer or away. The change in integration is assumed to be made through changes in the existing relations of the net and maybe an addition or switch of one relationship.

Drifting closer or away can be an effect of either strategic action or just a way to solve ad hoc problems. Some of these changes might be a result of gradual switching to or from specific agents at the dyadic level and having closer contacts with the indirect relationships. Another example of drifting closer might be as a result of an agent acquiring another agent or another agent's agent when suddenly a number of organizations both directly and indirectly related to the focal nets are part of the same group. Another situation would be that through an acquisition of a company with many international relationships, priorities may change among the indirect relationships of that net.

The importance of indirect or weaker relationships are well-known. Granovetter (1973) points at the strength of weak ties and their importance. In certain circumstances, such as looking for a new job,

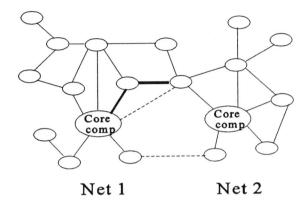

Net 1   Net 2

Figure 10.2. Drifting Closer and Drifting Away

NOTE: Dark bold line = Existing Relationship 1: Changed in degree of integration; dark line = Existing Relationship 2: Changed in degree of integration; line = unchanged relationship; dashed line = temporary, passive, or infrequent: changed relationship.

weak ties offer solutions to problems that the strong direct ties cannot. One of the reasons is that through the weak ties an actor has access to other networks.

Drifting does not change the size of the nets, but it affects the possibility for changing the net size in the future. Strategically drifting seems to be of importance when trying to come closer to indirectly related organizations and their relationships. Figure 10.2 illustrates that drifting closer or away are very much dependent on trust and the degree of complementarity or overlap between the nets in question. Furthermore, drifting between nets implies a knowledge of the existence, size, and design of the nets. There has to be an awareness of which nets the organizations are a part and how they are related to the focal net.

One of the advantages, according to Granovetter (1985), of being embedded in a network, however, is that information of organizations and their relationships is available. Such information can be gained through different direct and indirect relations. Furthermore, this advantage might turn also into a disadvantage for a specific firm.

Information gained this way can be used to influence a certain firm indicating the direction of change. In her dissertation, Young (1992) applies the reasoning of Heider (1958), saying that unbalanced situations strive to become balanced, toward trust in interorganizational relations. In this case it seems that change in one network has an effect on the balance with other networks, and that this will lead to new changes at the relationship and network levels. If relationships unbalanced in trust strive to become balanced, this would mean that efforts have to be made to increase trust. Therefore, it seems likely that when trust or distrust develops between two organizations, it will have an impact on development not only between these two organizations but on other direct and indirect relations in the same net as well.

Furthermore, the effects might lead to changes in positive or negative connectedness for the involved organizations on the relationship level and to changes in the structure of the nets. Positive and negative connections are easily understood at the relationship level based on changes in integration like switching representatives, new cooperation, and so on. On the other hand, nets can also be negatively or positively connected but this seems to be less readily understood. The concepts of *complementary* and *overlapping* will be used to describe positive and negative connectedness at the net level.

Both concepts have been used in the network approach. Complementarity is very common in interorganizational networks (Håkansson, 1987; Johanson & Mattsson, 1992); it means that the resources and activities of two organizations complement each other. Overlapping is a term that has been used mostly in social networks (Knoke & Kuklinski, 1982). Overlapping in this study is used in a slightly different sense because it concerns the characteristics of organizations rather than the organization as such. These characteristics are either their geographical location or types of activities performed. Two companies overlap geographically if they are represented in the same areas, and in their activities if they perform the same activities. The parts that overlap might be a basis for latent or open conflict between organizations and therefore lead to negative connectedness between nets. Overlapping in one sense, either geographical or in activities, and complementary in the other, might be positive and create possibilities. On the other hand, overlapping in both senses leads to full competition.

Drifting closer or away are dependent on the degree that two nets are complementary or overlapping. It is more natural for nets being complementary to drift closer to each other while overlapping would lead to drifting away.

Finally, there seem to exist some typical sequences of net changes similar to the relationship life cycle (Hertz, 1993). These sequences differ over time. These typical changes, which largely take place within nets, are important for the understanding of the changes going on between networks. During earlier decades when international interdependencies were lower, the dominant way for transport companies to develop internationally was to change gradually by adding relationships one by one. More recent developmental sequences show that joining nets is the more typical way. After a period of formation and settlement of relationships between the different companies in the former nets, the organizations move into a phase of closer cooperation, namely of adaptation and intensified cooperation to increase effectiveness and efficiency of the relationships. Closer cooperation is then followed by a closing up, which means moving toward a closure of a net leading to high interdependence between organizations and high complementarity in the net. It will then be increasingly difficult for new organizations to join the net. (The closing up can be compared to what ecology discusses as the closure of a net; Astley, 1985.)

Consistent with these findings, Fombrun (1982) had argued on a more general level that there are two basic types of evolutionary changes in networks; convergence and divergence (or contradiction). In the sequence, the convergence seems to be dominating. Over time, however, as cooperation with organizations outside the network becomes increasingly important, contradiction and divergence develop. In the end, this would result in a split of the net. The more integrated the net had been, the more radical this split may seem to be (Hertz, 1993).

Underlying the changes going on in the typical sequence of international growth moving toward a closing up, there are the gradual changes like drifting closer or away to or from other nets. Often it is a direct result of other changes going on within and between nets. Furthermore, as several nets in the total network of an industry become increasingly integrated, the cooperation between two nets involves more organizations. Does this mean that conflicts between nets as a result of drifting closer and away will involve more companies and will show more quickly? An empirical example will be used to demonstrate the importance and effects of drifting for the development of the involved organizations.

EMPIRICAL EXAMPLES

The empirical examples are taken from the freight forwarding industry. Even though the main part of the empirical material originates from Hertz's (1993) doctoral dissertation, new material has been added based on annual reports, protocols, personal meetings, pamphlets, and so on (cf. Forsgren & Kinch, 1970). We have chosen relationships between ASG, a large Swedish freight forwarding company, and three organizations, which obviously have their basic loyalty in another net. These changes span over a period of 40 years, and they involve both drifting closer and drifting away in combination with the joining and splitting of net(s). The focus in the examples is on relationships to international representatives, because they are the base of the international network of transport companies. These are ASG-Schenker, ASG-Emery, and ASG-Danzas, which all have or have had a relationship as cooperating partners. Schenker, Emery, and Danzas are three very large international groups of transport companies.

ASG-Schenker Networks

After World War II, rail and sea were initially the two dominant means of transportation. The lack of vehicles, the condition of the roads in Europe, and so on, made trucking transports less common. Therefore, the state railways played a very important role for the transport sector in Europe.

ASG and Schenker were two large international freight forwarding companies, owned by the state railways in Sweden and West Germany, respectively. After the war, expansion was very high and the relationships were strong between the state railways of Sweden and West Germany; that is, Svenska Järnvägarna (SJ) and Deutsche Bundesbahn (DB). During the same period, ASG and Schenker expanded very quickly in Europe as well as to other parts of the world.

1950s and 1960s

The cooperation during the 1950s and 1960s between ASG and Schenker concerned transports by rail between West Germany and Sweden. During this period ASG cooperated with Schenker. At this time, the vast majority of local offices in freight forwarding had little integration with other offices even in the same country. Thus it was necessary for ASG to have somewhere around 20 agents to cover only West Germany. These agents all worked separately and largely had different ownerships. In one of these places, Schenker was the representative of ASG's and then for a shorter time another Schenker office was added as a representative to ASG in West Germany. The relationship had a very positive development. The railway owners of the two core companies, ASG and Schenker, were interested in a closer cooperation between the two.

When ASG and Schenker were both in a process of developing airfreight services internationally to overseas markets, the possibility of widening the cooperation between the two networks evolved. In 1961, ASG and Schenker established a joint venture in the Far East for airfreight (ASG had 49%, Schenker 51%). During this period, ASG as a group considered widening the cooperation with the Schenker group worldwide, and the establishment of this joint venture in Hong Kong in the Far East was a sign of this. This was a result of common interests between two large companies. Even the two parent companies were involved in the discussions. After evaluating different alternatives of interest for future development, however, ASG decided to cooperate with another small group, Atege, in West Germany. As a result, the cooperation with the Schenker group in land transportation changed in the late 1960s from drifting closer to away.

1970s and 1980s

In the late 1960s or early 1970s, Schenker started its own organization in Sweden. Before that it had been cooperating with an agent representing the main part of Schenker international operations. When Schenker established its own operating subsidiary for land transportation in Sweden, ASG and Schenker became open competitors. Very quickly the Schenker offices worldwide pushed for development in air and sea freight, which caused further complications in cooperation between ASG and Schenker.

In spite of this, the cooperation in air transports via the joint venture in the Far East was expanding on its own. Several new offices were established in the Philippines, Bangkok, Taiwan, Korea, and so forth—some in the name of Schenker-ASG and some in Schenker's name only—but administrated by the Hong Kong office. Through the Hong Kong joint venture, there were many indirect relationships between ASG and Schenker. The two core companies helped each other in the process of finding new agents in other countries. In India and Japan, this led to a cooperation between ASG and the agents of Schenker. In many other countries, ASG and Schenker networks cooperated temporarily solving ad hoc problems for each of the two networks. As Schenker-ASG in Hong Kong developed over time, it became increasingly a part of the Schenker worldwide organization, and to a lesser extent a part of the ASG international network. The joint venture in Hong Kong, however, stagnated during 1980s partly due to the conflicts between the owners.

In the late 1970s, ASG decided to have their own salesforce in the Schenker-ASG office in Hong Kong and Bangkok to promote air and sea freight for ASG. By then the Schenker organization in Sweden had become quite a large organization and the two large international networks of ASG and Schenker had become almost fully overlapping. Only some ties were left to the Schenker group through the cooperation with some of the independent Schenker agents and the joint venture in Hong Kong.

The internationalization of Schenker-ASG Hong Kong and the continued development of the Schenker parent company and subsidiaries made it increasingly difficult to cooperate with ASG. This was especially true when ASG became part of a large, international chain of exclusively cooperating agents, WACO, the idea of the chain being to increase their activities worldwide. ASG, however, continued their cooperation with Schenker-ASG in Hong Kong but under strain. When in 1980 ASG broke cooperation with the WACO air-freight group, it started a number of new ASG offices in the United Kingdom, Australia, and so on. At that point the conflicts between ASG and Schenker international networks became too severe to continue. Schenker-ASG in Hong Kong split up in 1981; they divided the resources of the joint venture and set up their own offices there. ASG also established a representative office in Singapore, moving the salesforce from Schenker Bangkok to Singapore. The agent in India left with the Schenker group split but the agent in Japan continued.

ASG-Emery

A first crucial change in the development of airfreight for ASG came as a result of the cooperation with Emery Airfreight in 1959. This cooperation with Emery, as an exclusive agent, became very important for ASG as an airfreight forwarder. It gave ASG an opportunity to be very strong in the U.S. market, which was one of the most important markets for the Swedish customers. At the same time, the high-quality services that Emery offered with their 48-hour guarantee put high demands on the ASG organization. Emery had highly developed communication and information systems that ASG wanted to take part in.

ASG wanted to develop the relationship further. The ongoing discussions between ASG and Schenker about widening their cooperation during the mid-1960s and a combination of establishing its own office made Emery break its relationships with ASG. A couple of years later, Emery reestablished its relationship with ASG, covering Sweden and Denmark. The relationship expanded and much new direct traffic between different parts of the United States and Scandinavia were developed.

Over time ASG was also a passive agent for several Emery offices in other countries such as New Zealand, Australia, and South Africa, receiving routing orders, handling their cargo, and so on; Emery also helped when ASG was in temporary need of agents in countries, and so on. The two nets were drifting closer. This continued for almost a decade until the mid-1970s. In spite of the close relationship, their cooperation did not turn into a joining of the two nets. The number of direct established relationships between the two nets were few and too temporary.

In 1975, before ASG joined the WACO organization in airfreight, they reconsidered a development of joining networks with Emery worldwide. The decision turned in favor of another worldwide organization in development, WACO, which caused the two networks of ASG and Emery to drift away from each other. The relationship was dissolved in 1979.

ASG-Danzas

ASG has been cooperating with Danzas in France from the early 1980s. The establishment of the relationship was a result of breaking a 20-year-old cooperation with the former agent, Dubois et Fils. When ASG and Danzas started to cooperate in France, Danzas in France was its first and largest operation in Europe. Thus, it had had a specific status and importance for the Danzas Group with close direct contacts to the board of the Group. The cooperation with ASG, however, was only a question of a cooperation for France and no other country, so it stayed at the relationship level. To establish the cooperation, both ASG and Danzas had switched from a former agent in France and Sweden, respectively. The newly established cooperation developed well and integration increased. As a result of this cooperation ASG and Danzas had now and then talked about joining nets in Europe, and several indirect relationships were involved. At the time, however, it seemed difficult to work out.

Because a large competitor, Swedish-owned Bilspedition Group, merged its three fully owned international freight forwarding companies in 1988, a problem arose for the Danzas Group. This relationship had been established more than half a century ago. In the three merged parallel Swedish operations of Bilspedition, relationships to 56 European agents were dissolved. These agents all had to find new representation in Scandinavian countries. Including changes to the subsidiaries of the merging companies, the Bilspedition merger caused a dissolution of more than 100 relationships to international agents (e.g., Danzas in Switzerland lost its agent in Sweden).

ASG could not help Danzas, because it had an almost 50-year-old cooperation with another Swiss company named Natural AG. Therefore Danzas acquired 55% of another small Swedish forwarding company. This complicated the cooperation between ASG and Danzas and the two nets were drifting away from each other for a short time.

A couple of years later, the ASG agent in Holland went bankrupt. Additionally, the cooperation with Lassen in Germany and in Portugal became increasingly problematic, because the Lassen and ASG nets were drifting away from each other. In the process of looking for new agents, ASG asked for help from Danzas.

Finally, when ASG's established agent in Italy joined a net with another large group of companies, it turned to Danzas in an attempt to find a new agent. Danzas accepted the position of being the new agent in Italy. In doing this the two nets were drifting closer. At the same time, however, the widened cooperation enhanced the conflict between ASG and the Danzas joint venture in Sweden. The cooperation was standing at a crossroad and a discussion started concerning joining the two worldwide nets and not only cooperating in two separate relationships. The mutual understanding and trust between the two core organizations was said to be an important factor in the decision-making process of joining the two nets, because large and costly changes had to be involved before as well as after the joining.

In autumn of 1992, the two core organizations in the ASG and Danzas networks decided to form a worldwide strategic alliance and signed an agreement for a decade. The two nets overlapped, which implied many complications and necessitated changes. In some places, however, their strengths and weaknesses in the different geographical areas were more complementary. Thus, to join the nets, ASG and Danzas had to leave a large number of their existing agents in Europe. This in turn had implications for many other companies in Europe. Because the joining of nets would not be limited to Europe, many other changes in terms of selling existing subsidiaries, switching agents, and so on took place in other continents as well.

SUMMARY

In each of these three cases, the case began with a question of solving a specific situation in one country. Then this relationship expanded and developed along the relationship life cycle into a closer cooperation. Trust seemed to increase between the organizations; as the firms, or other organizations in their nets, needed a representative or specific knowledge, they drew on each others' networks. Changes in one net had effects on other nets. The combined changes of the ASG Schenker and Emery networks are illustrated in Figures 10.3 through 10.6. The Danzas changes are less complicated, took place more quickly, and therefore not illustrated.

Over time, temporary and infrequent relationships developed between the two nets; additionally, there seemed to be a large number of relationships of a passive sort, used when needed without much obligation, the sort of relationship that must also be taken into consideration when talking about drifting closer or away. Often a change toward joining networks is halted due to a close relation with other networks. Furthermore, drifting closer (e.g., toward the Schenker net) also meant drifting away (e.g., from the Emery net). As ASG was

Small Networks for Schenker, ASG, and Emery

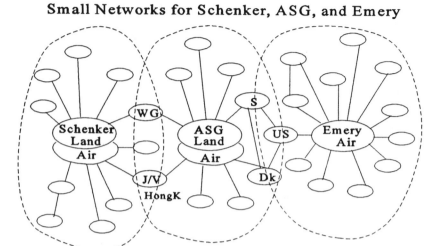

Figure 10.3. ASG Drifting Closer and Away From Schenker and Emery Small Networks: Early 1960s

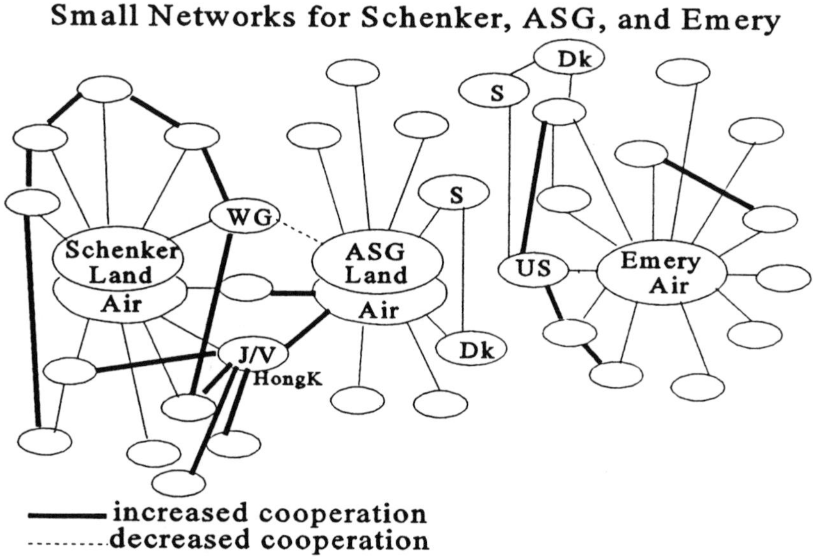

Small Networks for Schenker, ASG, and Emery

———— increased cooperation
············decreased cooperation

Figure 10.4. ASG Drifting Closer and Away From Schenker and Emery Small Networks: Mid-1960s

Small Networks for Schenker, ASG, and Emery

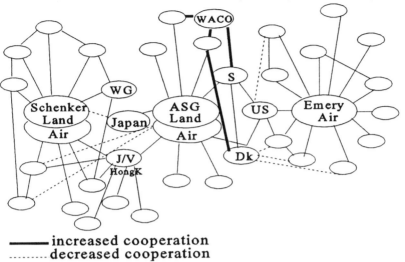

———— increased cooperation
········· decreased cooperation

Figure 10.5. ASG Drifting Closer and Away From Schenker and Emery Small Networks: Mid-1970s

Small Networks for Schenker, ASG, and Emery

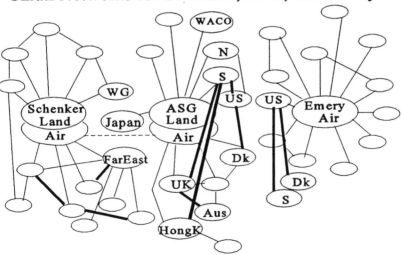

Figure 10.6. ASG Drifting Closer and Away From Schenker and Emery Small Networks: Late 1970s

drifting very close to another large international organization (WACO), both the Schenker and the Emery networks were drifting away, but stayed on at the relationship level through a reduction to one or two direct relationships. Both these relationships were subject to a decreasing degree of integration as a result of the drifting away. Finally, in the early 1980s, even those final direct relationships were dissolved; ASG had formed a number of subsidiaries of its own in the United Kingdom, the United States, Australia, and Norway, and the integration within the ASG network was increased.

RESULTS AND PROPOSITIONS

In this section, the tentative results of the three empirical examples are presented. From that, 10 propositions have been formulated that show the importance of drifting closer and away for the dynamics of networks and also an indicator of more radical changes.

There are some vital questions to be answered about drifting closer and away that must be answered. The examples illustrated what happened and how it happened. Now we consider to what extent drifting is a purposive and planned action, what the purpose could be, when drifting is used, and the possible effects in the total network. This information would give us a better understanding of the importance of drifting for a focal company and net. When analyzing the effects of drifting, we will dwell on the question of whether drifting is an indicator for radical changes or not. The discussion will be based on the former theoretical presentation and the examples.

The basic factors behind drifting closer or away in the empirical examples were the dynamics in the total international network and an interest in developing the focal net or organization. These changes were sometimes purposive by the focal net and at other times just an effect of relationship changes and drifting of other nets in the total network. Often nets went through periods of drifting closer or away several times due to changes going on from both sides.

To what extent then would such an ad hoc solution leading to drifting between two nets be purposive and planned? In some of the cases the focal net was the initiator, approaching a partner and its net for the purpose of searching for new, more stable, or temporary partner(s). At other times it was approached by one of the partners (in another net) looking for a new stable or temporary partner, or the partner's partner looking for a new relationship. From this it seems that the reasons for drifting can be anything from strategic, tactical, to a day-to-day solution. These examples yielded all three. Over time however, it seems that tactical and ad hoc solutions dominated. The purpose in these examples was to find new partner(s), either of more stable or temporary type.

All three examples start with relationship development and develop into changes between their nets. Gradual changes in direct and indirect relationships develop out of increasing integration in existing relationship(s) to a specific network. Developing along the relationship life cycle (Dwyer et al., 1987; Gadde & Mattsson, 1987; Hertz, 1993), trust in existing relationships is an important prerequisite for drifting closer, because discrete transactions, temporary, or passive relationships to relatively unknown organizations, may not be sufficient to ensure reliable performance. Therefore, the focal organization relies on the existing direct relationship to be sure that the agreement will be fulfilled. In a way, it can be seen as a guarantee of better behavior from the indirectly connected organization.

When there is a need of temporary, infrequent, or passive representative in a country, the partners draw on each others' nets. As a result, a number of indirect relationships are activated. Such behavior is consistent with the reasoning of Granovetter (1973), where weak ties offer solutions to problems that direct relationships cannot solve. Through the indirect relationships, the forwarding companies in the examples found a way to solve their ad hoc problems. These problems might include finding a representative in an area where the focal network is not represented but the firm desires a temporary or passive representative. This could be due to customers having temporary projects, infrequent transports or strikes, flooding, and so on, necessitating new procedures and partners. Furthermore, the exchanges were mutual in the examples.

A result of helping each other is that integration in the direct relationships increases further and the indirect relationships become closer. Sometimes the exchange with the indirect relationships might be a number of discrete transactions. At other times, the flow of transactions to the agent's agent might increase and turn into a temporary relationship or perhaps even an established direct relationship.

In the Schenker example, the ownership (i.e., Swedish and West German railways), was of importance for the interest to join the two networks. The fact that the companies were both owned by their respective state railway companies was seen as a link between them. Also, in the Danzas example, the management claimed a certain mutual understanding between the two organizations (ASG and Danzas), indicating that the similarity in corporate culture and company position in the network could be of importance for drifting closer.

Drifting closer is an important way to internationalize. Finding and developing a suitable solution for a specific country takes time and means both costs and benefits (Dwyer et al., 1987). Suitable relationships are perhaps not available during that period of time. Therefore, if a focal net lacks a representative in another country, but is related to an organization that is part of such a network, they use each others' networks. The net will be more international and the focal organization increases its degree of internationalization. Furthermore, the drifting allows for single organizations as well as nets to increase their commitment over time gradually, starting from a very low degree of commitment. The focal net and company get a period of trial and error without excessive costs. For example, in the empirical cases, we discussed levels of commitments not even recognized as a relationship, characterized by a high degree of flexibility, perhaps as a way to avoid a higher commitment.

Drifting closer to the nets of some of the existing partners seemed to be an important strategic action when looking for nets of interest for future development. The existing partner has the knowledge of the other net and a specific agent and connections. It also knows their historical behavior, reputation, and so on. In addition, the new or temporary partnership gives the focal net the possibility of reaching further out in the total network. This knowledge will then be communicated to the focal company and net, and will increase their knowledge about the network and suitable nets of interest for development.

In the ASG-Schenker example, the indirect relationships to the Schenker network, in combination with the existing joint venture, gave information about each other and the structure of the Schenker network as a whole, as well as other networks being indirectly connected to Schenker. It seems that the organizations involved make use of what Granovetter (1985) described as an important advantage of a network: to gain information and knowledge through the network.

As the nets became increasingly integrated, moving along the change sequence of nets toward closing up (Hertz, 1993), the direct and indirect relationships become closer, and the risk of spillover or leakage of important intangible assets increases. When Schenker increased its integration between their subsidiaries and agents worldwide during the 1970s, the ASG/Schenker joint venture in the Far East became closely related to the Schenker international network. Accordingly, Schenker operations in Sweden came to include not only land transportation but also airfreight and sea freight in direct competition with ASG. As a result, the conflicts between the two nets became more open where they were directly competing, and it complicated the situation for the joint venture in the Far East. At the same time, Emery was also increasing its degree of integration in its international network, which meant that ASG would have to choose either the Schenker or Emery network. As ASG in the late 1970s (with Emery and WACO) formed a number of subsidiaries of its own worldwide and integrated its international network, the cooperation with Schenker became too conflict laden and was dissolved. As long as cooperation was maintained at the relationship level, it seemed possible to be part of several competing nets.

Over time, development of new services and products in a net will change the relative importance of the organizations taking part in the net. Initially development is often made through the existing relationships and channels. Enlargement of the cooperation in the relationship life cycle seems to verify this. Anderson and Coughlan (1987) have the same reasoning for distribution channels. Some partners, however, are more suitable for development than others due to lack of knowledge, willingness to invest, and so on. This leads to a shift in the relative importance of the net. As services and products gradually increase, it seems natural that the focal net will drift closer to another net having the know-how and willingness to develop these services and products. If the products and services continue to grow together, the two nets will be joined, as happened between ASG and Schenker in airfreight. On the other hand, if the agents of a related net are already tied up, they might still give temporary assistance through existing relationships. In such a case, drifting closer might be an alternative to joining nets. Over time, if the cooperation is successful, or the situation changes, a switch in favor of the focal might even be considered.

Can drifting be an indicator of future cooperation? Both in the Schenker and Danzas examples drifting closer resulted in joining nets. Even though drifting closer does not necessarily lead to joining networks, in all examples, the core companies always took a deeper cooperation into consideration. In the Schenker example, the plans of joining on a worldwide basis only gave rise to a limited Far East cooperation. Obviously, management seemed aware that they had to make a decision as to which way the cooperation should go when they realized that the two nets were drifting closer. Therefore, it can be said that drifting closer will lead to a consideration of a closer cooperation; if timing and the circumstances are right, they will join their nets.

Complementarity and degree of overlap are very important in all three examples as a tool for understanding drifting as a phenomenon. As long as the two nets had complementary areas, the companies were willing to develop further together. The more the nets overlapped, the less they were interested in helping each other, even though they still had a joint venture or existing deeper cooperation in some area. Drifting closer or away might both be an effect and cause of development into more complementary overlapping between two nets. The effects and causes are often connected in that drifting closer to one net leads to drifting away from another.

Over time drifting closer and away were speeded up. In the Danzas example, fewer changes in indirect relationships were needed to come to a decision. One of the reasons for this phenomenon might be fewer alternatives when most companies are tied up internationally. Therefore timing becomes extremely important.

These discussions show that drifting is an important concept for nets, both for solving their day-to-day work and for their future development. It also helps organizations to develop in a more cautious way with less uncertainty and greater flexibility. At the same time, it increases the knowledge of the total network and the possibility of finding new nets to join.

PROPOSITIONS

Based on the results we formulate a number of propositions.

Proposition 1: Drifting closer is an important way to solve certain types of ad hoc problems.

Proposition 2: Drifting closer to one net often involves drifting away from another one.

Proposition 3: It is not unusual that nets go through periods of both drifting closer and away several times between each other.

Proposition 4: Drifting helps to avoid a higher level of commitment when internationalizing and allows for flexibility in decisions.

Proposition 5: Drifting closer is an important way for organizations to gain knowledge and information about the total network and to search for new nets to join.

Proposition 6: Drifting is an important way to expand or withdraw without informing negatively connected relationships in the focal networks or overlapping networks.

Proposition 7: The joining of nets is often foregone by drifting closer between two nets.

Proposition 8: The higher the degree of integration, the more aware organizations and nets are of drifting taking place.

Proposition 9: Drifting is an indicator of nets considering joining.

Proposition 10: Drifting is a result and a cause of overlapping and complementarity of two nets.

These are some of the more important results when combining the theoretical base with the empirical examples.

CONCLUSIONS

The purpose of this chapter was to look at the importance of drifting closer and away in nets. From the results and propositions we can see that drifting has many different effects and purposes for nets and focal companies. It seems to be very important as a complementary process to the joining or splitting of net(s). Although the more radical changes show a high complexity and many investments, drifting is a gradual change that gives nets and organizations a chance to develop on a trial and error basis, without excessive risk, and with some flexibility. In addition, drifting allows companies to gain experience and information about other parts of the total network.

Drifting has strong implications for companies in their strategic action, because it indicates in which direction the organization can develop in the total network. It also helps in the selection process of finding new future partners. This importance, in combination with the fact that drifting is the most common of changes taking place between nets at the net level, means that it should be a research area of high importance. There is still, however, very little research done on this concept. Hopefully, new studies focusing on this concept will be undertaken in the future.

CHAPTER

11

Marketing Networks

A New Entrant's
Approach to Network Equity

PHILIP C. ZERRILLO, Sr.
RAVI RAINA

The research and development team breathes a sigh of relief. They've done it, they have created a new product that offers greater performance with the added benefit of a lower cost. Sales has assured them that this new product is a "can't miss" winner. After all, how can it fail? Just look at the value proposition that such a product has to offer compared with its current rivals. But fail it may.

Too often, products that seem to offer exceptional value are unable to get a foothold in the marketplace. In spite of having a better mousetrap, managers at these firms often find themselves scratching their heads in amazement as competing firms, with seemingly inferior market offerings, continue to command a dominant position in the market. We would argue that the mistake that these firms most often make is that they fail to properly understand the network they are attempting to enter. The marketplace is full of operating networks and entering any one of them may be more difficult than would appear on the surface. As existing systems, these networks are com-

AUTHORS' NOTE: The authors wish to acknowledge their gratitude to Joseph J. Scarsi, Sr. His wisdom, patience, effort, and support made this chapter a reality. This project could never have been undertaken without his advice.

prised of actors that constitute its structure and carry out its processes. The success or failure of new market offerings depends on the
firm's understanding of both the social and economic functions that
the network members carry out, as well as the inherent inertia that
inevitably exists within such purposive networks.

Much network research conceptualizes networks in a horizontal
fashion, that is, as structures in which the actors interact with each
other on a parallel level. One type of network that has often been
overlooked in such research, however, is the vertical marketing system, popularly called a "marketing channel." In this chapter we
investigate vertical linkages by discussing network relationships in the
context of marketing channels. Channels are decidedly hierarchical
in nature. A vertical conceptualization is appropriate due to the
natural movement of goods from the point of production or extrac-
tion to the point of consumption or use (Stern & El-Ansary, 1992).
Various actors have positions in the channel network, either up or
downstream from other actors, because of the types of functions or
flows in which they participate.

Channels are networks that exist to efficiently and effectively
promote, modify, and move goods to markets or places of use. In
doing so, the channel participants add value to the product and share
the division of labor, rent, and risk. Unlike some other forms of
networks, channels are for the most part intentionally developed
networks. Although the actors may not always be conscious of their
membership in a particular network, the fact that they choose to
specialize in a certain function or process indicates that they are
purposely assuming a network position.

Research on networks and channel relations generally focuses on
either (a) the formation of relationships, evolving from the primary
static position, during which it is assumed that no network exists, to
the development of an "optimal" network, or (b) the conditions
under which the network relationships will be modified, evolving
from the current state, in which the general questions to be answered
center around how to move the current channel toward the normative structure. Very little channels research, however, has looked at
how potential channel members are admitted to, or precluded from
the network.

In this chapter we will first highlight relevant research on why
particular actors come together to form the network of interest and

why certain structures or arrangements evolve.[1] Second, we look at the reasons why networks may change. We discuss the internal and external conditions, considerations, and barriers to network change. Third, we analyze the implications that these structures and their resistance to change have for actors who are currently excluded from the network. And last, we introduce several concepts from the brand equity literature that may shed light on the networks' permanence and seeming lack of permeability to outsiders.

THE EMBEDDED NATURE OF FIRMS

No man is an island (Raspa, 1975), and no organization can be one either (Håkansson & Snehota, 1989). Firms have been characterized as operating in an environment of connectedness with other firms to ensure their survival and achieve their goals (Oliver, 1990; Starbuck, 1976). It has become apparent that to prosper in today's dynamic business environment, it is a virtual necessity for firms to seek some form of cooperative relations with other firms. We see an increasing number of firms entering into a variety of interorganizational relationships to attain their business goals (Ring & Van de Ven, 1994). Managers have continually moved away from discrete market transactions or hierarchical arrangements (Friar & Horwitch, 1985; Teece, 1986) toward interorganizational relationships such as partnerships, coalitions, strategic alliances, joint ventures, franchising arrangements, and trade or research consortia (Astley & Fombrum, 1983; Oliver, 1988). To conduct its day-to-day operations, an organization must interact with other entities (organizations, people, legislative bodies, and so on). This connectedness has often been popularly referred to as a network.

A casual review of the marketing or business literature would suggest that firms are entering into interorganizational relationships at an ever increasing rate as a conscious and focused strategy. But the explanation for why firms are entering into such relationships seems to vary.

In premarket societies, economic behavior was believed to be heavily embedded in social relations. Some researchers theorize that with modernization, behavior has become much more autonomous or transaction based (Granovetter, 1985). In the postmodern society, however, it appears that economic behavior is becoming socially based again. The nature of a firm's interaction with its environment has been perceived in vastly different ways by researchers belonging to different schools of thought. Sociologists maintain that firm-level behavior is socially constrained and that there is very little independence available to individual firm managers (Granovetter, 1985). At the other extreme, the utilitarian tradition of classical and neoclassical economics assumes rational, self-interested behavior affected minimally by social relations. The firm is expected to interface with the external environment to maximize its profit objectives, wherein the environment is defined as anything that is not a part of the organization itself (Miles, 1980).

A number of researchers have suggested that to avoid the problems posed by market uncertainty, organizations gradually adopt a more social orientation (Podolny, 1994). Managers attempt to hedge against uncertainty by forming exclusive partnerships with exchange partners with whom they have transacted in the past. Those holding to this view contend that individual transactions between firms need to be interpreted in reference to the long term social relationships between the actors. That is, transactions are seldom analyzed on an individual discrete basis, but rather in a continuous relational manner. This later format implies an expectation of continued exchange, which leads to permanence and inertia in the relationships that evolve.

Organizational theorists have paid increasing attention to the social embeddedness of interorganizational relations; research on how the socioeconomic environment affects organizational structure and processes has moved to the center stage (Hannan & Freeman, 1979). In addition, the study of organizations has moved from focusing on individual organizations to an examination of populations of organizations relating to their environment (e.g., Aldrich & Whetten, 1981; Burt, 1980, 1983).

A third view suggests that the rise in interorganizational relationships is motivated by the attainment of goals that would not be attainable by any firm independently (Litwak & Hylon, 1962; Van de Ven, 1976). By joining forces and developing a consensus on certain macro-level goals, it is expected that overall returns available to the group of firms will exceed those available to any firm acting independently. Zajac and Olsen (1993) posit that the recent proliferation of a wide variety of interorganizational arrangements is a function of anticipated value gains from such relations.

CAUSES OF NETWORK FORMATION

To date, most of the research on interorganizational relations has focused either on the antecedent conditions of a network, or on the structural properties inherent in an existing network. Van de Ven (1976) suggests that interorganizational relationships are formed either because of an internal need for resources or a commitment to an external problem or opportunity. In a review of the literature, Oliver (1990) lists the six reasons most commonly cited for the formation of interorganizational relationships. These determinants, which encompass both the internal motivations for organizations to establish relations, and the external factors that facilitate or impede the formation of such relationships, include the following.

First, firms often must establish relations out of necessity. This necessity could be at the request of external parties such as governments or legislative mandates, or even industry or professional regulatory bodies. Alternatively, the formation of interorganizational relationships may be driven by resource dependence (e.g., Gupta & Lad, 1983; Pfeffer & Salancik, 1978; Warren, 1967; Warren, Rose, & Bergunder, 1974; Zeitz, 1980). Firms are forced to establish relations to reduce the market risks inherent in the acquisition of critical resources.

The second factor is asymmetry. Rather than assuming that firms engage in relationships because of a dependence or a lack of power, several researchers advance the notion that firms are often motivated by the potential to exercise power or control over another organization and its resources. That is, by engaging in a relationship with a firm that has scarce resources, a firm may be able to exert power over other firms with which it either exchanges or competes (e.g., Benson, 1975; Blau, 1964; Pfeffer & Salancik, 1978; Whetten, 1981).

The third factor is reciprocity. Firms may cooperate, collaborate, or coordinate with each other for the purpose of pursuing common or mutually beneficial goals. Rooted in exchange theory (e.g., Emerson, 1962; Thibaut & Kelly, 1959), linkages among exchange members are expected to be characterized by mutual support, balance, and a common understanding, rather than self-seeking interest, conflict, or extreme uses of power.

Fourth, efficiency is important. Relationships are often the outcome of a firm's attempt to enhance its internal input/output ratio (Astley & Fombrun, 1983). In posing a "make or buy" decision for each process a firm performs, a naturally firm-centric network eventually evolves, in which a single actor occupies the central position (e.g., see Iacobucci & Zerrillo, Chapter 18, this volume). Although much of the theory of out-sourcing has focused on how external relations can make the firm more efficient, a parallel stream of literature has emphasized the potential drag that social interaction can have on performance and market competitiveness (e.g., Baker, 1990; Thorelli, 1986; Williamson, 1985).

A fifth factor is stability or predictability. As an adaptive response to environmental uncertainty, firms will engage in interorganizational relations. Environmental uncertainty may be due to a lack of perfect knowledge about environmental fluctuations, potential exchange partners, or available rates of exchange in an interorganizational field (Cook, 1977). By engaging in certain relationships or networks, firms are able to reduce the level of uncertainty they face (e.g., Aldrich, 1971, 1982; Burt, 1980).

Legitimacy is the sixth major factor. There may be a social need for firms to justify their activities or outputs. By engaging in certain relationships, the firm may wish to appear to conform to prevailing norms, rules, beliefs, or expectations of external constituents. The need for legitimacy may be based on an internal recognition that the enhancement of the firm's reputation may be beneficial, or at the request of external constituents such as other network members, government organizations, boards, and so on (DiMaggio, 1988; DiMaggio & Powell, 1983).

Oliver (1990) has confined her analyses to only those relationships that have been consciously and explicitly put in place. Other authors, however, offer an expanded view of interorganizational relationships as "psychological contracts," which may consist of "unwritten and largely nonverbalized sets of congruent expectations and assumptions held by transacting parties about each others' prerogatives and obligations," (Ring & Van de Ven, 1994, p. 100). Ring and Van de Ven's (1994) interpretation of Turner (1987) suggests that "identity (a sense of self in relation to others) and inclusion (constructing a common external factual order) are two fundamental forces that motivate human thought and action" (p. 100). They maintain that the development and evolution of cooperative relationships between organizations consists of a repetitive sequence of negotiations, commitment, and execution stages. Over time, network members develop behavioral expectations of each other regarding the rights and obligations of membership in the network (Van de Ven, 1976). That is, members of a network are expected to develop a common mindset.

BARRIERS TO NETWORK CHANGE
AND NETWORK ENTRY

So, what does this all mean to a firm that has invented a new product and wants to get it to the marketplace? Two aspects of networks are important to note. First, interorganizational networks are generally full systems; that is, at any point in time, the vast majority of channel or network positions are occupied. When looking at an existing marketplace and performing a general feasibility analysis, most forecasters fail to take into account the fact that in the network they are trying to enter, someone is currently performing that function. Furthermore, the actors involved in the network may have formal or informal ties and agreements regarding the division of labor and manner in which business is to be conducted. Second, once a network is in place, it becomes a self-sustaining system that may be much more resistant to change than would first appear (Anderson, Håkansson, & Johanson, 1994).

Environmental factors, the general market structure, social or kinship relations, and resource dependence tend to force the firms in a network to adapt and fit in (Aldrich & Whetten, 1981). This desire to avoid conflict leads to stability in a relationship. The fact that firms do not always possess the ability and desire to adapt, however, leads to inertia; that is, the resistance to change. The idea of interorganizational inertia was first suggested by Burns and Stalker (1961) and Stinchcombe (1965) as a reason why firms of one genesis do not fully adapt to a changing environment. Inertial pressures can arise from a firm's consideration of internal as well as environmental factors (Hannan & Freeman, 1977). We now discuss several forces that can cause a channel network to be inert, and the possible implications these forces may have on parties attempting to enter the channel.

Internal considerations comprise the first force. Investments in plant, equipment, and specialized personnel that are not easily transferable can cause firms to support the present network system. The level of assets that are not readily redeployable elsewhere can create a barrier to change within each firm of the network. These investments have also been referred to as transaction specific assets (cf. Willamson, 1985). Similarly, firms also accumulate stock assets (Dierickx & Cool, 1989), which are assets that are relationship specific and have no value outside that relationship (e.g., specialized training, knowledge of each others' operating procedures, and so on). Firms attempting to enter the network must be aware of the switching costs faced by each network member. Furthermore, it is essential that they understand the base value of these assets, referred to in accounting terms as the salvage value. If one were to analyze the operating cost for the member of the existing network, it is important to understand that a firm's resources are in place and one must essentially compete with them on their variable cost only. The fact that resources are in the marketplace nearly ensures their permanence. For example, when an older plant with inferior technology goes out of business it is often purchased at a fraction of its original cost and the new operators may enter the marketplace or network with minimal fixed costs to recover.

The second force is that of an internal information deficiency. A failure of the existing members of the network to recognize the need for change may make it that much more difficult for the new member to enter that network. One must realize that organizational leaders do not receive anything close to full information, and they may therefore not recognize the need for change. The fact that one firm's value proposition exceeds that of its rival incumbent is unimportant unless network members are aware of the difference and its implication.

Third, parties of a network must have a substantial motivational investment to entertain change. New entrants often fail to assess the threshold point at which a network member is willing to consider change. A product or service may provide superior value to the purchaser, but routinely such products are not adopted if they are of minimal concern to the purchaser. Managers often operate under considerable time constraints, so if the expected payoff from the decision to switch is not above a minimum threshold level, they will not be willing to engage in the decision-making task.

Political equilibrium comprises the fourth force. Change involves the redistribution of resources that may threaten an existing power structure. If adoption of a new product or firm into the network is likely to change the existing power structure of the network, the dominant existing actor may block such an adoption. Therefore, the probability of altering the products, processes, or actors of the channel, which may in any way diminish the power of the dominant firm, is reduced.

The fifth major force is that of established procedures. Once standards, procedures, and the allocation of tasks and authority have become the subject of normative agreement, the cost of change is greatly increased. Take, for instance, the steam engine. Although the new electric engines reduced the need for a worker to shovel coal into the engine furnace, this advantage did not count for much initially, as labor contracts with the railroad unions stated that two persons must always be present in the cab.

The final force that can also inhibit change is that of cost or demand interdependencies. Even if the new product outperforms and is less costly than the current product, these efficiencies may not materialize if the existing product has substantial cost (shared resources, buying efficiencies, and so on) or demand (shared customers, selling efficiencies, and so on) interdependence with other products carried by the channel. As a result, although the new product may enjoy certain advantages over the existing product, in a network context, it may actually suffer disadvantages.

EXTERNAL PRESSURES

There are several sorts of external pressures. First, legal and fiscal barriers to entry and exit may cause difficulties for those firms trying to enter a network. Many barriers to entry such as legal filings, antitrust clauses that preclude certain forms of vertical or horizontal integration, or host country considerations regarding the level of foreign ownership are easily recognizable.

Other legal barriers may not be as obvious. For example, certain simple legal considerations of the bankruptcy laws have created havoc for present channel networks. Many firms, which may have otherwise been forced to leave the marketplace, are temporarily kept in place due to statutes such as Chapter 11. A channel member faced with a finite period of reprieve will most likely engage in short-term volume building strategies, as opposed to long-term investments in value enhancing assets. By reducing their dedication of resources to marketing elements such as sales support, service, warranty support, and the maintenance of extensive inventory, a firm may be able to offer products at lower prices, although at an inferior level of service output. Such strategies can cause chaos for other network members who are attempting to provide value added services to the customer. But more to our issue, these regulations may also preclude potential new actors from entering or taking hold in an existing network.

Other legal barriers to exit may be due to constituent considerations. For example, a tobacco company in the United States may find it difficult to find a buyer. The firms most interested in purchasing such a company may be those firms currently involved in the industry. Antitrust law, however, would most probably preclude any mergers by companies in such an oligopolistic industry. Similarly, government regulations regarding vendor characteristics and vendor requirements may also exclude firms from entering a network.

Second, the network's collective rationality may not coincide with the rationality of its individual actors. Let's examine the case of a company that designs a new fiber that is less expensive than leather but has a 50% greater wear life. The company decides to make shoes and attempts to market them at lower prices through a channel that currently sells leather shoes at substantially higher prices. Although the manufacturer sees an opportunity, its potential trade partners may not share such enthusiasm. For the channel, a new lower cost product may translate into lower dollar margins, and an extended product life may mean reduced future volume. In addition to these obvious and directly estimable costs, other issues such as the effect the product may have on store image, clientele, inventory, and so forth must also be considered. Thus, although the manufacturer and the consumer view the product as beneficial, it may appear threatening to many other members of the trade, and is therefore unlikely to win support.

Third, the legitimacy of a network may be threatened by change. Take the case of a company like Ben and Jerry's ice creams. When considering the addition of low fat yogurts to their product line, they entertained the thought of using artificial sweeteners to make up for the loss of product flavor due to reduced milk fat. The company realized, however, that this was contrary to their "all natural" position in the marketplace, an important consideration for many of their distributive partners. Similarly, when one of their local dairy cooperatives encountered financial difficulty, Ben and Jerry's offered financial support to keep the concern active. Although it may have been more cost effective to allow the cooperative to fail and purchase dairy products elsewhere, the company has always claimed to support family farms. Thus an important and integral part of their network's legitimacy may have been at stake.

Fourth, sociocultural factors may also deter network change. An internal desire to change is often subject to sociocultural considerations. For example, a firm may locate a new foreign source of supply for one of the raw materials it employs. If, however, the potential supplier is from a country with which much of the host country's citizenry is disenchanted, using such a supplier may not be possible. Similarly, if consumers are boycotting products made by a certain firm or products that contain materials from a certain firm or host country, the opportunity to change the network may be blunted.

Fifth, change may require extensive knowledge of the environment external to the network. Information about the relevant external environment may be costly to obtain, particularly in turbulent situations. Additionally, to the extent that any individual actor is responsible for the costs (be they monetary or in the form of resource dedication) of obtaining this information, the probability of information acquisition will decline, unless the potential cost of risk is proportionally excessive.

NETWORK CHANGE

We have discussed why networks may form, and we have suggested a number of reasons why networks are resistant to change and therefore difficult to enter. To round out our discussion we feel that it is necessary to discuss how change takes place. Several factors either internal and external to the channel may be the cause of change. Many of the factors that prevent change can also be a cause of network change, such as the government, sociocultural factors, information availability, legal or legislative mandates, and increasing motivational investment by one party. We now consider several additional factors that may be harbingers of network change.

The internal considerations are several. First and foremost is a firm's recognition that the make or buy decision favors a change from a hierarchical arrangement to that of an exchange partner. Additionally, it may be the case that firms change exchange partners as they realize that superior returns are available from alternative exchange partners.

Second, a relationship with certain network actors may require extensive formalization and contractual explication. The degree of formalization in a network relationship may be cause for the members who interact with a particular party to seek alternative exchange partners (Van de Ven & Walker, 1984). For example, trying to enlist a government agency in a network may move network actors to seek alternative arrangements as the level of formalization and reporting may become excessive.

Third, a continued feeling of domain disensus between exchanging parties can create a situation ripe for change. Parties of the network that cannot agree on their scope of activities and responsibilities are likely to seek alternative hierarchical or exchange relations. Additionally, if they are not in agreement as to the nature of their business missions or their manner of conducting business, conflict will continue.

We now discuss the several external reasons for network change. First, Ring and Van de Ven (1994) suggest that interorganizational ties will often dissolve when there is a continued commitment to losing transactions. Eventually, other parties, which have an interest in the network, or are part of a connected network, may step in to change the current structure. For instance, Van de Ven, Venkataraman, Polley, and Garud (1989) found that firms are unwilling to terminate the relationships on their own and external parties (e.g., banks, factors, shareholders, suppliers, customers) must intervene to initiate change.

Second, an external network may begin to encroach on a focal network, forcing the focal network to change or adapt. Today many channel relationships are in a state of flux because actors in a competing channel, or even a tangential network, have forced change. For example, many manufacturing firms have begun to install on-package pricing, palletize for display, and offer immediate stock replenishment, satellite ordering, and so on for their retail trade. Although these practices have forced competing manufacturers to engage in similar activities, they have also forced noncompeting manufacturers who may also interact with the channel members to act similarly.

Third, an action in the external environment can cause a change in the functions to be performed. Government legislation, interest group protests, physical or economic conditions of the marketplace, and so forth may necessitate either temporary or permanent alterations in a channel configuration. For example, a product contamination scare may cause a temporary change in actors or network structure, whereas the North American Free Trade Agreement is expected to do away with many of the intermediate transactions that were previously required to cross national boundaries.

MANAGERIAL CONCERNS REVISITED

In discussing the potential reasons for network formation, inertia, and change, it should be apparent that any firm attempting to engage in business exchange must become aware of the network structures they will encounter. Taking our initial example of the firm that has developed a sure winner for the market, several considerations should now become apparent. First, does increased efficiency or product performance mean good things for all of the channel members? If the product performs better and lasts longer, is this really good for all of the parties concerned? Although this seems foreign to many firms specializing in research and development and marketing, a closer look at the local rationality of adjacent channel members may provide clues to the hurdles an innovator faces. The product innovator might ask: Can the downstream channel member accept the enhanced utility? Enhanced utility may cause organizational strains, or disutilities for their objective function. Take the case of an industrial lubricant that lasts longer; for example, a synthetic car oil that lasts 10,000 miles between check-ups instead of the standard 3,000; what does it mean to the channel network members? Would stores specializing in quick-stop oil changes be willing to accept this product? How rapidly would a product such as this be accepted by this group? What other existing channel members may be willing to accept this product?

It is important to understand that a product or actor will only be adopted into the network if they offer utilities to multiple levels of the channel or network. If they do not, then either (a) one of the members is going to have to be able to integrate forward or backward to take over the function; (b) an alternative or competing network which employs the actor or product must exist; or (c) the actor or product must make the scope of services and functions provided by the objecting channel member obsolete. That is, the innovator must often be prepared to replace multiple functions in the channel. Few firms are able to enter a network successfully without being prepared to perform multiple tasks.

New organizations must design their goals, technologies, domain definitions, and other activities to take account of preexisting organizations (Aldrich & Whetten, 1981). Warren et al. (1974) found that when new organizations adopted the definition of the situation held by older organizations, there was very little overt conflict (Aldrich & Whetten, 1981). Although it is essential to avoid destructive conflict when attempting to enter a network, it is also essential to understand the network position occupied by the firms one is trying to replace.

To the outsider, network decisions appear somewhat simple. "Simply do away with the network member" is often an easy decision for the objective, disconnected observer, but we must look at what each member adds to their network. Firms have a certain network position; that is, they have an equity position in their network, the extent of which may not always be apparent to outsiders attempting to penetrate the network. A loose paraphrasing of the brand equity literature may shed light on how firms can maintain their network position when offering seemingly lower value. It is suggested that the equity of a brand is derived from five bases (Aaker, 1993): (a) brand loyalty, (b) name awareness, (c) perceived quality, (d) brand associations, and (e) other proprietary assets, such as trademarks, logos, and so forth.

A network actor provides similar benefits to justify its position in the network. A firm might inspire loyalty among consumers of the channel or networks output. The fact that a retailer, which may be foreign owned and that buys from a foreign wholesaler and transacts with a foreign bank to finance their inventory, and so on, sells made-in-America blue jeans still may inspire loyalty among a segment of American shoppers.

Similarly, having a firm involved in a channel may afford name awareness to the channel. The fact that "Ace is the place for True Value hardware" or "Jiffy Lube uses Penzoil" indicates that the network is provided with awareness by having this actor associated with it. The fact that a network actor is a familiar name may serve as an indicator of reliability within the network. Additionally, this may bring attention to the efforts of the network.

Network actors also have a level of perceived quality, whether deserved or not. Actors are sometimes kept in a channel because of outside perceptions of quality. Although the firm's performance or product may be inferior, the perceptions of downstream channel members may dictate their continued association.

Certain network actors may also have associations that justify their continued position in a network. For instance, a tuna manufacturer that makes dolphin-safe tuna may be preferred to one that does not make such a claim. Or, the fact that one sports drink offers better fluid recapture than another may not be of consequence when the other is associated with professional sports leagues, events, celebrities, or life styles. The fact that "Pepsi is the drink of a new generation" may make it the drink of choice for a fun park catering to teenagers because its associations may be more in keeping with the target clientele.

CONCLUSION

The past several decades have been a period of great change as the level of competition in local markets around the globe has intensified. The turbulent economy of the 1980s to the present has forced many firms to rethink their business competencies and alter their approach to the marketplace. The majority of firms have analyzed, and eventually participated in, more interorganizational relationships than at any other time in the history of modern business. In doing so, these firms have intentionally, and sometimes unintentionally, created business networks. The importance of these networks is sometimes not apparent to outsiders. Although many channel linkages appear to be tenuous, their cumulative effect can often be a significant hurdle for outsiders to jump. In contemplating entry into a new market, actors must assess their core competencies not only in terms of the effect they will have on final users, but also in regard to their consequences for adjacent network actors. Firms that cannot offer substantial benefits to their potential trade partners face the prospect of network exclusion. This exclusion may force a very painful lesson in the importance and permanence of network structures.

NOTE

1. Throughout this chapter we will often refer to network actors. This term should be taken to be synonymous with firms. Although channel actors may indeed be individuals, the majority of analysis and literature in this area has focused on the firm as the unit of analysis, an orientation with which we will remain consistent.

Networks Analyses and Brand-Switching Behavior

The Ehrenberg Automobile Data

DAWN IACOBUCCI
GERALDINE HENDERSON
ALBERTO MARCATI
JENNIFER E. CHANG

Several researchers have examined Ehrenberg's "brand-switching data" representing the French and British automobile markets from 1986 to 1989. In this chapter, we model these data in a variety of ways. We present some basic contingency table analyses as baseline results against which to compare subsequent methods. We then consider these marketplaces as networks and explore some results that arise from network methodologies and philosophies. Finally, we model multiple networks simultaneously to study phenomena such as dynamic markets and cross-cultural competitive market structure.

INTRODUCTION

At the invitation of Professor Andrew Ehrenberg, then at the London Business School, 21 teams of researchers embarked on a project in which each team analyzed a contingency table using its own

AUTHORS' NOTE: We are grateful to the National Science Foundation for research support (Grant No. SES-9023445).

technique of expertise. The data are brand-switching data in the automobile manufacturing industries of France and Great Britain. There exist two-way classifications of purchases wherein the rows of each data matrix describe the owners' previous car makes, and the columns of the matrix describe the makes of the currently owned automobiles. Each cell entry is the number of consumers who had owned the row-brand car and who now owned the column-brand car. These data exist for 4 consecutive years, 1986 through 1989.

Ehrenberg's study was conducted primarily for methodological reasons, to see whether the various methods employed would converge on similar conclusions, and thus, furthermore, to see what substantive answers managers would find on using each method (cf. Colombo & Morrison, 1989). A preliminary summary of the project is presented in Colombo, Ehrenberg, and Sabavala (1994), but unfortunately that manuscript contains few analytical details. Colombo and his coauthors are planning to compile a more complete report, but until that material becomes available, we proceed with our research (at the worst, we may find that we have duplicated efforts with some methods reported in this chapter).

Among the approaches considered in that project, and of particular interest to the current research, was the investigation of several network methodologies by Alberto Marcati. In this chapter, we wish to pursue the further application of network methods to these brand-switching data. In addition to contributing another dimension to the methodological study of the automobile data, the current investigation is also a new direction for network analysts. Traditionally, actors studied in the network paradigm have been people or groups of people, for example, firms in business transactions or departments within organizations (e.g., Galaskiewicz, 1985a). In our application, the actors are car manufacturers, and the relational ties are the volumes of consumer purchases flowing to and from different car makes over time. Brand-switching data may have been analyzed by network proximities methods, but if they have been, we are not aware of such studies. These automobile data also include self-reflexive ties, a property unusual for networks, but one that is important for these data, because they will, in some form, represent repeat purchase and loyalty.

In our application of network techniques to these brand-switching data, we will analyze each of the eight matrixes separately (two countries, four time periods each), and perhaps more important, also analyze various meaningful subsets of the matrixes simultaneously (multivariately), to address such questions as change of structure over time and comparability of competitive structure across countries. These issues were not thoroughly addressed in the Ehrenberg project, nor have network analysts traditionally considered many multivariate issues. Many network researchers in marketing find such multivariate and dynamic questions of greatest interest (e.g., Gadde & Mattsson, 1987), however, and we at least concur that such issues should not be ignored when the data exist to examine them.

In this chapter, we will explore a variety of data analysis methods. We will present some basic methods that researchers might apply to any two-way contingency table, thereby serving as a benchmark against which to compare other methods. Such methods were not developed specifically as network analytic tools, but they are frequently applied to network data. We also present truer network methods, those that were developed with a focus on the interrelationships among actors in a network (e.g., the associations contained in the body of a contingency table).

In our comparison of various methods' analytical results, we also wish to be pragmatic. It is certainly true that the logic of network methods is quite distinct from that of other methods, and in general should result in different empirical performances. We are, however, curious to examine the extent to which simple analyses capture the essence of these data. That is, theoretically the methods have many different properties, but if we find, say, that the simple computations of row and column margins provide all the information obtained by more sophisticated network methods, an argument might be made against the more technical models based on redundancy, at least for these data.

The eight matrixes are presented in Table 12.1. These tables represent the raw frequencies as obtained directly from the Ehrenberg study. For the purposes of some methods and simplicity, we have also dichotomized the data, and the binary matrixes appear in Table 12.2. If the matrixes are difficult to read, the networks representing the binary ties are also presented in Figures 12.1 (for the French market) and 12.2 (for the U.K. market).

(text continued on page 231)

TABLE 12.1 Frequencies of Consumers Who Had Owned Row Cars and Now Own Column Cars[a]

	AL[b]	BMW[b]	CI[b]	FI[b]	FO[b]	GM[b]	LA[b]	ME[b]	PE[b]	RE[b]	RO[b]	SE[b]	VW[b]	VO[b]
French market 1986														
AL	82	6	16	16	15	11	0	3	37	24	4	7	25	1
BMW	1	138	1	7	6	1	0	16	22	31	3	4	13	3
CI	7	16	1,437	96	100	62	19	18	283	310	40	22	107	20
FI	8	7	46	358	38	33	6	5	67	116	19	24	29	5
FO	7	8	67	39	494	42	6	4	71	96	12	8	32	10
GM	3	5	19	7	28	245	2	2	41	42	4	7	20	6
LA	0	0	9	11	7	5	57	0	4	17	2	0	3	0
ME	0	11	2	1	3	1	0	89	5	19	0	4	12	4
PE	13	43	251	122	239	130	40	29	2,310	653	48	34	148	30
RE	21	49	312	219	310	295	44	34	817	3,944	88	87	241	34
RO	2	2	3	15	14	12	0	1	24	31	77	0	5	1
SE	0	0	0	4	1	0	0	0	9	5	0	17	1	0
VW	8	23	22	26	45	31	4	9	116	78	12	19	477	12
VO	1	4	0	3	3	4	0	2	4	12	2	4	0	49
French market 1987														
AL	96	10	18	13	17	13	0	3	30	40	4	6	19	3
BMW	2	126	8	9	5	5	0	13	24	35	4	4	29	3
CI	3	11	1,525	127	88	72	32	21	274	432	38	25	78	16
FI	11	5	34	397	44	24	5	4	112	165	17	25	40	5
FO	10	9	47	40	559	42	5	6	88	136	16	9	62	6

	AL	BMW	CI	FI	FO	GM	LA	ME	PE	RE	RO	SE	VW	VO
GM	3	6	24	24	25	277	10	3	64	107	6	7	23	6
LA	0	0	15	14	11	2	67	0	7	10	2	2	5	0
ME	1	6	3	1	5	3	0	97	6	12	2	0	10	6
PE	9	33	295	162	196	127	38	30	2,235	760	52	60	147	29
RE	23	37	367	243	271	223	45	28	801	4,349	79	78	225	36
RO	2	2	4	19	11	11	2	2	28	33	84	8	10	2
SE	2	0	5	6	7	1	2	1	7	9	2	13	1	0
VW	8	16	33	33	46	35	2	13	92	123	10	9	467	10
VO	0	1	10	4	7	2	0	1	24	25	3	0	2	63

French market 1988

	AL	BMW	CI	FI	FO	GM	LA	ME	PE	RE	RO	SE	VW	VO
AL	43	2	4	10	5	3	0	2	30	24	2	2	12	1
BMW	1	163	2	4	6	6	0	20	26	30	3	0	19	3
CI	8	12	1,708	132	106	99	10	18	332	385	36	19	80	12
FI	10	5	69	441	60	46	14	4	117	145	18	22	35	4
FO	5	9	39	51	518	56	7	8	180	121	20	13	48	6
GM	6	2	25	22	24	328	8	2	81	76	7	8	20	4
LA	0	0	2	13	8	6	31	0	18	20	2	3	0	1
ME	0	9	2	1	4	2	0	109	10	14	3	0	8	5
PE	16	25	260	186	198	172	35	23	2,437	705	53	37	159	21
RE	26	28	355	283	250	249	61	27	1,002	4,261	78	73	256	27
RO	2	3	11	23	11	23	1	3	34	42	86	6	5	1
SE	2	0	4	4	2	1	1	0	10	17	4	31	14	1
VW	5	19	25	37	52	41	12	12	141	126	17	11	575	8
VO	1	3	0	16	3	6	11	7	32	43	3	3	7	121

TABLE 12.1 *Continued*

	AL[b]	BMW[b]	CI[b]	FI[b]	FO[b]	GM[b]	LA[b]	ME[b]	PE[b]	RE[b]	RO[b]	SE[b]	VW[b]	VO[b]
French market 1989														
AL	97	5	19	19	14	7	0	3	27	35	5	6	17	4
BMW	4	163	20	9	14	6	0	19	39	40	6	4	29	4
CI	6	13	1,811	136	98	67	21	15	464	477	29	28	90	10
FI	11	5	69	526	50	49	12	3	134	148	27	17	82	5
FO	4	10	45	53	696	76	8	8	121	146	20	23	60	7
GM	2	7	20	23	50	362	7	4	68	80	7	12	39	4
LA	0	0	12	13	11	12	68	0	25	16	4	3	7	0
ME	2	17	3	3	5	2	0	136	4	10	3	1	5	3
PE	13	23	273	164	195	168	34	23	2,928	728	47	60	199	20
RE	22	37	353	334	308	254	40	33	896	4,861	78	106	310	24
RO	2	4	18	25	30	3	6	1	30	45	115	6	40	2
SE	2	0	13	10	10	11	0	0	10	29	3	36	13	0
VW	6	21	50	51	65	59	2	10	177	115	13	25	772	9
VO	1	3	11	5	4	6	0	3	9	17	3	4	18	78

	BMW^c	CI^c	FI^c	FO^c	GM^c	HO^c	ME^c	NI^c	PE^c	RE^c	RO^c	SA^c	TO^c	VW^c	VO^c
U.K. market 1986															
BMW	163	2	4	47	21	0	8	4	4	5	26	3	1	23	13
CI	1	109	10	23	12	1	1	9	14	18	33	2	4	12	10
FI	1	15	287	42	21	4	1	15	24	16	87	3	6	12	4
FO	11	32	58	3,329	264	21	11	106	164	84	528	11	42	79	26
GM	6	25	43	459	1,477	16	3	81	124	68	379	12	19	96	25
HO	6	0	2	19	13	68	0	29	5	3	5	0	8	5	5
ME	13	2	1	12	5	1	85	2	2	3	11	1	1	10	7
NI	12	12	23	116	45	8	0	562	35	18	144	0	7	13	3
PE	7	6	25	87	54	3	0	28	337	34	96	4	6	34	15
RE	8	8	23	69	36	7	1	17	32	322	66	5	6	27	8
RO	10	17	46	373	192	23	7	83	125	83	1,876	13	20	63	36
SA	3	1	0	5	5	1	1	1	1	3	6	47	0	4	5
TO	5	3	0	33	26	6	0	21	18	21	40	0	137	15	8
VW	18	10	18	108	60	3	5	29	39	34	112	6	8	546	15
VO	9	1	6	59	38	1	7	23	20	28	72	8	7	27	306
U.K. market 1987															
BMW	182	5	3	40	8	9	18	4	2	3	17	5	0	18	8
CI	2	135	14	28	16	1	2	17	20	13	18	2	0	5	4
FI	4	14	329	88	38	1	1	23	31	18	63	1	19	18	9
FO	47	39	60	3,981	396	4	14	165	121	76	342	7	41	122	84
GM	19	22	24	321	1,731	2	9	41	69	44	180	5	25	67	45
HO	3	4	4	11	5	0	2	17	4	8	12	0	25	4	7
ME	6	1	0	11	2	14	112	4	1	6	4	2	0	12	5

227

TABLE 12.1 Continued

	BMW^c	CI^c	FI^c	FO^c	GM^c	HO^c	ME^c	NI^c	PE^c	RE^c	RO^c	SA^c	TO^c	VW^c	VO^c
NI	5	12	15	137	53	1	1	557	47	26	61	1	15	24	27
PE	6	27	19	147	89	1	2	40	353	35	120	2	0	28	31
RE	4	18	28	88	34	1	2	39	39	388	64	3	10	38	17
RO	29	44	106	633	346	7	11	133	139	74	1,928	6	21	100	67
SA	2	4	4	21	5	1	2	0	6	4	8	56	6	5	8
TO	3	3	3	28	11	1	1	42	10	8	20	0	187	7	6
VW	23	13	23	114	66	3	12	47	48	24	50	9	6	614	23
VO	10	7	3	50	22	2	8	0	19	18	44	7	13	21	378
U.K. market 1988															
BMW	156	3	4	39	10	8	15	3	12	3	19	4	7	18	7
CI	1	170	18	13	12	6	1	14	10	6	13	1	0	6	3
FI	4	19	328	87	23	0	1	37	29	16	40	1	5	19	5
FO	35	51	50	3,494	304	20	13	138	136	71	250	6	24	87	89
GM	11	40	33	356	1,585	22	3	60	90	56	128	4	34	46	55
HO	2	1	3	17	10	87	2	8	1	6	11	1	7	9	4
ME	9	3	0	16	2	3	105	0	3	1	11	2	0	5	5
NI	5	24	19	104	49	17	0	459	38	23	55	1	13	12	13
PE	4	35	25	106	68	6	2	49	337	38	77	1	12	20	24
RE	9	26	18	75	47	14	2	28	38	355	46	1	0	17	17
RO	17	53	78	571	288	20	5	150	158	77	1,945	4	32	88	57
SA	1	4	5	5	10	0	1	8	3	2	4	55	0	4	2
TO	1	3	5	19	9	0	1	27	13	7	12	0	170	5	6
VW	20	20	17	109	60	20	13	41	62	26	51	5	10	588	28
VO	11	12	5	53	24	0	8	17	21	13	33	5	3	15	349

U.K. market 1989

	BMW	CI	FI	FO	GM	HO	ME	NI	PE	RE	RO	SA	TO	VW	VO
BMW	240	2	2	32	18	0	28	0	21	8	34	8	12	31	14
CI	2	226	13	28	22	0	2	9	16	15	23	2	3	9	10
FI	7	30	461	92	51	0	1	23	47	23	48	1	3	35	11
FO	63	107	64	4,216	629	14	23	221	289	119	395	15	83	160	120
GM	30	77	32	670	2,013	28	10	133	166	79	301	7	46	114	58
HO	5	3	2	12	10	132	3	0	4	8	9	1	23	7	3
ME	23	3	0	14	5	7	146	0	1	2	10	2	0	5	4
NI	6	18	21	70	68	15	2	789	28	21	48	1	17	20	22
PE	5	32	21	107	53	4	2	53	486	34	70	2	17	19	20
RE	11	24	27	99	43	12	6	37	57	381	55	4	9	33	23
RO	34	85	88	713	370	56	10	221	181	108	2,407	6	38	102	92
SA	7	1	2	6	4	3	4		1	4	6	58	3	5	8
TO	6	7	4	36	15	14	4	10	11	12	13	1	169	13	10
VW	30	36	21	128	94	9	18	57	88	32	57	11	33	748	35
VO	15	16	10	56	37	4	11	35	21	14	29	6	0	44	481

a. These networks contain 14 actors in the French market, and 15 in the U.K. market, due to our deletion of actors whose data were missing or otherwise incomplete in Ehrenberg's source data (i.e., Saab in the French data, and Mazda and Porsche in the U.K. data). As a result, the row margins for 198(t) do not perfectly equal the column margins for 198($t-1$).

b. AL = Alfa Romeo, BMW = BMW, CI = Citroen, FI = Fiat, FO = Ford, GM = GM, LA = Lada, ME = Mercedes, PE = Peugeot, RE = Renault, RO = Rover, SE = Seat, VW = VW/Audi, VO = Volvo.

c. BMW = BMW, CI = Citroen, FI = Fiat, FO = Ford, GM = GM, HO = Honda, ME = Mercedes, NI = Nissan, PE = Peugeot, RE = Renault, RO = Rover, SA = Saab, TO = Toyota, VW = VW/Audi, VO = Volvo.

TABLE 12.2 Dichotomized Data (1 = frequency exceeded 1% of market grand total,[a] 0 = frequency did not exceed 1% of grand total)

	A	B	C	F	F	G	L	M	P	R	R	S	V	V
French market 1986														
Alfa Romeo	1	0	0	0	0	0	0	0	0	0	0	0	0	0
BMW	0	1	0	0	0	0	0	0	0	0	0	0	0	0
Citroen	0	0	1	1	1	0	0	0	1	1	0	0	1	0
Fiat	0	0	0	1	0	0	0	0	0	1	0	0	0	0
Ford	0	0	0	0	1	0	0	0	0	1	0	0	0	0
GM	0	0	0	0	0	1	0	0	0	0	0	0	0	0
Lada	0	0	0	0	0	0	0	0	0	0	0	0	0	0
Mercedes	0	0	0	0	0	0	0	1	0	0	0	0	0	0
Peugeot	0	0	1	1	1	1	0	0	1	1	0	0	1	0
Renault	0	0	1	1	1	1	0	0	1	1	1	1	1	0
Rover	0	0	0	0	0	0	0	0	0	0	1	0	0	0
Seat	0	0	0	0	0	0	0	0	0	0	0	0	0	0
VW/A	0	0	0	0	0	0	0	0	1	1	0	0	1	0
Volvo	0	0	0	0	0	0	0	0	0	0	0	0	0	0
French market 1987														
Alfa Romeo	1	0	0	0	0	0	0	0	0	0	0	0	0	0
BMW	0	1	0	0	0	0	0	0	0	0	0	0	0	0
Citroen	0	0	1	1	1	0	0	0	1	1	0	0	0	0
Fiat	0	0	0	1	0	0	0	0	1	1	0	0	0	0
Ford	0	0	0	0	1	0	0	0	1	1	0	0	0	0
GM	0	0	0	0	0	1	0	0	0	1	0	0	0	0
Lada	0	0	0	0	0	0	0	0	0	0	0	0	0	0
Mercedes	0	0	0	0	0	0	0	1	0	0	0	0	0	0
Peugeot	0	0	1	1	1	1	0	0	1	1	0	0	1	0
Renault	0	0	1	1	1	1	0	0	1	1	0	0	1	0
Rover	0	0	0	0	0	0	0	0	0	0	1	0	0	0
Seat	0	0	0	0	0	0	0	0	0	0	0	0	0	0
VW/A	0	0	0	0	0	0	0	0	1	1	0	0	1	0
Volvo	0	0	0	0	0	0	0	0	0	0	0	0	0	0

TABLE 12.2 *Continued*

	A	B	C	F	F	G	L	M	P	R	R	S	V	V
French market 1988														
Alfa														
Romeo	0	0	0	0	0	0	0	0	0	0	0	0	0	0
BMW	0	1	0	0	0	0	0	0	0	0	0	0	0	0
Citroen	0	0	1	1	1	1	0	0	1	1	0	0	0	0
Fiat	0	0	0	1	0	0	0	0	1	1	0	0	0	0
Ford	0	0	0	0	1	0	0	0	1	1	0	0	0	0
GM	0	0	0	0	0	1	0	0	0	0	0	0	0	0
Lada	0	0	0	0	0	0	0	0	0	0	0	0	0	0
Mercedes	0	0	0	0	0	0	0	1	0	0	0	0	0	0
Peugeot	0	0	1	1	1	1	0	0	1	1	0	0	1	0
Renault	0	0	1	1	1	1	0	0	1	1	0	0	1	0
Rover	0	0	0	0	0	0	0	0	0	0	1	0	0	0
Seat	0	0	0	0	0	0	0	0	0	0	0	0	0	0
VW/A	0	0	0	0	0	0	0	0	1	1	0	0	1	1
Volvo	0	0	0	0	0	0	0	0	0	0	0	0	0	1
French market 1989														
Alfa														
Romeo	1	0	0	0	0	0	0	0	0	0	0	0	0	0
BMW	0	1	0	0	0	0	0	0	0	0	0	0	0	0
Citroen	0	0	1	1	1	0	0	0	1	1	0	0	0	0
Fiat	0	0	0	1	0	0	0	0	1	1	0	0	0	0
Ford	0	0	0	0	1	0	0	0	1	1	0	0	0	0
GM	0	0	0	0	0	1	0	0	0	0	0	0	0	0
Lada	0	0	0	0	0	0	0	0	0	0	0	0	0	0
Mercedes	0	0	0	0	0	0	0	1	0	0	0	0	0	0
Peugeot	0	0	1	1	1	1	0	0	1	1	0	0	1	0
Renault	0	0	1	1	1	1	0	0	1	1	0	1	1	0
Rover	0	0	0	0	0	0	0	0	0	0	1	0	0	0
Seat	0	0	0	0	0	0	0	0	0	0	0	0	0	0
VW/A	0	0	0	0	0	0	0	0	1	1	0	0	1	0
Volvo	0	0	0	0	0	0	0	0	0	0	0	0	0	0

(continued)

ANALYSES OF ROWS AND COLUMNS

We begin with a variety of methods that produce row scores and column scores as their end results. Such analyses would be a fairly

TABLE 12.2 *Continued*

	B	C	F	F	G	H	M	N	P	R	R	S	T	V	V
U.K. market 1986															
BMW	1	0	0	0	0	0	0	0	0	0	0	0	0	0	0
Citroen	0	1	0	0	0	0	0	0	0	0	0	0	0	0	0
Fiat	0	0	1	0	0	0	0	0	0	0	1	0	0	0	0
Ford	0	0	0	1	1	0	0	1	1	1	1	0	0	1	0
GM	0	0	0	1	1	0	0	1	1	1	1	0	0	1	0
Honda	0	0	0	0	0	1	0	0	0	0	0	0	0	0	0
Mercedes	0	0	0	0	0	0	1	0	0	0	0	0	0	0	0
Nissan	0	0	0	1	0	0	0	1	0	0	1	0	0	0	0
Peugeot	0	0	0	1	0	0	0	0	1	0	1	0	0	0	0
Renault	0	0	0	1	0	0	0	0	0	1	0	0	0	0	0
Rover	0	0	0	1	1	0	0	1	1	1	1	0	0	0	0
Saab	0	0	0	0	0	0	0	0	0	0	0	0	0	0	0
Toyota	0	0	0	0	0	0	0	0	0	0	0	0	1	0	0
VW/A	0	0	0	1	0	0	0	0	0	0	1	0	0	1	0
Volvo	0	0	0	0	0	0	0	0	0	0	1	0	0	0	1
U.K. market 1987															
BMW	1	0	0	0	0	0	0	0	0	0	0	0	0	0	0
Citroen	0	1	0	0	0	0	0	0	0	0	0	0	0	0	0
Fiat	0	0	1	1	0	0	0	0	0	0	0	0	0	0	0
Ford	0	0	0	1	1	0	0	1	1	1	1	0	0	1	1
GM	0	0	0	1	1	0	0	0	0	0	1	0	0	0	0
Honda	0	0	0	0	0	0	0	0	0	0	0	0	0	0	0
Mercedes	0	0	0	0	0	0	1	0	0	0	0	0	0	0	0
Nissan	0	0	0	1	0	0	0	1	0	0	0	0	0	0	0
Peugeot	0	0	0	1	1	0	0	0	1	0	1	0	0	0	0
Renault	0	0	0	1	0	0	0	0	0	1	0	0	0	0	0
Rover	0	0	1	1	1	0	0	1	1	1	1	0	0	1	0
Saab	0	0	0	0	0	0	0	0	0	0	0	0	0	0	0
Toyota	0	0	0	0	0	0	0	0	0	0	0	0	1	0	0
VW/A	0	0	0	1	0	0	0	0	0	0	0	0	0	1	0
Volvo	0	0	0	0	0	0	0	0	0	0	0	0	0	0	1

typical starting place in the analysis of brand-switching data. The row and column scores provide basic market share information at Times t and $t+1$, respectively. We will later proceed to analytical methods that examine the associations internal to the body of the table. The methods

TABLE 12.2 *Continued*

	B	C	F	F	G	H	M	N	P	R	R	S	T	V	V
U.K. market 1988															
BMW	1	0	0	0	0	0	0	0	0	0	0	0	0	0	0
Citroen	0	1	0	0	0	0	0	0	0	0	0	0	0	0	0
Fiat	0	0	1	1	0	0	0	0	0	0	0	0	0	0	0
Ford	0	0	0	1	1	0	0	1	1	1	1	0	0	1	1
GM	0	0	0	1	1	0	0	0	1	0	1	0	0	0	0
Honda	0	0	0	0	0	1	0	0	0	0	0	0	0	0	0
Mercedes	0	0	0	0	0	0	1	0	0	0	0	0	0	0	0
Nissan	0	0	0	1	0	0	0	1	0	0	0	0	0	0	0
Peugeot	0	0	0	1	1	0	0	0	1	0	1	0	0	0	0
Renault	0	0	0	1	0	0	0	0	0	1	0	0	0	0	0
Rover	0	0	1	1	1	0	0	1	1	1	1	0	0	1	0
Saab	0	0	0	0	0	0	0	0	0	0	0	0	0	0	0
Toyota	0	0	0	0	0	0	0	0	0	0	0	0	1	0	0
VW/A	0	0	0	1	0	0	0	0	0	0	0	0	0	1	0
Volvo	0	0	0	0	0	0	0	0	0	0	0	0	0	0	1
U.K. market 1989															
BMW	0	0	0	0	0	0	0	0	0	0	0	0	0	0	0
Citroen	0	0	0	0	0	0	0	0	0	0	0	0	0	0	0
Fiat	0	0	1	1	0	0	0	0	0	0	0	0	0	0	0
Ford	0	1	0	1	1	0	0	1	1	1	1	0	0	1	1
GM	0	0	0	1	1	0	0	1	1	0	1	0	0	1	0
Honda	0	0	0	0	0	1	0	0	0	0	0	0	0	0	0
Mercedes	0	0	0	0	0	0	1	0	0	0	0	0	0	0	0
Nissan	0	0	0	0	0	0	0	1	0	0	0	0	0	0	0
Peugeot	0	0	0	1	0	0	0	0	1	0	0	0	0	0	0
Renault	0	0	0	1	0	0	0	0	0	1	0	0	0	0	0
Rover	0	0	1	1	1	0	0	1	1	1	1	0	0	1	1
Saab	0	0	0	0	0	0	0	0	0	0	0	0	0	0	0
Toyota	0	0	0	0	0	0	0	0	0	0	0	0	1	0	0
VW/A	0	0	0	1	1	0	0	0	1	0	0	0	0	1	0
Volvo	0	0	0	0	0	0	0	0	0	0	0	0	0	0	1

a. Given the highly loyal purchase behavior, the diagonals were not included in the computation of the 1% share thresholds. (When diagonals are included, similar structural results occur for a .05% share threshold.)

we use are outlined in Table 12.3 and the outline corresponds to the section headings, for the reader's convenience.

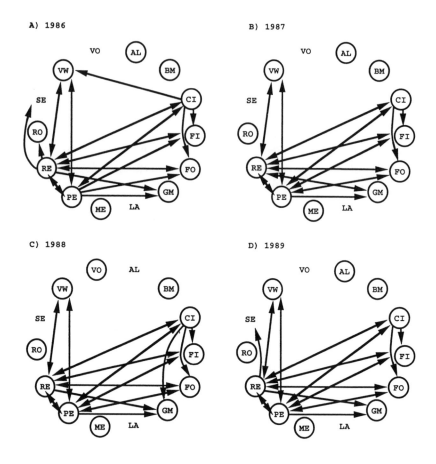

Figure 12.1. French Automobile Switching Networks

NOTE: AL = Alfa Romeo, BM = BMW, CI = Citroen, FI = Fiat, FO = Ford, GM = GM, LA = Lada, ME = Mercedes, PE = Peugeot, RE = Renault, RO = Rover, SE = Seat, VW = VW/Audi, VO = Volvo.

Row and Column Margin Percentages

Simple descriptive indexes include row and column marginal information, such as the row and column percentages of the grand

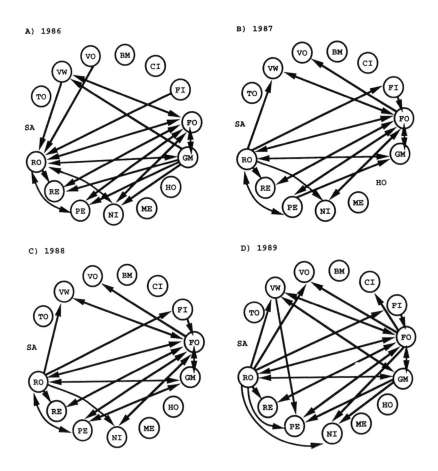

Figure 12.2. British Automobile Switching Networks

NOTE: BM = BMW, CI = Citroen, FI = Fiat, FO = Ford, GM = GM, HO = Honda, ME = Mercedes, NI = Nissan, PE = Peugeot, RE = Renault, RO = Rover, SA = Saab, TO = Toyota, VW = VW/Audi, VO = Volvo.

total: $\text{row}_i\% = \Sigma_j x_{ij}/\Sigma_i\Sigma_j x_{ij})*100\% = x_{i+}/x_{++}*100\%$, and $\text{column}_j\% = \Sigma_i x_{ij}/\Sigma_i\Sigma_j x_{ij})*100\% = x_{+j}/x_{++}*100\%$ for the I by J table $\mathbf{X} = \{x_{ij}\}$, with subscripts i denoting rows (i = 1, 2, . . . I) and j denoting columns (j = 1, 2, . . . J; I = J for these data). These row and column percentages

TABLE 12.3 Plan of Analysis Attack

Analyses of rows and columns
  Row and column margin percentages
  Correspondence analyses
  Network degree centrality
  Network closeness centrality
  Network betweenness centrality
Associations internal to table
  Log-linear models of independence and quasi-independence
  Network dyadic relations model
  Analyses of symmetry
   Log-linear models of symmetry and quasi-symmetry
   Quadratic assignment procedure (QAP) correlation between X and X'
Multivariate analyses
  Longitudinal
   Network sequential dyadic relations models
   QAP regressions predicting future market structures
   Clique and block evolution
  Cross-country market structure comparison

are found for both the French and British markets for all four time points in Table 12.4.

These descriptive statistics give us an opportunity to make some initial observations on these data. Both markets contain a small number of highly active players (i.e., in the French market, the three largest players are ordered: Renault, Peugeot, Citroen; and for the United Kingdom, the three largest are: Ford, Rover, GM). At the other extreme, both markets contain several players who capture only nominal markets (e.g., approximately 1% to 2% market share, including for the French market: Alfa Romeo, BMW, Lada, Mercedes, Rover, Seat, Volvo; and for the U.K. market: BMW, Citroen, Honda, Mercedes, Saab, Toyota). Both markets contain a few manufacturers who serve intermediate-sized markets, perhaps due to product segmentation or market insulation (approximately 5% shares, including for the French: Fiat, Ford, GM, VW/Audi; and in the United Kingdom: Fiat, Nissan, Peugeot, Renault, VW/Audi, Volvo).

These statistics are univariate in the sense of having been computed for one country at one point in time, but we can compare these basic characteristics across time or countries. For example, regarding

TABLE 12.4 Row and Column Percentages (from data in Table 12.1)

	Row Percentages				Column Percentages			
	1986	*1987*	*1988*	*1989*	*1986*	*1987*	*1988*	*1989*
French data								
Alfa								
Romeo	1.44	1.48	.72	1.18	.89	.99	.73	1.00
BMW	1.43	1.45	1.47	1.63	1.82	1.53	1.63	1.79
Citroen	14.78	14.93	15.31	14.92	12.73	13.91	14.60	15.83
Fiat	4.43	4.83	5.13	5.20	5.38	6.36	7.13	7.99
Ford	5.22	5.64	5.60	5.84	7.59	7.53	7.27	9.03
GM	2.51	3.19	3.17	3.13	5.08	4.88	6.05	6.30
Lada	.67	.74	.54	.78	1.04	1.21	1.11	1.15
Mercedes	.88	.83	.86	.89	1.24	1.29	1.37	1.50
Peugeot	23.83	22.72	22.40	22.28	22.20	22.09	25.93	28.74
Renault	37.84	37.05	36.11	35.00	31.33	36.33	35.01	39.31
Rover	1.09	1.19	1.30	1.49	1.81	1.86	1.93	2.10
Seat	.22	.30	.47	.63	1.38	1.43	1.33	1.93
VW/Audi	5.14	4.88	5.60	6.29	6.48	6.51	7.21	9.79
Volvo	.51	.77	1.33	.74	1.02	1.01	1.11	.78
U.K. data								
BMW	1.97	1.78	1.84	2.01	1.66	1.91	1.71	2.16
Citroen	1.58	1.53	1.64	1.70	1.48	1.92	2.78	2.98
Fiat	3.28	3.63	3.67	3.72	3.33	3.51	3.64	3.43
Ford	29.03	30.41	28.53	29.09	29.12	31.51	30.30	28.02
GM	17.25	14.40	15.10	16.80	13.82	15.61	14.96	15.32
Honda	1.02	.59	1.01	.99	.99	.27	1.33	1.33
Mercedes	.95	1.00	.99	.99	.79	1.09	1.03	1.21
Nissan	6.08	5.43	4.98	5.11	6.15	6.24	6.22	7.09
Peugeot	4.48	4.98	4.81	4.13	5.75	5.03	5.69	6.32
Renault	3.87	4.27	4.15	3.66	4.51	4.12	4.19	3.84
Rover	18.07	20.15	21.20	20.13	21.20	16.21	16.12	15.64
Saab	.51	.73	.62	.50	.70	.59	.54	.56
Toyota	2.03	1.82	1.66	1.45	1.66	2.04	1.90	2.04
VW/Audi	6.16	5.94	6.40	6.24	5.88	5.99	5.62	6.00
Volvo	3.73	3.33	3.40	3.48	2.96	3.98	3.97	4.07

the sequential nature of these data, the basic relative market share patterns just described are robust in being highly consistent across all four time periods, whether examining row (*t*) or column (*t* + 1) indexes. The mean Pearson product-moment correlation coefficient among the 4 years' row percentages is .99, as is the mean correlation among the 4 years' column percentages, and for the row to column comparisons within respective years. Clearly these margins suggest high stability. We will show, however, that this margin stability does not mean there are no interesting dynamic phenomena in these data. (We elaborate on the market stability in a later section in which we model these data longitudinally.)

In addition, consider cross-country comparisons, such as the national loyalties that are observed. For example, all three major players in France are French, and whereas Peugeot and Renault are also moderate players in the United Kingdom, the Citroen brand is purchased infrequently in the United Kingdom, suggesting differences between the countries in availability (e.g., exporting, distribution), or perhaps perceived quality. Similarly, Rover is one of the three most popular brands in the United Kingdom, but is purchased infrequently by the French. The other two popular brands in Britain (Ford and GM) have the same status in France as Peugeot and Renault have in the United Kingdom in that they are players of intermediary volume. Finally, the U.K.-U.S. manufacturing relationship appears to be more successful than the France-U.S. tie.

Marginal information, by definition, does not represent the internal workings of the data matrixes. For example, several auto manufacturers in both markets have large row margins (e.g., Peugeot in France), suggesting the loss of many customers, but their respective column margins are also large, indicating that the customers are being replaced in nearly equal quantities. These large share competitors simply see much incoming and outgoing action. One might hypothesize that the action of the Citroen, Peugeot, and Renault brands is reciprocal—that the French purchase primarily French cars, so former owners of Citroen will next buy Peugeot, for example. When we examine the associations within the body of the table, later in the chapter, we shall see that this "exchange" hypothesis is somewhat too simple to describe the structure of the transactions.

Correspondence Analyses

Correspondence analysis has become a popular method of data analysis among marketing researchers for the analysis of two-way tables (e.g., Carroll, Green, & Schaffer, 1987; Greenacre & Hastie, 1987; Hoffman & Franke, 1986), and it would be a likely candidate for an analytical tool to apply to these brand-switching data. The method is essentially a factoring of the matrix (via a singular value decomposition), analogous to a principal components analysis (after properly scaling the rows and columns of the matrix).

Following Carroll et al. (1987), we rescale the data matrix $\mathbf{X}$: $\mathbf{H} = \mathbf{RXC}$, where $\mathbf{R} = \mathrm{diag}(\mathbf{X1})^{-.5}$ and $\mathbf{C} = \mathrm{diag}(\mathbf{X'1})^{-.5}$, the vector $\mathbf{1}$ is $I \times 1$ ($= J \times 1$), and the scaling matrixes, $\mathbf{R}$ and $\mathbf{C}$ are $I \times J$ (i.e., 14×14 for the French car market, and 15×15 for the United Kingdom). A singular value decomposition of $\mathbf{H}$ is extracted: $\mathbf{H} = \mathbf{UDV'}$, and the first nontrivial singular values and vectors are retained to produce the $I \times 1$ row scores, $\mathbf{S}_r$ and $J \times 1$ column scores, $\mathbf{S}_c$: $\mathbf{S}_r = \mathbf{RU}(\mathbf{D} + \mathbf{I})^{.5}$ and $\mathbf{S}_c = \mathbf{CV}(\mathbf{D} + \mathbf{I})^{.5}$. Correspondence analysis draws on cell entries, but its focus is on obtaining these row and column score outputs.

The results are presented in Table 12.5. We make two observations. First, row scores resulting from a correspondence analysis are usually plotted against column scores in a two-dimensional space, to examine interpoint distances and the spatial properties inherent to the model. The row scores for these particular data are so highly correlated with the column scores that the supposed two-dimensional space collapses almost completely to a single line rising from the origin at 45 degrees. Specifically, the mean correlation between the row and column scores for respective time points is .99 for the French data and .97 for the British data. Again, these findings presumably reflect temporal stability, because the row scores (t) are so similar to column scores ($t + 1$).

Second, although this method yields a message consistent with the simpler row and column percentages (i.e., stability over time), the correspondence analysis scores are not significantly correlated with the respective percentages (all $ps > .10$). Thus, the distance-based logic of the correspondence analysis model provides information that is unique from the simple percentage calculations, even though both are aggregates across one dimension of the data. That unique information is apparently reflecting some aspect of these cars such as luxury, cost, or quality, because the one-dimensional-appearing plots (or the values in Table 12.5) position Mercedes and BMW at one end, with Volvo, Saab, and sometimes VW/Audi nearby, and Citroen, Lada, Fiat, Ford, and GM at the other end, with all other car

TABLE 12.5 Correspondence Analysis Results

	Row Scores				Column Scores			
	1986	1987	1988	1989	1986	1987	1988	1989
French data (raw frequencies in Table 12.1)								
Alfa								
Romeo	.005	.013	.002	.005	.006	.015	.001	.007
BMW	.043	.036	.056	.026	.038	.035	.055	.029
Citroen	−.015	−.008	−.006	−.003	−.017	−.009	−.007	−.003
Fiat	−.001	−.000	−.002	−.001	−.001	−.001	−.002	−.001
Ford	−.001	.004	.000	.001	−.001	.003	−.000	.000
GM	.001	.001	−.001	.000	.001	.001	−.001	−.001
Lada	−.007	−.007	−.002	−.003	−.006	−.007	−.001	−.003
Mercedes	.051	.073	.056	.082	.043	.060	.049	.070
Peugeot	.000	−.000	−.001	−.002	−.000	−.001	−.001	−.002
Renault	.002	−.002	−.002	−.002	.002	−.002	−.002	−.002
Rover	.001	.003	.001	.001	−.001	.001	.001	.001
Seat	.003	.001	−.001	−.001	.004	−.000	−.002	−.000
VW/Audi	.009	.012	.006	.003	.007	.010	.005	.002
Volvo	.014	.007	.013	.010	.009	.009	.015	.010
U.K. data (raw frequencies in Table 12.1)								
BMW	.033	.032	.028	.028	.038	.028	.027	.027
Citroen	.003	.002	.001	−.001	.002	.001	.001	−.001
Fiat	−.001	−.002	−.002	−.003	−.001	−.002	−.002	−.004
Ford	−.006	−.004	−.003	−.003	−.005	−.004	−.003	−.003
GM	−.003	−.005	−.005	−.003	−.003	−.005	−.005	−.003
Honda	.002	.004	.007	.011	.000	.042	.007	.010
Mercedes	.072	.073	.080	.064	.078	.069	.079	.059
Nissan	−.003	−.001	−.002	−.004	−.002	−.001	−.002	−.004
Peugeot	−.001	−.001	−.001	−.002	−.001	−.001	−.000	−.001
Renault	.002	.002	.000	.001	.002	.002	−.000	.000
Rover	−.002	−.002	−.003	−.003	−.002	−.003	−.003	−.003
Saab	.018	.014	.021	.025	.015	.017	.024	.023
Toyota	.001	.001	−.000	.005	.001	.001	−.000	.004
VW/Audi	.009	.010	.010	.007	.010	.010	.010	.006
Volvo	.017	.011	.010	.009	.019	.010	.008	.008

makes in between. It is possible that these ordered scores reflect a hierarchy of consumer car aspirations—the scores reflect a greater likelihood of trading *to* Mercedes and BMW (like a sink in graph theory), and trading *from* the Citroens, Ladas, and Fiats (like a source in graph theory). This pattern also gives us an initial indication that there might be substantial asymmetries in these data, a property we investigate in more detail shortly.

Network Degree Centrality

Network analysts, drawing from graph theory, have generated many indexes to describe the rows (actors sending "ties"—or volumes of car purchasers) and columns (actors receiving ties) of sociomatrixes such as those in Tables 12.1 and 12.2 (cf. Burt & Minor, 1983; Knoke & Kuklinski, 1982; Scott, 1991; Wasserman & Faust, 1994). An already classic exposition of several indexes is Freeman (1979), who described the conceptual differences between three indexes of centrality. The centrality indexes treated in his article are those we explore here.

The degree centrality of an actor in a network reflects the number of other actors to whom the focal actor is tied, or adjacent. Freeman uses the example of a communication network to describe the different indexes; an actor with a high degree centrality is described as a person who is "in the thick of things" (Freeman, 1979, p. 219), highly interconnected with many others, who would be a "major channel of information" for those other contacts. (For these car data, highly central manufacturers would be those that demonstrate high trading volumes to and from other makes of cars.) By contrast, actors with low degrees are more peripheral to the network. Out-degrees and in-degrees are computed as row and column marginal frequencies, excluding diagonals ($x_{i+} - x_{ii}$ and $x_{+j} - x_{jj}$). To illustrate, the in- and out-degrees computed on the binary data (in Table 12.2) are presented in Table 12.6.

For the raw frequency data in Table 12.1, out-degrees capture the number of outgoing ties per actor, weighted by the strengths of those ties (the frequencies of consumers switching out). For the binary data in Table 12.2, an out-degree represents more simply the number of car manufacturers to whom consumers traded, with no differential weighting. (For these data, the consumer trading consideration sets included all other car makes, but the binary data are based on frequencies exceeding a 1% market threshold.) Similarly, in-degrees for the raw data in Table 12.1 represent the weighted flows to each

TABLE 12.6 Freeman's (1979) Degree Centrality Computed on Binary Data in Table 12.2

	Row Degrees				Column Degrees			
	1986	1987	1988	1989	1986	1987	1988	1989
French data								
Alfa Romeo	0	0	0	0	0	0	0	0
BMW	0	0	0	0	0	0	0	0
Citroen	5	4	5	4	2	2	2	2
Fiat	1	2	2	2	3	3	3	3
Ford	1	2	2	2	3	3	3	3
GM	0	1	0	0	2	2	3	2
Lada	0	0	0	0	0	0	0	0
Mercedes	0	0	0	0	0	0	0	0
Peugeot	6	6	6	6	3	5	5	5
Renault	8	6	6	7	5	6	5	5
Rover	0	0	0	0	1	0	0	0
Seat	0	0	0	0	1	0	0	1
VW/Audi	2	2	2	2	3	2	2	2
Volvo	0	0	0	0	0	0	0	0
U.K. data								
BMW	0	0	0	0	0	0	0	0
Citroen	0	0	0	0	0	0	0	1
Fiat	1	1	1	1	0	1	1	1
Ford	6	7	7	8	6	7	7	6
GM	6	2	3	5	2	3	3	3
Honda	0	0	0	0	0	0	0	0
Mercedes	0	0	0	0	0	0	0	0
Nissan	2	1	1	0	3	2	2	3
Peugeot	2	3	3	1	3	3	3	4
Renault	1	1	1	1	3	2	2	2
Rover	5	7	7	8	7	3	3	2
Saab	0	0	0	0	0	0	0	0
Toyota	0	0	0	0	0	0	0	0
VW/Audi	2	1	1	3	2	2	2	3
Volvo	1	0	0	0	0	1	1	2

car make, and the in-degrees for the binary ties in Table 12.2 represent the simple count of flows to each car make. In- and out-degrees will of course be highly correlated with the column and row marginal percentages; even the in- and out-degrees in Table 12.6 (computed on the *binary* data in Table 12.2) are correlated with the column and row percentages presented in Table 12.4 (computed on the *raw frequency* data in Table 12.1; the mean correlation is .916, $p < .0001$).

Given the high correlation, it is not surprising that these indexes yield some similar results (e.g., the French market scores are largest for Citroen, Peugeot, and Renault, and the British market scores are largest for Ford, GM, and Rover). The degree centrality scores, however, also suggest some of the asymmetries discovered via the correspondence analysis; for example, in the French market, Citroen's row scores are high, but the column scores are lower, suggesting greater propensities for losing than gaining customers, and the reverse is true for Renault and Nissan in the British market.

Network Closeness Centrality

A second measure of centrality described by Freeman (1979) is closeness centrality. Closeness is a property that defines an actor as central to the extent that the actor is close enough to many others to communicate to them directly, and therefore not needing to rely on others to "relay messages" (Freeman, 1979, p. 224). If all actors in a network are close to each other, communications originating with any actor will flow through the rest of the network quickly, thus, high closeness centralities are associated with short flow times, low costs, high efficiencies, and the like, depending on the content of the relational tie being modeled (Freeman, 1979, p. 225). For these data, closeness might suggest the variance in the likelihood that the automobiles are interchangeable—that is, if all the cars were far from each other, then a consumer would be less likely to transition from one car all the way to a distant car, but if the cars are all close, a consumer's purchase patterns over time would demonstrate indiscriminate car-hopping. In a close network, the BMW brand manager can hope to persuade the former Citroen owner, say, but in a far network, the manager would need to be patient, knowing that the Citroen owner will go through ownership of many other cars before turning to the BMW.

Specifically, the farness of an actor is computed as the sum over the lengths of the (shortest) distances (i.e., geodesics) between the focal actor to all others in the network. The closeness of an actor is the reciprocal of farness: closeness$_i$ = $1/\Sigma_i d(i,j)$, where $d(i,j)$ is the geodesic (shortest distance between) actors i and j. Unlike the degree centralities, closeness indexes are not computed for rows separately from columns, so the single set of closeness centralities for these car manufacturers is presented in Table 12.7. The closeness indexes for these data are not graded very finely—there are essentially two scores—a low index for some cars (e.g., for the French market: Alfa Romeo, BMW, Lada, Mercedes, and Volvo), and a higher score for others. Even given their simple binary nature, these closeness centralities might be reflecting volume, because they are fairly highly correlated with the percentages (mean $r = .619$, $p < .018$).

Network Betweenness Centrality

Finally, the third major centrality index described by Freeman (1979) is the betweenness index, which reflects the frequency with which a particular actor is on the geodesic path between any other two actors. An actor with a high betweenness score is thought to be one who has "potential for control" of the group's communication, in that they could, for example, "influence the group by withholding or distorting information in transmissions" (Freeman, 1979, p. 221). For the brand-switching data, a car that is highly central according to this betweenness criterion would be a car that consumers are likely to own as a transition car (between owning some former make and later purchasing another make). The betweenness index is computed as: betweenness$_i$ = $g_{jk(i)}/g_{jk}$, where g_{jk} is the number of geodesics that link actors j and k, and $g_{jk(i)}$ is the number of those geodesics that contain actor i along the path.

The single set of betweenness centralities are presented in Table 12.8. They appear even more clearly dichotomous in scoring, and are even more highly correlated with the table percentages (mean $r = .881$, $p < .0001$). This correlation suggests these betweenness indexes reflect volume, but the interpretation that a car with a high betweenness score is an intermediary purchase is also plausible, and probably cannot be teased apart, given that these cars (e.g., Renault, Rover) are those consumers trade from and trade to in greater frequencies than other cars.

Other researchers have presented more recent treatises on additional measures (e.g., information centrality, Freeman, Borgatti, &

TABLE 12.7 Freeman's (1979) Closeness Centrality Computed on Binary Data in Table 12.2

	Closeness			
	1986	*1987*	*1988*	*1989*
French data				
Alfa Romeo	7.14	7.14	7.14	7.14
BMW	7.14	7.14	7.14	7.14
Citroen	16.05	12.26	12.38	13.83
Fiat	15.66	12.15	12.15	13.68
Ford	15.66	12.15	12.15	13.68
GM	15.48	12.04	12.15	13.54
Lada	7.14	7.14	7.14	7.14
Mercedes	7.14	7.14	7.14	7.14
Peugeot	16.25	12.50	12.50	14.13
Renault	16.67	12.50	12.50	14.29
Rover	15.29	7.14	7.14	7.14
Seat	15.29	7.14	7.14	13.40
VW/Audi	15.66	12.04	12.04	13.54
Volvo	7.14	7.14	7.14	7.14
U.K. data				
BMW	6.67	6.67	6.67	6.67
Citroen	6.67	6.67	6.67	15.22
Fiat	13.33	13.46	13.46	15.38
Ford	14.00	14.29	14.29	16.67
GM	14.00	13.59	13.59	15.91
Honda	6.67	6.67	6.67	6.67
Mercedes	6.67	6.67	6.67	6.67
Nissan	13.59	13.46	13.46	15.56
Peugeot	13.59	13.59	13.59	15.73
Renault	13.59	13.46	13.46	15.38
Rover	14.29	14.14	14.14	16.47
Saab	6.67	6.67	6.67	6.67
Toyota	6.67	6.67	6.67	6.67
VW/Audi	13.59	13.46	13.46	15.73
Volvo	13.33	13.33	13.33	15.38

White, 1991; flow betweenness, Stephenson & Zelen, 1989), but the three centrality indexes of Freeman (1979) still serve as a standard, and we believe they have been sufficient to give the reader a sense of

TABLE 12.8 Freeman's (1979) Betweeness Centrality for Binary Data in Table 12.2

	Betweenness			
	1986	*1987*	*1988*	*1989*
French data				
Alfa Romeo	0	0	0	0
BMW	0	0	0	0
Citroen	0	0	0	0
Fiat	0	0	0	0
Ford	0	0	0	0
GM	0	0	0	0
Lada	0	0	0	0
Mercedes	0	0	0	0
Peugeot	1.6	4.49	4.17	4.49
Renault	14.42	7.69	4.17	7.69
Rover	0	0	0	0
Seat	0	0	0	0
VW/Audi	0	0	0	0
Volvo	0	0	0	0
U.K. data				
BMW	0	0	0	0
Citroen	0	0	0	0
Fiat	0	0	0	0
Ford	7.42	18.96	18.68	17.31
GM	.82	0	0	.82
Honda	0	0	0	0
Mercedes	0	0	0	0
Nissan	0	0	0	0
Peugeot	0	0	0	0
Renault	0	0	0	0
Rover	9.34	5.22	4.95	3.3
Saab	0	0	0	0
Toyota	0	0	0	0
VW/Audi	0	0	0	0
Volvo	0	0	0	0

some network indexes that may be computed on sociometric data. (For the curious reader, we might mention that the information centralities were correlated with the percentages, mean $r = .590$, $p <$

.025, and the flow betweenness indexes were even more highly correlated, mean $r = .947$, $p < .0001$.)

These three sets of centrality indexes progress conceptually beyond the marginal percentage information to consider more of the dyadic and triadic interactive structure in the spirit of a true network analysis. We noted, however, the high empirical similarity of these indexes to the row and column percentages, which are simple aggregates of one dimension over the other. We turn now to additional methods, including more network methods, that examine the patterns internal to the table.

ASSOCIATIONS INTERNAL TO TABLE

Log-Linear Models of Independence and Quasi-Independence

The fundamental statistic an analyst examines in a two-way crosstabulation is the X^2 of fit for the model of independence. We refer to this model more generally as the log-linear model:

$$\text{Ln} \{E(x_{ij})\} = u + u_{1(i)} + u_{2(j)}$$
on $(I - 1)(J - 1)$ degrees of freedom.

Even cursory inspection of the matrixes in Table 12.1 might lead us to suspect that the model of independence will not fit these data. The hypothesis of independence would suggest that consumer purchases were random, and would yield no apparent pattern in the table. That is, knowing what brand a consumer purchased at Time t would be of no help in predicting what brand the consumer purchases subsequently (Time $t + 1$). A hypothesis of randomness appears implausible given the apparent structure in the data (even just looking at the matrixes), but we will test for randomness and then explore the structure.

Table 12.9 contains the fit statistics for the model of independence applied to these matrixes. In every case (for both countries and all four time periods), the G^2s indicate that the model of independence does not fit (all ps = .000; see the G^2s for the models labeled "independence"; $G^2 = \Sigma_i\Sigma_j o_{ij}\ln(o_{ij}/e_{ij})$, Fienberg, 1980).

TABLE 12.9 Log-Linear Models of Independence and Quasi-Independence
Fit to Data in Table 12.1 (raw frequencies)

	G^2	df	p	ΔG^2	Δdf	p
French market model						
1986 Independence	16032.309	169	.000	15488.535	14	< .001
Quasi-independence	543.774	155	.000			
1987 Independence	16447.653	169	.000	15991.761	14	< .001
Quasi-independence	455.892	155	.000			
1988 Independence	17933.864	169	.000	17411.511	14	< .001
Quasi-independence	522.353	155	.000			
1989 Independence	22043.764	169	.000	21403.105	14	< .001
Quasi-independence	640.659	155	.000			
U.K. market model						
1986 Independence	20768.760	196	.000	20070.358	15	< .001
Quasi-independence	698.402	181	.000			
1987 Independence	24113.260	196	.000	23107.187	15	< .001
Quasi-independence	1006.073	181	.000			
1988 Independence	23325.641	196	.000	22634.746	15	< .001
Quasi-independence	690.895	181	.000			
1989 Independence	29109.713	196	.000	27914.916	15	< .001
Quasi-independence	1194.797	181	.000			

To understand why the model of independence does not fit these data, we study the matrixes in Table 12.1 and see that at least one reason the purchase behavior appears nonrandom is that most of the diagonal values are large, and this suggests that consumers are purchasing with some loyalty (i.e., purchases at Time $t + 1$ are not independent of those at Time t). The diagonal values in the matrixes in Table 12.1 are not corrected for differential market shares, but standardized residuals after fitting the model of independence (i.e., after correcting for margins) are highly significant: exceeding "20" as a z-score value, indicating there is indeed high loyalty. In network terms, we would say that the self-reflexive ties are extremely strong.

Therefore, we proceed to fit the model of quasi-independence (Fienberg, 1980), to address the question: Even though the model of independence does not fit, due to the loyal purchase behavior reflected in the large diagonal values, is the brand switching random, or are there also predictable, structural patterns in the off-diagonal elements of these matrixes? This model is fit on $I(= J)$ fewer degrees of freedom essentially by fitting the model of independence around the structural zeros imputed into the diagonal cells (the self-reflexive cells), where the loyalty behavior is reflected.

Although the ΔG^2s in Table 12.9 indicate there is significant improvement in fit from the model of independence to quasi-independence (all ps < .001), the G^2s in the table indicate the model of quasi-independence still does not fit (all ps = .000 for the G^2s for the models labeled "quasi-independence"). Thus, we conclude the consumer purchasing is nonrandom over time, even after considering and correcting for loyalty.

To study the structural patterns in these data, we coded the standardized residuals cell by cell on fitting the model of quasi-independence to these data: "*" and "+" represent significantly positive residuals ($z > 4.00$, and $z > 2.58$, respectively), and "–" and "=" represent significantly negative residuals ($z < -2.58$ and $z < -4.00$, respectively). Thus, the first two codes represent those elements in the matrix where there are more consumers purchasing the column car after having owned the row car than would be expected if quasi-independence held, and the second two codes indicate very infrequent transactions. The coded tables are presented in Table 12.10.

As an example, note that BMW and Mercedes do more intertrading (in all eight matrixes) than the model (hypothesizing quasi-randomness) would predict. Consumers considering these car makes are also somewhat more likely to be trading-in or trading-to VW/Audi or Volvo in France, and Honda or Saab in Britain. These consideration sets tell the manufacturers who their most likely competitors are, as a subset of all possible competitors.

There are many phenomena in this table that finally give us a sense of the data's richness, beyond simple row and column scores. For example, earlier we briefly entertained the hypothesis that the cars within the trios of {Citroen-Peugeot-Renault} in France and {Ford-GM-Rover} in the United Kingdom were somehow interchangeable. There is some tendency (across the matrixes) for Peugeot owners to continue to purchase French brands (i.e., there are several "+"s in the Peugeot rows corresponding to Citroen columns, Renault columns, or both), but for example, Renault buyers are literally less

TABLE 12.10 Standardized Residuals From Quasi-Independence Models (described in Table 12.9)

	A	B	C	F	F	G	L	M	P	R	R	S	V	V
French market 1986														
Alfa Romeo		.	.	.	.	.	.	−	.	.	.	.	.	.
BMW	.		−	.	.	.	.	*	.	.	.	.	.	.
Citroen	.	.		.	.	−	.	.	.	.	.	.	.	.
Fiat	.	.	.		.	.	.	−	.	.	.	*	.	.
Ford	.	.	+	.		.	.	−	.	.	.	.	.	.
GM	.	.	.	.	.		.	.	.	.	.	.	.	.
Lada	.	.	.	+	.	.		.	.	.	.	.	.	.
Mercedes	.	*	.	.	.	.	.		.	.	.	.	+	+
Peugeot	.	.	.	.	.	.	.	.		+	−	.	.	.
Renault	.	.	.	.	.	+	.	.	.		.	.	.	.
Rover	.	.	.	.	.	.	.	.	.	.		.	.	.
Seat	.	.	.	.	.	.	.	.	.	.	.		.	.
VW/A	.	*	−	.	.	.	.	.	.	−	.	.		.
Volvo	.	+	.	.	.	.	.	.	.	.	+	.	.	
French market 1987														
Alfa Romeo		*	.	.	.	.	.	.	.	.	.	.	.	.
BMW	.		.	.	.	.	.	*	.	.	.	.	*	.
Citroen	.	.		.	.	.	+	.	.	.	.	.	.	.
Fiat	+	.	−		.	.	.	.	.	.	+	.	.	.
Ford	+	.	.	.		.	.	.	.	.	.	.	*	.
GM	.	.	.	.	.		.	.	.	.	.	.	.	.
Lada	.	.	+	+	.	.		.	.	.	.	.	.	.
Mercedes	.	*	.	.	.	.	.		.	.	.	.	+	*
Peugeot	.	.	+	.	.	.	.	.		.	.	.	.	.
Renault	.	.	.	.	.	.	.	.	.		.	.	.	.
Rover	.	.	−	+	.	.	.	.	.	.		+	.	.
Seat	+	.	.	.	.	.	.	.	.	.	.		.	.
VW/A	.	+	.	.	.	.	+	.	.	.	.	.		.
Volvo	.	.	.	.	.	.	.	.	.	.	.	.	.	

predictable in their subsequent purchases (i.e., Renault rows are composed nearly entirely of ".".s, meaning few significant departures from random behavior for Renault owners). Citroen buyers show more structural predictability (there are more clear patterns of

TABLE 12.10 *Continued*

	A	B	C	F	F	G	L	M	P	R	R	S	V	V
French market 1988														
Alfa Romeo	.	.	.	.	.	.	.	.	.	.	.	.	.	.
BMW	.	.	−	.	.	.	.	*	.	.	.	.	+	.
Citroen	.	.	.	.	.	.	.	.	.	.	.	.	.	.
Fiat	.	.	.	.	.	.	.	.	−	.	.	+	.	.
Ford	.	.	.	.	.	.	.	.	−	.	.	.	.	.
GM	.	.	.	.	.	.	.	.	.	.	.	.	.	.
Lada	.	.	.	+	.	.	.	.	.	.	.	.	.	.
Mercedes	.	*	.	.	.	.	.	.	.	.	.	.	.	*
Peugeot	.	.	.	.	.	.	.	.	.	.	.	.	.	.
Renault	.	.	.	.	.	.	.	−	.	.	.	.	.	.
Rover	.	.	.	.	.	+	.	.	.	.	.	.	.	.
Seat	.	.	.	.	.	.	.	.	.	.	.	.	*	.
VW/A	.	*	−	.	.	.	.	.	.	.	.	.	.	.
Volvo	.	.	.	−	.	.	*	*	.	.	.	.	.	.
French market 1989														
Alfa Romeo	.	.	.	.	.	.	.	.	.	.	.	.	.	.
BMW	.	.	.	.	.	.	.	*	.	.	.	.	+	.
Citroen	.	.	.	−	−	.	.	*	+	.	.	.	=	.
Fiat	+	.	.	.	.	.	.	.	.	.	+	.	+	.
Ford	.	.	.	.	.	*	.	.	.	.	.	.	.	.
GM	.	.	.	.	*	.	.	.	.	.	.	.	.	.
Lada	.	.	.	.	.	.	.	.	.	.	.	.	.	.
Mercedes	.	*	.	.	.	.	.	.	−	.	.	.	.	+
Peugeot	.	.	.	−	.	.	.	.	.	.	+	.	.	.
Renault	.	.	.	.	.	.	.	.	.	.	.	.	.	.
Rover	.	.	.	.	+	−	.	.	−	.	.	.	+	.
Seat	.	.	.	.	.	.	.	.	−	.	.	.	.	.
VW/A	.	*	.	.	.	.	.	.	.	=	.	.	.	.
Volvo	.	.	.	.	.	.	.	.	.	.	.	.	+	.

(continued)

especially high or low purchase frequency patterns—more "*+–="
codes in the Citroen rows), but not necessarily more national loyalty
in their purchases (i.e., not necessarily found in the Peugeot or
Renault columns). The British market demonstrates a greater extent
of the anticipated interpurchasing among the Ford, GM, and Rover
brands, particularly in the dyads between Ford and GM, and between

TABLE 12.10 *Continued*

	B	C	F	F	G	H	M	N	P	R	R	S	T	V	V
U.K. market 1986															
BMW	.	.	.	.	.	.	*	.	.	.	.	.	.	*	*
Citroen	.	.	+	.	.	.	.	.	.	+	.	.	.	.	+
Fiat	.	*	.	−	.	.	.	.	.	.	+	.	.	.	.
Ford	−	.	.	.	.	.	.	.	.	.	+	.	.	−	−
GM	−	.	.	*	.	.	.	.	.	.	.	.	.	.	.
Honda	+	.	.	.	.	.	*	.	.	.	=	.	*	.	.
Mercedes	*	.	.	.	.	.	.	.	.	.	.	.	.	+	*
Nissan	+	.	.	.	.	.	.	.	.	.	+	.	.	−	.
Peugeot	.	.	+	.	.	.	.	.	.	.	.	.	.	.	.
Renault	.	.	+	.	.	.	.	.	.	.	.	.	.	.	.
Rover	−	.	.	.	.	.	.	.	.	.	.	.	.	.	.
Saab	+	.	.	.	.	.	.	.	.	.	.	.	.	.	*
Toyota	.	.	−	.	.	.	+	.	+	.	.	.	.	.	.
VW/A	*	.	.	.	.	.	.	.	.	.	.	.	.	.	.
Volvo	.	.	.	.	.	+	.	.	+	.	+	.	.	.	.
U.K. market 1987															
BMW	.	.	.	−	*	*	.	.	.	.	.	*	.	+	.
Citroen	.	.	+	.	.	.	.	+	.	.	.	.	.	.	.
Fiat	.	.	.	.	.	.	.	.	.	.	.	*	.	.	.
Ford	.	.	.	.	*	.	.	.	.	.	.	.	.	.	.
GM	.	.	.	.	.	.	−	.	.	.	.	.	.	.	.
Honda	.	.	.	−	−	.	+	.	.	.	.	*	.	.	.
Mercedes	+	.	.	.	*	.	.	.	.	.	.	.	.	+	.
Nissan	.	.	.	.	.	.	.	.	.	.	.	.	.	.	.
Peugeot	.	+	.	.	.	.	.	.	.	.	+	.	.	−	.
Renault	.	.	+	.	−	.	.	.	.	.	.	.	+	.	.
Rover	.	.	+	+	.	.	.	.	.	.	.	.	−	.	.
Saab	.	.	.	.	.	.	.	.	.	.	.	+	.	.	+
Toyota	.	.	.	.	.	.	*	.	.	.	.	.	.	.	.
VW/A	+	.	.	.	.	.	+	.	.	.	−	+	.	.	.
Volvo	.	.	.	.	.	.	+	=	.	.	.	*	+	.	.

(continued)

Ford and Rover (i.e., more "+"s and "*"s in these row and column combinations).[1]

There are very few combinations that are particularly rare. The French 1989 market shows two (Citroen to VW/Audi, and VW/Audi

TABLE 12.10 *Continued*

	B	C	F	F	G	H	M	N	P	R	R	S	T	V	V
U.K. market 1988															
BMW	.	.	.	.	.	+	*	−	.	.	.	+	+	+	.
Citroen	.	.	*	−	.	+	.	.	.	.	.	.	.	.	.
Fiat	.	.	.	−	.	.	+	.	.	.	.	.	.	.	.
Ford	.	.	.	.	+	.	.	.	.	.	.	.	.	.	.
GM	.	.	.	+	.	.	−	.	.	.	.	.	.	.	.
Honda	.	.	.	.	.	.	.	.	.	.	*	.	.	.	.
Mercedes	*	.	.	.	.	.	.	.	.	.	.	+	.	.	.
Nissan	.	.	.	.	.	+	.	.	.	.	.	.	.	.	.
Peugeot	.	+	.	−	.	.	.	.	.	+	.	.	.	.	.
Renault	.	+	.	.	.	+	.	.	.	.	.	.	−	.	.
Rover	−	.	.	+	.	.	−	.	.	.	.	.	.	.	.
Saab	.	.	.	.	.	.	.	.	.	.	.	.	.	.	.
Toyota	.	.	.	.	.	.	.	*	.	.	.	.	.	.	.
VW/A	+	.	.	.	.	+	+	.	+	.	.	.	.	.	.
Volvo	+	.	.	.	.	.	*	.	.	.	.	+	.	.	.
U.K. market 1989															
BMW	.	.	−	−	.	*	=	.	.	.	*	+	*	.	.
Citroen	.	.	+	.	.	.	.	.	+	.	.	.	.	.	.
Fiat	.	+	.	.	.	.	.	.	.	.	.	.	.	−	.
Ford	.	.	−	.	*	=	.	.	.	.	.	.	.	.	.
GM	.	.	−	*	.	−	.	.	.	.	.	.	.	.	−
Honda	.	.	.	.	.	.	−	.	.	.	.	.	*	.	.
Mercedes	*	.	.	.	.	*	.	.	.	.	.	.	.	.	.
Nissan	.	.	+	+	.	+	.	.	.	.	.	.	.	.	.
Peugeot	.	+	.	.	−	.	.	+	.	+	.	.	.	.	.
Renault	.	.	+	.	−	.	.	.	+	.	.	.	.	.	.
Rover	−	.	.	+	.	+	−	+	.	.	.	−	−	.	.
Saab	*	.	.	.	.	.	*	.	.	.	.	.	.	.	+
Toyota	.	.	.	.	.	*	.	.	.	.	.	.	.	.	.
VW/A	+	.	.	−	.	.	+	.	+	.	−	+	+	.	.
Volvo	+	.	.	−	.	.	*	.	.	.	+	−	*	.	.

* > 4.00 (very frequent); + > 2.58 (frequent); − < −2.58 (infrequent); = < −4.00 (very infrequent).

to Renault); that is, it was highly unusual (less often than chance) for Citroen owners to purchase VW/Audis, or for VW/Audi owners to purchase Renaults. The U.K. market yields one rare purchase pattern in 1986 (Honda to Rover), one in 1987 (Volvo to Nissan), and two in 1989 (BMW to Nissan, and Ford to Honda). Again, it would be interesting to understand why these purchase patterns are so rare. One might argue that one car in each pair is in a different sort of market from the other in the pair, but that could be true of many dyads within these markets, and there were no a priori expectations that the data would flag these purchases as particularly unusual temporal dyads.

Finally, these structural patterns could be used by any one of the manufacturers' marketing managers to focus study on their brand in the marketplace compared with others, over time. For example, the BMW rows in the U.K. matrixes (for each year) have a fair number of marks ("*+−="s), indicating this competitor is more likely (than randomness) to lose consumers to Mercedes, VW/Audi, Volvo, Honda, Saab, and Toyota ("*" and "+"), and not likely to lose consumers to GM, Nissan, or Ford ("−" and "="). Although that list may seem like a good number of competitors to deal with, in trying to manage the loss of consumers to other manufacturers, at least the BMW manager's picture is clear. BMW knows the players in the market to and from whom it is most likely to lose and gain BMW owners. Contrast BMW's picture with say that of Saab. For Saab, the rows (if we are still focusing on where lost consumers are going), show far fewer strong indications of pattern. We see that Saab is likely to lose consumers to BMW, Volvo, Toyota, and Mercedes, but this is all we know, and even these patterns are not highly consistent over time. In a way then, Saab's management is more challenged because they are just as likely to be losing their consumers to all the other manufacturers. BMW's competitive picture was more crystallized compared with the near-random behavior of the Saab purchaser (according to the abundance of non-significant residuals—the "."s).

We can do a similar analysis *within* a competitor comparing its rows to its columns. For example, Volvo has twice the number of "codes" in its rows compared to its columns. Thus, information more clearly indicates where Volvo's customers are going than from which competitors Volvo's customers come. Such a market situation actually suggests that Volvo is not executing (or doing so successfully) a targeted marketing plan, but rather is attracting consumers from all sorts of previous car makes. Surely a car manufacturer could be happy in such a situation, as long as incoming volumes were high, but should volume drop off, or should the manager wish to understand the consumers she or he is likely to attract, this information picture is not clear. Because the outgoing (row) information is clear on the other hand, Volvo would know where to focus to stop the leaking customers (i.e., Mercedes, Renault, Saab, Toyota, BMW, VW/Audi, and not Nissan, Ford, or Toyota). That is, Volvo has a clearer means of identifying how to retain customers than to attract them.

This analysis of the independence and quasi-independence of the two-way contingency tables was fairly simple, but the results are rich and quite telling. In addition, these results can serve as a simple baseline against which to compare other methods, just as the row and column percentages served as a baseline for other row and column indexes.

Network Dyadic Relations Model

A network model proposed as a stochastic advance in an otherwise typically descriptive network literature is that of Wasserman and Iacobucci (1986). Details regarding this modeling approach are found in several sources, so we are brief here (cf. Iacobucci & Grace, 1993; Iacobucci & Hopkins, 1991, 1992, 1994; Iacobucci & Wasserman, 1987, 1988; Wasserman & Iacobucci, 1988). The network model

$$\text{Ln } P\{Y_{ijk\ell} = y_{ijk\ell}\} = \lambda_{ij} + \theta_k + \theta_\ell + \alpha_{ik} + \alpha_{j\ell} + \beta_{jk} + \beta_{i\ell} + \rho_{k\ell}$$

is fit via the hierarchical log-linear model

$$u + u_{1(i)} + u_{2(j)} + u_{12(ij)} + u_{3(k)} + u_{4(\ell)} +$$
$$u_{13(ik)} + u_{24(j\ell)} + u_{23(jk)} + u_{14(i\ell)} + u_{34(k\ell)}$$

to the four-dimensional y-array defined as $y_{ijk\ell} = 1$ for row actor i sending relational ties of strength k to column actor j and receiving at strength ℓ.[2] The α, β, and ρ parameters are of particular interest to the network researcher. The first two parameters reflect actor-level behavior of expansiveness and popularity respectively (tendencies for actor i to send and receive relational ties at strengths k and ℓ).

TABLE 12.11　Fitting Network Dyadic Relations Model and Variants to Data in Table 12.2

Test of	ΔG^2	Δdf	p	Test of	ΔG^2	Δdf	p
French market							
		1986				1987	
α	80.232	13	< .001	α	36.674	13	< .001
β	36.884	13	< .001	β	26.411	13	< .020
ρ	.998	1	< .900	ρ	2.419	1	< .900
		1988				1989	
α	56.027	13	< .001	α	57.221	13	< .001
β	34.173	13	< .010	β	28.142	13	< .010
ρ	3.466	1	< .100	ρ	1.777	1	< .900
U.K. market							
		1986				1987	
α	54.213	14	< .001	α	62.241	14	< .001
β	62.723	14	< .001	β	40.787	14	< .001
ρ	.385	1	< .900	ρ	.000	1	1.000
		1988				1989	
α	58.113	14	< .001	α	95.703	14	< .001
β	34.909	14	< .010	β	53.618	14	< .001
ρ	.000	1	1.000	ρ	.000	1	1.000

The ρ parameter is dyadic in nature, reflecting mutuality or the extent to which relational ties are exchanged.

Table 12.11 contains the ΔG^2 statistics that test the significance of each of these three vectors of parameters. (These tests are computed by comparing G^2s from hierarchically nested models; for example, the ΔG^2 for the α parameters is the difference in G^2s from the model containing all three sets of parameters, to the model in which the αs are dropped in which the effective hypothesis is that all αs equal zero. Thus, a significant ΔG^2 means that not all the actors are behaving in the same manner, but rather their α-estimates vary, and therefore the set of αs are significantly different from zero.) The fit statistics indicate that for every network, the α and β parameters are necessary in describing the data, but the ρs are not. We focus on the significant parameters first (i.e., the αs and βs) and return to ρs in a moment.

The α and β estimates are presented in Table 12.12. These parameters are somewhat analogous to out-degrees and in-degrees, but need not correlate perfectly with row and column marginal information because this model incorporates dyadic associations, not just aggregate row or column information. Nevertheless, for these data, the αs are highly correlated with the row percentages (mean $r=.914, p<.0001$), as are the β-estimates with the column percentages (mean $r=.810, p<.0005$). The estimates tell a picture of asymmetry similar to the degree centralities and correspondence analyses scores. For example, in the French market, Citroen's αs (reflecting roughly the volume of lost customers) are larger than its βs (gained customers), whereas Fiat's are the reverse. The signs are as interesting as the magnitudes of these estimates. For example, there appears some stability for BMW, Lada, Mercedes, Rover, and Seat in that none is losing or gaining customers in great volumes (both αs and βs are negative), and companies like Fiat and Ford are not losing customers (small αs) but are gaining them (positive βs), a good place to be indeed.

We now return to the ρ estimates. These parameters represent reciprocity and were not significant for any of the networks. This finding, in conjunction with the significance of the αs and βs, suggests that perhaps the only action in these data are in the margins, and that few relational associations are occurring in the body of the table. If this were true, all that need be known about each market would be described by the row and column marginal percentages, the simple starting point we have been using as a benchmark throughout this chapter. Luckily the data are more interesting. As we saw with the standardized residuals of the quasi-independence models (presented in Table 12.10), the results are not so simple, but rather there are structural patterns that appear consistently but at a microscopic level. The ρ parameter reflects action that is more dyadic than α or β to be sure, but it is an aggregate estimate across all dyads, and thus appears to be insufficiently sensitive in detecting the associations in these particular market transactions.

For example, in the French markets, the ρ's estimates were all near-zero, which is consistent with their being nonsignificant, but the ρs in the United Kingdom data (which were also not significant), were much larger, and highly negative. Thus, it is evidently not the case that every dyad of car manufacturers trades customers, but rather

TABLE 12.12 α, β Estimates From Data in Table 12.2 (models fit in Table 12.11)

French market	αs				βs			
	1986	1987	1988	1989	1986	1987	1988	1989
Alfa Romeo	−.127	−.130	−.085	−.085	−.224	−.144	−.063	−.221
BMW	−.127	−.130	−.085	−.085	−.224	−.144	−.063	−.221
Citroen	.259	.239	.227	.156	.004	.029	−.056	.119
Fiat	.046	.017	−.013	−.010	.232	.172	.118	.236
Ford	−.046	.017	−.013	−.010	.232	.172	.118	.236
GM	−.208	−.133	−.188	−.182	.082	.024	.125	.088
Lada	−.127	−.130	−.085	−.085	−.224	−.143	−.063	−.221
Mercedes	−.127	−.130	−.085	−.085	−.224	−.143	−.063	−.221
Peugeot	.403	.390	.224	.300	.167	.222	.126	.309
Renault	.557	.309	.224	.446	.320	.373	.126	.302
Rover	−.207	−.130	−.089	−.096	−.065	−.144	−.059	−.207
Seat	−.207	−.130	−.089	−.174	−.065	−.144	−.059	−.056
VW/Audi	.104	.074	.061	−.004	.236	.011	−.039	.075
Volvo	−.102	−.130	−.003	−.085	−.248	−.144	−.145	−.221

U.K. market	αs				βs			
	1986	1987	1988	1989	1986	1987	1988	1989
BMW	−.132	−.351	−.378	−.424	−.157	−.322	−.364	−.444
Citroen	−.132	−.351	−.378	−.358	−.157	−.322	−.364	−.296
Fiat	−.044	−.001	−.015	−.027	−.160	−.044	−.091	−.167
Ford	.333	.756	.856	.928	.312	.783	.868	.909
GM	.344	.339	.445	.530	.149	.322	.456	.513
Honda	−.132	−.351	−.378	−.424	−.157	−.322	−.364	−.444
Mercedes	−.132	−.351	−.378	−.424	−.157	−.322	−.364	−.444
Nissan	.026	.110	.039	−.169	.158	.097	.048	.112
Peugeot	.026	.338	.445	.222	.158	.242	.456	.483
Renault	−.059	.110	.039	−.014	.162	.097	.048	−.033
Rover	.183	.626	.728	.798	.319	.514	.572	.370
Saab	−.132	−.351	−.378	−.424	−.157	−.322	−.364	−.444
Toyota	−.132	−.351	−.378	−.424	−.157	−.322	−.364	−.444
VW/Audi	.029	.110	.039	.381	.002	.097	.048	.372
Volvo	−.044	−.283	−.310	−.169	−.160	−.176	−.219	−.053

there is some evidence that brand switching may be asymmetric. We have suspected some asymmetries from the correspondence analysis results as well, so we next pursue the hypothesis of asymmetry more explicitly.

Analyses of Symmetry

Log-Linear Models of Symmetry and Quasi-Symmetry

We will explore two means of testing symmetry. In this section, we apply the methods of Bishop, Fienberg, and Holland (1975), who present a log-linear model for a two-way table with elements x_{ij} in which a three-way table is created:

$$x_{ij1} = x_{ij} \quad i > j, 0 \text{ elsewhere},$$

and

$$x_{ij2} = x_{ji} \quad i > j, 0 \text{ elsewhere}.$$

The models fit to this three-dimensional array are symmetry:

$$\text{Ln } \{E(x)_{ijk}\} = u + u_{1(i)} + u_{2(j)} + u_{3(k)} + u_{12(ij)}$$

and quasi-symmetry (such as presented here, with a relaxation on the assumption of homogeneous margins):

$$\text{Ln } \{E(x)_{ijk}\} = u + u_{1(i)} + u_{2(j)} + u_{3(k)} + \\ u_{12(ij)} + u_{13(ik)} + u_{23(jk)}.$$

Table 12.13 contains the results of fitting these two models to each data set. We see that the matrixes do indeed evidently display some asymmetries. The model of symmetry does not fit any of the eight matrixes (see the G^2s for the models labeled "symmetry"), and although the relaxation of the assumption of marginal homogeneity in the quasi-symmetry model improves the fits significantly (see the ΔG^2s comparing the fits between symmetry and quasi-symmetry), the quasi-symmetry models nevertheless still do not fit the data (see the G^2s for the models labeled "quasi-symmetry").

TABLE 12.13 Log-Linear Analyses of Symmetry Fit to Data in Table 12.1

	Model	G^2	df	p	ΔG^2	Δdf	p
French market							
1986	Quasi-symmetry	131.507	260	< .001			
	Symmetry	1317.203	286	< .001	1185.696	26	< .001
1987	Quasi-symmetry	102.392	260	< .010			
	Symmetry	759.105	286	< .001	656.713	26	< .001
1988	Quasi-symmetry	101.724	260	< .010			
	Symmetry	792.848	286	< .001	691.124	26	< .001
1989	Quasi-symmetry	93.273	260	< .050			
	Symmetry	845.723	286	< .001	752.450	26	< .001
U.K. market							
1986	Quasi-symmetry	215.304	301	< .001			
	Symmetry	553.574	329	< .001	338.270	28	< .001
1987	Quasi-symmetry	253.257	301	< .001			
	Symmetry	515.026	329	< .001	261.769	28	< .001
1988	Quasi-symmetry	162.458	301	< .001			
	Symmetry	570.782	329	< .001	408.324	28	< .001
1989	Quasi-symmetry	205.496	301	< .001			
	Symmetry	1145.620	329	< .001	940.124	28	< .001

NOTE: All ps < .001, thus, models of symmetry and quasi-symmetry do not fit (according to the G^2), but the relaxation of the symmetry assumption of homogeneity of margins in the quasi-symmetry models does significantly improve the fits (according to the ΔG^2s).

Quadratic Assignment Procedure
(QAP) Correlation Between X and X′

For our second exploration of symmetry, we rely on the quadratic assignment procedure, a nonparametric means of comparing proximity matrixes, like sociomatrixes or brand-switching matrixes, that incorporate the inherent row and column interdependencies.[3] We took each of the eight networks as matrixes, **X**, and computed the correlation with its transpose, **X′**, reasoning that if **X** were symmetric, it would equal **X′**, and therefore would presumably predict it well. The results are presented in Table 12.14 and they confirm the log-linear method of inquiry into symmetry for these data. The correlations are very near zero, indicating that knowledge of one matrix, **X**, or its transpose **X′**, yields no information in predicting another.

TABLE 12.14 Quadratic Assignment Procedure (QAP) Analyses of Symmetry—
Correlations Between X and X': Fit to Data in Table 12.1

French Market		U.K. Market	
Year	r	*Year*	r
1986	−.055	1986	−.064
1987	−.061	1987	−.055
1988	−.065	1988	−.050
1989	−.067	1989	−.044

It may be the case that several dyads, triads, or even very small groups of car manufacturers symmetrically trade consumers back and forth (e.g., BMW and Mercedes as in Table 12.10), but these multiple results converge to demonstrate that symmetry is not a property that would describe these markets very well as a whole. We had suggested previously that consumer car purchases may appear hierarchical, in that some cars may be more desirable to trade-up to than others, and these asymmetries are consistent with this hypothesis.

MULTIVARIATE ANALYSES

Longitudinal

In this section, we study the dynamics of the car markets over time. We explore three methodologies: a statistical modeling procedure, a regression (predictive) use of the quadratic assignment nonparametric procedure, and a simpler qualitative examination of evolving pictures of clique and block formation across the time periods.

Network Sequential Dyadic Relations Models

For the first method, we fit the sequential generalization models of the network modeling results presented earlier. These models have been presented in detail in sources such as Iacobucci (1989), Iacobucci and Wasserman (1988), and Wasserman and Iacobucci (1988), so once again, we are brief here. A longitudinal network model such as

$$\text{Ln } P\{Y_{ijk1\ell1k2\ell2} = y_{ijk1\ell1k2\ell2}\} = \lambda_{ij} + \theta_{k1} \theta_{\ell1} +$$
$$\alpha_{ik1} + \alpha_{j\ell1} + \beta_{jk1} + \beta_{i\ell1} + \rho_{k1\ell1} + \theta_{k2} + \theta_{\ell2} +$$
$$\alpha_{ik2} + \alpha_{j\ell2} + \beta_{jk2} + \beta_{i\ell2} + \rho_{k2\ell2} + \omega_{k1k2} + \omega_{\ell1\ell2} + \omega_{k1\ell2} +$$
$$\omega_{\ell1k2} + \omega_{k1k2\ell2} + \omega_{\ell1k2\ell2} + \omega_{k1\ell1k2} + \omega_{k1\ell1\ell2} + \omega_{k1\ell1k2\ell2}$$

is fit via hierarchical log-linear models and now, in addition to the expansiveness, popularity, and reciprocity parameters fit to Times 1 and 2, parameters reflecting the dynamic behavior are also included. In this chapter, we have attempted to be readable and not too technical, so we wish to explain this model more fully.

These additional parameters (the ωs) are most readily understood by attending to the subscripts. The subscripts "k_1 and ℓ_1" represent the ties sent and received by actors i and j at Time 1, and "k_2 and ℓ_2" represent the relational ties at Time 2.[4] If the last parameter in the model above, $\omega_{k1\ell1k2\ell2}$, were significant, it would indicate that the dyad's joint behavior (both $\hat{k}$ and ℓ) at Time 1 were associated with, or predictive of, the dyad's joint behavior at Time 2. We call this effect "relational integration." Other parameters examine different behaviors. Each of the dynamic parameters (the ωs) are also illustrated in Figure 12.3.

For additional examples, the parameters $\omega_{k1\ell1k2}$ and $\omega_{k1\ell1\ell2}$ are referred to as "dyadic initiates" because the joint dyadic behavior (both k and ℓ) at Time 1 predicts one of the parties' behavior at Time 2. By way of contrast, the parameters $\omega_{k1k2\ell2}$ and $\omega_{\ell1k2\ell2}$ are referred to as "dyadic responses" because the initiating behavior by one party at Time 1 is responded to by the joint dyad at Time 2 (e.g., perhaps one actor strikes up a negotiation that results in a subsequent exchange). Perhaps the simplest dynamic parameters are the ω_{k1k2} and $\omega_{\ell1k2\ell2}$ terms, which reflect autocorrelative behaviors on the part of either actor (e.g., what actor i does at Time 1 is associated with, or can be used to predict, what the same actor does subsequently). Finally, the parameters $\omega_{k1\ell2}$ and $\omega_{\ell1k2}$ we have labeled "power" because the actions of one party at Time 1 influence the actions of the other party at the future point in time (cf. Iacobucci & Hopkins, 1992).

To test all these parameters, we fit the model above, and its variants (dropping each dynamic parameter in turn to test its significance). This method was somewhat temperamental on these data. First, the computers to which we had access were not large enough to estimate all the necessary parameters for the $14 \times 14 \times 2 \times 2 \times 2 \times 2$ and $15 \times$

Univariate Parameters:

Expansiveness (α):   Popularity (β):   Reciprocity (ρ):

Dynamic Parameters:

Autocorrelation (ω_{k1k2}, ω_{l1l2}):   Power (ω_{k1l2}, ω_{l1k2}):

Dyadic Initiate (ω_{k1l1k2}, ω_{k1l1l2}):   Dyadic Response (ω_{k1k2l2}, ω_{l1k2l2}):

Relational Integration ($\omega_{k1l1k2l2}$):

Figure 12.3. Depiction to Describe Dynamic Parameters

$15 \times 2 \times 2 \times 2 \times 2$ tables, so we fit these models to a network comprised of a subset of 7 actors common to the 14 and 15 actors in each market. The data are depicted in Table 12.15, and the fit statistics appear in Table 12.16.

TABLE 12.15 Subset of Seven Actors from French and U.K. Data in Table 12.2

	B	C	F	M	R	R	V	B	C	F	M	R	R	V
	French Market 1986							French Market 1987[a]						
BMW	1	0	0	0	0	0	0	1	0	0	0	0	0	0
Citroen	0	1	1	0	1	0	0	0	1	1	0	1	0	0
Ford	0	0	1	0	1	0	0	0	0	1	0	1	0	0
Mercedes	0	0	0	1	0	0	0	0	0	0	1	0	0	0
Renault	0	1	1	0	1	1	0	0	1	1	0	1	0	0
Rover	0	0	0	0	0	1	0	0	0	0	0	0	1	0
Volvo	0	0	0	0	0	0	0	0	0	0	0	0	0	0
	French Market 1988							French Market 1989[a]						
BMW	1	0	0	0	0	0	0	1	0	0	0	0	0	0
Citroen	0	1	1	0	1	0	0	0	1	1	0	1	0	0
Ford	0	0	1	0	1	0	0	0	0	1	0	1	0	0
Mercedes	0	0	0	1	0	0	0	0	0	0	1	0	0	0
Renault	0	1	1	0	1	0	0	0	1	1	0	1	0	0
Rover	0	0	0	0	0	1	0	0	0	0	0	0	1	0
Volvo	0	0	0	0	0	0	1	0	0	0	0	0	0	0
	U.K. Market 1986							U.K. Market 1987[b]						
BMW	1	0	0	0	0	0	0	1	0	0	0	0	0	0
Citroen	0	1	0	0	0	0	0	0	1	0	0	0	0	0
Ford	0	0	1	0	1	1	0	0	0	1	0	1	1	1
Mercedes	0	0	0	1	0	0	0	0	0	0	1	0	0	0
Renault	0	0	1	0	1	0	0	0	0	1	0	1	0	0
Rover	0	0	1	0	1	1	0	0	0	1	0	1	1	0
Volvo	0	0	0	0	0	1	1	0	0	0	0	0	0	1
	U.K. Market 1988[b]							U.K. Market 1989						
BMW	1	0	0	0	0	0	0	1	0	0	0	0	0	0
Citroen	0	1	0	0	0	0	0	0	1	0	0	0	0	0
Ford	0	0	1	0	1	1	1	0	1	1	0	1	1	1
Mercedes	0	0	0	1	0	0	0	0	0	0	1	0	0	0
Renault	0	0	1	0	1	0	0	0	0	1	0	1	0	0
Rover	0	0	1	0	1	1	0	0	0	1	0	1	1	1
Volvo	0	0	0	0	0	0	1	0	0	0	0	0	0	1

a. Note the 1987 French market is identical to its 1989 market.
b. Note the 1987 U.K. market is identical to its 1988 market.

TABLE 12.16 Fitting Sequential Network Models to Data in Table 12.15

Significance of:	G^2	Δdf	G^2	Δdf	G^2	Δdf
			Lag 1			
	1986, 1987		1987, 1988		1988, 1989	
French market						
Relational integration*	.000	1	.000	1	.000	1
Dyadic response	.000	1	.000	1	.000	1
Dyadic initiate	.000	1	.000	1	.000	1
Power	.000	1	.000	1	.000	1
Autocorrelation	1.537	1	1.314	1	1.314	1

	Lag 2				Lag 3	
	1986, 1988		1987, 1989		1986, 1989	
Relational integration	.000	1	.000	1	.000	1
Dyadic response	.000	1	.000	1	.000	1
Dyadic initiate	.000	1	.000	1	.000	1
Power	.000	1	.000	1	.000	1
Autocorrelation	1.537	1	1.314	1	1.537	1

	Lag 1					
	1986, 1987		1987, 1988		1988, 1989	
U.K. market						
Relational integration	.000	1	.000	1	.000	1
Dyadic response	.000	1	.585	1	.006	1
Dyadic initiate	.020	1	.278	1	.000	1
Power	.010	1	.822	1	.000	1
Autocorrelation	2.394	1*	3.274	1*	.818	1

	Lag 2				Lag 3	
	1986, 1988		1987, 1989		1986, 1989	
Relational integration	.000	1	.000	1	.001	1
Dyadic response	.000	1	.006	1	.000	1
Dyadic initiate	.020	1	.000	1	.034	1
Power	.010	1	.000	1	.000	1
Autocorrelation	2.394	1*	.818	1	.407	1

NOTE: The model "relational integration" is fit via hierarchical log-linear modeling:
[IJ][IK1][JL1][JK1][IL1][IK2][JL2][JK2][IL2][K1L1K2L2]. For the dyadic response model, the margin [K1K2L2][L1K2L2] is freed to test its significance. For dyadic initiate, the effect corresponding to the margin [K1L1K2][K1L2L2] is tested, for the power model, the effect corresponding to the margin [K1L2][K2L1] is tested, and for the autocorrelation model, the effect corresponding to the margin [K1K2][L1L2] is tested.
*$p < .15$.

The model-fitting troubles did not end, because the parameter estimates are not easily explained. Almost all of the parameters are zero, and almost none are significant. The autocorrelation effects in the British market are marginal ($p < .15$). The lack of dynamic effects suggest these markets are changing so greatly from year to year that knowing the relational structure in one year cannot help to predict the structure in years to come. The data in Table 12.15 make such results seem implausible. The French market is identical in years 1987 and 1989, and very few other structural changes occur (Volvo's loyalty changes from 1987 through 1989, but the diagonals are not considered in this model, so truly the only difference across the four matrixes is the Renault and Rover dyad differing in 1986 versus 1987). The U.K. market is somewhat more interesting, with the Ford-Volvo dyad changing from 1986 to 1987, and the Ford-Citroen dyad changing from 1988 to 1989, but overall, both markets look highly temporally stable, at least for these seven actors, with the ties made binary. Fitting these models leaves sufficient degrees of freedom, but we suspect the results and near-zero parameter estimates are a function of the lack of variance—it seems ironic because lack of variance over time should indicate high stability in these markets, but evidently the lack of variance reduced the effective degrees of freedom, affecting the estimates accordingly.

These results are also disappointing because we know the larger matrixes showed many interesting patterns across the years, but as we described with the reciprocity effect, perhaps these parameters are also not sensitive to change given that they are estimated by aggregating over the dyads. That is, even with significant interactions occurring between certain manufacturers, if not all dyadic relations are similar in direction or strength, then the parameters will reflect the dyadic heterogeneity and aggregate to nearly zero. In addition, of course, we might have simply selected a poor, uninteresting subset of seven actors in these two markets. Finally, it is of some assurance that the autocorrelative effects (which reflect within-actor stability) were large in at least the British market.

QAP Regressions Predicting
Future Market Structures

We now turn to a regression application of the quadratic assignment nonparametric procedure, using the same logic as the model-

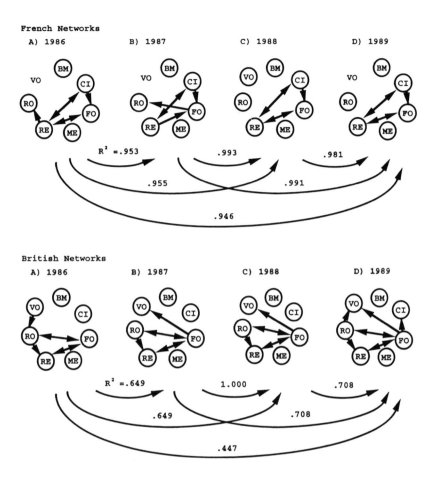

Figure 12.4. Quadratic Assignment Procedure (QAP) Regressions Examining Sequential Structural Prediction on Small Networks (data in Table 12.15)

NOTE: BM = BMW, CI = Citroen, FO = Ford, ME = Mercedes, RE = Renault, RO = Rover, VO = Volvo.

ing in the previous section, in which an early year is used to predict structure in later years (in lags one, 1986 to 1987, 1987 to 1988, 1988 to 1989; two, 1986 to 1988, 1987 to 1989; and three, 1986 to 1989). The correlations are presented in Figures 12.4 and 12.5. For com-

French Data   g=14

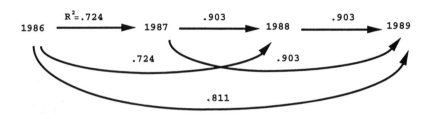

British Data   g=15

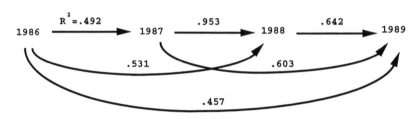

Figure 12.5. Quadratic Assignment Procedure (QAP) Regressions Examining Sequential Structural Prediction (on networks in Table 12.2)

parison, we begin with the same subset of seven actors, but later in the table we present the results for the larger, original networks.

These results suggest high stability in France. There was some movement from 1986 to 1987, but then a settling of the market structure, because 1987 predicts 1988 and even 1989 fairly well. The U.K. market appears less stable, because it is more difficult to predict future structure from points further back in time. Only the progression from the market structure in 1987 to that in 1988 appears stable or predictable. Note also that these correlations (e.g., .649 from 1986 to 1987) seem small and overly sensitive to the change of one dyadic value compared with 41 other matrix elements (correlations computed elementwise across the two matrixes).

Perhaps the networks of seven actors are indeed peculiarly small, because the correlations in Figure 12.5 (based on the original 14 and 15 member networks) are actually interesting. The French market is more stable than the British market (given its higher correlations overall), but the *r*s of .724, .903, and .903 in France defend the interpretation of early changes and then a market settling, with the British market bouncing around dramatically. It shows stability from 1987 to 1988, but its instability before or after certainly caution us as to generalizations or extrapolations in either direction.

Clique and Block Evolution

Our final longitudinal view of these data will be in examining the evolution of network subgroups and their composition over time. There are basically two major types of defining subgroups within networks: groups defined by their interconnective cohesiveness, or "cliques," and groups defined by the similarities of their actors' interconnections with others, or "structural equivalence" (cf. Hopkins, Henderson, & Iacobucci, 1995; Knoke & Kuklinski, 1982). Strict cliques are defined to be maximally complete subgraphs (the largest subset of three or more actors from the network population set who are all pairwise interconnected), derived by algorithms like the clique algorithm in UCINET (Borgatti, Everett, & Freeman, 1992, p. 86, a procedure based on Luce & Perry, 1949; also see Note 3). Structurally equivalent actors are found by computing some measure of similarity (e.g., correlations, distances) between pairs of actors based on both the rows and columns of the sociomatrix (the ties sent and received by each actor). Sets of equivalent actors can be found in a variety of ways, and we used the popular CONCOR algorithm in UCINET, which is based on iterative correlations.

For these brand-switching data, car manufacturers who are highly connected, and therefore would appear together in a clique, would be those alternate cars that consumers are most frequently trading directly to and from. For example, Ford, GM, and Rover would comprise a clique if trading were high between each pair, relative to other dyads of car trades. By contrast, two structurally equivalent car manufacturers would be car makes that are interchangeable in the sense that the consumer purchasing either car (e.g., Peugeot or Renault) is similarly likely to have come from the same previous car make (e.g., Citroen) and go to another same future car make (e.g., Volvo). In business-to-business ties, cliques and equivalence sets offer alternative operationalizations of competitor actors. Cliques suggest those competitors from whom a manager might wish to harvest

TABLE 12.17 Cliques Over Time Based on the Binary Data in Table 12.2

French market

1986	[Ci,Fo,Pe,Re]	[Ci,Fi,Pe,Re]	[GM,Pe,Re]	[Ci,Pe,Re,VW]
1987	[Ci,Fo,Pe,Re]	[Ci,Fi,Pe,Re]	[GM,Pe,Re]	[Pe,Re,VW]
1988	[Ci,Fo,Pe,Re]	[Ci,Fi,Pe,Re]	[Ci,GM,Pe,Re]	[Pe,Re,VW]
1989	[Ci,Fo,Pe,Re]	[Ci,Fi,Pe,Re]	[GM,Pe,Re]	[Pe,Re,VW]

U.K. market

1986	[Fo,GM,Ni, Ro]	[Fo,GM,Pe,Ro]	[Fo,GM,Re,Ro]	[Fo,GM,Ro,VW]	
1987	[Fo, Ni, Ro]	[Fo,GM,Pe,Ro]	[Fo, Re,Ro]	[Fo, Ro,VW]	[Fi,Fo,Ro]
1988	[Fo, Ni, Ro]	[Fo,GM,Pe,Ro]	[Fo, Re,Ro]	[Fo, Ro,VW]	[Fi,Fo,Ro]
1989	[Fo,GM,Ni,Ro]	[Fo,GM,Pe,Ro,VW]	[Fo, Re,Ro]	[Fo, Ro,VW]	[Fi,Fo,Ro]

Ci = Citroen, Fi = Fiat, Fo = Ford, GM = GM, Ni = Nissan, Pe = Peugeot, Re = Renault, Ro = Rover, VW = VW/Audi.

customers (or prevent losing to the competitor), and equivalence sets suggest those competitors that customers might see as substitutes. For more on the differences in interpreting cliques and equivalent actors with respect to competition, see Marcati (Chapter 13, this volume).

The cliques for these data are presented in Table 12.17, and the structurally equivalent actors are presented in Table 12.18. In the French market, we see two cliques that are stable over time—that comprised of {Citroen, Ford, Peugeot, and Renault} and that comprised of {Citroen, Fiat, Peugeot, and Renault}. The other cliques are comprised of primarily {GM, Peugeot, and Renault} and {Peugeot, Renault, and VW/Audi}. (Car makes not listed did not become a member of any clique due to lack of sufficient interconnections.) The only change over time is whether the Citroen brand is included in one of these latter cliques. The Peugeot-Renault dyad is especially strong in that it appears in each of these cliques. The nationalism we have suggested earlier is also somewhat apparent in that Citroen joins Peugeot and Renault for several of these cliques.

In the British market, we see more movement over time (consistent with previous results indicating the comparatively less stable U.K. structure). There is a clique comprised of {Ford, Nissan, and Rover} and sometimes GM. The second clique is primarily {Ford, GM, Peugeot, Rover} and in 1989, VW/Audi joins the group. The third clique is comprised of {Ford, Renault, and Rover} and in 1986 GM appears in the group. The fourth clique consists of {Ford, Rover,

TABLE 12.18 Structural Equivalence Over Time Based on the Binary Data in Table 12.2

French market

1986	[Al,BMW,GM,Me,Ro]	[Ci,Fi,Fo, Pe,Re,Se,VW]	[La, Vo]
1987	[Al,BMW, Me,Ro]	[Ci,Fi,Fo,GM,Pe,Re, VW]	[La,Se,Vo]
1988	[BMW,GM,Me,Ro,Vo]	[Ci,Fi,Fo, Pe,Re, VW]	[Al,La,Se,]
1989	[Al,BMW,GM,Me,Ro]	[Ci,Fi,Fo, Pe,Re,Se,VW]	[La, Vo]

U.K. market

1986	[BMW,Ci,Fi,Ho,Me,To,Vo]	[Fo,GM,Ro]	[Ni,Pe,Re,VW]		[Sa]
1987	[BMW,Ci,Fi, Me,To,Vo]	[Fo,GM,Ro,	Ni,Pe,Re,VW]		[Ho,Sa]
1988	[BMW,Ci, Ho, Me,To,Vo]	[Fo,GM,Ro,	Ni,Pe,Re,VW]	[Fi]	[Sa]
1989	[BMW,Ci, Ho, Me,To]	[Fo,GM,Ro,	Pe, VW]	[Fi,Ni, Re,Vo]

Al = Alfa Romeo, BMW = BMW, Ci = Citroen, Fi = Fiat, Fo = Ford, GM = GM, La = Lada, Me = Mercedes, Ni = Nissan, Pe = Peugeot, Re = Renault, Ro = Rover, Sa = Saab, Se = Seat, To = Toyota, Vo = Volvo, VW = VW/Audi.

VW/Audi, and again, in 1986 GM joins. After 1986, the cars by {Fiat, Ford, and Rover} form a fifth clique. Like the French market, we see the major British players consistently (Ford, Rover, even GM), and the variability in network structure from year to year reflects players that are somewhat peripheral to the groups—sometimes being more connected and sometimes less.

Table 12.18 shows the sets of structurally equivalent actors in these markets. Although there are fewer groups, the actors bounce around more from year to year. For example, in France, the first group is primarily {Alfa Romeo, BMW, GM, Mercedes, and Rover}, but Alfa Romeo is more similar to members of another group in 1988, when Volvo joins the first group. The second group is primarily {Citroen, Fiat, Ford, Peugeot, Renault, and VW/Audi}, but occasionally GM and Seat appear similar to these actors. Finally, Lada and Volvo appear somewhat similar, and they are sometimes joined by Alfa Romeo, Seat, or both.

In the U.K. market, the first group of actors with similar patterns of interactions with others is {BMW, Citroen, Honda, Mercedes, Toyota, Volvo} and perhaps Fiat. There is a second major group in 1987 to 1989 that is split in 1986. This group consists of {Ford, GM, Rover, Nissan, Peugeot, Renault, and VW/Audi}. Finally, there are occasionally isolates or a group of miscellaneous players (e.g., Honda and Saab).

It is not easy to see what these sets of actors have in common, so it is important to remember that the manufacturers are grouped as structurally equivalent because they are actors whose consumers have purchased similar alternative cars prior to or after purchasing the focal competitor car. For example, take the first group in the British market: {BMW, Citroen, Honda, Mercedes, Toyota, Volvo and sometimes Fiat}. It might be attractive to interpret this group as including cars to which a consumer aspires (e.g., BMW, Mercedes, Volvo), but that explanation does not fit the Citroen and peripheral group member, Fiat. These car makes share few apparent features—not volume of consumers, not country of origin, and so on. The property they share, by definition, is that a BMW purchaser is likely to have come from the same cars and in the future go to the same cars, as the purchasers of the other cars in the set. Although this might be believable for the Mercedes or Volvo, and so on, it seems less likely for the Citroens, and so on. Perhaps the cars such as Peugeot, Renault, Rover, GM, Ford, and the like are intermediary cars that Citroen and Fiat owners trade up from and from which BMW and Mercedes obtain their future purchasers. This description is not particularly satisfying because structural equivalence is supposed to function symmetrically in the sense that the previous car makes (from whom a focal actor obtains customers) *and* the future car makes (to whom the focal actor loses customers) should be identical.

Cross-Country Market Structure Comparison

Finally, although we have made many qualitative comparisons between the two countries' markets in discussing their parallel results, we now more directly compare their market structures. We created a super-matrix template with the 18 actors that comprise the union of the French and U.K. manufacturers, and filled the empty trading positions with zeros in the respective countries (e.g., Honda in France). We then computed the quadratic assignment correlations between the French and U.K. supersociomatrixes for each year, and the results follow.

For 1986, the correlation between the two countries' exchange structures was the lowest: $r = .080$, but the correlations did not increase substantially over future years. In 1987, the correlation was $r = .095$; in 1988, $r = .202$; and in 1989, $r = .104$. This lack of similarity in structure is due in part, of course, to the fact that the players in the two markets are not identical, so there are rows and columns of zeros in the supersociomatrixes in one market while there are ones and zeros in the respective rows and columns in the other market. (There are three actors in the French market that do not appear in the British market (Alfa Romeo, Lada, Seat) and four in the United Kingdom that are not in the French network (Honda, Saab, Nissan, Toyota).) We had also identified earlier, however, some different patterns between country alliances even for the manufacturers that exist in both markets (e.g., Citroen, Peugeot, Renault, Ford, GM, and Rover).

CONCLUSIONS

In this chapter, we examined several means of analyzing brand-switching data. We used methods created for contingency tables as well as methods developed specifically for network relations. Some methods focused on describing the margins and others focused on the internal associations of the tables.

Much like the conclusions drawn by Colombo et al. (1994), we found the methods sometimes converged in the tales they told, and yet they were by no means redundant. It would be inefficient for a researcher to use each of these methods for every matrix of brand-switching data, and there was sufficient overlap across the results that it would also appear to be unnecessary. Nevertheless, it is also the case that any one of these methods alone would not have told the full story that these data are capable of yielding. Thus some combination of several analytical methods seems to be warranted.

The correspondence analyses and the centrality indexes suggested asymmetries in the brand-switching behavior that was not obvious by the marginal percentages. The asymmetric structure was studied in greater depth using log-linear modeling and the correlational method of quadratic assignment popular in network analysis. Models focusing on the associative structures internal to the tables included fitting log-linear models of quasi-independence, with an enlightening view of standardized residuals, and the network dyadic relations modeling, which allowed for simultaneous examination of actor indexes and tendencies for reciprocal ties. Finally, we explored several means of analyzing these data multivariately, including the simple, qualitative analysis of the cliques and structural equivalence blocks apparent in these data.

Returning then to the statement that a combination of methods might be useful, we might suggest the following. The researcher should include one method to examine each of: (a) row and column margins (e.g., percentages, betweenness indexes); (b) possible asymmetries (e.g., correspondence analysis, degree centralities, log-linear models of symmetry, matrix correlations of X and X'); (c) internal table association (e.g., quasi-independence log-linear models, network dyadic relations models); (d) actor grouping methods (e.g., cliques, structural equivalence); (e) and some multivariate technique (e.g., longitudinal models).

NOTES

1. There also appears to be some of this interpurchasing among the Japanese brands of Honda, Nissan, and Toyota in the U.K. marketplace, and it would be interesting to understand whether this behavior was attributable to loyalty (e.g., perceptions of country-of-origin quality) or accessibility (e.g., trade-ins at homogeneously Japanese-make dealerships).

2. The model would be too large to fit and the results not particularly meaningful if fit to the raw data (requiring a table of size $14 \times 14 \times 817 \times 817$ for the French 1986 market, for example), so we fit these data on the binary matrixes in Table 12.2.

3. The QAP correlation of Hubert (1987) and Hubert and Baker (1978) is available in UCINET, a popular network program available for a nominal fee from Steve Borgatti, Department of Sociology, University of South Carolina, Columbia, SC 29208. For our purposes, we can simply refer to the correlation computed element-wise between pairs of matrixes.

4. Times 1 and 2 take on the years 1986 and 1987 for a time lag of 1 (or 1987 to 1988, 1988 to 1989), 1986 and 1988 for a time lag of 2 (or 1987 to 1989) and 1986 and 1989 for a time lag of 3.

Brand Switching and Competition

A Behavior-Oriented Approach to Better Identify the Structure of the Market

ALBERTO MARCATI

This chapter is about competitive relationships among brands, and it deals with the structure and extent of competition within a market. It purports to apply a network approach to the analysis of market structures to investigate similarities and dissimilarities among firms or brands and to identify product and market segments, by drawing on customer-derived information. It is in fact our contention that network analysis is especially suited for identifying competitive relations among firms and for increasing our understanding of competition, through the concepts of cohesion and structural equivalence.

We need not stress here the importance of market structure in orienting marketing activities and in determining their impact and their effects. Market structure defines the environment close to the firm and the system of relationships in which firms are embedded; it influences the working of strategies and the likely targets of marketing actions; it determines which competitors will affect each other's performance, reciprocally interfere with each other's marketing strategies and policies, address each other's clients, and so on.

Customer-based methods to identify market structure can be grouped into two categories, depending on their bases, either judgmental or behavioral, although hybrid methods combining those bases are increasingly used to get more operational, better, and richer

275

results (Bayrus, 1992; Day, Shocker, & Srivastava, 1979; McCarthy, Kannan, Chandrasekharan, & Wright, 1992; Shocker, Stewart, & Zahorik, 1990). Decision sequence analysis, perceptual mapping, judgments of similarity and substitutability, and the like belong to the first category and rely on the perceptions, representations, or preferences of customers, whereas cross-elasticity of demand, similarities in behavior, and brand switching belong to the second category and build on actual behaviors. The discussion of the advantages and limitations of both categories is outside the scope of our analysis, although it is our contention that, contrary to occasionally heralded beliefs, they are more complements than substitutes and add to each other to build a multifaceted representation of competitive context (Lehmann, 1972).

COMPETITION, BRAND SWITCHING, AND NETWORK ANALYSIS

In this chapter we focus on brand switching, addressing the same set of brand-switching data in the car industry as in Iacobucci et al. (Chapter 12, this volume; see also Colombo & Morrison, 1989). It is well-known, and has already been documented in this book, that brand-switching analysis builds on buying patterns and the sequence of successive purchases made by the same individual. Brand-switching data are presented usually in the form of a square matrix, in which values of each cell, x_{ij}, correspond to the number of customers that have bought Brand I at Time t and Brand J at Time $t + 1$. Those data represent the frequency of occurrence of individuals choosing Brand I at Time t and Brand J at a successive purchase at Time $t + 1$, and they are very often transformed into row percentages, so that they are interpreted as probabilities of buying Brand J at Time $t + 1$, conditional on the purchase of Brand I on previous occasion(s), at Time t or earlier. But the data can also be taken to show a flow of customers from the customer base or client portfolio of Brand I to that of Brand J.

A high probability of buying J for customers of Brand I, or the existence of a substantial flow of customers from Brand I to Brand J, points to a strong attraction of Brand J for customers of Brand I, and is therefore related to the strength of the competition between the brands under consideration. The probability can also be taken as an indicator of brand substitutability and homogeneity, based on the premise that switching is more likely between close substitutes than between dissimilar brands. By looking at joint purchases or at flows of buyers among brands, the analyst is able to suggest where competition is strongest, to work out the attraction capabilities of brands, to define customer-based distances among brands, to judge their similarities and dissimilarities and how closely they are associated to each other, and to determine groups of homogeneous brands, splitting the whole market into groups of brands that show different levels of reciprocal competition and homogeneity.

We stress the fact that the attraction capability of a brand is not related solely to its similarity to, or homogeneity with, other brands, because it has been suggested, and conclusively shown in a number of contexts, that "double jeopardy" is at work in that repeat buying and switching are both related to market penetration and market share. Flows among brands are influenced by similarity but also by sheer size, and switching between two brands therefore can be traced back to similarity or homogeneity of the brands, as well as size—that is, the attraction resulting from size and market share. In unstructured markets, that is, markets in which no strategic groups of competitors nor product/market segments exist, brands draw their customers proportionally to their market share (Urban, Johnson, & Hauser, 1984).

In the analysis of raw brand-switching data, the effects of size and homogeneity are pooled together. By using row or column percentages, the situation is not changed substantially, although the range of variation is reduced. It is only by taking deviations vis à vis market share that one can get rid of the effect of market share and uncover the underlying structure of the market, by relying on behaviors dictated only by perceived similarities or dissimilarities. Therefore, to account for those differences we deal with raw data and row-wise percentages, but we also transform the data to get rid of market share effects as much as possible. In addition, we work with binary data that are better fit to highlight the underlying structure of the network of relations, without distortions derived from intensities. It is fair enough to say that binary data introduce a different kind of distortion, because relations of different intensity and strength are treated in the same way, but also because the choice of the "cut-off" point, the value taken as a threshold "cutting off" an existing relation from a missing one, may impact on the representation of the network.

For the sake of our application, we focus on the French, 1989 market data. Table 13.1 presents the raw data, the row percentages, a binary version of the row percentages (using the rule $x_{ij} = 1$ iff $x_{ij} \geq$ 5%, = 0 otherwise), the binary version of the first matrix, and a binary market share matrix derived from the row percentages (using the rule $x_{ij} = 1$ iff $x_{ij}x_{i+}/x_{++}$, = 0 otherwise).

At this preliminary point, a first very general comment is in order about the overall characteristics of those networks. The first two networks in Table 13.1 are very dense, because car makes are widely and diffusely connected to each other, whereas the third, fourth, and fifth networks are much more sparse. Car makes compete widely with each other and it is not surprising that customers move freely among almost all of them, even among those that common sense may judge very different—a small, economy car or a smart and luxurious sedan, because all goods compete to a certain extent for customers' resources, and even very different products can be put against each other, as it has been very appropriately pointed out (Shocker et al., 1990).

Density can also derive from variety-seeking behavior or joint consumption, or parallel joint purchase, of products by individual customers or by households, when data are taken at the household level. We know that individuals do not behave necessarily in a mono- lithic way, not only because they are at times curious and "variety seekers" and they want to try different ways and means, but also because they experience their needs in different context, they need to fulfill different functions, and the way they respond to a same basic need may vary widely according to the context. They buy different products of the same class not only because they are or may be multiloyal and perceive the products in similar ways but also because those different products play a different role within their consump- tion system and are part of a wider portfolio, that is bought and consumed to fulfill a whole set of needs and functions (Feinberg, Kahn, & McAlister, 1994; Givon & Muller, 1994; Jain & Niu, 1974; Srivastava, Alpert, & Shocker, 1984; Trivedi, Bass, & Rao, 1994; Uncles, Hammond, Ehrenberg, & Davis, 1994). In this sense, a small, city car or a large 4-wheeler can be owned by the same individual in conjunction with a sedan to perform completely different functions. This is even more true when a multiplicity of individuals are involved, as it is the case in the car industry, where the unit of analysis is the household, and we know that multiple car ownership is widely diffused.[1]

The analysis of competition from brand-switching data rests on the additional simplifying assumption of a "steady state," or stationary behavior, for customers and competitors alike, meaning on one hand that customers do not change their choice criteria and behaviors in the time period under consideration, and that they buy at period $t + 1$ a brand that they might have bought as well at Time t, or vice versa, and on the other hand that competitors do not change their strategy (for instance, targeting, positioning, and so on) or marketing mix within the same time period (Lehmann, 1972; see also Novak, 1993; Zahorik, 1994). Of course, this may be a strong assumption to make, on both counts, when the time horizon is wide and allows for deep and far-reaching changes in purchasing strategy on the part of customers and in marketing strategy on the part of competitors. As far as the change of strategy on the part of car vendors is concerned, we can mention as an example the change in product breadth by many a competitor, adding new cars at the top or bottom of their product lines to capture new segments of customers.

There is an additional limitation to our study, deriving from the level of aggregation of our data. By working at the vendor level and not at the level of each individual product, we are missing some of the subtleties and excitement of "real-life" competition and we are building ambiguity into the analysis, ending up with coarse-grained results that may be not directly applicable, because we are mixing up products with very different characteristics. This is especially confusing when putting together vendors with product portfolios of different breadth, because competitors differ by product lines.

The traditional analysis of joint probabilities of purchasing Brand I at Time t and Brand J at Time $t + 1$ or of conditional probabilities of buying Brand J, given the previous purchase of Brand I, captures "direct" competitive relationships among brands, by focusing on switching to and from each individual brand and by isolating brands competing directly, almost "head on," against each other. By direct competition we refer to the competition between two brands that are *substitutes* to each other, and exchange customers in one or the other direction, or reciprocally.

But such an analysis is unable to uncover a different, more subtle and less evident kind of competition that does not come out easily by

TABLE 13.1 Network 1: Raw Frequency Data for French 1989 Market

	AL	BMW	CI	FI	FO	GM	LA	ME	PE	RE	RO	SE	VW	VO
AL	97	5	19	19	14	7	0	3	27	35	5	6	17	4
BMW	4	163	20	9	14	6	0	19	39	40	6	4	29	4
CI	6	13	1,811	136	98	67	21	15	464	477	29	28	90	10
FI	11	5	69	526	50	49	12	3	134	148	27	17	82	5
FO	4	10	45	53	696	76	8	8	121	146	20	23	60	7
GM	2	7	20	23	50	362	7	4	68	80	7	12	39	4
LA	0	0	12	13	11	12	68	0	25	16	4	3	7	0
ME	2	17	3	3	5	2	0	136	4	10	3	1	5	3
PE	13	23	273	164	195	168	34	23	2,928	728	47	60	199	20
RE	22	37	353	334	308	254	40	33	896	4,861	78	106	310	24
RO	2	4	18	25	30	3	6	1	30	45	115	6	40	2
SE	2	0	13	10	10	11	0	0	10	29	3	36	13	0
VW	6	21	50	51	65	59	2	10	177	115	13	25	772	9
VO	1	3	11	5	4	6	0	3	9	17	3	4	18	78

Network 2: Row Percentages(based on the raw frequencies in Network 1)

37	1	7	7	5	2	0	1	10	13	1	2	6	1
1	45	5	2	3	1	0	5	10	11	1	1	8	1
0	0	55	4	3	2	0	0	14	14	0	0	2	0
0	0	6	46	4	4	1	0	11	13	2	1	7	0
0	0	3	4	54	5	0	0	9	11	1	1	4	0
0	1	2	3	7	52	1	0	9	11	1	1	5	0
0	0	7	7	6	7	39	0	14	9	2	1	4	0
1	8	1	1	2	1	0	70	2	5	1	0	2	1
0	0	5	3	4	3	0	0	60	14	0	1	4	0
0	0	4	4	4	3	0	0	11	63	1	1	4	0
0	1	5	7	9	0	1	0	9	13	35	1	12	0
1	0	9	7	7	8	0	0	7	21	2	26	9	0
0	1	3	3	4	4	0	0	12	8	0	1	56	0
0	1	6	3	2	3	0	1	5	10	1	2	11	48

Network 3: Binary Row Percentages

1	0	1	1	1	0	0	0	1	1	0	0	1	0
0	1	1	0	0	0	0	1	1	1	0	0	1	0
0	0	1	0	0	0	0	0	1	1	0	0	0	0
0	0	1	1	0	0	0	0	1	1	0	0	1	0
0	0	0	0	1	1	0	0	1	1	0	0	0	0
0	0	0	0	1	1	0	0	1	1	0	0	1	0
0	0	1	1	1	1	1	0	1	1	0	0	0	0
0	1	0	0	0	0	0	1	0	1	0	0	0	0

TABLE 13.1 *Continued*

0	0	1	0	0	0	0	0	1	1	0	0	0	0
0	0	0	0	0	0	0	0	1	1	0	0	0	0
0	0	1	1	1	0	0	0	1	1	1	0	1	0
0	0	1	1	1	1	0	0	1	1	0	1	1	0
0	0	0	0	0	0	0	0	1	1	0	0	1	0
0	0	1	0	0	0	0	0	1	1	0	0	1	1

Network 4: Binary Data Version of Network 1

1	0	0	0	0	0	0	0	0	0	0	0	0	0
0	1	0	0	0	0	0	0	0	0	0	0	0	0
0	0	1	1	1	0	0	0	1	1	0	0	0	0
0	0	0	1	0	0	0	0	1	1	0	0	0	0
0	0	0	0	1	0	0	0	1	1	0	0	0	0
0	0	0	0	0	1	0	0	0	0	0	0	0	0
0	0	0	0	0	0	0	0	0	0	0	0	0	0
0	0	0	0	0	0	0	1	0	0	0	0	0	0
0	0	1	1	1	1	0	0	1	1	0	0	1	0
0	0	1	1	1	1	0	0	1	1	0	1	1	0
0	0	0	0	0	0	0	0	0	0	1	0	0	0
0	0	0	0	0	0	0	0	0	0	0	0	0	0
0	0	0	0	0	0	0	0	1	1	0	0	1	0
0	0	0	0	0	0	0	0	0	0	0	0	0	0

Network 5: Binary Market Share Transformation

1	1	0	1	0	0	0	0	0	0	1	1	0	1
1	1	0	0	0	0	0	1	0	0	1	0	1	1
0	0	1	0	0	0	0	0	0	0	0	0	0	0
1	0	0	1	0	0	1	0	0	0	1	0	0	0
0	0	0	0	1	1	0	0	0	0	0	1	0	0
0	0	0	0	1	1	1	0	0	0	0	1	0	0
0	0	0	1	0	1	1	0	0	0	1	1	0	0
1	1	0	0	0	0	0	1	0	0	0	0	0	1
0	0	0	0	0	0	0	0	1	0	0	0	0	0
0	0	0	0	0	0	0	0	0	1	0	0	0	0
0	0	0	1	1	0	1	0	0	0	1	1	1	0
1	0	0	1	1	1	0	0	0	0	1	1	1	0
0	1	0	0	0	0	0	0	0	0	0	1	1	0
0	1	0	0	0	0	0	1	0	0	1	1	1	1

NOTE: AL = Alfa Romeo, BMW = BMW, CI = Citroen, FI = Fiat, FO = Ford, GM = GM, LA = Lada, ME = Mercedes, PE = Peugeot, RE = Renault, RO = Rover, SE = Seat, VW = VW/Audi, VO = Volvo.

looking at high switching among brands and adds on the top of direct competition. This is the "indirect" competition that takes place via "third parties." In fact, brands are embedded into systems of competitive relationships and can be affected by the activities of other competitors, even if they do not exchange customers directly and do not compete reciprocally for each other's customers, because they compete to acquire customers from the same brands, or, on the contrary, they become the target of offensive moves from the same brands and lose customers to them.

To clarify this problem, let us consider a simple hypothetical situation involving three brands, Renault, Lada, and Seat. Suppose switching goes on from Renault to Lada and from Renault to Seat, but not from Lada to Seat, or vice versa, meaning that Renault customers are attracted by Lada and by Seat and switch to those new makes. Although the customers choosing Lada are different from those choosing Seat, as a whole, Renault customers at Time t have both Lada and Seat as a possible choice at Time $t + 1$, and they can choose either of them interchangeably. Therefore, Lada and Seat draw their customers at least partially from Renault customers and compete for the same pool of customers.

Now suppose instead that switching goes on from Rover to Renault and from Seat to Renault, but not from Rover to Seat, or vice versa. Previous customers of both Rover and Seat consider switching to Renault, and Renault customers at Time t have bought Renault, Rover, or Seat previously, and therefore they are attracted by those brands. On the other hand, Renault draws its customers from both Rover and Seat and may direct its action to each one of them, or both, so that Rover and Seat compete for attention and the allocation of marketing effort on the part of Renault.

In what follows, we will first highlight the concepts of cohesion and structural equivalence, applying the proposed framework to the analysis of the car industry to hint at its advantages and to stress its limitations. Cohesion addresses direct relationships and direct competition among brands, by giving new insights and providing more formal tools to common sense, but it is not new vis à vis more traditional analytical techniques that are now widely used and well established. Real value added, we believe, is in the notion of structural equivalence, dealing with indirect competition by looking at positions within the system.

THE ANALYSIS OF
INDIVIDUAL POSITIONS

In network analysis, researchers have traditionally focused their attention on the notion of individual positions, making this concept one of the building blocks of network analysis and giving it widespread coverage in the network analytic literature. Two different orientations have emerged so far and have received increased recognition, that have been termed, perhaps slightly inappropriately, relational and positional approaches (Burt, 1978).

The former approach rests on the idea of individual (sometimes mediated) relations among actors, and the homogenizing and cohesive effect coming therefrom, and pivots around the notion of "cohesion." Cohesion refers to adjacency, proximity, or reachability (Wasserman & Faust, 1994) among actors and it purposefully identifies cohesive subgroups—that is, "subsets of actors among whom there are relatively strong, direct, intense, frequent, or positive ties" (Wasserman & Faust, 1994, p. 249).

The latter approach builds on connections to third parties, and stands on the notion of "equivalence." Equivalence is associated with similarities and dissimilarities of ties to third parties and results in the definition of equivalent actors—that is, "subsets of actors who are similarly embedded in networks of relations" (Wasserman & Faust, 1994, p. 348), by holding the same, or similar, patterns of relations to the rest of the group.

Analysis of Cohesion

To group actors on the basis of direct connections, a number of concepts have been devised that allow for varying intensities and strengths of relations and for a different integration within the group. One such concept is that of "component," which refers to a maximal complete subgraph in which any two vertexes are connected by a "semipath" meaning a subset of the set of relations constituting the network, that is at the same time complete (i.e., all nodes are connected by a semipath) and maximal (i.e., with this property holding for the subgraph, but not holding if additional nodes are added to the subgraph). A semipath is a sequence of arcs in which direction does not matter. Thus, components are made of actors who may be connected to each other even indirectly, via any number of connections in any direction, to or from any of them. In our application to the car industry, each component encompasses those makes who are loosely, at times very loosely, linked to each other, because they belong to the same hypothetical purchasing trajectory or sequence of purchases.

As Table 13.2 clearly indicates, many connected components are found in our networks, and most of the car vendors share membership of a number of components with many others.[2] Also in line with what we might expect, binary matrixes are characterized by a smaller number of components than are valued matrixes. The implication of these results is that again at a very general level, all car makes compete against all others, but for a few exceptions that have to deal with each other. Of particular interest, consider the network treatments in matrixes 4 and 5. In Network 4, Alfa Romeo, BMW, Lada, Mercedes, Rover, and Volvo (the marginal low-volume players) are excluded from the only component with more than three members. In Network 5, missing are Citroen, Peugeot, and Renault.

We can sketch here briefly what will be one of the themes of the whole analysis: When raw data are involved, very consistently cohesion is stronger among bigger vendors, whereas marginal players have looser connections. When the impact of size is lessened (i.e., through the use of binary data), a completely different picture emerges and a less traditional and familiar product-market structure comes out. By getting rid of the effect of size and market share, the connections among Citroen, Peugeot, and Renault (the main French broad-line high-volume vendors) lose most of their strength, and their integration or apparent homogeneity disappear or is lessened.

Traditionally, network analysis has also addressed the notion of a "clique," that is, the maximal complete subgraph of 3 or more actors who are "adjacent" to each other. Remember that adjacency between actors simply means that there is a direct link between the two actors Cliques are groups of actors related tightly and directly to each other. In our car application, cliques refer to sets of makes directly related to each other, in either direction, and therefore identify a much stronger and more direct relationship than the one which is implied by components. As we have seen, the number of cliques varies widely across networks (i.e., different treatments of the data). In general, they involve Peugeot, Renault, Citroen, Fiat, Ford, GM, and so on,

TABLE 13.2 Cliques

				Network 1 (raw frequencies)								
1:	AL	BMW	CI	FI	FO	GM	ME	PE	RE	RO	SE	VW	VO
2:	CI	FI		FO	GM	LA	PE	RE	RO	SE	VW		

				Network 2 (row percentages)								
1:	AL	BMW	CI	FI	FO	GM	ME	PE	RE	RO	VW	VO
2:	AL	BMW	CI	FI	FO	GM	PE	RE	RO	SE	VW	VO
3:	CI	FI	FO	GM	LA	PE	RE	RO	SE	VW		

			Network 3 (binary row percentages)		
1:	CI	FI	LA	PE	RE
2:	AL	CI	FI	PE	RE
3:	CI	FI	PE	RE	RO
4:	CI	FI	PE	RE	SE
5:	BMW	CI	PE	RE	
6:	CI	PE	RE	VO	
7:	FO	GM	LA	PE	RE
8:	FO	GM	PE	RE	SE
9:	AL	FO	PE	RE	
10:	FO	PE	RE	RO	
11:	GM	PE	RE	SE	VW
12:	AL	FI	PE	RE	VW
13:	FI	PE	RE	RO	VW
14:	FI	PE	RE	SE	VW
15:	BMW	PE	RE	VW	
16:	PE	RE	VW	VO	
17:	BMW	ME	RE		

			Network 4 (binary data)	
1:	CI	FO	PE	RE
2:	CI	FI	PE	RE
3:	GM	PE	RE	
4:	PE	RE	VW	

			Network 5 (binary market share transformed data)	
1:	FI	LA	RO	SE
2:	AL	FI	RO	SE
3:	FO	RO	SE	
4:	RO	SE	VW	VO
5:	AL	RO	SE	VO
6:	BMW	RO	VW	VO
7:	AL	BMW	RO	VO
8:	GM	LA	SE	
9:	FO	GM	SE	
10:	AL	BMW	ME	VO

NOTE: AL = Alfa Romeo, BMW = BMW, CI = Citroen, FI = Fiat, FO = Ford, GM = GM, LA = Lada, ME = Mercedes, PE = Peugeot, RE = Renault, RO = Rover, SE = Seat, VW = VW/Audi, VO = Volvo.

TABLE 13.3 2-Cliques

						Network 1								
1:	AL	BMW	CI	FI	FO	GM	LA	ME	PE	RE	RO	SE	VW	VO
						Network 2								
1:	AL	BMW	CI	FI	FO	GM	LA	ME	PE	RE	RO	SE	VW	VO
						Network 3								
1:	AL	BMW	CI	FI	FO	GM	LA	ME	PE	RE	RO	SE	VW	VO
						Network 4								
1:	CI	FI	FO	GM	PE	RE	SE	VW						
						Network 5								
1:	AL	BMW	FI	FO	LA	RO	SE	VW	VO					
2:	AL	BMW	FI	ME	RO	SE	VW	VO						
3:	AL	FI	FO	GM	LA	RO	SE	VW	VO					

NOTE: AL = Alfa Romeo, BMW = BMW, CI = Citroen, FI = Fiat, FO = Ford, GM = GM, LA = Lada, ME = Mercedes, PE = Peugeot, RE = Renault, RO = Rover, SE = Seat, VW = VW/Audi, VO = Volvo.

that is, the large broad-line vendors. In Network 5, on the contrary, joint clique membership involves Rover and Seat, BMW and Alfa Romeo, and the like, that is, the low-volume restricted-line specialists.

Cliques imply a very tight definition of cohesive subgroups, that does not hold very often in practice, because actors may be close to others and yet be connected indirectly to them (by a short path), or subgraphs may be very close to being a clique but lack a few connections. To deal with this problem, researchers have loosened the definition of clique, in either of the following two ways. They have defined "n-cliques"—cliques in which actors are not adjacent to each other but are connected to the other members of the clique by a path of length n. (The length of a path is the number of arcs in it—the length from i to k in a path i to j to k is three.) Clearly, a clique is a special case of an n-clique, where n = 1. In general, given that our Networks 1, 2, and 3 are dense, we find that a single 2-clique links all the vendors; in Network 4, the only 2-clique links Citroen, Fiat, Ford, GM, Peugeot, Renault, Seat, Volkswagen; in Network 5 there are 3 2-cliques, as in Table 13.3.

As an alternative strategy to loosen the notion of clique, researchers have set a limit to the maximal degree required for each actor in the clique, defining what came to be called "k-plexes." By degree of an actor, it is simply meant the number of connections of an actor and therefore the number of relations with other actors. In k-plexes, each actor is adjacent to no fewer than g_s-k actors in the subgraph, where g_s is the number of actors in the subgraph, such that for each actor no more than k ties can be lacking. Again, a clique is a special case of k-plex, where k = 1. As Table 13.4 indicates, the number of 2-plexes varied widely within our networks, although not so their members. The only exception, consistent with our previous findings, is Network 5, where Rover and Seat, Alfa and Volvo, BMW, Volkswagen, and the rest of vendors appear to be decreasingly cohesive.

A completely different approach to identifying cohesive groups has been followed at times by examining ties within and across groups, in the belief that cohesion derives as much from strength and intensity of linkages among members of a group as from the weakness and dispersion of linkages to members of a different group. Among the prominent notions devised with this objective in mind is the "lambda set." The analysis of lambda sets addresses the number of links connecting individual actors, and structures the whole network according to the number of individual links existing between actors: The higher the number of links, the stronger the association between those actors and the higher the number of lambda sets in which they share membership.

Lambda set membership matrixes are shown in Table 13.5, for all networks. The resulting picture is consistent with previous representations. In Networks 1 to 4, Peugeot and Renault, Citroen, Volkswagen, Ford, Fiat, Seat and the like belong to common lambda sets in decreasing numbers. In Network 5, joint membership describes Rover and Seat, Alfa, Volvo, BMW, Volkswagen, Fiat, Lada, and so on, while Citroen, Peugeot, and Renault are less cohesive.

Analysis of Equivalence

In keeping with the tradition of social network analysis, we are especially concerned with the notion of equivalence, which is where, in our opinion, lies most of the value added of our approach. As has

TABLE 13.4 2-Plexes

							Network 1					
1:	AL	BMW	CI	FI	FO	GM	ME	PE	RE	RO	SE	VW	VO
2:	AL	CI	FI	FO	GM	LA	PE	RE	RO	SE	VW
3:	BMW	CI	FI	FO	GM	LA	PE	RE	RO	SE	VW
4:	CI	FI	FO	GM	LA	ME	PE	RE	RO	SE	VW
5:	CI	FI	FO	GM	LA	PE	RE	RO	SE	VW	VO

							Network 2					
1:	AL	BMW	CI	FI	FO	GM	ME	PE	RE	RO	SE	VW	VO
2:	AL	CI	FI	FO	GM	LA	PE	RE	RO	SE	VW
3:	BMW	CI	FI	FO	GM	LA	PE	RE	RO	SE	VW
4:	CI	FI	FO	GM	LA	ME	PE	RE	RO	VW
5:	CI	FI	FO	GM	LA	PE	RE	RO	SE	VW	VO

						Network 3	
1:	AL	BMW	CI	PE	RE	VW
2:	AL	CI	FI	LA	PE	RE
3:	AL	CI	FI	PE	RE	RO	VW
4:	AL	CI	FI	PE	RE	SE	VW
5:	AL	CI	FO	LA	PE	RE
6:	AL	CI	FO	PE	RE	RO
7:	AL	CI	FO	PE	RE	SE
8:	AL	CI	PE	RE	VW	VO
9:	AL	FI	FO	LA	PE	RE
10:	AL	FI	FO	PE	RE	RO
11:	AL	FI	FO	PE	RE	SE
12:	AL	FO	GM	PE	RE	VW
13:	AL	FO	PE	RE	RO	VW
14:	AL	FO	PE	RE	SE	VW
15:	AL	ME	RE
16:	BMW	CI	FI	PE	RE	VW
17:	BMW	CI	LA	PE	RE
18:	BMW	CI	ME	RE
19:	BMW	CI	PE	RE	RO	VW
20:	BMW	CI	PE	RE	SE	VW
21:	BMW	CI	PE	RE	VW	VO
22:	BMW	FO	PE	RE
23:	BMW	GM	PE	RE	VW
24:	BMW	ME	PE	RE
25:	BMW	ME	RE	VW
26:	CI	FI	LA	PE	RE	RO
27:	CI	FI	LA	PE	RE	SE

TABLE 13.4 *Continued*

28:	CI	FI	PE	RE	RO	SE	VW
29:	CI	FI	PE	RE	VW	VO	
30:	CI	FO	LA	PE	RE	RO	
31:	CI	FO	LA	PE	RE	SE	
32:	CI	FO	PE	RE	RO	SE	
33:	CI	GM	LA	PE	RE	SE	
34:	CI	LA	PE	RE	VO		
35:	CI	PE	RE	RO	VW	VO	
36:	CI	PE	RE	SE	VW	VO	
37:	FI	FO	LA	PE	RE	RO	
38:	FI	FO	LA	PE	RE	SE	
39:	FI	FO	PE	RE	RO	SE	
40:	FI	GM	LA	PE	RE	SE	
41:	FI	GM	LA	PE	RE	VW	
42:	FI	GM	PE	RE	SE	VW	
43:	FI	ME	RE				
44:	FO	GM	LA	PE	RE	SE	
45:	FO	GM	PE	RE	RO	VW	
46:	FO	GM	PE	RE	SE	VW	
47:	FO	ME	RE				
48:	FO	PE	RE	RO	SE	VW	
49:	FO	PE	RE	VO			
50:	GM	ME	RE				
51:	GM	PE	RE	VW	VO		
52:	LA	ME	RE				
53:	ME	RE	RO				
54:	ME	RE	SE				
55:	ME	RE	VO				

Network 4

1:	CI	FI	FO	PE	RE
2:	CI	GM	PE	RE	
3:	CI	PE	RE	VW	
4:	CI	RE	SE		
5:	FI	GM	PE	RE	
6:	FI	PE	RE	VW	
7:	FI	RE	SE		
8:	FO	GM	PE	RE	
9:	FO	PE	RE	VW	
10:	FO	RE	SE		
11:	GM	PE	RE	VW	
12:	GM	RE	SE		
13:	PE	RE	SE		
14:	RE	SE	VW		

(continued)

TABLE 13.4 *Continued*

			Network 5			
1:	AL	BMW	FI	RO		
2:	AL	BMW	ME	RO	VO	
3:	AL	BMW	RO	SE	VW	VO
4:	AL	FI	LA	RO	SE	
5:	AL	FI	ME			
6:	AL	FI	RO	SE	VO	
7:	AL	FO	RO	SE		
8:	AL	GM	SE			
9:	AL	ME	SE	VO		
10:	BMW	FO	RO			
11:	BMW	LA	RO			
12:	BMW	ME	VW	VO		
13:	FI	FO	RO	SE		
14:	FI	GM	LA	SE		
15:	FI	RO	SE	VW		
16:	FO	GM	LA	RO	SE	
17:	FO	RO	SE	VW		
18:	FO	RO	SE	VO		
19:	GM	SE	VW			
20:	GM	SE	VO			
21:	LA	RO	SE	VW		
22:	LA	RO	SE	VO		

NOTE: AL = Alfa Romeo, BMW = BMW, CI = Citroen, FI = Fiat, FO = Ford, GM = GM, LA = Lada, ME = Mercedes, PE = Peugeot, RE = Renault, RO = Rover, SE = Seat, VW = VW/Audi, VO = Volvo.

already been pointed out, the notion of equivalence is intriguing and has to do with commonalities and similarities not deriving from direct interaction and the direct exchange of products, information, knowledge, affect, and the like, but instead from being located similarly within the network of relations. Equivalence analysis leads to the identification of "equivalence classes"—that is, groups of actors who are tied in the same way to the remaining actors, by relying on one of the many alternative definitions of equivalence that have been suggested.

The long-standing definition of equivalence has been termed "structural equivalence"—that is, the equivalence deriving from being tied to the "same" individual actors. Such a situation is seldom realized in practice, so this strong definition has been relaxed to achieve a more realistic approach, by referring to similarity (and not identity) of relational ties and identifying "approximately" structurally equivalent actors.

Structural equivalence can be measured in two different ways, by computing Euclidean distances or correlations. Euclidean distance between ties to and from actors is defined as $d_{ij} = (x_{ik} - x_{jk})^2 + (x_{ki} - x_{kj})^2$ and shows the properties of a distance metric: $d_{ii} = 0$, $d_{ij} = d_{ji}$, $d_{ij} \neq 0$ for $i \neq j$. Correlations are defined as the Pearson product-moment correlation of rows and columns corresponding to two different actors. In working with Euclidean distances, a distance matrix is derived that is successively treated with clustering methods. In working with correlations, the whole network may be partitioned into blocks of actors that share a similar profile. In our application, the outcome of the analysis is blurred, because both methods and data sets affect the results and do not give a coherent representation. (Results are shown in Tables 13.5, 13.6, and 13.7.)

Consider first structural equivalence derived from the analysis of Euclidean distances. Equivalence is stronger for Alfa, Lada, Rover, Seat, Volvo, BMW, and Mercedes, and so on, when valued relations are considered (Networks 1 and 2); it is strong again for BMW and Mercedes; Alfa and. Rover; but it is also so for Fiat, Ford, and GM; Peugeot and Renault; when binary relations are used instead (Networks 3 and 4). In general we could say that when market share is taken into account (Network 5), we get hybrid results, with Ford and GM; BMW, Volvo, and Mercedes; Citroen, Peugeot, and Renault; and so on, linked in decreasing order.

Consider then the analysis derived from correlations. BMW and Mercedes are usually in the same block, as are Citroen, Peugeot, and Renault, and GM and Seat, but the remaining vendors are spread over different blocks, depending on the network, without any coherent or consistent pattern. The partitioning also carries widely different ability to account for the actual pattern, as measured by the varying R^2s. As an example consider Network 5 in Table 13.6 where the impact of market share is removed: Blocks are formed by Citroen, Peugeot, and Renault; Fiat, Lada, and Rover; Ford, GM, and Seat; Alfa, BMW, Mercedes, Volkswagen, and Volvo; and R^2 equals 0.465.

Ties between and within partitions are described using density tables; tables whose values (entries) record the proportion of actual versus potential ties among actors. Structural equivalence is defined

TABLE 13.5   Lambda Sets

Hierarchical Lambda Set Partitions

Network 1

```
                1 1        1   1 1
Lambda      8 7 1 2 1 2 6 5 4 3 0 9 3 4
------      - - - - - - - - - - - - - -
2336        . . . . . . . . . . XXX . .
1475        . . . . . . . . . XXXXX . .
951         . . . . . . . . XXXXXX .
911         . . . . . . . XXXXXXXXX .
902         . . . . . . . XXXXXXXXXX .
728         . . . . . . XXXXXXXXXXXX .
295         . . . . . XXXXXXXXXXXXXX .
287         . . . . XXXXXXXXXXXXXXXX .
196         . . . XXXXXXXXXXXXXXXXXX .
161         . . XXXXXXXXXXXXXXXXXXXX .
147         . XXXXXXXXXXXXXXXXXXXXXX .
125         XXXXXXXXXXXXXXXXXXXXXXXX .
109         XXXXXXXXXXXXXXXXXXXXXXXXX
```

Network 2

```
                1       1     1   1 1
Lambda      8 2 1 7 6 1 5 2 4 3 0 9 3 4
------      - - - - - - - - - - - - - -
126         . . . . . . . . . . XXX . .
91          . . . . . . . . . . XXXXX .
82          . . . . . . . . XXXXXX .
79          . . . . . . . XXXXXXXXX .
76          . . . . . . . XXXXXXXXXX .
72          . . . . . . XXXXXXXXXXXX .
64          . . . . . XXXXXXXXXXXXXX .
61          . . . . XXXXXXXXXXXXXXXX .
57          . . . XXXXXXXXXXXXXXXXXX .
56          . . XXXXXXXXXXXXXXXXXXXX .
52          . XXXXXXXXXXXXXXXXXXXXXX .
46          . XXXXXXXXXXXXXXXXXXXXXXXXX
25          XXXXXXXXXXXXXXXXXXXXXXXXX
```

Network 3

```
                1       1     1   1 1
Lambda      8 2 1 6 7 1 5 2 4 3 0 9 3 4
------      - - - - - - - - - - - - - -
12          . . . . . . . . . . XXX . .
9           . . . . . . . . . XXXXXXX .
8           . . . . . . . . XXXXXXXXX .
7           . . . . . . XXXXXXXXXXXXXX .
6           . . XXXXXXXXXXXXXXXXXXXX .
5           . XXXXXXXXXXXXXXXXXXXXXX .
4           . XXXXXXXXXXXXXXXXXXXXXXXXX
2           XXXXXXXXXXXXXXXXXXXXXXXXX
```

TABLE 13.5 *Continued*

Network 4

```
              1 1             1   1 1
Lambda   1 2 7 8 1 2 6 4 5 3 0 9 3 4
------   - - - - - - - - - - - - - -
    6    . . . . . . . . . XXX . .
    4    . . . . . . . . . XXXXX . .
    3    . . . . . . . XXXXXXXXX . .
    2    . . . . . . XXXXXXXXXXXXX .
    1    . . . . . XXXXXXXXXXXXXXX .
    0    XXXXXXXXXXXXXXXXXXXXXXXXXXXXX
```

Network 5

```
            1           1   1 1 1
Lambda   3 9 0 5 6 8 4 7 3 2 1 1 2 4
------   - - - - - - - - - - - - - -
    8    . . . . . . . . . . . XXX .
    6    . . . . . . . . . . . XXXXXX
    5    . . . . . . . . . . XXXXXXXXX
    4    . . . . . . XXXXXXXXXXXXXX
    3    . . . XXXXXXXXXXXXXXXXXXXX
    0    XXXXXXXXXXXXXXXXXXXXXXXXXXXXX
```

NOTE: 1 = Alfa Romeo, 2 = BMW, 3 = Citroen, 4 = Fiat, 5 = Ford, 6 = GM, 7 = Lada, 8 = Mercedes, 9 = Peugeot, 10 = Renault, 11 = Rover, 12 = Seat, 13 = VW/Audi, 14 = Volvo.

by setting a strong condition for equivalence to hold, because relationships are individualized and meant to carry a sort of personal flavor, and are considered to be equal only if they associate actors with the same individual. At times this is not really required, because what is at stake is the "role" of an actor; the actor's position within the structure of the system, and the actual characteristics and attributes of other actors are irrelevant, so that actors who hold the same position within the system are taken to be equal.

To take this into account, researchers have devised the notion of "automorphic equivalence"; the equivalence of actors holding positions that are not distinguishable from one another when individual attributes and characteristics of actors are not considered. Automorphisms are mappings of graphs into themselves, which do not affect the structure of relations, irrespective of the actual identity of actors involved by each relation. For automorphic equivalence to hold, therefore, only relations matter, and not specific individuals, so that relationships are the same, although connecting different individuals, if they hold the same position within the system.

TABLE 13.6 Structural Equivalence Based on Euclidean Distance

Hierarchical Clustering of Equivalence Matrix

Network 1

```
        1   1           1  1  1
Level   0 9 3 3 5 4 6 2 8 1 1 2 7 4
------- - - - - - - - - - - - - - -
 132.797  . . . . . . . . . . . XXX .
 152.553  . . . . . . . . . . . XXXXX
 174.279  . . . . . . . . . . XXXXXX
 202.576  . . . . . . . . . XXXXXXXXX
 229.254  . . . . . . . . XXXXXXXXXXX
 260.985  . . . . . . . XXXXXXXXXXXXX
 596.134  . . . . . . XXXXXXXXXXXXXXX
 843.438  . . . . . XXXXXXXXXXXXXXXXX
1053.324  . . . . XXXXXXXXXXXXXXXXXXX
1168.685  . . . XXXXXXXXXXXXXXXXXXXXX
2647.854  . . XXXXXXXXXXXXXXXXXXXXXXX
4235.544  . XXXXXXXXXXXXXXXXXXXXXXXXX
6834.251  XXXXXXXXXXXXXXXXXXXXXXXXXXX
```

Network 2

```
        1   1           1 1 1
Level   8 9 0 3 5 3 6 2 4 7 1 1 2 4
------- - - - - - - - - - - - - - -
 60.141  . . . . . . . . . . . XXX .
 65.307  . . . . . . . . . . . XXXXX .
 70.774  . . . . . . . . . . XXXXXX .
 74.125  . . . . . . . . . XXXXXXXX .
 81.083  . . . . . . . . XXXXXXXXXX .
 85.078  . . . . . . . . XXXXXXXXXXXX
 92.957  . . . . . . XXXXXXXXXXXXXXX
 94.243  . . . . . XXXXXXXXXXXXXXXXX
 96.120  . . . . XXXXXXXXXXXXXXXXXXX
 97.450  . . . XXXXXXXXXXXXXXXXXXXXX
 99.669  . XXX XXXXXXXXXXXXXXXXXXXXX
104.830  . XXXXXXXXXXXXXXXXXXXXXXXXX
121.149  XXXXXXXXXXXXXXXXXXXXXXXXXXX
```

Table 13.8 shows, as is usually the case in our equivalence analyses, results are mixed and representations deriving from our networks differ widely, although some similarities emerge, in particular, in Networks 1 to 4, the linkages among Alfa, Lada, Rover, and Volvo and the low equivalence between Peugeot and Renault. Again, Network 5 stands out clearly, because it shows a strong equivalence between Citroen, Peugeot, and Renault, as well as between Fiat and Volks-

TABLE 13.6 *Continued*

```
                          Network 3

         1 1             1   1 1
Level    3 0 9 3 2 8 5 6 4 1 1 7 2 4
-----    - - - - - - - - - - - - - -
1.414    . XXX . . . . . . . . . . .
1.732    . XXX . XXX XXX . . . . . .
2.000    . XXX . XXX XXX . XXX . . .
2.236    . XXX . XXX XXX . XXX XXX .
2.300    XXXXX . XXX XXX . XXX XXX .
2.307    XXXXX . XXX XXX . XXXXXXX .
2.621    XXXXX . XXX XXX XXXXXXXXX .
2.646    XXXXXXX XXX XXX XXXXXXXXX .
2.656    XXXXXXX XXX XXX XXXXXXXXXXX
3.000    XXXXXXX XXX XXXXXXXXXXXXXXX
3.121    XXXXXXX XXXXXXXXXXXXXXXXXXX
3.436    XXXXXXXXXXXXXXXXXXXXXXXXXXX
```

```
                          Network 4

         1       1   1       1   1
Level    9 0 3 4 5 3 6 1 8 2 1 2 7 4
-----    - - - - - - - - - - - - - -
0.000    . . . . . . . . . . . . XXX
1.000    XXX . . . . . . . . . XXXXX
1.494    XXX . . . . . . . . XXXXXX
1.595    XXX . . . . . . . XXXXXXXXX
1.662    XXX . . . . . . XXXXXXXXXXX
1.711    XXX . . . . . XXXXXXXXXXXXX
1.732    XXX XXX . . . XXXXXXXXXXXXX
1.911    XXX XXXXX . . XXXXXXXXXXXXX
2.191    XXX XXXXX . XXXXXXXXXXXXXXX
2.265    XXX XXXXXXX XXXXXXXXXXXXXXX
2.676    XXXXXXXXXXX XXXXXXXXXXXXXXX
2.955    XXXXXXXXXXXXXXXXXXXXXXXXXXX
```

```
                          Network 5

           1     1     1 1         1
Level      4 7 1 6 5 2 3 9 0 3 1 8 2 4
-----      - - - - - - - - - - - - - -
1.732      . . . XXX . . . . . . . XXX
2.000      . . . XXX . XXXXX . . . XXX
2.157      . . . XXX . XXXXX . . XXXXX
2.449      XXX . XXX . XXXXX . . XXXXX
2.702      XXXXX XXX . XXXXX . . XXXXX
2.737      XXXXX XXX . XXXXX . XXXXXXX
2.943      XXXXX XXXXX XXXXX . XXXXXXX
2.995      XXXXX XXXXX XXXXX XXXXXXXXX
3.053      XXXXXXXXXXX XXXXX XXXXXXXXX
3.384      XXXXXXXXXXX XXXXXXXXXXXXXXX
3.726      XXXXXXXXXXXXXXXXXXXXXXXXXXX
```

TABLE 13.7 Structural Equivalence Based on Correlations

Partition Diagram

		Network 1	

```
                1           1   1 1 1
Level   1 4 2 8 3 9 7 4 6 0 5 2 3 1
-----   - - - - - - - - - - - - - -
    2   XXX XXX XXXXX XXXXXXXXXXXX
    1   XXXXXXX XXXXXXXXXXXXXXXXXX
R-squared = 0.163
```

		Network 2	

```
              1 1   1         1 1
Level   1 9 3 4 2 0 6 1 5 7 8 2 3 4
-----   - - - - - - - - - - - - - -
    2   XXXXXXXXXXX XXXXXXX XXX XXX
    1   XXXXXXXXXXXXXXXXXXX XXXXXXX
R-squared = 0.237
```

		Network 3	

```
            1     1   1       1 1
Level   1 2 6 4 1 7 4 2 8 3 9 0 3 5
-----   - - - - - - - - - - - - - -
    2   XXXXXXXXXXXXX XXX XXXXXXX .
    1   XXXXXXXXXXXXXXXXX XXXXXXXXX
R-squared = 0.603
```

		Network 4	

```
            1     1   1   1       1
Level   1 2 1 8 7 4 3 3 9 0 5 4 2 6
-----   - - - - - - - - - - - - - -
    2   XXXXXXX XXX XXXXXXXXXXX XXX
    1   XXXXXXXXXXX XXXXXXXXXXXXXXX
R-squared = 0.556
```

		Network 5	

```
          1 1     1   1       1
Level   1 2 3 4 8 3 0 9 1 4 7 2 6 5
-----   - - - - - - - - - - - - - -
    2   XXXXXXXXX XXXXX XXXXX XXXXX
    1   XXXXXXXXXXXXXXX XXXXXXXXXXX
R-squared = 0.465
```

wagen and Ford and GM, at odds with the results coming from previous networks, but in line with those from structural equivalence.

Comparison of Cohesion
and Equivalence Analyses

A few comments are in order at this stage, to compare and contrast results from cohesion and equivalence analyses. Cohesion analysis groups competitors along two very different lines, depending on data used, and the picture derived from Networks 1 to 4 clashes with that derived from Network 5, where market share is taken into account. In the first case, cohesion is stronger among larger players, and smaller ones add to this core incrementally; in the second, groupings differ widely and linkages among actors who did not appear previously as competitors emerge. In any case, cohesion analysis allows for finer groupings than the ones we are used to in the traditional categories.

Equivalence analysis is apparently able to uncover linkages that are not immediately apparent by looking only at direct flows of customers among makes, because they are blurred by the impact of size and market share. It can also be pointed out that results of equivalence analysis of Networks 1 to 4 are not completely dissimilar by those emerging from cohesion analysis of Network 5 (where the impact of market size has been disposed of), and they all point to intense competition between restricted-line specialists, that is, vendors of 4-wheelers, sporty, or luxury cars. Alfa, BMW, Lada, Mercedes, Rover, Seat, and Volvo, to a different extent and in different combinations, are consistently put against each other.

The market is fragmented and its structure is marked by deep cleavages, with small groupings of competitors pitted against each other, and connected only loosely to the rest of the network. Strong competitive relationships exist, first of all, among a few key players—Citroen, Peugeot, and Renault—but also among some of the restricted-line specialists we have been referring to earlier and among a few additional medium-sized middle-of-the-road competitors, like Fiat, Ford, and GM. It must also be stressed that results from equivalence analysis differ for different networks, but they are not as polarized as those of cohesion analysis (where results from Networks 1 to 4 stand against those from Network 5), suggesting a lesser influence of market share.

TABLE 13.8 Automorphic Equivalence

Hierarchical Clustering of (non)Equivalence Matrix

Network 1

```
             1       1 1 1         1
Level        9 0 3 6 4 5 3 1 2 1 2 7 8 4
--------     - - - - - - - - - - - - - -
  18.493     . . . . . . . . . . . . XXX
  26.723     . . . . . . . . . . . XXXXX
  30.741     . . . . . . . . . . XXX XXXXX
  41.759     . . . . . . . . . . XXXXXXXXX
  46.011     . . . . . XXX . . XXXXXXXXX
  54.635     . . . . . XXX XXX XXXXXXXXX
  78.224     . . . . XXXXX XXX XXXXXXXXX
  85.076     . . . . XXXXX XXXXXXXXXXXXX
 140.382     . . . XXXXXXX XXXXXXXXXXXXX
 356.634     XXX . XXXXXXX XXXXXXXXXXXXX
 369.091     XXX . XXXXXXXXXXXXXXXXXXXXX
 699.925     XXX XXXXXXXXXXXXXXXXXXXXXXX
1229.797     XXXXXXXXXXXXXXXXXXXXXXXXXXX
```

Network 2

```
             1       1 1       1 1
Level        9 0 3 4 5 6 3 2 8 2 1 7 1 4
------       - - - - - - - - - - - - - -
  3.317      . . . . . . . . . XXX . .
  5.292      . . . XXX . . . . . XXX . .
  5.927      . . . XXX . . . . . XXXXX .
  6.108      . . . XXXXX . . . . XXXXX .
  7.359      . . . XXXXX . . . . XXXXXX
  8.325      . . . XXXXX . . . XXXXXXXXX
  8.491      . . XXXXXXX . . . XXXXXXXXX
  9.679      . . XXXXXXXXX . . XXXXXXXXX
 10.677      XXX XXXXXXXXX . . XXXXXXXXX
 11.162      XXX XXXXXXXXX . XXXXXXXXXXX
 13.564      XXX XXXXXXXXX XXXXXXXXXXXXX
 19.739      XXX XXXXXXXXXXXXXXXXXXXXXXX
 35.047      XXXXXXXXXXXXXXXXXXXXXXXXXXX
```

CONCLUSIONS

A number of tentative conclusions can be drawn from our application, some of which are methodological, others substantive. Among the methodological conclusions, let us mention the contribution of network analysis to our understanding of market structures. To this end, equivalence analysis performs pretty well and adds nontrivial aspects to traditional results. It is our opinion that it has to be included in

TABLE 13.8 *Continued*

```
                          Network 3

        1   1           1   1   1
Level   9 0 3 3 4 5 6 8 1 1 7 2 2 4
------  - - - - - - - - - - - - - -
0.000   . . . . . . . . XXXXX . . .
1.414   . . . . . . . . XXXXXXX . .
2.000   XXX . . . . . . XXXXXXX XXX
2.828   XXX . . XXX . . XXXXXXX XXX
3.051   XXX . . XXXXX . XXXXXXX XXX
3.692   XXX . . XXXXX . XXXXXXXXXXX
4.000   XXX XXX XXXXX . XXXXXXXXXXX
4.768   XXX XXX XXXXX XXXXXXXXXXXX
6.517   XXX XXX XXXXXXXXXXXXXXXXXXX
6.962   XXXXXXX XXXXXXXXXXXXXXXXXXX
14.225  XXXXXXXXXXXXXXXXXXXXXXXXXXX
```

```
                          Network 4

        1       1   1     1     1
Level   9 0 3 4 5 3 6 2 8 1 1 2 7 4
------  - - - - - - - - - - - - - -
0.000   . . . XXX . . . XXXXXXXXXXX
1.414   XXX . XXXXX XXX XXXXXXXXXXX
2.962   XXX XXXXXXX XXX XXXXXXXXXXX
7.209   XXXXXXXXXXX XXX XXXXXXXXXXX
7.744   XXXXXXXXXXX XXXXXXXXXXXXXXX
10.785  XXXXXXXXXXXXXXXXXXXXXXXXXXX
```

```
                          Network 5

        1   1 1       1         1
Level   0 9 3 1 2 1 5 4 3 8 6 7 2 4
------  - - - - - - - - - - - - - -
0.000   XXXXX . . . . . . . . . . .
1.414   XXXXX . . . . XXX . XXX . .
2.000   XXXXX XXX . . XXX . XXX XXX
2.702   XXXXX XXX . XXXXX . XXX XXX
3.483   XXXXX XXX XXXXXXX . XXX XXX
3.916   XXXXX XXX XXXXXXX . XXXXXXX
4.918   XXXXX XXX XXXXXXX XXXXXXXXX
5.429   XXXXX XXX XXXXXXXXXXXXXXXXX
5.775   XXXXX XXXXXXXXXXXXXXXXXXXXX
16.855  XXXXXXXXXXXXXXXXXXXXXXXXXXX
```

our existing tool-kit for competitive and structural analysis of brand-switching data. Its promise does not go without limitations, though, due to the lack of robustness to transformations of data and to change of analytical techniques, because they both influence results in a rather dramatic way. This problem is not unbeatable in itself, but it requires that applications are realized in controlled environments and calls for a continuing intervention on the part of the researcher.

Cohesion analysis does not carry any specific problem, if it is not for limitations deriving from the need to symmetrize data, resulting in the loss of important information. From a substantive point of view, the first result has to do with the groupings themselves, which are at times different from those derived from a cursory analysis, common sense or popular wisdom: In particular, the role of "marginal players" Alfa, Lada, Rover, Seat, Volvo, comes out more clearly and improves more traditional partitions of vendors in "locals," "luxury" manufacturers, and the like.

Another important result consists in lending support, even from our very specific standpoint, to the impact of market share on brand switching. When market share is brought into the picture, the traditional groupings based on size disappear and new ones emerge that stand more on similarities. But strangely enough, at that point, new groupings derived from equivalence analysis bring big players back into the picture, because they apparently perform a similar function within the system.

NOTES

1. According to the French National Statistical Office (INSEE), in 1989, 23.9% of French households had no car, 50.6% had just 1 car, 23.1% had 2 cars, and the remaining 2.4% had 3 cars or more.

2. These data were analyzed using the software package UCINET IV developed by Borgatti, Everett, and Freeman (1992). The software has some limitations in cohesion analysis, because it makes symmetric relationships, disregarding the direction of relationships, and transforms valued relationships into binary ones. Equivalence analysis does not suffer those limitations, because directed relationships can be taken into account. In identifying automorphic equivalence, maxsim or geodesic distances are considered depending on the kind of relationships used (valued or binary, respectively).

PART V

Consumer Networks

A Network Perspective on Crossing the Micro-Macro Divide in Consumer Behavior Research

JAMES C. WARD

PETER REINGEN

Consumption is neither individual, social, nor cultural in origin. Instead, consumption results from the reciprocal interaction of all three of these forces, each creating the other. In this chapter, we will propose the network concept as a conceptual and analytical means of bridging individual, social, and cultural levels of analysis. Historically, consumer researchers have focused their study on one of these levels, usually on the individual level, without considering its relation to the other two. Thus, the relation of micro to macro processes has been slighted, even though the interplay of the individual in his or her sociocultural context lies at the heart of many phenomena of vital interest to consumer researchers. We will suggest that conceiving of consumer behavior as a multilevel network phenomenon deepens insight into the "interrelatedness" of phenomena across levels, and also within each level of analysis. Thus, our vision of the interrelations of micro to macro phenomena entails a catholic application of the network idea to not only the social, but also the individual and cultural aspects of consumption.

Better understanding the relation of micro to macro processes has been called the "holy grail" of the social sciences. The greats of early social science, scholars such as Wundt, Durkheim, and Mead, were fascinated by the question of how individual thought and behavior produced society and culture, which in turn molded the individual

(Forgas, 1983). After a long hiatus, perhaps produced by the specialization of the social sciences, the question of how micro and macro
processes interrelate has reasserted itself. A renaissance of scholar-
ship, more often theoretical than empirical, is producing innovative
conceptual approaches to bridging levels of analysis (Cole, 1991;
Howard, 1994; Morgan & Schwalbe, 1990).

Our objective is to outline how relating networks at the individual,
social, and cultural level to one another provides new insights into
concepts central to the study of consumer behavior. The chapter will
proceed by tracing present conceptualizations of phenomena at each
level of analysis, outlining a "wheel of networks" perspective on the
interplay of networks from the individual to the cultural, and then
discussing the insights offered by studying across levels networks: the
cognitive-cultural network, the social-cognitive network, and the
social-cultural network. Thus, we will discuss cognitive networks
originating from culturally inspired and socially shared networks of
logic, and we will conceive of culture as a pattern of variation in the
sharing of individual cognitive networks. We will go on to discuss the
influence of social networks on the formation of individual cognitive
networks and the influence of individual initiative in the construction
of social networks. Finally, we will discuss the influence of cultural
belief systems on social structure and the role of social networks in
the creation of culture. Our intent is to provoke new perspectives and
critical discussion, but not to suggest that our approach is the only
or superior one.

THE PSYCHOLOGICAL, THE SOCIAL,
AND THE CULTURAL IN CONSUMER RESEARCH

Progress in the social sciences has come at the expense of a
splintered view of the human condition. The founders of social
science were fascinated by the relations of individuals with larger
sociocultural phenomena. Forgas (1983) reminds us that Wundt, a
founder of experimental, intraindividual psychology, was also a stu-
dent of "collective psychology," which he wrote of in his 10-volume
opus *Volkerpsychologie*. Many of the early greats of social science,
including Durkheim and Mead, visited Wundt's laboratory at Leipzig
University and were influenced by his fascination with the individual.

and the collective. This influence can be seen in Durkheim's concepts of *"representations individuelles"* and *"representations collectives,"* and Mead's rejection of a separation of individual and social phenomena in favor of the argument that self and society continuously create one another, a cornerstone of the symbolic interactionist perspective.

But especially after the second world war, the social sciences in America became increasingly specialized and increasingly insular. The social sciences began to resemble "closed shops" in which union rules prohibited each trade from doing the other's work or using its tools. Reflecting trends in its "source" disciplines, consumer behavior became specialized also. The result of specialization can be seen from a brief review of how the terms psychological, social, and cultural have come to be defined in the marketing literature.

Consumer researchers overwhelmingly view the psychological level of analysis through the lens of cognitive psychology. Research inspired by this lens regards the internal "information processing" operations of individuals as the focal phenomena, typically measures these as self-reports of isolated individuals in laboratory settings, and rarely concerns the influence of macro processes on micro phenomena. The embeddedness of psychological processes in larger schemes of relations such as culturally shared and socially communicated networks of reasoning has been largely ignored.

The social is a rare focus among consumer researchers. When social relations are the primary focus of inquiry, three approaches are typical: (a) laboratory studies of how the individual consumer reacts to fictive others, (b) descriptions of social structure, perhaps based on participant observation or a literature review, and (c) analyses of how individual consumers are influenced by social ties and their network structure (Brown & Reingen, 1987). In all of these approaches, social structure is usually treated as a given whose interaction with other levels of analysis is rarely examined. What is most missing is a focus on network structure as a dependent variable—a structure shaped by cultural belief systems and individual initiative.

Recent ethnographic studies have provided more insight into the individual-group dynamic (e.g., Schouten & McAlexander, 1995). But perhaps because of the notion of "incommensurability," ethnographic studies have not exploited structured methods for exploring social networks and their interaction with other levels of analysis in systematic detail and depth.

At the cultural level of analysis, the bias toward focusing on one level, culture, as the independent force creating the others persists. In consumer research, culture is usually defined as the beliefs that some collectivity shares. Interpretive ethnographies (e.g., Belk, Sherry, & Wallendorf, 1988) often focus on shared meanings as organizing principles of consumption behavior, even if they are rarely articulated by the participants themselves. Such analyses view (a) culture as a mysterious haze, floating above the sociocognitive matrix, influencing those below but not influenced by them; and (b) culture as uniformly shared among participants. Although the most widely shared elements of culture are critical to understand, as is their "invisible hand" influence, culture can also be conceived and studied in ways that highlight the uneven sharing created by its constant, mutually procreative interactions with other levels of analysis.

Our review of consumer behavior approaches to the psychological, social, and cultural aspects of consumption reveals a persistent insistence on viewing each level as a discrete phenomena, particularly in studies relying on structured measures. Far from being the focus of investigation, their reciprocal relations are either ignored, treated as methodological nuisances, or perhaps forced into an independent-dependent variable relation. Ethnographic research has shown far more sensitivity to bridging levels of analysis, but much opportunity remains to study how the particular is translated into the general and vice versa.

NETWORKS AS AN APPROACH TO BRIDGING MICRO TO MACRO LEVELS OF ANALYSIS

We will next outline the power of the network concept for studying the *interrelatedness* of phenomena, in particular the interrelatedness of individual, social, and cultural phenomena, but also the interrelatedness of phenomena within each level of analysis.

How can these levels of analysis be conceived as networks? The idea of conceiving of social structure as a network comprising actors (nodes) and the social ties between them (links) is familiar. But the network concept is just as apropos for characterizing the individual and cultural levels of analysis. At the individual level, reasoning, mental models, schemas, and memory processes have all been represented as networks of linked concepts (Galotti, 1989; Gentner, 1983; Lunt & Livingstone, 1991). At the cultural level, the network metaphor is novel, but not without precedent. In particular, the 19th-century notion of "group mind" implies a collective mental network (Wegner, 1987). In our view, if we search for the core of a culture, we often find a belief system, a network of reasoning relating actions, events, and objects to end goals. Such belief systems include religions, political ideologies, moral philosophies, and other systems of reasoning about how to live such as health fads, cults, and personal success schemes.

How is conceiving of culture and other levels of analysis as networks facilitative of revealing their interaction? As a metaphor, and as an analytic perspective, the network idea promotes understanding of how a node, tie, or subgraph at any level of analysis relates to the presence, frequency, or network position of a node, tie, or subgraph at other levels of analysis. The generality of the network idea enhances its power for across-levels analysis. Nodes may be people or concepts. Links may be social or logical. This across-levels network perspective encourages questions about how network structure at one level influences network structure at another level. For example, how does the cognitive network centrality of a particular pattern of reasoning relate to the social centrality of individuals, and vice versa? Besides facilitating across-levels analysis, the network perspective encourages understanding the relatedness of elements within any single level of analysis.

THE WHEEL OF NETWORKS

Networks at the individual, social, and cultural levels continuously interact in creating one another. Thus, the network concept supplies the *leitmotif* for an across-levels perspective on consumer endeavor, which we illustrate by the "Wheel of Networks" shown in Figure 14.1. We trisect the circle by the cultural, social, and cognitive networks. The choice of a circle to represent their relation was not a graphic convenience, but an attempt to suggest that these networks (a) continuously recreate one another, (b) are not in a "higher-lower" hierarchical relationship suggested by the term "levels," and (c) together create the gestalt or "worldview" through which an individual or group perceives the world.

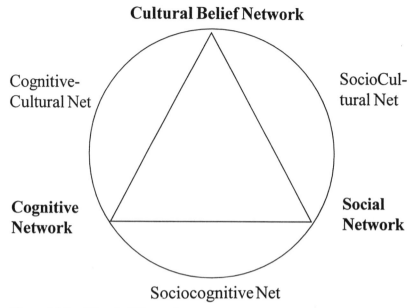

Figure 14.1.   Wheel of Networks

The wheel illustrates our concern with the interrelation of networks. As we traverse the wheel, the link from the cultural to the cognitive defines the cognitive-cultural net, the link from cognitive to social defines the social-cognitive net, and the link from social to cultural defines the social-cultural net. Our cardinal interest is in these intersections.

We will illustrate the insights gained from across-levels network analysis with data from a study of participants in two subcultures—macrobiotics and animal rights activists who were customers of a natural food store. The study, Sirsi, Ward, and Reingen (1996), traces variation in the sharing of causal reasoning about food consumption to three sources: cultural belief networks, social networks, and individual differences in belief system expertise. Each phenomenon is conceived as a network. The study began with a lengthy ethnography resulting in a broad, qualitative understanding of the cognitive, social, and belief system networks operant in the macrobiotic and animal rights subcultures. Based on this understanding, we measured individual cognitive networks via cognitive mapping and social networks via interaction measures. These networks were related to one another by the analysis of sharing at one level while holding the others constant. We will rely on a subset of the findings, maps of variation in sharing in reasoning about food avoidance, to illustrate the potential insights offered by analyzing the intersection nets in the wheel of networks.

These maps of sharing and variation are based on individual participants' "cognitive maps," which capture their causal reasoning about food consumption. The individual maps were constructed by a task that proceeded as follows: Participants were presented with a large board displaying stickers each containing a belief statement about food. These belief statements were selected on the basis of the ethnographic study to represent a broad range of beliefs relevant to food consumption in each microculture. The board also contained arrow stickers. On a second large board, four behaviors were listed on four stickers: never consume, generally avoid, consume occasionally, and consume regularly.

After a participant was shown the boards, the mapping task was explained. For each of the foods, the participant was asked to choose a behavior that he or she engaged in toward the product (e.g., never consume), and then select the belief statements relevant to explaining his or her behavior. The participant then arranged the belief statements on a board to reflect his or her emic view of the reasoning behind the behavior. Belief statements were linked with arrow stickers to indicate their perceived direction of causality. The initial outputs of the mapping task were individual cognitive maps showing the participants' causal reasoning about why they avoided or consumed various foods. Each of these maps could be viewed as a network of nodes (belief statements) connected by causal relations (the arrow stickers). The individual cognitive networks for each of the foods were then analyzed for sharing of nodes and causal relations. The analysis of sharing was conducted across expert and novice participants within each subculture, across subgroups defined by social network analysis, and across subcultural belief systems.

Figure 14.2 is a map of shared cognitions for macrobiotic experts and macrobiotic novices. Figure 14.3 shows maps for animal rights experts, intermediates, and novices. Each map shows the concepts and causal connections shared by at least 50% of map contributors about why they avoid a food.

In the maps, concepts are shown as circles. The percentage of participants sharing a concept for each avoided product is shown

MACROBIOTIC EXPERTS

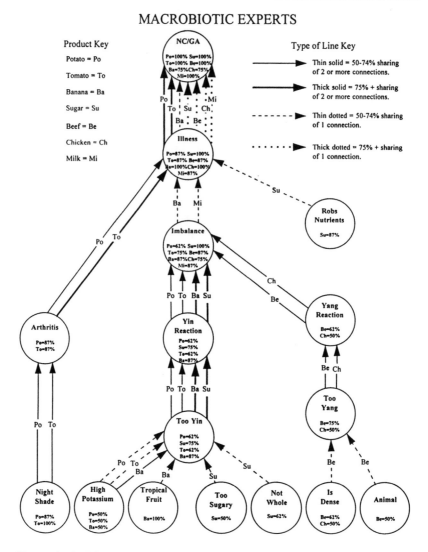

Figure 14.2. Macrobiotic Cognitive-Cultural Network

within the circle (e.g., Figure 14.2 shows that 87% of macrobiotic experts identified potato as a nightshade vegetable). Causal relations between concepts are shown by directed lines. The lines show variance in sharing by their thickness and continuity. The thickness of

MACROBIOTIC NOVICES

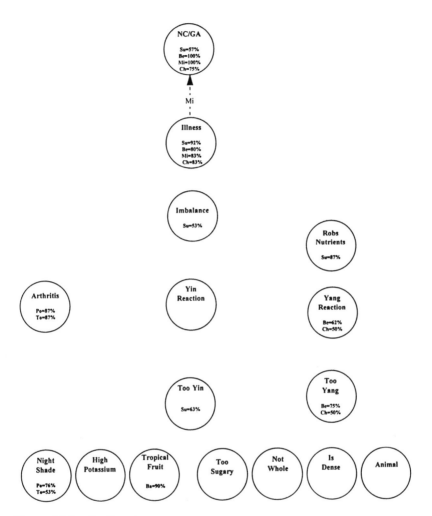

Figure 14.2. *Continued*

the lines indicates the degree to which the casual connections are shared. A thin line indicates the connection is shared by 50% to 74% of respondents (e.g., the thin line for tomato in Figure 14.2 indicating "nightshade" causes "arthritis"). A thick line indicates the connection is

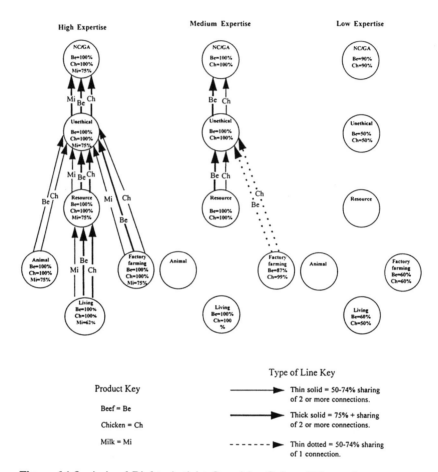

Figure 14.3. Animal Rights Activist Cognitive-Cultural Network

shared by 75% or more of respondents (e.g., the thick line for tomato in Figure 14.2 indicating that "arthritis" causes "illness"). Solid lines indicate shared connections of more than two concepts. Dotted lines indicate a shared connection between just two concepts.

We will refer to these maps to illustrate the power of the network perspective for revealing the relations of micro and macro phenomena, and the relatedness of phenomena at each level. We will begin by discussing how a multilevel network perspective can shed new light on some traditional streams of consumer research.

THE COGNITIVE-CULTURAL NETWORK

The links "downward" from cultural belief networks to individual cognitive networks, and the links "upward" from individual cognitive networks to cultural belief networks have not been a focus of inquiry in consumer research. Cultural belief systems not only have a pervasive influence on individual cognition, but individuals also influence sharing and variation in culture through their roles as its keepers and creators.

Our maps of shared reasoning structures provide insight into both the effects of culture on cognition and the effects of individuals on the distribution of sharing of a culture's belief system. The maps thus can be viewed as representations of "cultural mind" and as representations of intracultural variation due to individual differences.

The influence of cultural belief networks is apparent in the maps of expert macrobiotics and animal rights activists. The most shared concepts and paths of reasoning in these maps reflect the core principles of each subculture. During our ethnographic investigation, we noted that participants in either belief system, once they accepted a premise highly central in the cultural belief net (e.g., that animals have rights), felt a logical pressure to organize all their cognitions and behaviors to be consistent with the belief system. The power of cultural belief networks to channel cognition is suggested by this observation: Despite the propinquity of the macrobiotics and activists at the natural food store, and despite similar behaviors and their mutual concern about the environment, the two sets of subcultural participants share virtually nothing in the intersection of their cognitive maps.

The maps also suggest the influence of individuals on the sharing of culture. Comparing the expert and novice maps reveals a startling contrast between the shared reasoning structures of experts and novices. In both subcultures, the experts seemed to be the repository of what many ethnographers would be tempted to characterize as the culture, that is, shared meanings, beliefs, and logics of action. In contrast, the novices in each culture share little of the belief system. The figure shows that they share primarily concepts (often those also shared by experts) but not the more complex chains of reasoning linking products to behavior. In each subculture, experts were a minority of members, yet they seemed to exercise influence disproportionate to their numbers on group reasoning and action. The influence of cultural belief networks on individual cognitive structures and processes also suggests a fresh perspective on such staples of consumer research as attribution, categorization, and attitude models.

Attribution

Attributions can be viewed as merely one aspect of the broader phenomena of everyday reasoning guided by cultural theories about the causes of events. The marketing literature has continued to study attribution from the perspectives of paradigms developed by Kelley, Weiner, and Jones (Folkes, 1988). Each of these approaches focuses on people's retrospective attributions about some outcome or behavior to a few causal dimensions such as internal/external, stable/unstable, and control/uncontrollable. By reducing the study of attribution to a few causal dimensions, these approaches tend to obscure the influence of elaborate and specific cultural belief networks on individual reasoning about causality. A glance at the macrobiotic expert map suggests the complex influence of cultural belief systems on causal reasoning. To illustrate, if a person not sharing the macrobiotic belief system eats a hamburger at a fast food restaurant and gets sick, he or she would be likely to attribute the event to an external, controllable, perhaps unstable cause—that is, a "bad" hamburger, clearly the fault of the restaurant. If a participant in the macrobiotic belief system has the same experience, he or she would likely attribute the sickness to the body's natural reaction to a yang imbalance, an internal, controllable, stable attribution, clearly not the restaurant's fault.

In addition to illustrating how cultural belief networks shape individual reasoning, our maps show that the network of such reasoning is far more complex than can be captured by a few simple causal dimensions (Kelley, 1983a). We see that specific causes are linked to specific effects, these cause-effect linkages are networked together, some causes are more central than others, some causes are more proximate to behavior and some are more distal, and some cause-effect linkages are only potential in the sense that they depend on prior causes to be invoked. The networks of culturally inspired reasoning captured by the maps suggest some interesting prospects for deeper insights into the origin of consumer causal attributions.

Categorization

Cultural belief networks influence categorization, although the theory and methods used to study categorization rarely recognize this influence. Instead, they adopt a particularistic view of the origins of classification in individuals and object attributes. For example, prototype approaches represent category members as a list of the features most commonly listed for category members. We suggest that this approach does not highlight the logical relations among features arising by socioculturally transmitted networks of reasoning. If Product A (e.g., sugar in the macrobiotic expert map) is characterized by features X (too sugary), Y (too yin), and Z (causes imbalance), and if X causes Y and Y causes Z, we are missing an important aspect of category structure if we ignore the causal relations among attributes. Also, feature list approaches do not emphasize the issue of feature selection: Why are some features listed for many category members, some for a few, and some for none at all? Once again, the network approach suggests that broader networks of causal reasoning influence the assignment of features to objects. For example, the macrobiotic expert map shows that macrobiotic theory creates at least three broad categories of foods to be avoided—too yin, too yang, and nightshade. The belief system assigns foods to these categories because they are perceived to possess characteristics specified by macrobiotic theory to be diagnostic of inclusion. Once assigned to a category, theory also specifies the food to have many other features. Relative to the "traditional" approaches to categorization extant in the consumer literature, the network approach emphasizes a search for the relatedness of object features to one another, and a search for the origin of this relatedness in culturally shared theory networks.

Attitude

Cultural belief systems also are likely to strongly influence consumer attitudes in ways that the network metaphor highlights. In consumer behavior, we have conceived of and measured attitudes using a model incorporating ratings of a set of five to nine "salient beliefs" about an action or object. The network perspective accentuates several aspects of attitude the traditional model does not. First, the network perspective draws attention to the origins of salient beliefs evoked by larger systems of reasoning. Second, awareness of cultural belief systems naturally emphasizes the possible relations among salient beliefs. In traditional attitude models, once belief ratings are elicited, they are usually analyzed as if they are independent of one another. For example, a macrobiotic's salient beliefs about foods might concern their effects on health, their effects on the body's "balance," and their yin/yang properties. What this list does not reveal is the causal relations among these beliefs and their sociocultural origins. For instance, if potato is judged too yin, then it is also judged as imbalanced and thus bad for health. Furthermore, our maps show that salient beliefs may be cued by "trigger" beliefs. To illustrate, the macrobiotic expert map shows that the belief "high in potassium" for potato cues a shared chain of reasoning that includes all three of the above noted salient beliefs.

Our purpose in the preceding brief discussions of attribution, categorization, and attitude research in consumer behavior is not to point out the failings of past work but to highlight alternative aspects of these cognitive phenomena—namely, their relatedness to networks of reasoning within the individual and broader networks beyond the individual.

SOCIAL-COGNITIVE NETWORKS

The concept of social-cognitive networks suggests that the individual and the group—cognitive structure and social structure—act on one another. Sirsi et al.'s (1996) study of macrobiotic and animal rights activist microcultures found intimate links between cognitive and social networks. In both groups, expertise (the complexity of cognitive nets) was strongly related to structural position in social nets. In each microculture, one subgroup consisted primarily of high-expertise participants, whereas dyads and isolates were usually of lower expertise. Furthermore, in each microculture, expertise was positively related to prestige, or the receipt of social ties. Figure 14.4, from Sirsi et al. (1996), illustrates the relations among expertise, social network structure, and the sharing of reasoning about milk consumption among an animal rights subgroup (top) and strong-tie isolates (bottom). Numbered boxes are individuals. Experts are delineated by thick lines, intermediates by thin. Cognitive maps for milk consumption are shown in circles (never consume, generally avoid, consume occasionally, consume regularly). The top map shows that experts are tightly linked to one another, that they share key paths of reasoning about milk, and that none consumes milk. Cognitive and social structure are strongly related. The bottom graph of activist isolates shows that social isolation, a lack of expertise, and a paucity of sharing seem all to be related. These graphs clearly show the reciprocal influence of social and cognitive networks, influences we will next discuss from the perspective of the social and then the individual.

Social Network Influences on the Individual

The image of the lone individual mulling over a purchase decision is implicit in the majority of consumer research studies, but likely characterizes a subset of actual purchase decisions. Many individual consumer choices are influenced by groups—family, neighbors, coworkers, or friends. Ward and Reingen (1990) introduced the concept of sociocognitive analysis to consumer research. They assessed changes in sorority sisters' individual and shared cognitions about their choice of a party theme from Time 1 (prior to social interaction) to Time 2 (after social interaction). The study found relationships between social network structure, social communication, changes in shared positive and negative beliefs, and preference change.

Individual Influences on Social Networks

Turning from the influence of social networks on the individual to the influence of the individual on social networks, we suggest that the network metaphor often encourages a passive view of the individual as caught in a web of ties not of his or her personal making, playing his or her role as a "node" that receives, accepts, and transmits whatever information or influence that travels along the net. An emphasis on cross-levels interaction promotes a different, more proactive

STRONG-TIE ANIMAL RIGHTS SUBGROUP

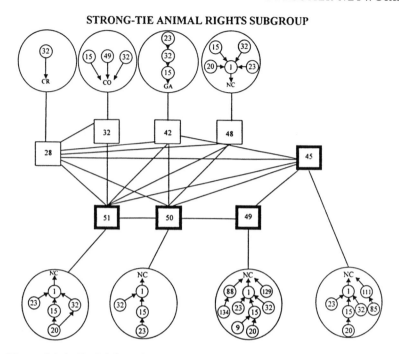

Figure 14.4. Social-Cognitive Network

view of the individual. We are daily confronted with individuals actively constructing, pruning, and using their networks to achieve multiple objectives with the cooperation of others who may share less with them than might by suggested by the notion of homophily. For example, professionals often assume roles in their community seemingly unrelated to their work to construct far-reaching networks of referral among the "right" people (Callero, 1994). Entrepreneurs commonly network with the owners of a wide range of other types of businesses in their community because of the potential of such ties to generate help, information, or revenue in unexpected ways. Consumers often construct networks of neighbors or coworkers who have little in common beyond their propinquity and the broadest demographic characteristics. These networks are frequently nonoverlapping groups constructed to facilitate specific activities: nights out on Friday, garage sales on Saturday, volunteer activities on Sunday.

STRONG-TIE ANIMAL RIGHTS ISOLATES

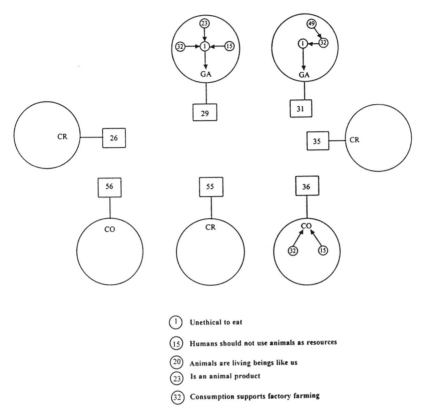

Figure 14.4. *Continued*

Furthermore, some consumers are much more involved in net-working activities than others. The concept of "market maven" (Feick & Price, 1987)—an expert on what and where to buy—could be expanded by the concept of "social maven"—a person who is highly involved in understanding and using social networks, often to facili-tate consumption activity. Virtually every established neighborhood has such a social maven—a person who knows which neighbor has a sought-after tool, which neighbor to ask for advice about wallpaper-ing, and which neighbor knows an attorney who handled a particular problem successfully. Social mavens seem to not only specialize in constructing large personal networks of direct ties, they also seem interested in developing expert knowledge of other people's networks, resulting in elaborate cognitive representations of their direct ties and also indirect ties. Research on social mavens may yield fresh insight into the sociocognitive dynamics of consumer behavior.

Sociocognitive Mind as a Meta-Network

The relationship between the individual and group in consumer decision making is more intimate than might be suggested by the foregoing discussions of network influences on individual cognition and individual influences on network structure. In everyday consumer situations, individuals rely on groups to an extent that blurs the boundaries between individual and group cognition. The notion of "group mind" is one that many researchers almost automatically dismiss with the comment, "Of course, groups don't think."

A new wave of thought about the nature of group mind, however, has emerged in recent years (Larson & Christenson, 1993; Wegner, 1987). Contemporary theorists avoid the claim that a group mind is a conscious entity, but they do observe that people commonly rely on knowledge beyond the contents of their own memory to make decisions. In particular, people often use their social networks as external memory, thus blending the social and cognitive seamlessly into a sort of social hard drive capable of holding vast amounts of information outside organic memory. All the user needs to access this hard drive is a database in his own memory listing file names (who knows what) and file relations (who knows whom). Detailed knowledge of file contents is not needed. Consumers commonly access their sociocognitive mind to help make consumption decisions. For example, suppose Neighbor A wants to buy a cellular phone, but is a novice about this product category. He or she recalls that Neighbor B, two blocks away, is a ham radio operator who is likely expert about cell phones. A has no social tie to B, but A knows that Neighbor C is friends with B. Of course, A gets C to introduce him or her to B, who is pleased to provide the requested expertise. This scenario is mundane, yet illustrates the simultaneous operation of networks at several levels—networks of product knowledge, social networks, and "cognitive" social networks (cognitive networks about who knows whom). This latter type of net has not been a focus of research in the social networks literature in consumer research, but may be a crucial determinant of whether a socially connected individual exploits the mental resources available in a network effectively or not. To use a group memory system effectively, a member needs to know its social structure, to know what direct and indirect ties know, and to be socially central to minimize the steps to reach any one knowledge store.

Wegner (1987) defines what he calls a "transactive memory system" as "a set of individual memory systems in combination with the communication that takes place between individuals" (p. 186). Although not captured in this definition, Wegner regards "metamemory," the memory for who knows what, to be a crucial determinant of whether individuals are effective in their use of group memory, and collectively, whether an organization has an effective collective memory system. Suppose, for example, that the person who answers the phone at a service organization, say, a marketing department in a business school, has only a hazy idea of which professor is expert at what. The phone answerer is then likely to make inefficient and problematic referrals of callers to faculty. Suppose further that the faculty have an incomplete idea of the research projects, areas of expertise, and professional contacts of one another. Once again, the group's memory system is inefficient, perhaps creating other inefficiencies in the department's work. Clearly, the memory systems of groups can also be viewed as networks.

The latter assertion is also supported by the tendency of groups to assign members "responsibility" for remembering information about different topics. Typically, a tightly knit group becomes knowledgeable about who within the group is expert about various topics. For example, Larry is the expert fisherman among a group of friends who often go trout fishing. The group is getting "skunked" one weekend, but learns from other fishermen that the trout are biting on a type of fly the group did not bring. Of course, Larry is joshingly blamed for not knowing what type of fly would be "hot" that day. Ted, on the other hand, is known to be handy with cars. If the old pickup truck the group took to the stream breaks down, Ted will be blamed by Larry and the others for not anticipating the problem. Once again, these examples are mundane, but they illustrate that once group members come to know one anothers' expertise, they assign informal responsibility for the category of "fishing knowledge" or "automotive knowledge" to the expert group member. Research on how larger social networks divvy up responsibility for remembering is lacking, but could reveal fascinating interactions among social network position, group memory "responsibilities," and attributions for blame.

SOCIAL-CULTURAL NETWORKS

Cultural belief networks and social networks interact in ways we have so far not emphasized. Just as cultural belief systems shape individual cognitive structures, they may also influence individuals' propensity to forge social ties with one another, and a group's preference for one form of social organization over another. Social networks, in turn, are the conduits through which belief change spreads in subcultures and outward to the wider culture.

The cultural universe of a pluralistic society contains many subuniverses defined by the cultural belief networks, the "worldviews," of the participants. These cultural belief networks are likely to have a "core" set of beliefs, high in network centrality, and more "peripheral" beliefs. The extent to which participants in these belief systems share core beliefs is likely to be closely related to their propensity to form close social ties. The force of this point is more apparent if we consider the likelihood of a highly committed pro-life activist, a member of NOW, and an "outlaw" biker becoming close personal friends. Their core beliefs are simply so repugnant to one another that interaction, perhaps even propinquity, is offensive. In our investigation of macrobiotics and animal rights activists, we found that despite the participants' many peripheral commonalities and ready access to one another at the store, they formed no social ties. In both groups, reasoning about food was at the core of their belief system. In particular, the macrobiotics evaluated food, including animal products, by the potential of the food to contribute to balance or imbalance in their bodies. They usually avoided meat as too yang, but occasional servings of white meat fish to correct a yin imbalance were to them not only moral but necessary. Committed animal rights advocates, vegans, held the clashing core belief that consuming any animal product was a moral sin. Given these conflicting core beliefs, social discourse between participants in these subcultures was not likely.

So far, we have focused on the influence of the cultural net on the social net. Just as important are the ways in which social networks influence cultural learning and change. In our study, we found that in each subculture, experts—macrobiotic "gurus" and activist "vegans"— were situated in relatively dense cliques at the center of their subcultures' social network. Not accidentally, we also noted that the few culture-relevant concepts novices shared at the 50% level were also those most shared in expert maps. In each subculture, the experts were ideally situated in the social network to shape novice cognitive networks to their liking.

On a broader scale, social innovation may be most likely to occur in local groups that share a belief system. We have called these local groups of belief system participants "microcultures." The sociocultural conditions in such groups are remarkably similar to what a group facilitator might recommend as ideal to encourage creativity: a face-to-face group, familiar enough with one another to facilitate communication, highly involved in a particular issue, and sharing core beliefs but also including much variation in ideas about the topic (Moore, 1994). Such local groups are often the source of new ideas that "bubble up" to the broader culture. The operation of these local forces, and perhaps their relevance to marketers, is illustrated well by the rock music industry in which many creative trends originate in local cultures, for example, the Seattle "grunge rock" movement that swept the nation. Such "sounds," although often identified with a city, may originate among relatively small networks of musicians and their followers within a metropolis. Thus, "microcultural analysis," with its focus on the local study of the relation of cultural belief networks to social networks and individual cognitive networks, holds promise for the study of the relation of culture to consumption behavior.

CONCLUSIONS

We began with the intent of showing how a multilevel network perspective could provoke novel insights into the origins of consumption behavior. We described how networks at different levels of analysis interrelate, and thus help build bridges across the "micro-macro" divide in the study of consumption behavior. The conception of individual, social, and cultural phenomena as networks facilitated analysis of their interrelatedness both between and within levels of analysis. In particular, the concepts of cognitive-cultural, social-cognitive, and social-cultural networks led to suggestions about the reciprocal character of these phenomena that are conducive to further research.

CHAPTER 15

Examining the Embedded Markets of Network Marketing Organizations

KENT GRAYSON

A n "embedded market" is one in which economic and social exchange are intermingled (Frenzen & Davis, 1990; Granovetter, 1985). The embeddedness of marketing exchanges has long been recognized (e.g., Bagozzi, 1975) and has recently been given considerable prominence by researchers focusing on relationship marketing (e.g., Dwyer, Schurr, & Oh, 1987; Moorman, Zaltman, & Deshpande, 1992; Morgan & Hunt, 1994). The purpose of this chapter is to highlight the potential research value of a highly embedded marketing strategy called "network marketing," which is sometimes also called "multi-level marketing" or "MLM." Network marketing organizations are likely to foster highly embedded exchange because they build their sales and distribution via the social network of their sales agents.

The chapter is divided into two sections. Because network marketing is not a generally well-known or well-understood marketing strategy, the first portion outlines some of the industry's basic elements, and addresses some of the concerns that are sometimes raised about network marketing. The second portion of the chapter highlights two potential research questions about network marketing, both of which address the ways in which the industry's social aspects may foster or hinder profitability. To develop and support these research issues, exploratory interviews were conducted with 17 net-

AUTHOR'S NOTE: The author is grateful to London Business School's Centre for Marketing for its support of this project and to Richard Berry for his helpful comments.

325

work marketing salespeople in the United Kingdom, paying particular attention to the social network implications of their profession. These interviews were analyzed in light of additional data collected as part of an ongoing study of the network marketing industry, and provide a basis for this chapter's conclusions and recommendations.

A NETWORK
MARKETING PRIMER

Network marketing organizations rely almost wholly on independent sales agents to market their products. Thus, these products are rarely (if ever) advertised via mass media or found in retail outlets. Instead, products are promoted, sold, and often personally distributed by individuals whose full- or part-time job is to act as an independent agent for the organization. What makes network marketing sales agents different from other direct-sales agents is that the former are rewarded for playing many more marketing roles than the latter. In particular, a network marketing agent, often called a "distributor," is encouraged to play not only the role of salesperson, but also that of personnel recruiter, sales manager, and end-user. These four roles and the reward structures that support them are outlined next.

Selling Product

Like other direct-selling agents, network marketing distributors are rewarded for selling products to end users. This reward comes in two forms: sales margins and sales commissions. Sales margins are earned when network marketing distributors buy company products at a discount and sell them at a higher retail price. These margins are usually no lower than 20% of wholesale and can be as high as 100% of wholesale. This element of network marketing is similar to the standard arrangement between a retailer and a manufacturer. In addition, network marketing distributors earn a commission on the products they sell. This rate usually begins at about 3% to 5% and increases with volume, sometimes exceeding 30% at the highest volume levels.[1]

Recruiting Others
to Sell Product

Network marketing distributors are rewarded not only for their own sales, but also for the sales of others whom they have recruited into the network. To understand this portion of the network marketing reward structure, imagine that you are a network marketing distributor and that your friend, Mary, is interested in becoming a distributor as well. If you sponsored Mary as a distributor, then Mary would become part of your "downline." From then on, Mary's sales would increase your earnings in two ways. First, you would earn a commission on Mary's sales, based on a commission rate that would change depending on Mary's sales relative to yours (This rate, however, would rarely fall below 3% to 5%.) Second, your parent company would determine your personal commission rate by combining your sales with Mary's. Because commission rates increase with volume, adding Mary's volume to yours would increase the percentage commission you earn on your own sales. Of course, Mary would also receive commissions according to the same plan, but only on those sales for which she or her downline were responsible.

Managing a Network
of Distributors

Your expanding commission potential would not stop with Mary. As a network marketing distributor, you would have the option of sponsoring a number of people in addition to Mary, each of whom would impact your earnings in the same way. And if Mary sponsored a third person, Joe, into the network, then commissions on his sales would be earned not only by him and Mary, but also by you. In fact, most companies would give you commission on up to five or six "levels" below you. Furthermore, the sales volume of all individuals in your downline would be added to your own volume for determination of your commission rate. Thanks to all of these factors, the network marketing compensation system explicitly rewards distributors for using their recruitment, training, and management skills to develop a thriving and growing sales network.

Using the Product

Unlike many other direct-selling agents, network marketing distributors are strongly encouraged to use the product(s) offered by the organization they represent. Because most network marketing products are consumer-targeted repeat-purchase items, members of the salesforce are generally eligible to become loyal product consumers. By developing a growing salesforce of individuals who are also product users, a network marketing company increases its volume as quickly as it increases its distribution range.

Encouragement to use the product comes in three forms: financial, managerial, and psycho-social. Financial encouragement is offered via product discounts and commissions. As mentioned previously, distributors can buy their company's products at a discount, which often means an opportunity to enjoy quality products at a reasonable price. In fact, many individuals first sign up to become distributors solely for this reason—they like the product and would prefer not to pay retail prices for it. Also, because a distributor earns commission on his or her personal purchases, buying product for personal consumption increases that distributor's commission check.

Although sales managers of all kinds advise using products as a way of developing product familiarity (e.g., Ogilvy, 1983, pp. 56-57; Wasserman, 1985, pp. 41-43), this encouragement is stronger in network marketing. Most network marketing managers advise that product usage is the only way to develop the genuine excitement that is necessary for sales success. Carmichael's (1991, p. 65) assertion is a typical reflection of this ethos: "If you use [the product] yourself and can genuinely enthuse about it, you are endowing it with a veritable seal of approval. Your belief will sell the product more effectively than any advertising" (see also Clothier, 1994; Failla, 1984).

Last, as Biggart (1989), Butterfield (1985), and Peven (1968) have documented, network marketing organizations often establish strong social pressures and rewards for distributor consumption of company products. For example, Biggart (1989, pp. 105-120) describes the way in which some network marketing companies equate product usage with patriotism and good parenthood. In sum, these three factors (financial, managerial, and psycho-social) provide a complex set of reasons and encouragements for personal product usage.

The Economic and Legal Viability
of Network Marketing

Network marketing companies like Amway Corporation and Shaklee Corporation have each operated prosperously in the United States for over 30 years (Roha, 1991). Amway, with sales of nearly $5 billion annually, has been among the most aggressive in terms of international expansion, having entered 10 new countries during the 1980s, and having launched in 10 more countries between 1990 and 1994 (Doebele, 1994). Other successful network marketing companies include: Nu Skin International, whose 1994 sales were $500 million (von Daehne, 1994); Herbalife International, a publicly traded company with 1992 sales of $405 million (Linden & Stern, 1993); Cabouchon, a U.K.-based jewelry company with $120 million in sales ("A Good Idea," 1995); and Melaleuca Inc., which has been named five times to *Inc.* magazine's 500 fastest-growing privately owned companies (Inc., 1994). Although network marketing companies have marketed everything from jewelry (Eskin, 1991) to legal insurance (Thompson, 1987), they are probably best known for their successful marketing of health and beauty products.

In the United Kingdom, network marketing accounts for £292 million ($453 million) annually, which is nearly 31% of total annual direct-selling revenues in that country (Direct Selling Association/U.K. Research Unit, 1995). In the United States, the percentage is much higher, with 70% of annual direct-selling volumes ($11.6 billion) generated by network marketing (Direct Selling Association/U.S.A., 1995). Despite this economic success, there is a perception among many consumers, practitioners, and researchers that network marketing is, at heart, an illegal business strategy. This is in part because network marketing is often confused with its illegal cousins, such as the pyramid scheme, the chain letter, and the Ponzi scheme (Grafton & Posey, 1990, pp. 599-600). Many of these schemes are illegal because they often do not require the selling of a product, and instead reward individuals for simply signing up others into the network. Even if a product is offered, a scheme can still be illegal if it encourages distributors to develop extensive product inventories, thus generating sales for the company without actual end-user purchases. In addition, a scheme is illegal if it promises unrealistically high incomes to potential distributors.

Such illegal schemes are sometimes confused with network marketing because, like network marketing organizations, these depend on social networks for developing revenue and distribution. Confusion is further enhanced by the fact that, during network marketing's infancy, no useful guidelines had been developed for distinguishing a viable network marketing company from an illegal one. Thus, even some well-intentioned organizations engaged in practices that were later deemed illegal (e.g., rewarding distributors for recruitment alone or encouraging the development of inventories).

Since that time, however, in the United States, the Federal Trade Commission has clarified the distinction between a legal and illegal network business—primarily in decisions rendered for Ger-ro-mar Inc. (1974), Holiday Magic Inc. (1974), and Koscot Interplanetary Inc. (1975). These decisions made explicit the following guidelines for viable network marketing organizations:

a. Compensation plans should strongly encourage each and every distributor, regardless of level, to personally generate significant retail sales.

b. Distributors should be protected from overbuying inventory, for example, via recourse to a company buy-back policy.

c. Distributors should not be compensated for the recruitment of new agents per se, but can be compensated for the product sales of these agents and their networks.

d. Nothing more than a nominal fee should be required for becoming a distributor, and distributors should not be allowed to purchase status at any given network level.

e. Extraordinary or unrealistic incomes should not be promised.

The history and impact of these legal decisions are more fully explored in Bartlett (1994, pp. 54-63), Griffin (1981), Hines (1988), and Stone and Steiner (1984), and are reflected in guidelines throughout the world (e.g., the U.K. Direct Selling Association's Code of Business Conduct, and Clothier, 1994). Yet, because few people keep abreast of legal and professional developments in the direct-selling industry, most are still not aware of the distinction between a legal and illegal network marketing plan. This is exacerbated by the fact that, still today, network marketing organizations face legal ramifications for alleged violations of the above regulations (e.g., Behar, 1985; Yamada, 1992). Thus, network marketing organizations are often seen as operating "on the borderline of what is legal and ethical" (Bonoma, 1991).

These legal concerns have helped to foster other negative impressions about the viability of network marketing. One of the most pervasive concerns is that network marketing organizations are prone to exponential growth and will therefore quickly saturate their markets. It is therefore argued that it is easy for those who join early to be successful, and nearly impossible for those who join late. Simple exponential mathematics are often used to support these claims: If 5 distributors sign up 5 friends who in turn recruit 5 more friends, and so on for 10 levels, then this single network would account for more than 12 million people. Furthermore, because the start-up costs for a network marketing organization are much lower than for many other businesses, distributors expand their businesses more quickly than managers of other franchises or start-ups. Last, the growth of a network marketing distribution system is highly decentralized, and this lack of central control will increase the likelihood that the business will expand beyond what is economically justifiable.

These perspectives emphasize the differences between network marketing organizations and other businesses. To put these claims in perspective, however, it is also useful to recognize the similarities. In their summary of legal issues related to network marketing, Grafton and Posey (1990) reflect this spirit:

> Nearly every manufacturing firm uses a system of middlemen to distribute its products. A pyramid shape emerges, with the manufacturer on top, supported by an ever-widening group of wholesalers and retailers, with a broad base of consumers at the pyramid's foundation. Multilevel [or network marketing] franchises combine both traditional distribution and direct door-to-door selling techniques. . . . Neither the existence of a large direct sales force nor a market system that forms a pyramid shape indicates that a distribution system is illegal. (pp. 599-600)

In this same vein, it is important to acknowledge that the opportunities inherent in any given business will change as the business becomes more prevalent and successful. Marketing and operating the first McDonald's in a city is much different from managing the 35th. Yet both can be successful.

Second, like other businesses, network marketing organizations are slow to reach a complete saturation point because of the standard market frictions that result from differing human abilities, motivations, and preferences. Even when a network marketing organization is starting out in a market, selling and recruiting is a difficult sales process. For example, network marketing executives estimate that 70% of the adult population is unlikely to become a new recruit and that a majority of the remaining 30% do not aggressively build a network (Coughlan & Grayson, 1994). This same research suggests that time constraints are a major factor in determining success, although differing skill levels certainly also play a role. Personal goals will also influence individual success and overall network growth—many people join network marketing organizations to generate only a moderate amount of part-time income.

Last, although distribution growth in network marketing organizations is indeed decentralized, this does not imply that individual distributors haphazardly or irresponsibly develop their business without regard for market viability. Signing up new recruits is only the first step toward building a successful network and usually nets a distributor little or no income. Having joined a network, a new distributor must be trained and managed to both sell product and recruit new distributors—an activity that consumes between 40% and 50% of a distributor's time (Coughlan & Grayson, 1994). Given these realities of salesforce management, some network marketing managers advise distributors to focus on recruiting and developing a small number (e.g., five) of excellent distributors rather than on signing up any and all takers (Failla, 1984).

NETWORK MARKETING
AND SOCIAL NETWORKS

To understand how network marketing sales strategies use social networks, consider the way in which most new distributors are encouraged to build their business. Most new network marketing distributors are encouraged to launch their business by making a list of all the people they know, and to consider everyone on the list to be a potential prospect. "Divide your life into a number of headings," advises Carmichael (1993, p. 41), "Who was I at school with? Who do

I work with? Who do I play sport with? Who do I know from a club, church, political party, and so forth? Who do I know through my marriage or children? Who do I buy goods or services from? Who is the most successful person I know?" Clothier (1994) is even more specific:

> Your list will include your ex-boyfriend/girlfriend/husband/wife, the hi-fi dealer, the television repairman, the window cleaner, your children's teachers, the squash club owner, the bank cashier, your doctor, your estate agent, your plumber, your postman, shop assistants whom you see regularly, the man who walks his dog past your house every morning, the garage attendant, the librarian, the publican, your hairdresser, the trading standards officer; in fact, anyone with whom you can conveniently start a conversation. When you add these people to those you "know"—all of your family, friends, relatives, neighbors, and colleagues—and all the people that you "have known," you will have quite a formidable list. If there are less than 100 people on the list it is quite likely that you have not thought hard enough. (p. 91)

Behind this advice is the recognition that existing social relationships often provide an open, and often trusting, environment in which sales topics can be raised as a matter of course. Metaphorically, the distributor's foot is already in the door, thus reducing the potential for initial sales resistance. Broadly speaking, most businesspeople use a similar strategy to build and maintain a client base: Personal and professional contacts provide a network of relationships that both supports and governs the success of industrial salespeople, professional service providers, and entrepreneurs alike (Granovetter, 1985). Network marketing organizations are unique, however, because they bring business concerns into social domains that are generally averse to commercial activity (Biggart, 1989). The remainder of this chapter more fully describes the intermingling of these domains, and highlights two research issues that result.

As mentioned earlier, these research issues are supported by exploratory interviews initiated with 17 network marketing distributors (7 women and 10 men) in the United Kingdom. Three different network marketing companies were represented in this group of informants, all three of which had, at the time of the interviews, an international presence that included both the United Kingdom and the United States. (Although three companies were represented, a majority of the informants worked for only one of the three.) Nearly half of these informants lived and worked in heavily populated urban areas, while slightly more than half lived and worked in smaller towns and suburban areas. Informants' level of experience with network marketing ranged from just under one year to over 11 years. The informants are identified by their gender and their years of experience as a network marketing distributor. Those with the same gender and years of experience are further distinguished by the letter A, B, or C. Thus, 2 men with 7 years of experience would be identified as (M/A, 7 years) and (M/B, 7 years).

The Intermingling of Contrary Domains

By using social networks for business growth, network marketing challenges the exchange rules that distinguish friendships from professional relationships. Researchers of interpersonal relationships have noted that the benefits associated with more intimate relationships, for example, love and unconditional acceptance, cannot generally be exchanged for the benefits associated with more commercial relationships, for example, money and goods (Argyle & Henderson, 1985; Brinberg & Wood, 1983; Foa & Foa, 1980). Network marketing organizations often challenge these exchange rules by emphasizing the social benefits that come from being part of a network marketing business. As Biggart (1989) observed, relations in network marketing organizations "are not just friendly, but highly personal. Distributors become involved in each other's private lives and often describe themselves as 'family' " (p. 4).

In addition, researchers of domestic social life have highlighted the way in which Westerners draw a clear line between the commercial activities of the public sphere and the personal activities of the private sphere (Barley, 1963; Daunton, 1983; Kent, 1990; Lawrence, 1990; Shorter, 1976). Most network marketing activity, however, occurs in the home—in the United Kingdom, for example, 72% of total sales are accomplished in the home (Direct Selling Association/UK Research Unit, 1995). Thus, network marketing blurs the distinctions between the commercial and the social by bringing commercial activity into a realm in which it is not usually found (Grayson, in press).

The sometimes uneasy balance that network marketers must strike between the personal and the social has been recognized in the popular press (e.g., Vogel, 1992), and was mentioned by a number of the informants for this project. As one informant explained, after joining a network marketing organization, friends "sort of treat you slightly differently, as though, you know, 'What are you doing?' " (M/B, 3 years). Another informant, who marketed her product by wearing a badge pinned to her clothing every day, found that her friends reacted negatively to her bringing commercial activity into the private domain:

> I have some friends who will not go out with me when I wear the badge. . . . And so, it happens that I stopped seeing them. . . . When a friend says to me, "I'm not going out with you with this badge," I say, "Fine, so we're not going out." You know, that's all, because I can tell you I lost some friends, I will put it this way. But it's really, I think it's narrow-mindedness on their behalf. And so, you know, we don't see the same things. So, I may as well not be friends with them. (F/C, 1 year)

These issues and concerns raise questions about the best way to build and manage a network marketing organization. On one hand, social relationships may facilitate the sales and recruitment process, and on the other, these relationships clearly raise sales barriers. This seeming paradox is more fully described in the following two sections. In the first, the question of recruitment is addressed, while the question of network management is addressed in the second.

Growing the Network: Strong Ties or Weak?

The list of potential prospects developed by most new network marketing distributors will contain not only individuals whom the distributor knows very well, but also individuals known only in passing. Knowing the potential benefits and drawbacks of selling to those whom the distributor knows well, this raises the question of whether one type of person is more likely to join than another. Although there will certainly be individual differences, previous research on social networks suggests that general tendencies may also exist. For example, Granovetter's (1973) well-known study of job referrals suggests that new information is more likely to be communicated via weak social ties rather than strong ones. Weak ties tend to link individuals who otherwise travel in different social circles, and who therefore are likely to have access to different information sources. In contrast, some studies in marketing have shown that more personal information, such as a referral for a professional service, is likely to be transmitted via strong ties (Brown & Reingen, 1987; Reingen & Kernan, 1986). Is network marketing more likely to grow via strong ties or weak?

Informants for this project were divided about whether strong or weak ties were better sales facilitators. Some reported that they depended almost wholly on weak ties for their business. This choice can be explained in part by the simple fact that people generally have more weak ties than strong ones. As one distributor explained,

> I would say for the first 2 years, most of the people who got involved with me, I knew either very well or reasonably well. Then, I would say after that—the next sort of 2 or 3 years—I tended to concentrate on strangers, people I didn't know. Because I basically ran out of people I knew. (M/B, 8 years)

This raises the important point that any research comparing the success of strong ties versus weak must take into account that the pool of strong ties is likely to be much smaller than the pool of weak ones.

In addition, several other respondents said that they focused on weak ties because of the social exchange concerns outlined above: It is often socially uncomfortable to raise business issues in a personal setting (Argyle & Henderson, 1985; Brinberg & Wood, 1983; Foa & Foa, 1980). One distributor said that he did not present the business to his closer friends because he was "scared of upsetting friendships" (M, 3 years), and another did not want to seem as if he was trying to "take advantage of close relationships" (M, 9 years). Still another distributor cited "fear of rejection" as a reason for depending more on weak ties than on strong ones: "I think it's a fear of their friends turning round and saying, 'Oh my god, you didn't get involved in one of those deals did you?' " (M, 11 years). This kind of thinking leads to what another informant (F, 5 years) described as a "block" about talking to friends about the business.

Another explanation for reliance on weak ties comes from role theory (Sarbin & Allen, 1968; Solomon, 1983). A role is a set of expectations about a person's behavior, including "that a person be what he claims to be, and that he be appropriately committed and involved in his role" (Sarbin & Allen, 1968, p. 520). A new distributor's close friends are well aware that a role change has recently taken place, and therefore believe that their friend cannot make a legitimate claim to the new identity (see, e.g., Goffman, 1959, pp. 43-51, 70-76). Thus, friends may be less willing to accept the person in his or her new role: "One week they are an ordinary person and the next week they are a . . . nutritional expert," explained one distributor (M/A, 4 years), "and the person they're trying to impress [wonders] how has this person all of a sudden become a nutritional expert?" In contrast, "if . . . they don't know me from Adam, they take whatever I say as gospel because I'm the expert distributor." Another distributor offered a similar account:

> They know me as, you know, [name], and they probably knew me from my previous work maybe. So they see me from a different viewpoint. And suddenly, I'm going to start talking about health and nutrition and business, that issue, it comes as a surprise to them. (M/B, 8 years)

As still another distributor explained, the preconceptions sometimes take years to wear off: "I have had people who are friends come into the business recently. Because they can see, even though I've told them about it years ago, it's only now that they're interested because they've seen the influence that it's had on me" (F, 7 years).

The foregoing comments suggest that the effort and potential social cost associated with selling to friends are too high for distributors, and that successful networks are more likely to grow via weak ties. In contrast with these distributors, however, others reported generating most of their network growth via strong ties, what some network marketers call their "circle of influence." Their explanations for this success run parallel with relationship marketing theory, which emphasizes the importance of trust in developing long-term exchange relationships. "Their center of influence will trust them more than a stranger" said one distributor (F/C, 1 year), whereas another distributor claimed that "you've got more credibility [with people who know you], or they can see more of you, or they know what you're about" (M/B, 3 years).

Ironically, role theory also provides an explanation for the value of strong ties—especially for transformational products like cosmetics, vitamins, and diet aids. If a distributor makes personal claims about the transformational value of a product or business, then friends know whether or not these claims are true. They can see that the person, who used to lay claim to a particular role, no longer fits the role or plays the part. One distributor explained his success with friends and relatives as follows:

> They'd seen me before and after. They'd seen me all sort of listless and fat and then they see me sort of slim and energetic. And the change is quite, sort of remarkable and swift basically. So the proof—there was my inner circle seeing me all the time sort of thing. Whereas people outside it, I suppose, you know, couldn't believe that I had lost the weight in the first place. (M, 2 years)

In sum, these interviews, combined with the research cited, suggest that network marketing organizations offer an interesting arena for testing and extending theories about the value of social ties in the diffusion of products and services. Qualitative evidence suggests that a key question relates to the relative value of strong versus weak ties in network growth.

Managing the Network: Professional or Personal?

A network may grow via strong ties or weak, but it can then be managed in a number of different ways. Informants for this project indicated that network management styles exist on a continuum from personal to professional, and that styles tend to fall toward one or the other extreme.

On the more personal side of the scale, one distributor talked about "becoming good mates" with members of his downline (M/B, 3 years), while another said that her relationship with her sponsor was becoming more like a friendship because they worked together so much (F/C 1 year). "He knows everything about me," said another informant about her distributor (F, 7 years). "He knows *everything* about me. And uh, he's really made it his business to do that." In describing his downline, another respondent said that "We know each other's birthdays, we go to each other's social occasions. . . . This person rings me if she's got a problem, nothing to do with business, so on. So we've gotten to know each other extremely well" (M/B, 8 years). Last, a question about distributor relations drew the following response:

A: Yeah, um, all of the people on my first line have become friends. They're not just my distributors.

Q: What's the distinction?

A: Well, I just I think it depends on the amount of time you spend with someone. I mean, if it's just someone who's on the end of a phone, and you don't get to see them very often, then you might look at them as someone who is just putting a few pounds in your bank account every month. I don't look at it like that. When I sign someone up, I mean, I look to see how I can get them to put money in their bank account, not how they can put money in my bank account. (M, 11 years)

This finding is not entirely surprising, given the accounts of authors such as Biggart (1989), who is cited earlier as comparing network marketing relationships with family relationships. What was slightly more surprising was the number of informants who contrasted themselves with this style, and instead described their management approach as more professional. "I think some people do get much closer socially, than perhaps I do" said one distributor (M/A, 4 years). "I tend to be warm but professional . . . I don't think that I'm, perhaps, as close as some people are." Another (M, 3 years) offered the following observation:

> I think friendships, you can probably leave a lot of that out. I would say, for the most part, friendships don't occur. I would say it's good acquaintances and sociable acquaintances. Friendships are the bonus.

Part of the reason for keeping network relationships more professional than social is that good salesforce management is not always kind and gentle. One respondent (M/B, 3 years) described his sponsor's management style as the following:

> It was good because it was very professional. Uh, at times it, it was a bit—you know, I found it a bit bullying. But, just that was my own viewpoint. Just do this and you gotta do that. But, uh, he was right (laughs). I need to do things, more things. It doesn't come if you sit on your bum does it?

In another case, this more professional approach was viewed as a way of keeping network marketing from dominating one's social life. "There are people in network marketing who probably hardly have friends out of the network," explained one informant (F, 5 years). "I would not allow that to happen in my life."

Building in part from the issues highlighted in the previous section, this section raises a further question about the best approach to managing a network. A partial answer to this question comes from a study by Frenzen and Davis (1990) on the embeddedness of party-plan sales.[2] Their research supported a model in which stronger social ties were correlated with greater likelihood of *purchase*. but not with greater purchase *quantity*. In other words the social obligation associated with friendship seemed to require a purchase of some sort, but not necessarily the spending of a lot of money. This finding suggests that networks reflecting a generally more personal management style may have more frequent purchases, but not necessarily purchases of greater quantity. Here again, these comments and findings raise some interesting theoretical and managerial questions.

CONCLUDING SUMMARY

The purpose of this chapter was to both outline the basics of the network marketing industry and to highlight some of its elements as valuable for marketing researchers, particularly those interested in the ways in which social networks and marketing management work together. Network marketing sales agents were contrasted with other sales agents because of the multiple roles that they are expected to play, and for which they are rewarded. These distributors are expected not only to sell, but also to recruit other distributors, manage a network, and consume products themselves. Concerns about the economic and legal viability of network marketing were also raised, along with some information that puts these concerns into better perspective.

Network marketing is a strategy in which social and marketing goals and rewards intermingle, and Westerners are sometimes uncomfortable when commercial and social realms overlap. This notion was explored using previous research along with exploratory interviews with distributors. Two clear perspectives emerged: that social relationships facilitate the success of network marketing organizations but at the same time hamper that success. Although it is certainly possible that both perspectives are correct to some degree, it would be valuable both theoretically and managerially to study which factor (if any) has a more powerful influence on network marketing organizations. Findings in this regard would not only shed light on the ways in which commercial and personal exchange can (or cannot) work together, but also on the ways in which network marketing organizations might best be managed.

NOTES

1. Descriptions of compensation plans throughout this chapter are based on a review of several industry compensation plans, as well as the results of a network marketing study implemented by Coughlan and Grayson (1994).

2. A party-plan system is similar to network marketing because it uses social networks and is centered in and around the home. Party plans do not, however, usually encourage or reward their sales agents for recruiting and managing their own salesforces, and do not offer multilevel commissions.

CHAPTER

16

Networks of Customer-to-Customer Relationships in Marketing

Conceptual Foundations and Implications

CHARLES L. MARTIN

TERRY CLARK

Customer-to-customer relationships are individual and group in-teractions and impressions between customers encountered in the acquisition and consumption of goods and services. They range from casual, brief encounters, to pleasant banter, to hostile ex-changes. Such relationships are significant because they set tone and expectations and, in many cases, are part and parcel of the customer's total experience with the firm. In the first two sections of this chapter, we discuss the nature of these customer-to-customer (c-c) relation-ships and argue for their relevance to marketing and to network analysis. The remaining three sections delve into classificational and causal analysis issues. Given the vast number of marketing-relevant relationships, we attempt to identify the general characteristics of c-c relationships and highlight their implications for marketing. Next, to develop additional marketing insights, we further dissect c-c rela-tionships and present classification guidelines. Finally, the antece-dents of c-c relationships are discussed to provide a theoretical base for future research.

342

BACKGROUND: EMERGENCE OF
THE RELATIONSHIP MARKETING PARADIGM

Increasingly, the marketing discipline is adopting a relationship perspective. This movement is evidenced in the publication of books (e.g., Christopher, Payne, & Ballantyne, 1991; Jackson, 1985; McKenna, 1991; Vavra, 1992); special issues of journals devoted to relationship marketing (e.g., *Journal of the Academy of Marketing Science, Journal of Business Research, Journal of Services Marketing,* and *Journal of Marketing Theory and Practice*); and the establishment of centers and conferences (e.g., the recently established Center for Relationship Marketing at Emory University sponsors a biannual relationship marketing conference).

Interest in the relationship approach is partially a result of closer scrutiny and criticism of the transaction orientation of traditional marketing (Parvatiyar & Sheth, 1992). Influenced by economic theory, the transaction approach views the steps in the value chain as arm's length, discrete exchanges between a series of buyers and sellers. Under this rubric, the marketer's task is primarily to (a) identify and attract customers, (b) negotiate the competitive environment, and (c) manage the exchange process with customers. In the extreme, the transaction approach degenerates into a "one-night stand" mentality, in which markets are trawled for profits. Customers become incidental necessities to this process, and a win-lose mentality dominates.

Although some have questioned whether the paradigm is truly new and truly different, or whether it simply represents a movement to refocus or repackage marketing (Fisk, 1994; Iacobucci, 1994), for many others, the relationship paradigm promises to revolutionize marketing by focusing on long-term win-win relationships, based on mutuality of promise and trust (Gronroos, 1990). Because it replaces the exchange with the relationship as the foundational concept, the role of marketing is at least refocused toward the task of managing multiple relationships relevant to the firm. Put simply, relationship marketing "attempts to integrate customers, suppliers, and other infrastructural partners into the firm's developmental and marketing activities. Such integration results in close interactive relationships with suppliers, customers or other partners of the firm" (Sheth & Parvatiyar, 1993, p. 2).

In this context, several key relationships present in most commercial value-chains are of interest: with suppliers, customers, competitors, regulators, and the firm itself. The temptation is to atomize these and treat them as separate, isolated phenomena. It is doubtful, however, whether marketing can be fully understood unless viewed from a broader or more comprehensive perspective. Network analysis provides a formidable tool for gaining such perspective in relationship marketing.

Clark and Martin (1994) offer a classification of first-, second-, and third-order relationships within which the myriad of all possible marketing relationships can be placed. As shown in Figure 16.1, first-order relationships are those occurring between the focal firm and other parties within its environment (firm-suppliers, firm-customers, firm-competitors, firm-regulators). Second-order relationships occur between parties in the firm's environment, excluding the focal firm itself (suppliers-competitors, suppliers-customers, suppliers-regulators, competitors-customers, competitors-regulators, customers-regulators). Third-order relationships include all relationships internal to each of the four parties (inside the firm, inside and between suppliers, inside and between competitors, inside and between regulators, between customers). Clark and Martin conclude that although first- and second-order relationships have received considerable attention in the literature, third-order customer-to-customer relationships remain relatively underresearched, with the exception of the extensive literature regarding word-of-mouth communications.

CUSTOMER-TO-CUSTOMER RELATIONSHIPS

Customer-to-customer (c-c) relationships are of considerable interest to marketers whose customers encounter one another either away from the business location (e.g., manufacturers' customers) or on-site (e.g., retail stores, many service businesses), for at least two interrelated reasons.

First, customers' purchase decisions and shopping or service experiences are routinely affected by other customers. For example,

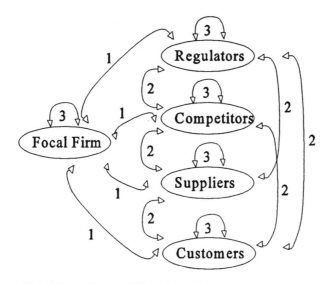

Figure 16.1. Three Levels of Relationships

NOTE: 1 = first-order relationship; 2 = second-order relationship; 3 = third-order relationship.

recommendations by other consumers are often seen as the most credible and influential sources of prepurchase information (Haywood, 1989; Quelch & Ash, 1981; Schlissel, 1985), and in general, the social dimensions of the shopping or service experience can be significant (either positive or negative) for customers (Harris, Baron, & Ratcliffe, 1995; Martin, in press; Tauber, 1972). In short, what customers say and do in one anothers' presence can enhance or inhibit customer satisfaction, and as a result affect the long-term profitability of the firm.

Second, the potential number of c-c relationships is staggering. Each relationship is embedded in a network of other relationships. For example, on-site encounters between retail customers can multiply quickly. Ten customers yield 90 (i.e., 10 × 9) possible dyadic encounters, and each dyad may experience multiple encounters within the context of their relationship. Moreover, before entering or after leaving the business encounter arena, a customer could easily interact with hundreds of other customers. In turn, each of these interactions becomes a link to a personal network of family, friends, coworkers, and other acquaintances. For the typical customer, this network ranges from 500 to 1,000 people (Raye-Johnson,

1990). Thus, even for a very small business with only 1,000 customers, social networks of up to one million people (1,000 × 1,000) are tapped.

The potential of exploiting these extensive social networks in one way or another has not been overlooked by firms such as MCI (i.e., the "Friends and Family" program), Mary Kay Cosmetics, Tupperware, and Amway, who aggressively encourage customers to recruit new customers from their social networks. Perhaps it is this realization of the network potential that prompted Christopher et al. (1991) to assert that the ultimate objective of relationship marketing is not simply repeat patronage, but ultimately the conversion of customers into active, vocal advocates for the business. The likely reason c-c relationships have received so little scholarly attention is that their management lies outside the direct control of the business. Like all third-order relationships (see Figure 16.1), the firm and its principals remain third parties in these relationships. Nevertheless, as argued throughout this chapter, it is possible for firms to influence c-c relationships by establishing behavioral parameters, framing c-c encounters, selectively targeting customers, encouraging group formation, and controlling the physical and social environments within which c-c encounters take place.

HOW CUSTOMER-TO-CUSTOMER
RELATIONSHIPS DIFFER

By definition, all relationships have some common characteristics. At a minimum, actors in common relationships are interdependent in that they might influence each others' thoughts, feelings, and behaviors (Kelley, 1983b). In addition, marketing relationships are usually discussed in terms of their longevity and their affect. That is, a relationship extends over time (e.g., repeat purchase behavior), and ideally the parties maintain a genuine interest and concern for one another and want to continue the relationship.

What then distinguishes c-c relationships from those more commonly recognized by marketers? There are several distinctions that imply formidable challenges for marketers. Many of these distinctions stem from the fact that customers play different roles while in the business environment. In this context, we offer the following eight axioms of c-c relationships.

A1: For Most Service and Retail Environments, the Volume of C-C Interactions Greatly Outnumbers That Between Customers and Employees

Jan Carlzon (1991) of Scandinavian Airlines System (SAS) observed that 137,000 interactions occur daily between his company's employees and customers. For a single flight, a passenger will interact with baggage handlers, ticketing agents, gate attendants, on-flight attendants, and other customer-contact employees. Recognizing the potential these types of interactions have to affect passengers' relationships with SAS, Carlzon challenged employees to heighten their sensitivity to each one of these "moments of truth." Carlzon failed to recognize the even greater number of potential interactions between his passengers. These verbal and nonverbal encounters occur as passengers compete for a baggage handler's attention, wait in line together, bump into one another on a crowded concourse, share the same armrest on the plane, exchange pleasantries and conversation, listen to one another's crying infants, and so on. The number and duration of such c-c encounters exceeds that of employee-customer encounters by an order of magnitude, and clearly, they contribute immensely to the passengers' flying experience.

The number of c-c encounters is further leveraged in business environments frequented by groups of customers (shopping malls, theme parks, bowling centers, restaurants, and so on). In these situations, the social interaction experience represents an important patronage motivation. In others, it can have the opposite effect.

A2: Customers' Roles Are Often Poorly Defined

Customers expect employees to be responsive, to provide service, and possibly to engage in some suggestive selling. Through formal training programs, employees can be made keenly aware of the impact their behavior has on customers. Indeed, they are often provided with specific scripts to guide their encounters with customers.

In contrast, customers often have little awareness and assume no responsibility for the effect their behaviors have on others. They may have few social skills and no training or scripts to guide their behavior. They may not recognize or articulate their roles. If they were recognized and articulated, customers might reject them.

A3: The Selection Process for Customers
Often Fails to Address the Question of C-C Compatibility

Prospective employees are usually chosen quite carefully. Depending on the industry, various types of interpersonal and social skills are sought. In some cases, job applicants for customer-contact positions are screened using scales to measure compatibility (Martin, 1995), awareness of others as measured by the "Fundamental Interpersonal Relations Orientation" scale (FIRO-B; Schutz, 1966), behavioral flexibility (Snyder, 1974), and other desirable traits. In contrast, the criteria for becoming a customer are rarely so stringent. Indeed, most businesses willingly serve anyone who walks in the door. Consequently, it should come as no surprise when dissatisfaction and conflict result after interaction-inept customers come into contact with each other. Businesses' pursuit of growth further leverages problems of c-c incompatibility. That is, to fuel growth, service businesses often find themselves targeting and catering to increasingly diverse mixtures of customers who are prone to be incompatible with one another (Martin, 1996).

A4: The Roles Played
by Customers Vary Substantially

Because standards of appropriate social behavior vary from city to city (Levine, 1993) and from culture to culture (Banton, 1965), customers tend to view their roles quite differently—possibly causing role confusion or conflict when customers from different cities or cultures interact. Roles and role perceptions vary over time as well, as customers become more confident and assertive as they gain experience and familiarity with the business and its environment. For example, in the role of "club member" in a service firm's frequency marketing program, a high-volume customer may develop a sense of property rights ("this is *my* table") or expect preferential treatment (breaking in line) that could alienate other customers.

Customers' perceived roles can be largely situation specific. For example, the role of a customer shopping alone will be quite different than the same customer shopping with his or her 4-year-old child. In the latter, more complex "parental customer" role, other customers' profanity and smoking behavior will be less tolerable. The large number of possible customer roles, many of which may be played simultaneously, further magnifies the variability and volatility of c-c relationships. For example, within one's own party or group, a customer might assume the role as contact person for the group, friend or adversary, spouse or parent, cheerleader or defender, influencer or decision maker, host(ess) or guest, discussion leader or sympathetic listener, designated driver, and so on. Or, in a broader sense, customers may accept or reject roles associated with their demographic or other characteristics, such as age, gender, marital status, occupation, religious affiliation, and, according to Banton (1965), even race.

A5: Rules of Social Interaction Are Not Clearly Defined for C-C Encounters

It is considered quite appropriate for the organization or its representatives to initiate contact with customers, or vice versa. Both customers and employees may feel free to approach one another even if they have never met previously (Czepiel, Solomon, Surprenant, & Gutman, 1985). Designated service counters, signage, employee uniforms, and name tags all help to facilitate customers' interaction with employees.

In contrast, customers may find it odd, even offensive or threatening, if other customers approach them or initiate conversation (Levine, 1993; Martin & Pranter, 1989). Knowing this, some customers are hesitant to interact with other customers, whereas others may check for customers' subtle cues such as eye contact, facial expressions, and other nonverbal behaviors indicative of whether or not interaction is welcome. Because these cues are sometimes barely perceptible, if at all, at least a few unexpected and unwelcome c-c interactions are inevitable whenever customers are in close proximity to one another.

A6: C-C Relationships
Can Be Highly Credible

Although there is growing evidence to suggest that society is generally becoming less trusting (Putnam, 1995; Russell, 1993), word-of-mouth communications among consumers are still seen as highly credible. For example, in a study of retail store shoppers, Davies, Baron, and Harris (1995) found that consumers were more likely to seek reassurance from other customers than from employees. Other studies have consistently found word-of-mouth to be an influential source of information, especially for intangible services that consumers find difficult to otherwise evaluate prior to purchase (Langeard, Bateson, Lovelock, & Eiglier, 1977; Quelch & Ash, 1981; Schlissel, 1985).

A7: C-C Relationships Are Difficult
to Identify, Monitor, and Control

It is difficult for the organization to fully know when and how customers interact with one another, and whether or not customers are satisfied with those interactions. Inconsiderate customers may perceive little or no benefit in monitoring and controlling their own behavior in the presence of other customers. Moreover, customers may not be aware of how other customers affect their own behavior or their impression of the business. Consequently, traditional survey research may be limited in its ability to provide comprehensive feedback concerning c-c relationships. Even with adequate data, it may be more difficult to shape customers' behaviors than that of the firm or its employees.

A8: C-C Information Exchanged Is More Varied
Than That in Customer-Employee Relationships

As Czepiel et al. (1985) note, encounters between employees and customers are characterized by the importance of the task-related information exchanged. This information exchange is typically directed toward specific goals, such as reaching a purchase decision. In contrast, the informational content of c-c relationships may or may not be task-related. Often, c-c relationships are purely social and have little to do with any impending decision. Indeed, the process of c-c interactions may be satisfying in and of itself.

CLASSIFYING C-C ENCOUNTERS
TO GAIN MARKETING INSIGHTS

The c-c encounter can be viewed as the building block of c-c relationships. A relationship is born when customers are affected by one another (i.e., are interdependent) in some way, in an encounter. Subsequent encounters further shape the relationship. C-c encounters, and hence c-c relationships, can be classified in numerous ways. The questions in Figure 16.2 serve as a useful basis for classification.

Where Do the Encounters Take Place?

Borrowing from the dramaturgical perspective (Grove & Fisk 1983), c-c encounters may occur either "off-stage" or "on-stage." Off-stage c-c encounters occur away from the business environment in customers' homes, workplaces, or other settings. Such encounters may be thought of in the context of word-of-mouth communications (Haywood, 1989), the influence of family (Stilley-Hopper, 1995), other peer groups and cultural or societal norms (Banton, 1965). The relationships stemming from off-stage encounters can exert strong influence on the probability a person will enter the shopping environment, and can influence how they act, and what they expect to find when they arrive. Programs to leverage word-of-mouth and influence public opinion may be the most appropriate tools for influencing off-stage c-c relationships. For example, businesses may target marketing efforts at opinion leaders in hopes of infiltrating consumers' networks.

On-stage encounters occur at the business location. Such encounters are an integral part of the shopping experience in many industries. Numerous studies confirm the effects of such public contacts. For example, too little or too much eye contact between strangers has been shown to have negative effects (Albas & Albas, 1989). Standing too close to others and crowding can create anxiety (Bateson & Hui, 1986; Fisher & Byrne, 1975; Hall, 1966). Breaking into line causes frustration (Caballero, Lumpkin, Brown, Katsinas, & Werner,

- Where do the encounters take place?
  On stage or off stage
- How frequently do encounters between the same customers occur?
  Frequently or infrequently encountered
- What is the duration of each encounter?
  Brief or extended duration
- Are encountered customers members of the same group or party?
  Intragroup or intergroup encounters
- How do customers react to c-c encounters?
  Satisfaction and approach, inconsequential effect, or dissatisfaction
  and avoidance
- What roles do customers play in the encounters?
  Decision maker, influencer, end user, opinion leader, trendsetter,
  first-time customer, solo shopper, group member, designated driver,
  host(ess), guest, and so on, or other roles related to age, gender,
  occupation, religion, culture, marital status, and so forth
- How do third parties affect c-c encounters (and the approach/avoid-
  ance for each)?
  High intragroup valences, high intergroup valences, low intragroup
  valences, low intergroup valences
- What is the content of the encounters (and the verbal/nonverbal for
  each)?
  Task-related content, nontask content, or a combination of task and
  nontask

Figure 16.2. Classifying Customer-to-Customer Encounters

1985). Public smoking is often seen as unacceptable (Gallup, 1990).
Even personal appearance has been shown to prompt others to feel
warm or threatened (Aronoff, Woike, & Hyman, 1992), or to evoke
stereotypical evaluations (Anderson & Sedikides, 1991).

Because they occur in the context of the business premises, on-
stage encounters are usually more controllable than off-stage encounters. Under the rubric of "customer compatibility management,"
Pranter and Martin (1991) suggest a number of approaches to
influence on-stage c-c encounters, including (a) targeting homogeneous, compatible customers; (b) attending to facility decor and
atmosphere; (c) grouping customers with homogeneous behaviors
or characteristics; (d) creating rules for compatible behavior to

protect customers' health and safety, and to position the organization; (e) communicating rules for compatible behavior via signage, employee contact, advertising, and so on; (f) leading compatible behavior by conveying a sense of belonging and togetherness, and by offering examples of compatible behaviors; (g) rewarding compatibility by recognizing customer acts of courtesy, patience, sharing, conviviality, and so on; and (h) enforcing rules of compatibility when broken.

How Frequently Do Encounters Between the Same Customers Occur?

When encounters are infrequent or largely random, customer relationships may fail to solidify, or they do so very slowly. Infrequent interactions lack intimacy and are usually superficial. Moreover, physical characteristics, observable behaviors, initial impressions, and perceived roles become significant in influencing such encounters.

Customers' coping behavior and willingness to tolerate others is also affected by frequency of encounter. For example, customers may ignore another's "inappropriate" behavior if they believe it is not likely to occur again. If the behavior does recur, customers may react aggressively or confrontationally, or they may dramatically alter their patronage behavior.

What Is the Duration of Each Encounter?

The duration of encounters affects the likelihood that customers will establish relationships. Duration also affects customers' (dis)satisfaction with c-c encounters. What is tolerable in a brief encounter (e.g., crying infants, smoking) might become intolerable in an extended encounter. Encounters of brief duration are likely to be less intimate, more role based, and more likely to hinge on impressions formed by physical characteristics and overt behaviors than those of longer duration.

To the extent customers can exercise control over frequency and duration, satisfaction with c-c encounters is likely to improve. Marketers and management can give customers such control by (a) providing spacious facilities so customers can avoid one another if they wish, and (b) providing point-of-purchase information, instructional signage, and personnel so that customers will not have to interact with one another.

Are Customer Encounters With Members of the Same Group or Party?

The distinction between inter- and intragroup c-c relationships may be substantial, with far-reaching marketing implications. Intergroup encounters often lack intimacy, frequency, and duration, because the actors are usually strangers. In contrast, intragroup members frequently know one another; therefore, their encounters are more likely to be intimate, frequent, and lengthy in duration. If intragroup members formed the group voluntarily (e.g., friends going out to dinner together) they probably view themselves as compatible. Indeed, their intragroup social interaction may be one of the primary benefits of the service experience.

The large volume of intragroup encounters leverages their importance. In many cases, the number of intragroup encounters exceeds those between members of different groups or between customers and employees. In fact, the presence of intragroup relationships may minimize the number and intimacy of customer- employee contacts. In a restaurant, for example, some customer group-members may have no interaction with employees, leaving the interaction entirely to other members.

The distinction between inter- and intragroup customers raises some interesting issues and implications about the nature of group dynamics and decision making that are central to the network perspective. First, because intragroup relationships are a primary benefit of the shopping experience, marketers should encourage group formation. This can be achieved by offering group discounts and other incentives, or otherwise affecting c-c encounters to encourage group formation. Some restaurants, for example, offer free meals to customers on their birthdays, realizing that most patrons will invite friends and family to join them in their birthday celebrations. A particularly insightful approach was initiated by a chain of family recreation centers in Canada. They succeeded at increasing the average party size by refusing to accept weekend reservations after midweek. By making their weekend reservations early in the week, customers were more likely to use the balance of the week to expand their group size by tapping into their social networks.

Second, the dynamics of group interaction affect the decision-making process. That is, successful marketers understand the roles that intragroup customers play in terms of influencing customer choices and facilitating purchases. A prime example is the recognition of the family as an intragroup decision-making unit (Moore-Shag & Wilkie, 1988; Stilley-Hopper, 1995). For example, most fast-food restaurants aim appeals at children knowing that these budding consumers exert considerable influence on the family's decision to dine out and their choice of restaurants (Nelson, 1978). Similarly, many salespeople use the "puppy dog" close to sway an unconvinced prospect. In using the close, the salesperson suggests that the prospect take the product (i.e., the puppy) home for the weekend, without obligation—knowing that other family members will fall in love with the "puppy" and then persuade the reluctant prospect to purchase.

Third, intragroup relationships can lead to group decisions quite different from those group members would make individually. In such situations, the selection criteria and the decision-making heuristics frequently differ. That is, individuals rank competing alternatives according to personally relevant considerations, while group members accept a compromise or advocate a choice based on criteria that are in the group's best interest. For some customers, maintaining group harmony may be regarded more highly than the importance of the immediate purchase decision, per se.

Research conducted under the auspices of the National Bowling Council illustrates how widely individual and group perceptions can differ. In one study, customers were asked individually to indicate their attitudes toward smoking behavior in the bowling center (Broh, 1989). In a related study, a comparable sample of customers responded as organized bowling teams (Martin, 1993). Although respondents in both studies were bowling team members, the individual responses favored a ban on smoking while team respondents rejected the notion of smoking bans. The majority of teams reported that their team would bowl elsewhere if smoking were banned at their bowling center. Apparently, as team members, smokers and non-smokers alike believed that banning smoking would represent too harsh a penalty for teammates who smoked. For nonsmokers, ties with their teammates were apparently stronger than their preference for smoke free environments.

How Do Customers React to C-C Encounters?

Whether customers believe their encounters with other customers contribute to, detract from, or else have no impact on the purchase decision or shopping experience depends, of course, on their evaluative judgments of the encounters. Although such judgments are often subjective, they are nevertheless highly relevant in understanding c-c interactions, and ultimately in understanding purchase decisions and patronage patterns. Attitudinally, the evaluative aspects of c-c relationships can be investigated by measuring customers' (dis)satisfaction with the relationships, encounters, or specific behaviors. Behaviorally, customers' evaluative reactions may be classified as either approach or avoidance behaviors.

(Dis)satisfaction

Using a scale introduced to marketing by Westbrook (1980), Martin (in press) measured 554 customers' (dis)satisfaction with 32 selected on-stage behaviors of other customers. "Violent" behaviors (e.g., in a restaurant, striking the table with one's fist) and "grungy" behaviors (e.g., smelling as if they had not showered in several days) were found to be the most dissatisfying, whereas "gregarious" behaviors (e.g., introducing themselves) were found to be the most satisfying.

It is managerially relevant to note that the (dis)satisfaction ratings in the Martin study varied across business settings, suggesting that consumers' perceptions of appropriate public behavior is somewhat situation-specific (e.g., shouting at a football game is seen as acceptable behavior, whereas shouting in a public library is not). Even in the context of a particular environment, however, consumers did not always agree on which behaviors were satisfying and which dissatisfying. Of the behaviors examined, smoking and the telling of racial or ethnic jokes had the greatest variation in ratings. Understandably, conflict may arise when customers within the c-c network have divergent views on the appropriateness of behaviors.

Approach-Avoidance

Mehrabian and Russell (1974) proposed the approach-avoidance dichotomy be used in examining individual behavioral reactions to the business environment. Building on this framework, Bitner (1992) uses approach-avoidance to classify behaviors in service businesses' physical environments.

The same conceptualization has proven useful in examining customers' evaluations of their relationships with other customers. For example, Baker (1987) uses approach-avoidance in examining service businesses' social environments, and concludes, "from the consumer's standpoint, social factors that enhance (inhibit) the service experience will increase the probability of approach (avoidance) behavior" (p. 81).

In a c-c context, approach relationships or encounters are those evaluated favorably. They are actively sought or welcomed, because they enrich the shopping experience. They are characterized by open communication, cooperation, courtesy, and helping behavior. Customers probably seek out business environments that offer desirable approach encounters. In contrast, c-c avoidance relationships or encounters are those that are seen as negative and undesirable. They detract from the shopping experience and customers probably avoid the environments in which they are likely to occur.

What Roles Do Customers Play in the Encounters?

As noted above, c-c encounters cannot be fully understood without an appreciation of the various roles played by customers. In situations where customers are strangers, their perceived roles serve as an interpretive guidebook of behavioral and relational rules and expectations. Thus one type of behavior might be considered appropriate in the context of one role, but not in another. Similarly, various behaviors may be seen as bothersome, tolerable, or enjoyable—depending on the roles they emanate from.

A key marketing challenge is to catalogue, describe, and generalize the various roles customers play. Customers can play more than one role simultaneously, or they may switch back and forth between some roles. On stage they may play the role of host(ess), guest, discussion leader, designated driver, and so on. Off stage they may play the role of opinion leader, trendsetter, decision maker, influencer, and so on. Some roles associated with demographic or other characteristics (e.g., age, gender, occupational status, marital status, and religious affiliation) may influence both on- and off-stage encounters.

Complicating the task of understanding customer role-playing is the possibility of role rejection. Role rejection occurs when customers fail to adopt social behaviors traditionally associated with certain roles. Understanding role rejection is complicated when role behaviors are not universally rejected. For example, when seating space is limited, some younger customers may subscribe to the role behavior of forfeiting their seats for senior citizens, while other young customers do not. The water becomes more muddied yet when senior citizens are split on accepting or rejecting the expected role behavior of accepting the forfeited seats. C-c conflict will likely arise between the two factions in each group—the role acceptors and the role rejectors. Similarly, traditionally gender-related role behaviors such as holding the door, paying the check, and "ladies first," among others, are in a state of flux—creating uncertainty and confusion in many c-c relationships and outright conflict in others.

How Do Third Parties Affect C-C Encounters?

Most of the discussion of c-c relationships thus far has been implicitly couched in terms of customer dyads. A broader network perspective of c-c relationships, however, suggests an intricate web of marketing-relevant relationships. Particularly germane to these web-like networks are the effects third parties have on c-c relationships. For example, a surly employee angers a customer who, in turn, disturbs other customers with his use of profanity. Consider the situation outlined in Figure 16.3.

In Figure 16.3, "on-stage" refers to the physical environment in which the business transactions are conducted. In this arena, customers and firm employees mix, mingle, and interact. "Off-stage" refers to c-c interactions away from the physical business environment, and employee interactions out of public arena in "the back room." In this context, "on-stage" could be the passenger cabin of an airplane, the dining area of a restaurant, a bank lobby, the men's department at

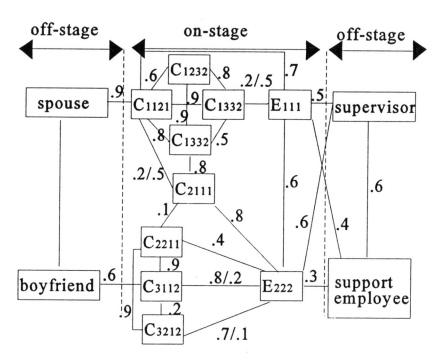

Figure 16.3. Network Analysis of C-C Relationships

NOTE: C_{ijkl} = Customer j in Group i, with role expectations k = 1 (single adult), 2 (parent), 3 (child), and attributes l = 1 (male), 2 (female). E_{abi} = employee contact person A, with role expectations b = 1 (sales), 2 (cashier), and attributes l = 1 (male), 2 (female).

JCPenney, or around the fountain at the mall. In Figure 16.3, on-stage individual customers *j* in group *i* with role expectations *k* and attributes *l* (C_{ijkl}) interact intra and inter group through approach (-), avoid (-), or approach/avoid (-) relationships. These relationships have valences, ranging from 0 (*no approach/avoid effects*) to 1.0 (*very strong approach/avoid effects*).

Many levels of analysis are possible with this type of framework. For example, when intragroup valences are all high, the likelihood of intergroup interaction is low. This is true, because as Granovetter (1973) has shown, strong intragroup ties are not as conducive to network wide diffusion of phenomena as are weak ties. Thus, in Figure 16.3, *ceteris paribus* we should expect Group 1 to remain insular in the on-stage environment precisely because of their strong ties. Because of the weak ties in Group 3, however, we should expect a greater degree of intergroup interaction or at least attempts to establish it. Moreover, because of the relatively low valences between employees in the back room and those on-stage, we should expect an on-stage partitioning of the customer population and a reduction in c-c interaction.

Going beyond the particulars of the case sketched out in Figure 16.3, we offer the following general propositions:

P1: Intragroup valences supersede intergroup valences, *ceteris paribus*.

P2: Weak intragroup valences increase intergroup c-c interactions.

P3: Customer groups form to maximize intragroup valences and to minimize intergroup valences.

P4: Increased c-c interactions are more likely when intergroup attributes are either similar or complementary.

P5: Combinations of strong intra- and intergroup valences make it unlikely newcomers will fit easily.

P6: Strong off-stage individual customer valences affect on-stage group behavior subject to the person's on-stage role.

Clearly, marketing programs can be designed to affect both off-stage and on-stage outcomes. Central to such efforts, internal marketing indirectly affects the quality and extent of c-c relations by carefully crafting the management-employee relationships (Gronroos, 1981; Bowers, Martin, & Luker, 1990). Similarly, the teamwork literature recognizes the impact that employee-employee relationships have on customer service and employee-customer relationships (Bak, Vogt, George, & Greentree, 1994; Berry, Zeithaml, & Parasuraman, 1990; International Customer Service Association [ICSA], 1995). It follows that c-c encounters also should be considered an integral part of the relationship ripple effect found within the interpersonal social structure of business environments.

What Is the Content of the Encounters?

The content of c-c encounters may be task related, nontask related, or some combination of task and nontask elements. Task encounters are related to the purchase and consumption of goods and services and include, for example, store orientation, purchase recommendations, referrals, and product demonstrations. They can occur on stage or off stage. Marketers can leverage the effectiveness of task encounters by developing customer satisfaction programs, implementing product and service quality initiatives, and stimulating positive word-of-mouth communications between customers.

Nontask encounters are not directly related to consumption or purchase, but contribute nevertheless to customers' evaluation of the on-stage shopping experience. Examples include customers' chit-chat about the weather, news of the day, and one anothers' children. Nontask encounters also include many nonverbal behaviors such as smoking or smiling in the presence of other customers. With nontask encounters, the marketing challenge is to cultivate compatible customers who will interact with one another in a mutually satisfying manner and will avoid behaviors that other customers find bothersome. Compatibility management strategies are appropriate, such as creating a relaxing, spacious atmosphere with conversational decor, and establishing and enforcing codes of conduct.

In their analysis of intergroup verbal communications between 1,101 retail store customers, Davies et al. (1995) found that at least 70% of the c-c encounters were task related, including product discussions (28%), product advice (21%), directions (13%), physical assistance (5%), and procedures (3%). Nontask communications ("pleasantries") accounted for around 21% of the verbal encounters. It seems likely that an investigation of *intra*-group or *non*verbal c-c encounters would yield a different mix of task and nontask content.

CAUSAL CONDITIONS
FOR C-C RELATIONSHIPS

Kelley (1983b) identifies three categories of relationship antecedents: personal, environmental, and relational. Building on this, valuable insight into the nature of c-c relationships can be gained. We posit that the interaction of personal, environmental, and relational factors produce the valences in c-c relationships, and that the network perspective is relevant to the understanding of all three categories of causal conditions.

Personal Causes

Personal causes are the relatively enduring characteristics of customers. As such, they may be thought of as the predispositions customers bring with them to the business setting. That is, they provide a baseline valence matrix that will be carried on stage. Personal causes include, for example, personality traits, interpersonal skills, physical characteristics, prejudicial attitudes, role expectations, normative beliefs, and memories of past experiences.

To the extent customers' personal characteristics are compatible, the stage is set for satisfying c-c relationships. If, however, customers' backgrounds and frames of reference clash, if they do not have interpersonal skills to deal with one another effectively, or if they are insensitive to others' needs, customer incompatibility can be a problem. The incompatibility can lead to intolerance and conflict, and when it does, c-c relationships suffer.

Several concurrent demographic and societal trends suggest that many consumer groups are on a collision course of incompatibility. For example, Martin and Pranter (1989) speculate that the shrinking size of households in the United States and the depersonalization of the marketplace (e.g., self-service operations, drive-through windows, catalogue shopping) creates fewer opportunities for customers to fine-tune their interpersonal skills and develop tolerance for other people's behavior. Putnam (1995) concurs, further noting that the average number of group memberships per American has dropped by almost 30% from 1967 to 1993. The increasing diversity of today's consumers is another trend with potential for conflict and incompatibility. As Boardman and Horowitz (1994) warn, "it appears likely that much of the conflict in the 1990s and beyond will involve cultural diversity on some level, whether the diversity arises from gender, race, religion, ethnicity, socioeconomic status, sexual orientation, culture, language, nationality, or other group identity factors" (p. 3).

If marketers have ever been able to assume that customers would get along with one another, or at least tolerate one another, it appears that such assumptions are under attack today. In this sense, marketers cannot afford to ignore or passively acknowledge c-c relationships.

Environmental Causes

Environmental causes are features of the physical or social surroundings within which c-c relationships are embedded.

Physical Environment

The physical environment includes the on-site facilities where customers come into contact with one another, so nonpersonal factors that affect customers' senses are highly relevant. For example, these include issues of building decor, layout, color, cleanliness, lighting, material texture, acoustics, smell, and temperature.

The effect of the physical environment or "servicescapes" on customers' perceptions and behaviors has been well-documented in the marketing literature (Bitner, 1992; Wakefield & Blodgett, 1994; Wener, 1985). The interaction of customer and physical environment is an integral part of the service experience (Eiglier, Langeard, Lovelock, Bateson, & Young, 1977; Turley & Fugate, 1992). For example, one study of consumers' experiences with fast-food restaurants revealed that three of the five most irritating aspects of the fast-food experience were physical environment issues, for example, "room is too hot or too cold," "noisy and loud music," and "lack of cleanliness" (McCarthy & Straus, 1992). With respect to c-c relationships in particular, the physical environment can affect the way customers interact with one another (Pranter & Martin, 1991), and the extent to which customers are attracted to or believe they are compatible with other customers in the environment (Donovan & Rossiter, 1982; Johnson, 1993).

Social Environment

In most retail and service businesses the physical environment coexists with a social environment (Baker, 1987; Kotler, 1973). Narrowly construed, the social environment includes the presence and behaviors of other people, primarily personnel and customers. In a broader context, the social environment may also include virtually anyone with whom customers might interact in other settings (hence the importance of the spouse to C_{1121} in Figure 16.3). In this sense, customers' social networks including family, friends, coworkers, and other acquaintances are part of the social environment.

The nature and extent of the social environment is relevant to a proper understanding of c-c relationships. Indeed, social learning theorists maintain that the role of the social environment in shaping behavior is greater than that played by the physical environment (Christensen, 1983). To many consumers, the appeals of the social environment may be as important, or more important, than those of the physical environment or the goods and services for sale. As alluded to, however, throughout this chapter, prospective customers can find social environments dissatisfying and avoid them.

Nonetheless, evidence of the presence and the potency of the social environment is undeniable. Tauber (1972) has identified five specific social motives for shopping: (a) social experiences outside the home, (b) communication with others having a similar interest, (c) peer group attraction, (d) status and authority, and (e) pleasure of bargaining. More recently, a study of 600 mall shoppers revealed 42% had "socialized with friends or others" while at the mall and 23% "had a conversation with other shoppers I just met today" (Bloch, Ridgway, & Nelson, 1991). Another survey of a retail store's customers found that 25% reported that talking with other customers added to their shopping experiences (Harris et al., 1995). A sports marketing study of baseball fans found that 55% were more attracted to the ball park by other fans than by the lure of the game itself (Mullin, Hardy, & Sutton, 1993). Still another study found customers were very satisfied with several gregarious behaviors of other customers in the social environment, for example, holding the door, introducing themselves, and asking about the well-being of one's family (Martin, in press). Finally, Maister (1985) shows that waiting for service is much more tolerable when customers are able to share the waiting experience with others.

Relational Causes

Relational causes stem from the process of two or more customers interacting with one another. Routine conversation is largely relational in that what customers say to one another affects the course of the dialogue. Nonverbal and paralinguistic behaviors can also be relational. For example, customers might react by shaking hands, sitting next to someone who establishes eye contact and smiles, responding in a like manner to customers who shout or laugh, or distancing themselves physically from smoking customers. Clearly, customers' interpersonal skills play an integral role in the development of c-c relationships. As Christensen (1983) notes, relational tools may be used by the actors (customers) to cope with their potential incompatibility. For example, they may try to influence each other by using a set of social skills, (e.g., compromise, turn taking, charm, persuasion) or coercive skills (e.g., threats, complaints, guilt). Ultimately, the interaction process can greatly influence customers' trust and attraction for one another, their willingness to share information and engage in cooperative or helping behaviors, and their purchase and patronage behaviors.

Although c-c interaction may be unpredictable and only indirectly controlled by the firm, cultural norms, role expectations, and generally accepted codes of conduct help guide and sometimes frame these relational processes if the customer mix is relatively homogeneous or complementary. The course of c-c interactions further depends on a number of situational considerations such as the frequency and duration of interactions, their content (e.g., product recommendations, pleasantries), the roles played and expected by customers (including whether or not the customers are strangers), and so on. The condition, however, that qualifies customer encounters as relational is that of interdependence. Customers are most interdependent when their valences are high, suggesting they impact each other's thoughts, feelings, or behaviors. Normal conversation between customers would pass the interdependency test because each customer's comments are (at least in part) a response to the other customer's comments or actions. A more subtle and perhaps less influential case of interdependency occurs simply when customers mentally acknowledge one anothers' presence. Because consumers' perceptions of the shopping experience and their purchase behaviors are so routinely interdependent, it is a mistake for marketers to assume that consumers act independently. Yet, it is interesting to note that most consumer research treats consumers as isolated units of analysis without regard for the myriad of c-c relationships within which "individual" consumer behavior is deeply embedded, hence, the necessity of the network perspective.

SUMMARY

Customer-to-customer relationships are individual and group interactions and impressions between customers encountered in the acquisition and consumption of goods and services. The way customers relate to one another affects their evaluation of and (dis)satisfaction with the shopping experience, their purchase and patronage behavior, and consequently, their relationship with the business and its employees. As such, networks of customer-to-customer relationships are highly relevant to the emerging relationship marketing paradigm. C-c relationships differ from those of other relevant marketing relationships in that (a) the volume of c-c encounters can greatly outnumber those between customers and employees; (b) customers' roles are often poorly defined; (c) the selection process for customers generally fails to address the question of customer compatibility; (d) the roles played by customers vary substantially; (e) rules of social interaction are not clearly defined for c-c encounters; (f) the credibility of c-c relationships is high; (g) c-c relationships are difficult to identify, monitor and control; and (h) their informational content varies considerably. These distinctions pose both marketing challenges and opportunities.

Additional marketing insights are gleaned from further classifying c-c encounters. As outlined in Figure 16.2, relational c-c encounters occur on stage or off stage, frequently or infrequently, briefly or for extended periods of time, and between members of the same group or between different groups. They may contribute to customer satisfaction or dissatisfaction, and they may stem from a multitude of roles that customers play. They may be affected by third parties leading to approach or avoidance behaviors, and their content may or may not pertain to the purchase and consumption process.

The antecedents or causal conditions that produce the valences in c-c relationships can be classified as well, as either (a) personal, (b) environmental, or (c) relational causes. The network perspective is relevant to the understanding of all three categories.

Network Analyses of Hierarchical Cognitive Connections Between Concrete and Abstract Goals

An Application to Consumer Recycling Attitudes and Behaviors

RICHARD P. BAGOZZI

GERALDINE HENDERSON

PRATIBHA A. DABHOLKAR

DAWN IACOBUCCI

In this chapter, we use network methods to analyze means-end chains from consumers regarding their attitudes toward recycling. Some of the recycling goals of these consumers (e.g., saving resources) are considered concrete means to more abstract goals (e.g., providing for future generations), and we explore the applicability of several network procedures to identifying hierarchical patterns in these relational ties. We compare the cognitive goal structures of recyclers and nonrecyclers with respect to their associative linkages.

INTRODUCTION

Bagozzi and Dabholkar (1994) studied consumers' attitudes toward recycling in a comparative test between the theory of "reasoned

AUTHORS' NOTE: We are grateful to the National Science Foundation grant awarded to the fourth author for research support (NSF Grant No. SES-9023445).

action" (Ajzen & Fishbein, 1980), in which attitudes and subjective norms influence behavioral intentions, which in turn determine behavior, and an augmented model in which past consumer behavior serves as an additional predictor variable (e.g., Bagozzi & Warshaw, 1990). Past behavior indeed improved prediction.

To obtain data for their tests, Bagozzi and Dabholkar (1994) elicited from consumers reasons why they recycle (for consumers who recycled) or reasons why one should recycle (for those who did not). The data collection was conducted using the "laddering" interview technique[1] in which each of the initially stated reasons (for recycling) is pursued in-depth for subsequent implications; that is, "Why is [the previously stated reason for recycling] important?" Due to this structured nature of questioning, goals stated early in the protocol are considered concrete means to the more abstract goals or values elicited later, hence the resulting data are referred to as "means-end" chains.[2] For example, one consumer's means-end chain began with the reason that recycling would "avoid filling up landfills (and running out of land)," which the consumer thought to be important to "save resources," which in turn was thought to be important to "give to future generations," and so on.

Bagozzi's and Dabholkar's (1994) comparative theory tests were conducted via regressions, but of greater interest to the current research was their consideration of the connections between the stated goals. A frequency matrix was created with each goal serving as an index for both a row and column, and the matrix elements described the number of times the row goal was stated as a means to the column goal.[3]

In the current research, we wish to examine some of the possibilities that network analyses hold for these data. The network paradigm provides many methods that may be applicable to such data and in particular may address concerns as yet unresolved in the analysis of implications matrixes. For example, one issue in the methodology of means-end chains is whether one analyzes only the direct linkages or also includes the indirect linkages (Reynolds & Gutman, 1988), an issue for which networks may be well suited. Another issue is the desire to obtain an analytical, hierarchical ordering of the goals from those thought to be most concrete to those considered most abstract. Selecting proper network indexes could prove to be the challenge in this current research because hierarchical data are fairly unusual for networks; that is, most of the goal linkages in this chapter are strictly unidirectional, whereas communications or interfirm trade linkages, for example, are often bidirectional. We now describe the data in more detail and begin their analysis.

THE DATA

In this chapter, we compare recyclers to nonrecyclers to extend Bagozzi and Dabholkar (1994), who studied recycling goals common to both groups.[4] Recyclers' and nonrecyclers' network matrixes are presented separately in Table 17.1 and will be analyzed separately throughout this chapter. The resulting comparisons will allow us to examine structures of cognitive associations thought to connect goals for two groups of consumers whose behaviors differ. We do not make claims regarding the temporal causal chain between attitudes and behaviors; that is, if it turns out in our analyses that recyclers' goal associations differ from those of nonrecyclers, we would not know whether these differences motivated the different behavior, or whether the differences were a result of their differential recycling behavior. Nevertheless, it is conceivable that training nonrecyclers to understand the linkages that recyclers perceive may enhance likelihood of recycling participation; perhaps emulation in attitude contributes to emulation in behavior. In any case, we are interested in studying similarities and differences in the recyclers' and nonrecyclers' network patterns.

Even before network indexes or subgroups are computed and derived, simple observations can be made on the raw data that begin to tell a story. First, in comparing the matrixes in Table 17.1, we see that the cells that are equal to zero in the recyclers' matrix—meaning that no recyclers mentioned a link between some particular pair of row and column goals—are also, for the most part, equal to zero in the nonrecyclers' matrix, and vice versa. (And cells that are nonzero in one matrix are usually also nonzero in the other.) Thus, we first note fairly high similarity between the groups in terms of basic structure, or the "type" of linkages.[5] For example, a tie from "1" (reduce waste) to "3" (save environment) is perceived by both groups. The exceptions are important because they demonstrate the associative links that recyclers make that nonrecyclers do not, and vice versa, and we will describe them shortly.

TABLE 17.1 Frequencies of Consumers Who Believe the Row Goal Leads to the Column Goal

	1	2	3	4	5	6	7	8	9	10	11	12	13	14	ODI[a]	OD2[b]
Beliefs among consumers who are recyclers																
(1) Reduce waste	0	0	1	0	6	0	0	0	0	0	6	4	0	0	17	4
(2) Reuse materials	0	0	0	0	0	0	0	0	0	0	0	0	0	0	15	3
(3) Save environment	0	0	0	2	9	0	0	5	4	3	0	12	0	4	32	5
(4) Save planet	0	0	0	0	0	0	0	0	0	0	0	6	0	4	10	2
(5) Avoid landfills	0	0	6	3	0	0	4	10	0	0	12	5	4	0	44	7
(6) Reduce cost living	0	0	0	0	0	0	0	0	0	7	0	0	0	0	7	1
(7) Save resources	0	0	0	0	0	0	0	0	0	0	0	0	0	3	9	2
(8) Reduce pollution	0	0	0	0	0	0	0	0	0	0	0	6	4	8	12	2
(9) Right thing to do	0	0	0	0	0	0	0	0	0	0	0	0	0	0	0	0
(10) Save money	0	0	0	0	0	0	0	0	0	0	0	0	0	0	0	0
(11) Reduce messy trash	0	0	0	0	0	0	0	0	0	0	0	0	3	0	3	1
(12) Future generations	0	0	0	0	0	0	0	0	2	0	0	0	0	0	2	1
(13) Promote health	0	0	0	0	0	0	0	0	0	0	0	0	0	0	0	0
(14) Life sustaining	0	0	0	0	0	0	0	0	0	0	0	0	0	0	0	0
IDI[c]	0	0	7	5	15	0	12	15	6	10	18	33	11	19		
ID2[d]	0	0	2	2	2	0	2	2	2	2	2	5	3	4		
Beliefs among consumers who are NOT recyclers																
(1) Reduce waste	0	0	2	0	6	0	0	0	0	0	2	1	0	0	11	4
(2) Reuse materials	0	0	0	0	0	0	0	0	1	1	0	0	0	0	5	3
(3) Save environment	0	0	0	3	3	0	0	2	0	0	0	4	0	2	14	5
(4) Save planet	0	0	0	0	0	0	0	0	3	0	0	4	0	1	8	3

370

													OD1	OD2
(5) Avoid landfills	0	1	0	0	1	1	0	0	4	1	0	0	8	5
(6) Reduce cost living	0	0	0	0	0	0	0	0	0	0	0	0	0	0
(7) Save resources	0	0	0	0	0	0	0	0	0	5	0	2	7	2
(8) Reduce pollution	0	0	0	0	0	0	0	0	0	0	1	2	3	2
(9) Right thing to do	0	0	0	0	0	0	0	0	0	0	0	0	0	0
(10) Save money	0	0	0	0	0	0	0	0	0	0	0	0	0	0
(11) Reduce messy trash	0	0	0	0	0	0	0	0	0	0	1	0	1	1
(12) Future generations	0	0	0	0	0	0	0	1	0	0	0	0	1	1
(13) Promote health	0	0	0	0	0	0	0	0	0	0	0	0	0	0
(14) Life sustaining	0	0	0	0	0	0	0	0	0	0	0	0	0	0
ID1	0	3	3	9	4	3	5	1	6	15	2	7		
ID2	0	2	1	2	2	2	3	1	2	5	2	4		

a. OD1 = out-degree 1—the sum of each row computed on these raw frequencies.
b. OD2 = out-degree 2—the sum of each row computed on the binary data.
c. ID1 = in-degree 1 —the sum of each column computed on the raw data.
d. ID2 = in-degree 2 —the sum of each column computed on the binary data.

In addition, we will see that these groups differ in the "strengths" of some of their linkages—more recyclers tend to believe in connections between certain goals. One might expect it to be true that a person who participates in the focal behavior (i.e., recycling) necessarily holds stronger convictions, which would suggest stronger ties in their associative network. Although initially this result might seem intuitive, consider that these frequencies represent numbers of consumers holding each linkage belief, not strength of beliefs within a person. In addition, the hypothesis that stronger beliefs lead to certain behaviors would predict nothing more specific than large frequencies (many ties, or many strong ties) with no a priori prediction regarding particular patterns in the ties. We will describe differences in strengths after describing differences in "type."

Differences in Type of Links

There are four major differences in the two network structures in terms of links that exist for one group that do not for the other (temporarily ignoring strengths of ties). Three of these structural differences are linkage beliefs that recyclers have that nonrecyclers do not. Specifically, recyclers believe that: "avoiding filling up landfills" helps to "save the planet" (the link from row 5 to column 4) and to "promote health and avoiding sickness" (row 5 to column 13), whereas nonrecyclers do not see that causal link. Similarly, recyclers believe that "reducing the cost of living" contributes to "saving money" (6 to 10) and nonrecyclers do not see that link.

Each of these links is a causal association that a recycler believes that a nonrecycler does not. For some purposes, it does not even matter whether the recyclers' beliefs are "true" or "correct." If one sought to develop a social marketing educational campaign, one might begin by highlighting these three links to the nonrecyclers hoping to enhance recycling "thinking," and thereby, perhaps, subsequent recycling behavior. The three links are even of different content (global, health, financial), which would allow for thematic approaches targeted at three different segments. Given their diversity, presumably one of the three themes might appeal to most nonrecyclers.

The remaining structural difference between the groups is that nonrecyclers believe that we should "save the planet" because it is "the right thing to do." Surely recyclers believe that saving the planet is proper as well, but this link does not appear in their networks. Perhaps the recyclers have internalized their own attitudes regarding the importance of recycling and therefore do not feel compelled by normative arguments.

Differences in Strength of Links

The belief networks of recyclers and nonrecyclers also differed in the strengths of eight links. In all cases, these were beliefs that occurred at least five more times among the recyclers than the nonrecyclers. Specifically, more recyclers saw ties

from "reuse materials" to "save resources" (2 to 7),

from "save environment" to "avoid landfills" (3 to 5) and to "provide for future generations" (3 to 12),

from "avoid landfills" to "save environment" (5 to 3), "reduce pollution" (5 to 8), and "reduce messy trash" (5 to 11),

from "reduce cost of living" to "save money" (6 to 10), and

from "reduce pollution" to "sustain life" (8 to 14).

Most of these links were seen by some nonrecyclers, but not in the frequency found among recyclers. One explanation might be that the reason recyclers recycle is that they have a dense network of associations of goals that may be achieved by recycling or that support recycling behavior. Nonrecyclers may be aware of most of the same goals and interconnections, but the strengths of beliefs do not exceed thresholds to either participate in recycling or to provide rich elaborations on reasons for recycling, as in the data collection task for this study.[6]

In sum thus far, the examination of the two data matrixes has suggested that there are some differences between the types and strengths of goal links that recyclers and nonrecyclers perceive. Density network indexes support these interpretations. The densities on the binary data indicate somewhat richer tie structures for the recyclers than the nonrecyclers, but the difference is slight (.15 vs. .14).[7] By comparison, densities for the raw frequency data (which reflect strengths of associations) show more dramatic differences between the two types of respondents (the density for the recyclers' network is .83, and for the nonrecyclers, .32).[8]

NETWORK INDEXES

In addition to presenting the matrixes, Table 17.1 also contains the in-degrees (the sum within a column across rows) and out-degrees (the sum over columns for each row) for both the raw data, as presented in Table 17.1, and for the binary data (all values in Table 17.1 greater than 1 become 1). In this application, an in-degree represents the number of times the column goal was said to be achieved by some row goals, and an out-degree represents the number of times the row goal was said to be a means to some column goals.[9]

Given these interpretations, it is easy to identify those goals that were frequently cited as instrumental to others (i.e., those with large out-degrees), as well as those goals that were seen more often as the ends to be attained (i.e., those with large in-degrees). For example, in terms of the out-degrees, more recyclers saw instrumental uses of reusing materials (15 recyclers vs. 5 nonrecyclers), saving the environment (32 vs. 14), and avoiding landfills (44 vs. 8). In terms of in-degrees, the goals that were more often seen by recyclers than nonrecyclers as desirable ends to be achieved included reducing pollution (15 vs. 3), reducing messy trash (18 vs. 6), providing for future generations (33 vs. 15), and sustaining life (19 vs. 7).

The goals on which the recyclers differ from the nonrecyclers (for either the in- or out-degrees) are a complex mixture of goals that are fairly concrete, immediate results of recycling, and those that are more abstract and therefore perhaps more difficult to see a personal impact or connection between one's behavior and the abstract long-term outcome. This mixture is interesting because one might have expected that recyclers recycle because they can understand more clearly the abstract and long-term results, so that they are better able to regulate their short-term behavior (e.g., in overcoming the inconvenience of recycling) to strive for long-term outcomes (e.g., good environmental results). Conversely, one might have expected that recyclers recycle because they focus on the connections between the more immediate, concrete goals, whereas nonrecyclers do not recycle because they only consider goals that are too abstract and therefore seem too unlikely to be achieved. These results are more interesting because neither simple explanation is sufficient.

Finally, the degrees allow classification of the goals into three useful categories. First, some goals had in-degrees of zero, meaning they were only thought to be instrumental to the achievement of other goals, and were never considered ends in themselves. These instrumental goals included reducing waste, reusing materials, and reducing the cost of living.[10] Second, other goals had out-degrees of zero, meaning they were never thought to be instrumental to the achievement of other goals, but rather they were the more abstract goals to which the others led. These end goals included being the right thing to do, saving money, promoting health, and sustaining life. Third, the remaining goals were "intermediate" in that they sometimes served as means and sometimes as ends. These goals included saving the environment, saving the planet, avoiding filling up landfills, saving resources, reducing pollution, reducing messy trash, and providing for future generations. This identification of groups of goals is related to a natural task in network analyses, which is the derivation of subgroups, a topic to which we now turn.

NETWORK SUBGROUPS

Subgroups of actors are derived from networks usually based on one of two criteria (Knoke & Kuklinski, 1982). Cliques are defined as groups of (3 or more) actors who are highly interconnected among themselves.[11] Structurally equivalent actors are those who may or may not be connected to each other, but who share similar patterns of connections with others. For these particular data, cliques might not be particularly meaningful. The data are hierarchical (i.e., mostly asymmetric dyads), so ties from goal "i" to goal "j" are rarely reciprocated, but this becomes particularly true as one extends the length of the means-end chain. That is, for a given chain from i to j to k, and so on, it may be that some consumers also saw links from j to i or k to j, but they probably did not mention a link from k to i. Thus, it is likely that there would be no clusters of goals that fit a strict definition of a clique.[12]

So instead, we wish to explore the application of structural equivalence to these data. In an example of say, a communications network, two persons would be identified as structurally equivalent if they sent communications *to* the same other actors, *and* if they were sent communications *from* the same other actors. In this means-ends analysis, two goals would be structurally equivalent if they were thought to be produced by the same prior instrumental goals and if they were thought to induce the same next end goals in the chain. This logic seems applicable, so we will describe its results momentarily. It may also be fruitful, however, to consider the components of structural equivalence separately. We will describe groups of goals that are structurally equivalent vis à vis their shared instrumental causal goals, and separately, we will also consider groups of goals that are equivalent vis à vis the goals to which they are thought to commonly lead.

Using the method of Breiger, Boorman, and Arabie (1975), whereby goals are clustered according to the similarities of their profiles (by iterative correlations), we derived the groups of goals depicted in Table 17.2. The first set of equivalent goal groups are based on the similarities of the goals' row profiles—that is, two goals are in a common cluster (I, II, III, or IV) if they are considered as essentially interchangeable means to achieving the same other goals as ends. For example, for the first cluster (I), the three goals of reducing waste, saving the environment, and avoiding filling up landfills are thought to be means to similar ends. Knowing these similarities among the instrumental actions could help the social marketer in many ways. For example, striving toward "saving the environment" is fairly intangible and not as easily communicated as say, showing landfills and projecting their expected growth and volume. Even if environmental researchers believed that the goal of "saving the environment" was say, a more direct causal link toward the other desired goals, it may be in the environment's best interest to prompt consumers to "avoid filling the landfills," given their evident ready acceptance toward the causal linkages (of course, with time the environmentalist would wish the consumer to be better educated to see the closer, "truer" link).

The remaining clusters differ for the recyclers and nonrecyclers. Cluster II has goals of saving the planet and resources and reducing pollution, to which nonrecyclers add providing for future generations. The associations recyclers make instead cluster future generations with cluster III, reducing the cost of living and reusing materials. Cluster IV for both groups is comprised mostly of the goals that

TABLE 17.2 Structural Equivalence Groups of Goals

Equivalence Sets for:	Recyclers				Nonrecyclers			
	I	II	III	IV	I	II	III	IV
Goals that are thought to affect the same consequential goals (structurally equivalent rows)								
(1) Reduce waste	I				I			
(2) Reuse materials			III				III	
(3) Save environment	I				I			
(4) Save planet		II				II		
(5) Avoid landfills	I				I			
(6) Reduce cost living			III					IV
(7) Save resources		II				II		
(8) Reduce pollution		II				II		
(9) Right thing to do				IV				IV
(10) Save money				IV				IV
(11) Reduce messy trash				IV			III	
(12) Future generations			III			II		
(13) Promote health				IV				IV
(14) Life sustaining				IV				IV
Goals that share the same instrumental causal goals (equivalent columns)								
(1) Reduce waste	I				I			
(2) Reuse materials	I				I			
(3) Save environment			III				III	
(4) Save planet			III					IV
(5) Avoid landfills				IV			III	
(6) Reduce cost living	I				I			
(7) Save resources		II				II		
(8) Reduce pollution			III					IV
(9) Right thing to do		II				II		
(10) Save money		II				II		
(11) Reduce messy trash			III				III	
(12) Future generations				IV				IV
(13) Promote health			III		I			
(14) Life sustaining				IV				IV
Goals that share both (standard structural equivalence)								
(1) Reduce waste	I				I			
(2) Reuse materials			III				III	
(3) Save environment	I				I			
(4) Save planet	I				I			
(5) Avoid landfills	I					II		
(6) Reduce cost living			III				III	
(7) Save resources	I				I			
(8) Reduce pollution		II				II		
(9) Right thing to do				IV				IV
(10) Save money				IV			III	
(11) Reduce messy trash		II				II		
(12) Future generations		II						IV
(13) Promote health		II						IV
(14) Life sustaining		II						IV

had all zeros in their rows, previously described as those goals that were not instrumental, but ultimate value states.

The second set of results in Table 17.2 describes the similarities among the goal structures vis-à-vis their roles as ultimate end goals (achieved by similar sets of instrumental goals). Once again, we see some similarities and some differences in the perceptions of recyclers and nonrecyclers—clusters I and II are the same, and III and IV differ. Cluster I contains those goals that had had entire columns of zeros, previously described as those goals that were seen only as instrumental, and not ends in themselves (i.e., reducing waste, reusing materials, and reducing the cost of living). Clusters III and IV, in particular, show how recyclers differ from nonrecyclers. For example, nonrecyclers think that the goal of avoiding filling up landfills is like other directly environmental goals of saving the environment and reducing messy trash. For recyclers, the avoidance of filling landfills is considered to be a goal like the much more abstract, futuristic goals of providing for future generations and sustaining life. Similarly, recyclers see reducing pollution as a goal that is achievable by the same means as the fairly mundane "reduce messy trash." Nonrecyclers might think of reducing pollution too abstractly, given that they believe it is achieved in the same way as the abstract goals of saving the planet, providing for future generations, and sustaining life.

These differences would also have implications for a social marketing campaign. If the ultimate goal is considered to be sustaining life, and the marketer sought concrete means of expressing the desire to achieve this goal, they could focus on landfills (to appeal to the recyclers) and pollution (to appeal to the nonrecycling segment). These results do not indicate that landfills or pollution are means to sustaining life, but if a recycler is attempting to reduce landfills and a nonrecycler is attempting to reduce pollution, the life sustaining goal will be achieved all the same.

The final set of results in Table 17.2 are those for which any set of goals tended to share both common antecedent goals and common consequential goals. This criterion is clearly more stringent, because both rows and columns must appear similar, and a quick surveyance of the matrixes in Table 17.1 with the equivalence sets in Table 17.2 indicate the clusters are fairly fuzzy. For example, Cluster I contains goals 1, 3, 4, 5, 7 for recyclers and 1, 3, 4, 7 for nonrecyclers. Examining the first matrix in Table 17.1 shows that for recyclers, the rows 1, 3, and 5 have some common column entry points, and the columns 3, 4, 5, and 7 share some common row structure. The conjunctive fits between the pairs of rows and columns, however, are not terribly precise, so not surprisingly, the resultant clusters are not trivially interpretable.

In a way, this finding is interesting in itself, because it suggests that there is little complete redundancy among these 14 goals in that no goal is completely substitutable with another vis à vis both their means and their ends. If any goals were completely interchangeable, the researcher would want to examine the content of the equivalent goals. If their contents were different in a substantively or theoretically meaningful way, they may be worth retaining as separate (but future empirically distinguishing evidence would be nice). If their content appeared similar, it could well be that the structural equivalence testing essentially identified categories of codes that should be aggregated before further analytical processing. If structural equivalence has ever been used in this way, it is unknown to these authors, but there is no reason it could not be a useful tool in preprocessing thematic codes obtained by respondents to research methods that produce qualitative data, such as these in-depth interviews.

DIRECT AND INDIRECT LINKS

When interviewers are recording consumer responses to this in-depth means-ends probing, they will record links of the sort i to j to k (e.g., i causes j, which causes k). In addition to creating matrixes representing the direct causal links, i to j, and j to k, they may be interested in the indirect implications, i to k (Reynolds & Gutman, 1988). Keeping track of the indirect links can be cumbersome, particularly if one considers links across the combinations offered by a single consumer, or certainly by the time one aggregates across consumers. Network analysis allows straightforward computation and examination of indirect links, even though most network research focuses on direct linkage structure.

It has long been known that when using a Boolean algebra logic, if one begins with the matrix of direct ties between goals i and j, that is, elements x_{ij} in **X**, one can derive the number of times goals i and j are connected by a link of distance two (i.e., through one other goal), via X^2 or three (i.e., through a path containing two intermediate goals), via X^3, and so on (Hage & Harary, 1983; Harary, 1969). In addition, the positive elements in $X - X^2$ would represent the indirect ties (of length two) between goals that had not previously been directly linked in X, and so on. This simple matrix algebra is a quick means of separating those goals that are richly interconnected from those that are sparsely connected.

We do not provide these results in this table, but they are easy enough to replicate given that we provide the raw data in Table 17.1. For these data, most goals are directly connected, or connected via few links, to the goals previously referred to as "intermediate," such as saving the environment (3) or avoiding landfills (5), and so by X^2, X^3, and X^4, most of the goals are fairly densely connected (going to the maximum possible of X^{13}, for 14 goals, seems completely unnecessary).

There are two exceptions, however, and they are particularly interesting because they share similar content. For both the recyclers' and nonrecyclers' networks, the goals of "reducing the cost of living" (6) and "saving money" (10) are not highly connected in X (the raw matrix of direct ties presented in Table 17.1), and when indirect ties are examined in X^2, both goals are disconnected. Once a goal becomes isolated, subsequent matrixes (X^3, X^4, etc.) will not reintegrate the goal. Thus, the financial goals remain separated from the other goals.

Marketers know that many, many consumers are motivated by financial concerns—we study price as one of the fundamental four Ps, we examine price elasticities, price sensitive segments, promotions, and corporate strategies such as everyday low pricing (EDLP). If, therefore, the way to many consumers' hearts is through their pocketbooks, perhaps environmentalists hoping to attain such goals as sustaining life and saving the planet need to address consumers using terms they can understand, that is, financial goals. Even for the recyclers in this sample, financial goals were peripheral to the environmental goals, but the nonrecyclers saw almost no connections. Forming a connection between financial goals and environmental goals may take the form of offering incentives for recycling behaviors, or educating the consumer that behaving in environmentally enhanced manners helps consumers financially (e.g., perhaps keeps pricing down due to reduced packaging costs).

DISCUSSION

In this chapter, we used network methods to represent means-ends chains collected via in-depth interviews. The hierarchical nature of the data is fairly unusual for networks, and of course network methods requiring symmetry are therefore not applicable (e.g., some measures of centrality, such as betweenness). If, however, data are clear and have a story to tell, simple methods should suffice. We examined recycling goal network matrixes, in-degrees and out-degrees, and structural equivalence sets. We interpreted each of these network methods in terms of these goal-structured data, and obtained some insight into recycling associations.

We were able to see some differences in how recyclers and non-recyclers think about recycling. Nonrecyclers are not simply ignorant of the benefits of recycling—many of the linkages stated by recyclers were also cited by at least a few nonrecyclers. Thus, a social marketing campaign aimed at increasing recycling behavior stating some of the recyclers' links would not be so much "news" to the nonrecyclers, as simply reinforcement of the nonrecyclers' apparently latent beliefs. Nevertheless, common cognitive interpretations of education and persuasive communications is that of creating or strengthening associative linkages, so it seems to be a perfectly reasonable goal for such an educational campaign to make nonrecyclers associations appear more like those of recyclers. It is of course another step to assume the resultant cognitive restructuring will help induce more recycling behavior—the differences in the two groups' behaviors is evidently more a function of how much the consumer takes the recycling values to heart.

NOTES

1. Gutman (1982) and Reynolds and Gutman (1988) describe the laddering interview technique, and position it as a means of investigating consumer categorization and values, respectively. For a discussion of yet unresolved issues with the methodology, see Gutman (1991); for a recent application, Walker and Olson (1991), and for an earlier article dealing with related issues, Bettman (1974). Also see the special issue of the *International Journal of Research in Marketing* guest edited by Jerry C. Olson (1995) on means-end chains.

2. This approach is consistent with Huffman and Houston's (1993) definition of goals as abstract, global benefits sought by consumers, enabled by features of the specific, immediate, local behavior (e.g., purchasing a certain product, or for our purposes, engaging in recycling behavior) to fulfill those more abstract goals.

3. In networks, this matrix is referred to as an adjacency- or sociomatrix. In these means-ends applications, the matrix is termed an implications matrix (Reynolds & Gutman, 1988), because of the relation between the row and column goals (row goals imply column goals).

4. Bagozzi and Dabholkar worked with 19 recycling goals. We retained 14 goals, having deleted those mentioned by fewer than 3 persons (to enhance our confidence in each tie's validity). Deleting goals also results in deleting their links (like a node cut in graph theory), and sometimes their contributors. Our sample size was 111: 74 persons recycled and 37 did not.

5. The similarity between matrixes of the zero-nonzero patterns also suggest the denigration that would occur to this study if we were to dichotomize the ties, as is frequently done in network research. Binary data are simpler, and the network indices simpler to interpret, than when working with network ties that indicate "strength" of tie. These data, however, are an example of the value of examining strengths of ties. The differences between the groups would be less compelling if the two matrixes were made binary.

6. To be fair, we must note that an alternative reason for there being more ties in the recyclers' network may be because there were more recyclers. Recall that our sample has twice as many recyclers as nonrecyclers (74 vs. 37). When the values in Table 17.1 are converted to proportions (by dividing by respective sample sizes, or by total number of goals mentioned—151 among the recyclers and 58 by the nonrecyclers), z tests of the differences only approach significance. The use of z tests here, however, is only rough because it tests micro (dyadic) relations in a macro (network) comparison, the elements of which are not independent, for example. Furthermore, the frequencies in the recyclers matrix are not simply two times the respective frequencies among the nonrecyclers' goals—rather, the additional recyclers gravitated toward the linkages that apparently reflect their beliefs, doing so in a nonrandom manner. Finally, the cutoff we have selected—that there be at least 5 more recyclers than nonrecyclers before we comment on their difference—is admittedly subjective, but it is fairly conservative given that it results in an average ratio of frequencies among recyclers to nonrecyclers of 4:1, which certainly exceeds the 2:1 ratio on the sample sizes.

7. Density is the proportion of ties that exist relative to the number of possible ties.

8. Another network index comparing the recyclers' and nonrecyclers' networks is the correlation computed elementwise between the two matrixes. For the raw data matrixes, $r = .778$, and for the binary data, $r = .914$. These correlations are useful because they remove the overall level of the numbers in the matrixes and reflect only their relative patterns—an important property if one is worried about a larger sample size imputing larger frequencies.

9. Degrees computed on the raw data also consider the strengths of the associations (as measured by the number of consumers who identified each row goal

as a means to each column goal). Degrees computed on the binary data reflect more simply the number of other goals to which each goal was tied.

10. Reducing the cost of living is an interesting goal, because although recyclers saw its utility to saving money, nonrecyclers saw no connection of any sort, as a means or end. The goal is an isolate actor in the nonrecyclers' network.

11. Properly, a clique is a complete subgraph—all pairwise connections exist.

12. There were, of course, some rough approximations, and not surprisingly, these "cliques" were comprised of the intermediate goals—the only nodes in the graphs that were connected in more than one direction (i.e., including the following: save the environment, avoid landfills, provide for future generations, save the planet).

PART VI

Final Issues

CHAPTER

18 Multiple Levels of Relational
Marketing Phenomena

DAWN IACOBUCCI

PHILIP C. ZERRILLO, SR.

In the United States and abroad, much of the enterprise of marketing is characterized as relational, whether defined as generalized
exchange (Bagozzi, 1975; Kotler & Levy, 1969) or a network of
interconnected firms (Axelsson & Easton, 1992; Håkansson, 1989;
Mizruchi & Schwartz, 1987; Stern & El-Ansary, 1992). Research on
distribution channels and business marketing has a particularly strong
tradition of focusing on relational constructs such as trust, cooperation, and power (cf. Anderson, Lodish, & Weitz, 1987; Anderson &
Narus, 1990; Dwyer, Schurr, & Oh, 1987; Etgar, 1976; Stern & Scheer,
1991). Thus, although relationships certainly exist in other realms of
marketing (e.g., service provider-client interactions, Iacobucci &
Ostrom, 1993, 1996), in this chapter we focus on interfirm relationships, for constancy throughout the chapter and to reflect the relative
wealth of this literature.

Marketers studying interorganizational behavior examine relational constructs at different levels, depending on what entity is taken
to be the unit of observation and analysis: actors (individual firms),
dyads (two partner firms, such as a manufacturer and distributor),
groups (three or more interacting firms), or networks (larger groups,

AUTHORS' NOTE: We are grateful to Louis Stern for suggesting this research topic
and his comments on an earlier draft; he has always been a source of inspiration and
kindness. We are also grateful to the National Science Foundation for research
support (NSF Grant No. SES-9023445).

defined shortly). We begin with a brief overview of some types of marketing research questions that have been posed at each level. We then consider methodological issues and their impact on the content that may be studied at each relational level.

Actors

One class of examples from the marketing literature of actor-level relational constructs would be those studies in which key informants at one firm report the extent to which they trust their partner firms, or attempt to influence them, and so on. (Anderson & Narus, 1984). Each relation exists in the body of a dyad, and each dyad in the context of a larger network environment, but the focus of such studies is on a firm's view of its relation to another. Another class of examples would be those studies that consider the structure of other actors tied to a focal firm, termed "organization sets" (Aldrich & Whetten, 1981). The structural ties resemble a "fan," with all relations radiating from, or converging on, the focal firm. Such studies allow examination of two research questions: within a single fan, the researcher can compare the utility of the focal firm's multiple dyads (e.g., "has this supplier been more cooperative than that one?"), or across several fans (i.e., several focal firms and their respective partners), the researcher can compare firm to firm vis à vis their relational structures (e.g., "does this firm have a more stable set of partners than that one?"). These studies examine a larger relational frame, and begin to address the broader network structure, but the focus is still on a single actor.

Dyads

Studying dyads allows for new opportunities. Methodologically, researchers can obtain parallel corresponding perceptions from both partners in a dyad and investigate the convergence of the two firms' views of their mutual relationship or embedding environment (Anderson & Narus, 1990). Judging dyadic consensus is critical for many empirical reasons, for example, understanding the "true" nature of the relationship or aggregating the data for subsequent analyses (John & Reve, 1982; Reve & Stern, 1986; Silk & Kalwani, 1982). Conceptually, many researchers believe that dyads are gestaltlike in that the joint relationship has character beyond the sum of two individual actors (Ring & Van de Ven, 1994; Van de Ven, 1976; Zajac & Olsen, 1993). Ring and Van de Ven (1994) state that an interorganizational relationship will "act as a social unit and has a unique identity separate from its members" (p. 24). Zajac and Olsen (1993) state that "opportunities for joint gains can be realized over time through the emergence of shared interests" (p. 133). In addition, a dyadic paradigm allows us to define precisely concepts such as power and interdependence, as we shall demonstrate. Although an individual firm can certainly report on its perceptions regarding power, dyadic data are required for a researcher to observe the full phenomenon, the interactive essence of the functioning relationship.

Groups

Still other relational phenomena may be studied within higher-order collections of firms such as triads or larger groups (e.g., action-sets, Aldrich & Whetten, 1981). Theoretical issues of balance, generalized reciprocity, coalition formation, and group negotiations become relevant as do market structure issues including the identification of competition and substitutable and complementary partners. As complex as dyads may be compared to the individual firms comprising the dyads, interconnections within groups are clearly all the more complex. Concerns for identifying subgroups within networks have led network researchers to define cliques (clusters of interconnected actors) and equivalence sets (actors with similar patterns of interactions with others), among other criteria.

Networks

Some researchers use the term *network* to describe the set comprised of a focal firm and all the firms to which it is connected, and the interconnections thereby implied, to compare one firm's network to another firm's network. The properties of a firm's set of dyadic relations and its structure of interconnections are studied and perhaps compared to other structures. Such research begins to incorporate aspects of networks, but often it is predominantly actor-focused, as previously described (i.e., the "fan" structure), so when we refer to this type of structure, we will call it a "firm-centric network," like the current use by social network researchers of "ego-centric networks" on individuals. Most researchers reserve the term network to refer to the largest set of interconnections, for example, to refer to an entire marketplace, including all competitors, and all their connections (e.g., suppliers, resellers, and so on). This use of the term resembles most closely that of the classic network methodology tradition, which begins with an assumption of a closed set of actors. As we shall describe later, in application the pragmatic issues regarding collecting such complete sets of data can cause enormous difficulty and nontrivial network sampling issues are not yet satisfactorily resolved.

Here ends our overview of the different levels of relational phenomena marketing researchers may wish to study. We now turn to methodological issues, but later we will revisit these levels applying the methodological concerns.

METHODOLOGICAL ISSUES

In this section, we discuss basic principles of statistical logic. This review might seem unnecessary, but it is important to point out that a network approach and network methods must follow certain logical conventions just like any other research method. It is true that network methods have properties that are different from, say, regression, but then regression is also different from say, content analysis: Different data are required, different scientific questions may be addressed, different assumptions made, and so on. And although we confidently state that network methods are superior in addressing certain questions regarding interconnected actors, and thus are inherently more appropriate tools for addressing certain marketing phenomena, we also very clearly state that network methods cannot bypass logic.

Statistical tools traditionally have been very important in the scientific activities of developing, testing, and revising theory. In the iterative scientific pursuit, a phenomenon is observed and described, an explanation or general laws sought, new deductions and predictions derived from the explanation and tested to see what is upheld and what must be modified. Sampling and inferential methods yield quantification of the extent to which phenomena might be general and reliable. Three properties of research methods are particularly important: random sampling, large samples, and relevant referent comparisons. We discuss each in turn, first for standard data, then for network data.

Consider the issue of random sampling in classic survey data. If we wished to understand the country's leaning toward some political candidate, we might ask our neighbor for his or her opinion. This opinion is a data point, to be sure, but we would not feel confident that our neighbor spoke for the country (i.e., lack of generalizability to the population) because this spokesperson was chosen by convenience, and not by random sampling. Thus, in a study where external validity may be important, we typically are concerned with random sampling from properly defined populations.[1]

We would also expect a more accurate prediction if we had polled many persons rather than just one. We gain confidence in results as sample sizes increase; single data points, or "cases," are not as compelling as multiple data points. Certainly whole disciplines are devoted to the analysis of single cases (e.g., medicine, clinical psychology, sociology), but none of us would be persuaded that a clinical psychologist understood our nature or human nature because he or she had conducted an in-depth analysis of a single other human being. Case analyses of networks are no different in this regard. (We are, however, completely sympathetic to the difficulty in gathering data on multiple networks, as we discuss later.) Sample size is not just an issue for quantitative modeling; qualitative descriptions also are more compelling if they span multiple observations. A sample size of one is simply too small to be telling; for example, a case study profiling one computer firm may not speak even for another computer firm, much less another industry, thus the researcher would have learned only how one particular firm functions. The golden rule in sampling is: More is always better. Networks are not different in this regard, and we will see the implications of sample size at each relational level shortly.

Continuing with the political survey example, imagine the pollster has drawn a random sample (hoping to enhance generalization) and has collected opinions from a large number of voters in that sample (to enhance the precision of the predictions). We now arrive at a new issue. The pollster analyzes the data and comes up with a number: say, 45. This number has little meaning without a comparison point. Either analytically or empirically, the business of statistical inference is to create referent numbers and distributions to which our observed measure is compared to gauge its size. Even as implicit scientists, we process phenomena such as numbers by comparing them to other relevant numbers, observations are judged relatively.

If the number "45" is known to be a percentage, then it might be judged against referent points such as "0%" or "100%" or "50%" in terms of proportions of voters leaning toward a given candidate. The referent might be derived from other empirical sources, such as the candidate's rating from past polls. And almost certainly, the pollster would also wish to compare the number to the values obtained for the other candidates. These comparisons are analogous to the computation of a descriptive statistic, such as a mean $\bar{x}$ (the "45"), a t-test comparing the observed mean to some hypothetical value, μ_0 (the candidate's past performance), and a t-test comparing the observed mean to another observed mean ($\bar{x}_1$ and $\bar{x}_2$; another candidate's index). No survey researcher would rely on the presentation of a descriptive mean, $\bar{x}$ to argue a point when a t-test comparing $\bar{x}$ to μ, or $\bar{x}_1$ to $\bar{x}_2$ was available. Similarly, a description of a network is most satisfying when compared to a referent benchmark—either a null hypothesis case or another observed case(s)—that is, either theory or data.

In sum, we have argued that random sampling is important, large sample sizes are important, and the comparison of a data point to another index is important. In terms of these basic statistical logical premises, note: Network methods are no different. Network methods have their unique vantage, certainly, but that which sets the methodology apart from classic multivariate methods lies in the ability of network methods to model interconnections, not in some ability to override fundamental logical statistical requirements. We now consider the issues as applied to network research.

METHODOLOGICAL ISSUES
IN NETWORK ANALYSES

A network is defined as a set of actors (e.g., individuals, departments in an organization, firms, and so on) and the relational ties between them (Knoke & Kuklinski, 1982; Scott, 1991). The interconnections are relational in nature (e.g., one worker "respects" another, one firm "does business with" another as indicated by flowing monies or memos, and so on). Networks have come to provide an important paradigm within which to study relational ties. Networks, however, are not necessary to study relational phenomena. A research project may focus on relational *content* or not, and the philosophical *paradigm* of the research approach relies on networks (sampling and methodology) or not.

Consider the contrasting cases. The political pollster from our earlier example could ask each of the voters whether the voter trusted his or her spouse, cooperated with his or her spouse, and so on. The methodology employed in such a study is a classic survey technique, and the data would be analyzed using standard analytical methods because each observational unit (the voter) would be assumed to be independent of the next voter polled from down the street. The content of this questionnaire though, is most certainly relational— the researcher is trying to characterize constructs of trust and cooperation from an individual's perspective. These are concepts that characterize relationships. Thus, relational content is present, in the absence of a network.

Similarly, a network could be present without relational content. For example, imagine a network defined by the set of all interconnected employees in a department within an organization. If these members were surveyed as to their job satisfaction and corporate loyalty, for example, the resulting research would reflect no apparent consideration of relational constructs. The relationships defining the network are ignored, the network simply serves as a sampling frame.

Certainly each of these studies could integrate the network structure with the relational content. For the first example, if both spouses were polled, and their answers compared, the research becomes dyadic in nature, and methods that incorporate interdependence would be important. For the second example, if the responses to job satisfaction were correlated with the centralities of the employees' positions in their departmental network ties, the research becomes relational in nature.

Distinguishing between the content of research as relational or not, and a research paradigm as involving networks or not is important—it gives researchers flexibility in how they might study relational phenomena. Networks have certain advantages for studying relationships, but of course they also have certain disadvantages, and we do not wish to take the position that they are the only means of studying relational phenomena. The type of relational phenomena studied at each level (i.e., actor, dyad, group, network) differs, and each level carries its own methodological challenges. Thus, the researcher must decide what relational phenomena are sought, and whether the methodological issues for the desired level can be resolved, or, if not, whether the interest in the focal relational phenomenon can be modified accordingly. We now consider the four levels.

Actors

To illustrate various issues at each relational level, we refer to Figure 18.1, which depicts a number of actors (labeled A through I) and various ties between them. The figure may represent an entire network, or part of a network, as a sample of firms from a much larger population and their network ties, depending on our needs. The diagram focuses primarily on features regarding Firms A and B and their dyadic relation. The other firms are drawn to suggest the typical complexity of additional ties. Some of the firms are labeled arbitrarily (e.g., E through I), and others are labeled in an attempt to depict their special status vis à vis a focal actor (e.g., C and D, A's distributor and retailer). If there were room in the figure, we would also draw a similarly complex set of ties linking each of the other firms to their various other partners.

A relational study focusing on actors would be one that modeled data from (all or some of) the respondent firms labeled A through I. For an actor-level study and the appropriate application of classic analytical methods, the fact that these firms are themselves interconnected is not relevant, so the classic models would treat each actor as separate and independent (e.g., just as one voter might know another's vote, or even influence another's vote, their data are nonetheless assumed independent and modeled accordingly). The actor-level analyses would focus on the individual firms and their perceptions of various relational states. For example, manufacturers might be asked about their typical relations with each other, or with their suppliers (e.g., their top supplier, their worst, and so on).

There are two very important reasons why the individual actor is a highly desirable level at which to study relational phenomena: Both

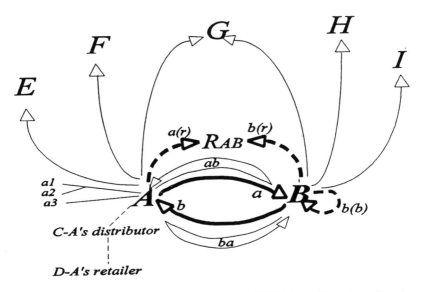

Figure 18.1. A Network of Interconnections With Focal Firm A, or Focal Dyad A-B

data collection and data analysis are simpler. First, because this unit of analysis and sampling is the smallest—one actor (not two as in a dyad, or more as in a group or network)—these units are the easiest to come by and the most plentiful. Thus, issues of random sampling and large sample sizes should not present overwhelming challenges. (We recognize that we are focusing on interorganizational phenomena, and obtaining a data point representing a firm presents more challenges than obtaining data on the example voter, but this additional difficulty is attributable to the type of focal respondent, not the relational content nor a network paradigm.)

Second, if the actor is the unit of analysis, then a standard database is created in which multiple respondents or informants are measured on a battery of variables, and the researcher is interested in the associations between those variables. The respondents are assumed to be independent observations; the units may be reporting on properties of relationships, but linkages are not the units of analysis. This assumption of independent observational units allows the use of classic statistical procedures as valid means of inquiry: Network methods are not necessary, standard methods are sufficient.

One of the common types of actor-level research described earlier was that of asking key informants at firms to respond with perceptions of relational properties (e.g., extent to which the firm trusts its partner firm, and so on). A questionnaire is sent to Firm A. If "a1" and "a2" (in the figure) represent two top-level managers, and "a3" represents a middle-level manager, then the survey gets routed to whomever fills the desired role of the researcher; for example, if mid-level managers are targeted, the survey goes to Actor a3. This surveying would be replicated at numerous (!) randomly sampled (!) firms, each of which has its representative employee-role like a3. The researcher gathers the data and conducts sophisticated analyses (e.g., structural equations modeling) or simple calculations (e.g., means and correlations). Either way, the results depict (the aggregation of) firms' perceptions regarding the measured relational phenomena. The researcher probably also investigates how the relational perceptions covary with firm-demographic variables (e.g., size, industry), or firm-attitude variables (e.g., expectations, strategy). Some of the covariates could themselves be relational, such as a firm's self-reported average relational duration.

Another type of actor-level relational study described earlier is the firm-centric perspective that considers the interconnected relational structure of other actors tied to a focal firm. In Figure 18.1, this sort of study corresponds to noting all relational ties Firm A has (B, C, E through G) and comparing properties of that structure to the respective ties of the other surveyed firms; for example, Firm B's ties to A, G, H, and I. This research question begins to envelope more of a network "feel" to it, but the data are rather spartan (only the surveyed firm's perspective is reflected), and the leverage of network methods may be meager (e.g., a network inquiry into an actor's "centrality" would not make sense for studies in which the contacted focal firm is by definition central to the connections it yields). The researcher, however, can measure actor indexes that reflect numbers and strengths of ties to other firms.

We had stated earlier that such studies would allow addressing two types of research questions. First, we could focus on Firm A, and diagnose which of its dyads (A-B, A-C, A-E, A-F, A-G) is most effective, costly, enduring, trustworthy, profitable, and so on. This investigation could be done for each surveyed firm (e.g., B-A, B-G, B-H, B-I), and the variability compared and explained via known properties of A and B. The second sort of research question is the comparison of A's firm-centric network linkages to the B-centric linkages. For example, B may have ties that are fewer but mightier. We would examine the correlations of indexes of relational structure with measures of firm performance, for example, to see whether there might be structures that enhance corporate success.

If actor-level research had only advantages (the ease with which large, random samples may be obtained, and the ease of familiar data analysis), we would stop here and study all relational phenomena from the perspective of the individual firm. Most relational researchers acknowledge, however, that certain phenomena come into being only in dyads or larger groups. Research on dyads, groups, and networks is complementary to actor-level research because they share the advantage that new research questions may be addressed, and they share the disadvantage of sampling difficulties just described as a strength of actor-level relational studies.

Dyads, Groups, and Networks

As the unit of analysis increases to two or more interconnected actors, it becomes increasingly difficult to sample intact groups. In actor-level research (i.e., standard survey methods), response rates do not approach 100%, but when one actor fails to complete a survey, it does not affect the data from another actor, given their independence. Unfortunately, for research on dyads or larger groups, when one actor fails to complete a survey, the entire unit of analysis is destroyed. If a manufacturer completes a survey but its distributing partner does not, the dyad is not intact, and the manufacturer's data are essentially wasted. For larger groups, say a "group" of size seven, a missing actor takes the group size down to six, but is probably still presentable as a "group." (Nevertheless, when the seventh member drops out, so does the information regarding the ties between that actor and the intact six; the deletion of an actor also deletes relational ties by implication.)

In addition, as the unit of analysis increases in size, the number of units in the relevant population is smaller than populations of individual actors. By definition, each larger order group is comprised of a number of the lower order units (e.g., a group is comprised of several actors). There are fewer coalitions of firms than there are firms, and fewer firms than there are employees, and so on. The number of candidate groups can be far smaller than the number of actors in the actor population, sometimes such that complete representation of the population may be preferable to sampling. Let us now consider these larger units.

Dyads

To illustrate research focusing on the dyad as the unit of observation and analysis, consider the dyad comprised of Actors A and B depicted in Figure 18.1. The link emanating from Actor A to Partner B that is labeled "a" denotes a relational tie from A to B that might represent Actor A's perception of its partner B (e.g., "Do you trust your partner B?") or Actor A's perceptions of its own behavior toward B (e.g., "Do you cooperate with B?"). The corresponding questions are also asked of Actor B about its partner, Firm A, and these relational responses are labeled by the link "b." In a dyadic study, these corresponding data points "a" and "b" obtained from Actors A and B would be linked in the analyses.

There are additional types of relational ties depicted in Figure 18.1. The links labeled "a(r)" and "b(r)" from A and B to the unit labeled "R_{AB}" represent the characterizations that Firms A and B would yield, respectively, about their joint relationship "R_{AB}."[2] For example, both firms might be asked to comment on the extent to which they believe their business partnership has been effective. Such questions begin to address the gestalt nature of the dyad, whereby the relationship between two parties becomes an entity unto itself, and must be described in joint, mutually dependent terms.

The links in the figure drawn from Actor A to B and back again (labeled "ab") and that from B to A and back (labeled "ba") depict metareflections of an actor on itself through its perception of its partner's eyes. For example, the relational link "ab" may represent Firm A's response to a recursive question such as, "To what extent do you think your partner . . . trusts you?" (There could be additional levels, say "aba," such as, "Do you think that your partner thinks you are trustworthy;" asking A for B's perception of A's outgoing attitudes, and so on.)

Various combinations of these dyadic perspectives could keep marketers in relational studies for years to come. Previously we had described two common sorts of dyadic studies. The first focused on the correspondence between the perceptions of both actors. Depending on the actual semantics of the questionnaire items used, the researcher might wish to test dyadic consensus by comparing the links "a" to "b," "a" to "ab," "a" to "ba," or "a(r)" to "b(r)."

For example, imagine a study conducted on trust with the following relational ties:

"a": represents the question to "A, do you trust your partner B?"

"b": to "B, do you trust your partner A?"

"ab": "A, do you think your partner B trusts you?"

"ba": "B, do you think your partner A trusts you?"

"a(r)": "A, do you think there is trust in your relationship (with B)?"

"b(r)": "B, do you think there is trust in your relationship (with A)?"

The comparison of "a" to "b" expresses the mutuality of the relationship, or the extent to which there is (self-reported) trust exchange (i.e., "A, do you trust B?, B, do you trust A?"). This notion of reciprocity in joint behavior is taken to be a substantively interesting phenomenon among network researchers, but it also might be what some researchers seek in measures of concordance.

Other researchers might prefer to examine the extent to which an actor perceives reciprocity (regardless of whether "a" actually resembles "b"). This view would suggest the researcher compare "a" to "ab" (i.e., "A, do you trust B, and, do you think your partner, B, trusts you?"). One might argue that even if "a" does *not* resemble "b," both parties would probably appear fairly content, at least in the short run, if each believed that their view "a" (or "b") resembled their perception of their partner's view "ab" (or "ba").

The cross products would provide another interesting comparison; for example, "a" to "ba," or, "A, do you trust B, and B, do you think A trusts you?" This comparison is one between an actor's stated perspective, and the partner's estimate of the actor's state. These ties resemble the classic communication model in which an intended message is sent by one party and interpreted and reacted to by another, and the goodness of the communication, or relationship, is partly a function of the sent intentions being similar to the received interpretations.

Finally, the two actors' views of their joint relationship would provide another comparison, "a(r)" to "b(r)" (i.e., "A and B, do you believe your relationship to be a trusting one?"). This comparison takes dyadic data and asks most directly the extent to which the two parties' perspectives are replications of each other's.

For any of these examinations, the researcher may be tempted to take the dyadic data and aggregate them if there is sufficient apparent agreement between partners. That is, with high consensus, a single dyad score might be generated with loss of little information, and subsequent analyses simplified by using standard (i.e., nonnetwork) methods for data analysis. This action is defensible, albeit probably not optimal for two reasons. First, most data sets will probably not yield "high consensus," as judged by the researcher. Marketing lore has suggested that two interrelating firms will demonstrate strong empirical consensus when reporting on fairly objective properties of their mutual arrangement (duration of relationship, volume of trade, and so on), but that their perspectives will diverge more for subjective properties of the relationship (cooperation, communicative openness, and so on). Recent research, however, has suggested greater complexity—that the dyadic perspectives even on the objective relational properties may exhibit strong differences (Anderson & Weitz, 1992; Zerrillo, 1995). Thus, understanding and measuring both firms within the dyad may be critical for eventual modeling.

Second, the researcher had gone through the bother of collecting the dyadic data, and it seems wasteful to aggregate over actors within the dyad to obtain a single value for the dyad. One exception to this occurs if one considers a technical point within network methods. The relational ties depicted in Figure 18.1 are "directed" from an originating actor toward the recipient partner (Figure 18.1 is termed a directed graph or digraph). There are other types of links that are not directed, and although it can be a matter of semantics, it could have implications for analysis. For example, we have been discussing directed relations (e.g., "Do you trust your partner?"), but a nondirected relational tie would be something like, "Are Firms A and B in business together?" (Presumably one could ask the directed forms of the question; "A, are you in business with B?" and "B, are you in business with A?" and although it might seem peculiar to get disagreement on such objective properties, according to the research referred to earlier, it appears it would be possible. Thus, a purist would say that both parties' perspectives should be sought on all criteria.) Thus, instead of two data points, "a" and "b," there would be the single data point "d" that would be common to the actors.[3]

We had also described dyadic research beyond tests of convergent view points. For example, we had suggested that the dyadic unit can enable clearer conceptualization of the concept "power." If the relational tie in Figure 18.1 labeled "a" measures the extent to which "A attempted to influence B's behavior at Time t," and "b" taps the extent to which "B behaved in the desired manner at Time $t + 1$," then the association between these two relational ties, "at 0" and "bt + 1" measures precisely the degree of success of the power play. These data can be truly sequential (i.e., more than one wave of data collection), or cross-sectional proxies (i.e., self-reported behaviors of Actors A and B at two points in time; "A, did you attempt to influence B at Time t?" and "B, how did you behave at Time $t + 1$?").

Other dynamic phenomena are also easily modeled, such as multivariate reciprocity (e.g., "If Actor A cooperates at Time t, does B report more trust at Time $t + 1$?"), autocorrelation (i.e., "Does actor A behave consistently over time?"), and so on (Iacobucci & Hopkins, 1992). Static multivariate questions are equally interesting, including modeling multiplexities (e.g., "Do actors who communicate more also tend to cooperate more, or trust more?"), generalized exchanges (e.g., "Is Actor A's trust negatively associated with Partner B's attempts to influence A?"), and so on.

Modeling these phenomena presumes some sort of replication. Recall that just as we do not wish to predict an election outcome on the basis of the single viewer, we cannot address these dyadic research questions by examining a sole pair of firms interacting at a single point in time.[4] Replication here simply means multiple units of analysis are observed; typically multiple dyads. It would, however, be equally valid to measure two interacting firms at multiple points in time, to focus on a single dyad, modeling its dynamic behavior and history. The richest data set would be one that combines measures of multiple dyads at multiple points in time (on multiple variables or relational ties).

Before leaving this discussion of the dyadic perspective, note the self-reflexive link at Actor B labeled, "b(b)." This tie denotes B's perception about its own properties; that is, it is not dyadic. For example, it might represent, "B, to what extent do you think you are generally a cooperative firm?" Note the question characterizes B as an actor, its general relational nature, not specific to any of B's particular relationships. These data provide anchors against which to compare actors' responses to their dyadic data. If B characterizes itself as generally cooperative, any resistance in the dyadic relationship will more likely be attributed to the Partner A, with implications of B's subsequent likely behavior toward A, for example.

Groups

Groups are usually defined as being comprised of three or more members, to distinguish them from dyads. For example, many disciplines have studied properties of balance; if the links in Figure 18.1 represent a partnership comprised of Firms A, B, and G, and the A-G and B-G linkages were effective, it would be problematic to all three parties if the A-B link is not. For directed relational data, balance can be somewhat like transitivity (e.g., if A says it trusts B, and B trusts C, does A trust C). In marketing, some linkages will represent particular linear structures (e.g., channels), which may make the A-C direct link irrelevant (e.g., in Figure 18.1, Firm A is connected to its distributor C, and C to its retailer D, but at least in this figure, A has no direct link to D). That is, the substantive arena of study can superimpose constraints on the structure of the triad A-B-C so that all pairwise relations may or may not be possible (cf. Valley, White, & Iacobucci, 1992).

Other new phenomena include generalized reciprocity, coalition formation and group negotiations, and market structure issues such as identifying competition and complementary partners. Generalized reciprocity would describe, say, Firm A receiving something good from B (e.g., cooperation, a price deal) in turn doing good to a third or fourth party within their common group. Although the term reciprocity has positive connotations, certainly negative phenomena may be reciprocated among actors as well; if A displeases B and B displeases another, the entire group may escalate upward to heated confrontations. Indeed, game theory has been helpful in deriving predictions for group (or dyadic) behavior for positive or negative interactions. Coalition formation is a pursuit of games on three or more parties; if A, B, and C are linked in business, but A and B begin to deal with each other more favorably, they gain leverage power over C (Iacobucci & Hopkins, 1994). Coalition formation and group negotiations are group manifestations of generalized power.

Market structure issues are another sort of relational phenomenon that might be examined at the group level. Network researchers have focused predominantly on the identification of groups within networks that might represent competitors or substitutable actors (e.g., Hopkins, Henderson, & Iacobucci, 1995). Two different criteria have been used in locating clusters of actors: The group of actors may be densely interconnected, or they may share similar relations with other actors in the larger network. The first of these objectives, seeking actors who are interconnected, is the pursuit of cliques. The second objective, seeking actors who interact with similar sets of others, is the pursuit of identifying structurally equivalent actors (Knoke & Kuklinski, 1982; Scott, 1991.)

Groups yield interesting methodological questions. For example, the network researcher can select a method that creates exclusive clusters, or clusters that overlap (cf. Arabie, Carroll, DeSarbo, & Wind, 1981). For the former, every actor belongs to only one group, but for the latter, each actor could belong to multiple groups. This decision regarding methodology has implications for subsequent modeling because the former choice results in independent units, whereas analysis of the latter would require incorporation of the nonindependence.[5]

Networks

We now turn to networks, the biggest unit of observation and analysis, anchoring the opposite extreme of actor-level research. Recall the three main methodological issues: random sampling, large sample sizes, and a comparison point for a datum (a hypothesized value or another empirical value). Random sampling need not be an overwhelming obstacle for network research. We recognize that most networks studied in detail are selected because the researcher is given access, or because the focal actor (e.g., in a firm-centric network) is a market leader or otherwise has special properties. On the face of it, these selection criteria appear systematic, not random, and would thereby likely provide a biased perspective, limiting generalizations to other networks. It is conceivable, however, that certain assumptions could be made to alleviate the apparent problems. For example, when researchers are given access to a network, it would appear that "convenience" drives the data. Still, most network researchers contact multiple firms in hopes to find a cooperative research setting, and it might not be unreasonable to assume that there was no a priori reason to believe that firm "A" would cooperate with the researcher, rather than firm "Q," and that therefore natural, random (or at least unexplainable) processes were underway to yield Firm A and not Q. Other researchers might not feel comfortable with this assumption, arguing that a firm willing to participate in an academic study might be atypical (interested in research, desperate for consultation, and so on), and therefore certainly not representative.

If a network is selected for its special properties, for example, focusing on a market leader, the selection criterion is clearly purposive and not random, and yet the researcher might redefine the sampling frame. For example, rather than seeking a computer firm that is representative (in a typical, average sense), for which the market leader computer firm would *not* be representative, perhaps the researcher redefines the study as one that investigates "market leaders." Then, it may be random to select the computer market leader rather than, say a telecommunications market leader.

Regarding the second issue, if we are to have confidence in recorded network phenomena on the basis of multiple data points, we must obtain replications, that is, more than one network. Although obtaining large samples for survey data takes effort, obtaining data on intact dyads or larger groups or networks requires more. Sampling is difficult on these macro units of observation and analysis, and observing whole, functioning networks in sufficient number as to make valid comparisons may often be impractical. The impracticalities are several: First, certainly the cost and effort would be great, but second, recall our point earlier that there are simply fewer units as the units become more macro (e.g., networks), so obtaining "large" sample sizes may be impossible.

Thus, it is not coincidence but rather a direct consequence of the macro problem of the unit of analysis and its data collection that many network researchers focus their methods on descriptions of a single network. The argument for such in-depth analysis of single observational units usually revolves around the richness of the resultant data. The network case analyst draws for us the tapestry of the interconnected actors and concludes that we now know these actors well. Note, however, the shift in logic. For descriptions of actors within a network, actors become the unit of analysis and the sample size is the number of actors. And we might indeed feel confident that "we know these actors well" because we observed a good number of them. For more macro research conducted on networks, however, networks are the unit of analysis, and sufficient numbers of networks must be sampled to be logically convincing or statistically sound. Note too that if networks are the focus of research, it matters not how many actors are in any of the sampled networks. It is easy to be sympathetic to the study of a single network when one realizes just how difficult data are to obtain from a single network, much less additional, replicate networks. Nevertheless, we have argued that more units, whether actors or networks, are better than fewer.

What, then, is a network researcher to do? We offer five suggestions. First, we recognize that for some purposes, a case analysis may suffice. For example, if asked to consult for a firm, a marketing researcher can offer a description of relationships in a firm's network or industry structure with little concern for statistics. In addition, a single-case network can yield a rich opportunity for substantive or methodological illustration.

Second, if only one network exists, then its structure cannot be compared to other empirical networks, but the existing network can be compared to a hypothesized structure (Hubert & Baker, 1978; Wasserman, 1987). This approach holds promise for theoretical progress at the macro network level. Presumably, clear theoretical deductions regarding what a network structure "should" look like could be compared to what the observed network "does" resemble. (Nevertheless, recall our analogy to the survey approach, in which we would seek a comparison of $\bar{x}$ to μ, or $\bar{x}_1$ to $\bar{x}_{12}$, not X_i—a single datum—to μ, which is the situation here with a single network. Theory can generate a network version of μ, and a single empirical network would be the counterpart to X_i, but only with additional networks could we obtain something like a network mean, $\bar{x}$, or any sense of variance about that mean, to assist in judging the size of any discrepancy.)

Third, a single network can yield its own comparison structure if multiple ties are measured on the actors. In a multivariate sense, we would compare the network's structure on its "cooperative" ties to its structure on its "power" ties, and so on. We had described earlier that modeling requires replications, and we had used the example of multiple dyads and multiple points in time. Measuring more than one relational variable also offers the network researcher opportunity for comparison, and appropriate network methods are available (Hubert & Baker, 1978; Iacobucci & Wasserman, 1988; Wasserman, 1987; Wasserman & Iacobucci, 1988).

Notice that these last two suggestions have essentially used the third methodological issue (referent points) to help assist likely shortcomings of network studies on the second issue (sample size). That is, if we cannot obtain more than one network, we can at least obtain a relevant comparison to assess fit of theoretical expectations. The suggestion of measuring multiple relational ties seems particularly fruitful for two reasons: First, the previous suggestion requires deductive predictions, which in turn requires theory, and second, it seems reasonable that a researcher would measure multiple network ties, requiring the actors in the network to yield perceptions of multiple structural relations. Even a 5-minute phone interview could yield information about trust, cooperation, and power ties, as well as properties of the actor, for example.[6,7]

A fourth suggestion would be to rely on the definition of network that we had characterized as firm centric, because even though the research and methods would focus on the structural ties in the firm's network, the firm is still essentially the sampling unit, and clearly firms are more abundant than networks of firms. This focus would allow comparison of firms' interconnections and the examination of the firms' networks' variability, and how the variability in network structures might be explained by other properties measured on the same firms.

Fifth, taking the fourth suggestion even further, a researcher might simply switch units of analysis. A network might be used as a cluster sample frame, but with a focus to study and model actors as the relevant unit of observation and analysis. This content of such research could clearly still be relational, and would thereby be characterized as "network research" (e.g., see the journal *Social Networks*). Indeed most of what is referred to as network research simply means that it focuses on understanding interconnections between sampled units, which distinguishes it from classic statistical methods that require assumptions of independence between those units. There is nothing improper or incorrect about referring to research that focuses on interconnections and relational ties as network research. Nevertheless, note that neither the links nor the network per se are the unit of analysis.

SUMMARY

In sum, we have tried to make and defend the following assertions: First, marketing is relational. Second, interorganizational marketing phenomena may be studied at the actor, dyad, group, or network levels. Third, network methodological issues for multilevel phenomena include random sampling (if one wishes to generalize to a population of the sampled units), large samples (for greater stability and precision in estimation), and some comparison point against which to judge the network data (either a hypothetical data point or another empirical data point). Fourth, networks are an ideal paradigm for studying certain relational phenomena, but the relational content and the network paradigm are separable. Fifth, many relational phenomena may be studied, including dyadic effects (e.g., convergence, power, multivariate reciprocity) and group effects (e.g., balance, coalition formation). Sixth, replications are important—either multiple units, multiple points in time, or multiple relational ties. Seventh, ideally, multiple replicate networks would be obtained to have empirical comparisons at the network level, but without replicates, other options exist: (a) one case network may be sufficient for certain purposes, (b) the network may be compared to a hypothetical network structure derived from theory, (c) the network structure on one relation tie may be compared to the structure on another relational tie measured on the same set of actors, (d) the researcher might focus on firm-centric networks, and (e) the researcher might focus on actors within the network.

There exists no method that can make a silk purse of a sow's ear; there are of course methods that if improperly used can tatter either. Rich and rigorous network data can yield great insights via network methods. Those same strong network data input into improper methods, however, will yield only basic patterns, and probably even those with intractable bias. And conversely, weak network data input into strong, capable network methods will result only in the strong, capable network analyses of weak network data. Certain inferences will not be possible if the data do not exist to address them. Some marketing researchers have criticized network studies for having little theory; many network researchers consider much in networks to be theoretical. Our stance given the issues raised in this chapter is that although we certainly hope for the continued strengthening of theory development, in the testing of such hypotheses and arguments, it will be the data, or lack thereof, not the existence of theoretical premises nor the already extant network methodology, that will almost surely prove to be the challenge in studying certain network phenomena. We hope this exposition highlights and clarifies substantive and methodological opportunities in the study of relational issues.

NOTES

1. If one wishes to generalize findings to a population, the sample must be representative, approximated via random sampling. External validity need not be a research goal, as in theory testing for which the enhancement of internal validity takes greater priority, and convenience samples are logically sufficient (Sternthal et al., 1987, and homogeneous samples such as students may be particularly desirable when attempting to parse small bits of explained variance). Whether the population is random or convenient, however, there is variability (error, noise, individual differences, heterogeneity) in a distribution and units must be sampled randomly from the relevant population to use statistical theory. Tables of critical values, for example, would be unusable if samples were drawn with any systematic bias.

2. R_{AB} is a hypothetical, nonsampleable unit, drawn into the figure for exposition.

3. Nondirected relations are also called "symmetric" because the sociomatrix of actors (A through I in Figure 18.1 as rows) by partners (A through I as columns) would be a symmetric matrix; a tie from A to B is also a tie from B to A, so the X_{ab} cell must equal the X_{ba} cell, hence symmetry. We prefer not to use this term because matrixes describing directed ties that are generally asymmetric (because A's ties to B X_{ab} may differ from B's ties to A, X_{ba}), could nevertheless happen to be symmetric if there was indeed agreement on the perspectives (i.e., if A's ties to B are identical to B's ties to A, for all actors A and B). Note that this observation suggests another means of testing for convergence in two parties' perspectives: If all actors agree in their views, then the directed relational ties should comprise a symmetric matrix ($X = X'$).

4. A single dyad at a single point in time violates both the need for a large sample and the need for a comparison point. Presumably, a theoretical prediction could be created against which this dyad could be compared, but in survey research, that would be like comparing a single person's data point, X_i to the hypothesized value for the population mean, μ, whereas normally we compare $\bar{x}$ to μ. We had described comparison sources as either theoretical or empirical, but a single dyad at a single point in time is essentially a case study of the dyad, with no contrast dyads. A single dyad yields no variance to enable modeling; trying to model a single pair of firms recorded at a single point in time would be like trying to regress a single X score on a single Y score.

5. Independence between units of observation is relevant to dyads too. In a series of manufacturer-distributor dyads in which each manufacturer partners with only one distributor, and vice versa, the dyadic units would be independent. If a manufacturer responds to a relational survey for each of its distributing partners (e.g., firm-centric networks), the dyads would not be independent.

6. The comparison of a network structure on one relational tie (e.g., trust) to the same network's on another relation (e.g., cooperation) is like a survey correlation of two data points measured on the same respondents. The analysis is a within-, not a between-subjects comparison, and there are methods for comparing a network to a hypothesized structure or to itself on a different set of relational ties, in this within-networks sense (Hubert & Baker, 1978; Iacobucci & Wasserman, 1988; Wasserman, 1987; Wasserman & Iacobucci, 1988). The between-networks comparisons can be made using the newer statistical methods in Iacobucci and Hopkins (1994).

7. Some network researchers create sociograms of interconnected actors where the content of the interconnection varies with each dyad; for example, A trusts B, C sends customers to D, E cooperates with B, and so on. This approach is fine for the goal of communicating an interesting case study, but it yields no replication and therefore no ability to compare data points or create network models.

References

Aaker, D. (1991). *Managing brand equity.* New York: Macmillan.

Aiken, M., & Hage, J. (1968). Organizational interdependence intraorganizational structure. *American Sociological Review, 33,* 912-930.

Ajzen, I., & Fishbein, M. (1990). *Understanding attitudes and predicting social behavior.* Englewood Cliffs, NJ: Prentice Hall.

A good idea grows into profits. (1995, May 15). *Evening Standard,* p. B1.

Alba, R. D. (1982). Taking stock of network analysis: A decade's results. *Research in the Sociology of Organizations, 1,* 39-74.

Albas, D. C., & Albas, C. A. (1989). Meaning in context: The impact of eye contact and perception of threat on proximity. *Journal of Social Psychology, 129,* 525-531.

Alderson, W. (1965). *Dynamic marketing behavior.* Homewood, IL: Irwin.

Aldrich, H. E. (1971). Organizational boundaries and interorganizational conflict. *Human Relations, 24,* 279-293.

Aldrich, H. E. (1979). *Organizations and environments.* Englewood Cliffs, NJ: Prentice Hall.

Aldrich, H. E. (1982). The origins and persistence of social networks. In P. V. Marsden & N. Lin (Eds.), *Handbook of organizational design* (pp. 281-293). Beverly Hills, CA: Sage.

Aldrich, H., & Whetten, D. A. (1981). Organization-sets, action-sets, and networks: Making the most of simplicity. In P. C. Nystrom & W. H. Starbuck (Eds.), *Handbook of organizational design, 1* (pp. 385-408). New York: Oxford University Press.

Aldrich, H., & Zimmer, C. (1986). Entrepreneurship through social networks. In D. L. Sexton & R. W. Smilor (Eds.), *The art and science of entrepreneurship* (pp. 3-23). Cambridge, MA: Ballinger.

Alford, R. R. (1975). *Health care politics.* Chicago: University of Chicago Press.

Allen, M. P. (1978). Economic interest groups and the corporate elite structure. *Social Science Quarterly, 58,* 597-615.

Allen, N. J., & Meyer, J. P. (1990). The measurement and antecedents of affective, continuance, and normative commitment to the organization. *Journal of Occupational Psychology, 63,* 1-18.

Alter, C., & Hage, J. (1993). *Organizations working together.* Newbury Park, CA: Sage.

Amin, A., & Thrift, N. (1992). Neo-Marshallian nodes in global networks. *International Journal of Urban and Regional Research, 6,* 571-587.

410

Anderson, C. A., & Sedikides, C. (1991). Thinking about people: Contributions of a typological alternative to associationistic and dimensional models of person perception. *Journal of Personality and Social Psychology, 60,* 203-217.

Anderson E., & Coughlan, A. T. (1987). International market entry and expansion via independent or integrated channels of distribution. *Journal of Marketing, 51,* 71-82.

Anderson, E., Lodish, L. M., & Weitz, B. A. (1987). Resource allocation behavior in conventional channels. *Journal of Marketing Research, 24,* 85-97.

Anderson, E., & Weitz, B. (1986). Determinants of continuity in conventional channel dyads. *Marketing Science, 8,* 319-325.

Anderson, E., & Weitz, B. (1992). The use of pledges to build and sustain commitment in distribution channels. *Journal of Marketing Research, 29,* 18-34.

Anderson, J. C., Håkansson, H., & Johanson, J. (1994). Dyadic business relationships within a business network context. *Journal of Marketing, 58,* 1-15.

Anderson, J. C., Jain, D. C., & Chintagunta, P. K. (1993). Customer value assessment in business markets: A state-of-practice study. *Journal of Business-to-Business Marketing, 1,* 3-29.

Anderson, J. C., & Narus, J. A. (1984). A model of the distributor's perspective of distributor-manufacturer working relationships. *Journal of Marketing Research, 48,* 62-74.

Anderson, J. C., & Narus, J. A. (1990). A model of distributor firm and manufacturer firm working relationships. *Journal of Marketing Research, 54,* 42-58.

Aoki, M. (1990). Toward an economic model of the Japanese firm. *Journal of Economic Literature, 28,* 1-27.

Aoki, M., & Dore, R. (Eds.). (1994). *The Japanese firm: The sources of competitive strength.* Oxford: Oxford University Press.

Arabie, P., Carroll, J. D., DeSarbo, W. S., & Wind, J. (1981). Overlapping clustering: A new method for product positioning. *Journal of Marketing Research, 18,* 310-317.

Arabie, P., & Wind, Y. (1994). Marketing and social networks. In S. Wasserman & J. Galaskiewicz (Eds.), *Advances in social network analysis: Research in the social and behavioral sciences* (pp. 254-273). Thousand Oaks, CA: Sage.

Argyle, M., & Henderson, M. (1985). *The anatomy of relationships.* New York: Penguin.

Aronoff, J., Woike, B. A., & Hyman, L. M. (1992). Which are the stimuli in facial displays of anger and happiness: Configurational bases of emotion recognition. *Journal of Personality and Social Psychology, 62,* 1050-1066.

Astley, W. G. (1984). Toward an appreciation of collective strategy: Social ecology of organizational environments. *Academy of Management Review, 9,* 526-535.

Astley, W. G. (1985). The two ecologies: Population and community perspectives on organization evolution. *Administrative Science Quarterly, 30,* 224-241.

Astley, W. G., & Fombrun, C. J. (1983). Collective strategy: Social ecology of organizational environments. *Academy of Management Review, 8,* 576-587.

Axelsson, B., & Easton, G. (Eds.). (1992). *Industrial networks: A new view of reality.* London: Routledge.

Baba, Y., & Imai, K. (1993). A network view of innovation and entrepreneurship: The case of the evolution of VCR systems. *International Social Science Journal, 45,* 23-34.

Bacharach, S., & Lawler, E. J. (1980). *Power and politics in organizations.* San Francisco: Jossey-Bass.

Badaracco J. L. (1991). *The knowledge link: How firms compete through strategic alliances.* Boston: Harvard Business School Press.

Bagozzi, R. P. (1975). Marketing as exchange. *Journal of Marketing, 39,* 32-39.

Bagozzi, R. P., & Dabholkar, P. A. (1994). Consumer recycling goals and their effect on decisions to recycle: A means-end chain analysis. *Psychology and Marketing, 11,* 313-340.

Bagozzi, R. P., & Warshaw, P. R. (1990). Trying to consume. *Journal of Consumer Research, 17,* 127-140.

Bak, C. A., Vogt, L. H., George, W. R., & Greentree, I. R. (1994). Management by team. *Journal of Services Marketing, 8,* 37-47.

Baker, J. (1987). The role of the environment in marketing services: The consumer perspective. In J. A. Czepiel, C. A. Congram, & J. Shanahan (Eds.), *The services challenge: Integrating for competitive advantage* (pp. 79-84). Chicago: American Marketing Association.

Baker, W. (1984). The social structure of a national securities market. *American Journal of Sociology, 89,* 775-811.

Baker, W. (1990). Market networks and corporate behavior. *American Journal of Sociology, 96,* 589-625.

Baker, W. (1992). The network organization in theory and practice. In N. Nohria & R. G. Eccles (Eds.), *Networks and organizations* (pp. 397-429). Boston: Harvard Business School Press.

Banton, M. (1965). *Roles: An introduction to the study of social relations.* New York: Basic Books.

Barley, M. W. (1963). *The house and home.* London: Vista.

Bartlett, R. C. (1994). *The direct option.* College Station: Texas A&M University Press.

Bass, F. M. (1969). A new product growth model for consumer durables. *Management Science, 15,* 215-227.

Bateson, J., & Hui, M. K. (1986). Crowding in the service environment. In M. Venkatesan, D. M. Schmalensee, & C. Marshall (Eds.), *Creativity in services marketing: What's new, what works, what's developing* (pp. 85-88). Chicago: American Marketing Association.

Bayus, B. L. (1992). Brand loyalty and marketing strategy: An application to home appliances. *Marketing Science, 11,* 21-38.

Beamish, P. W. (1984). *Joint venture performance in developing countries.* Unpublished doctoral dissertation, University of Western Ontario.

Behar, R. (1985, March 25). Cleaning up? *Forbes,* pp. 94-95.

Belk, R., Sherry, J., & Wallendorf, M. (1988). A naturalistic inquiry into buyer and seller behavior at a swap meet. *Journal of Consumer Research, 14,* 449-470.

Belussi, F. (1992). Benetton Italy: Beyond Fordism and flexible specialization to the evolution of the network firm model. In M. Swasti (Ed.), *Computer-aided manufacturing and women's employment: The clothing industry in four EC countries* (pp. 73-91). Berlin: Springer Verlag.

Benson, J. K. (1975). The interorganizational network as a political economy. *Administrative Science Quarterly, 20,* 229-249.

Berry, L. L., Zeithaml, V. A., & Parasuraman, A. (1990). Five imperatives for improving service quality. *Sloan Management Review, 29,* 29-38.

Best, M. (1990). *The new competition: Institutions for industrial restructuring.* Cambridge, MA: Harvard University Press.

Bettman, J. R. (1974). Toward a statistic for consumer decision net models. *Journal of Consumer Research, 1,* 71-80.

Biggart, N. W. (1989). *Charismatic capitalism: Direct selling organizations in America.* Chicago: University of Chicago Press.

Biggart, N. W., & Hamilton, G. G. (1992). On the limits of a firm-based theory to explain business networks: The Western bias of neo-classical economics. In N. Nohria & R. G. Eccles (Eds.), *Networks and organizations: Structure, form, and action* (pp. 471-490). Cambridge, MA: Harvard Business School Press.

Birley, S. (1985). The role of networks in the entrepreneurial process. *Journal of Business Venturing, 1,* 107-117.

Bishop, Y. M. M., Fienberg, S. E., & Holland, P. W. (1975). *Discrete multivariate analysis: Theory and practice.* Cambridge: MIT Press.

Bitner, M. J. (1992). Servicescapes: The impact of physical surroundings on customers and employees. *Journal of Marketing, 56,* 57-71.

Blau, P. (1964). *Exchange and power in social life.* New York: John Wiley.

Bleeke, J., & Ernst, D. (1993). *Collaborating to compete: Using strategic alliances and acquisitions in global markets.* New York: Free Press.

Bloch, P. H., Ridgway, N. M., & Nelson, J. E. (1991). Leisure and the shopping mall. *Advances In Consumer Research, 18,* 445-449.

Boardman, S. K., & Horowitz, S. V. (1994). Constructive conflict management and social problems: An introduction. *Journal of Social Issues, 50,* 1-12.

Boje, D., & Whetten, D. A. (1981). Effects of organizational strategies and constraints on centrality and attributions of influence in interorganizational networks. *Administrative Science Quarterly, 26,* 378-395.

Bonacich, P. (1987). Power and centrality: A family of measures. *American Journal of Sociology, 92,* 1170-1182.

Bonoma, T. V. (1991, February 18). This snake rises in bad times. *Marketing News, 25,* 16.

Borch, O. J., & Arthur, M. (1995). Strategic networks among small firms: Implications for strategy research methods. *Journal of Management Studies, 32,* 420-441.

Borgatti, S. P., Everett, M. G., & Freeman, L. C. (1992). *UCINET IV version 1.0 reference manual.* Columbia, SC: Analytic Technologies.

Bowers, M., Martin, C., & Luker, A. (1990). Trading places: Employees as customers, customers as employees. *Journal of Services Marketing, 4,* 55-69.

Brass, D. (1984). Being in the right place: A structural analysis of individual influence in organizations. *Administrative Science Quarterly, 29,* 518-539.

Brass, D., & Burkhardt, M. (1992). Centrality and power in organizations. In N. Nohria & R. G. Eccles (Eds.), *Networks and organizations* (pp. 191-215). Cambridge, MA: Harvard Business School Press.

Brass, D., & Burkhardt, M. (1993). Potential power and power use: An investigation of structure and behavior. *Academy of Management Journal, 36,* 441-470.

Brealey, R. A., & Myers, S. C. (1991). *Principles of corporate finance* (4th ed.). New York: McGraw-Hill

Breiger, R. L., Boorman, S. A., & Arabie, P. (1975). An algorithm for clustering relational data, with applications to social network analysis and comparison with multidimensional scaling. *Journal of Mathematical Psychology, 12,* 328-383.

Brinberg, D., & Wood, R. (1983). A resource exchange theory analysis of consumer behavior. *Journal of Consumer Research, 10,* 330-338.

Broh, I. (1989). *Bowling motivation study.* Washington, DC: National Bowling Council.

Brown, J. J., & Reingen, P. H. (1987). Social ties and word-of-mouth referral behavior. *Journal of Consumer Research, 14,* 350-362.

Burgers, W. P., Hill, C. W., & Kim, W. C. (1993). A theory of global strategic alliances: The case of the global auto industry. *Strategic Management Journal, 14,* 419-432.

Burkhardt, M., & Brass, D. (1990). Changing patterns or patterns of change: The effect of a change in technology on social network structure and power. *Administrative Science Quarterly, 35,* 104-127.

Burns, T., & Stalker, G. M. (1961). *The management of innovation.* London: Tavistock.

Burt, R. S. (1978). Cohesion versus structural equivalence as a basis for network subgroups. *Sociological Methods and Research, 7,* 189-212.

Burt, R. S. (1980). Co-optive corporate actor networks: A reconsideration of interlocking directories involving American manufacturing. *Administrative Science Quarterly, 25,* 557-582.

Burt, R. S. (1982). *Toward a structural theory of action.* New York: Academic Press.

Burt, R. S. (1983). *Corporate profits and cooptation: Networks of markets constraints and directorate ties in the American economy.* New York: Academic Press.

Burt, R. S. (1987). Social contagion and innovation, cohesion versus structural equivalence. *American Journal of Sociology, 92,* 1287-1335.

Burt, R. S. (1988). The stability of American markets. *American Journal of Sociology, 94,* 356-395.

Burt, R. S. (1992). *Structural holes.* Cambridge, MA: Harvard University Press.

Burt, R. S., & Minor, M. J. (1983). *Applied network methods.* Beverly Hills, CA: Sage.

Burt, R. S., & Uchiyama, T. (1989). The conditional significance of communication for interpersonal influence. In M. Kochen (Ed.), *The small world* (pp. 67-87). Norwood, NJ: Ablex.

Butterfield, S. (1985). *Amway: The cult of free enterprise.* Boston: South End Press.

Byrne, J. A., Brandt, R., & Port, O. (1993, February 8). The virtual corporation. *Business Week,* pp. 98-102.

Caballero, M. J., Lumpkin, J. R., Brown, D., Katsinas, R., & Werner, S. (1985). Waiting in line: A primary investigation. In D. M. Klein & A. E. Smith (Eds.), *Marketing: The next decade* (pp. 46-49). Boca Raton, FL: Southern Marketing Association.

Callero, P. (1994). From role-playing to role-using: Understanding role as resource. *Social Psychology Quarterly, 57,* 228-243.

Callon, M. (1986). The sociology of an actor-network: The case of the electric vehicle. In M. Callon, J. Law, & A. Rip (Eds.), *The dynamics of science and technology: Sociology of science in the real world* (pp. 19-34). London: Macmillan.

Callon, M. (1987). Society in the making: The study of technology as a tool for sociological analysis. In W. E. Bijker, T. P. Hughes, & T. J. Pinch (Eds.), *The social construction of technical systems: New directions in the sociology and history of technology* (pp. 83-103). London: MIT Press.

Callon, M. (1992). The dynamics of techno-economic networks. In R. Coombs, P. Saviotti, & V. Walsh (Eds.), *Technology change and company strategies: Economic and sociological perspectives* (pp. 72-102). London: Academic Press.

Callon, M. (1993). Variety and irreversibility in networks of technique conception and adoption. In D. Foray & C. Freeman (Eds.), *Technology and the wealth of nations: The dynamics of constructed advantage* (pp. 232-268). London: Pinter.

Callon, M., & Latour, B. (1981). Unscrewing the big leviathan: How actors macro-structure reality and how sociologists help them to do so. In K. Knorr-Cetina & A. Cicourel (Eds.), *Advances in social theory and methodology: Toward an integration of micro- and macro-sociologies* (pp. 277-303). London: Routledge & Kegan Paul.

Camagni, R. (Ed.). (1991). *Innovation networks: Spatial perspectives.* London: Belhaven.

Capecchi, V. (1989). A history of flexible specialization and industrial districts in Emilia-Romagna. In F. Pyke, G. Becattini, & W. Sengenberger (Eds.), *Industrial districts and interfirm cooperation in Italy* (pp. 20-36). Geneva: International Institute for Labour Studies.

Carlzon, J. (1991). Putting the customer first: The key to service strategy. In C. H. Lovelock (Ed.), *Services marketing* (2nd ed., pp. 424-432). Englewood Cliffs, NJ: Prentice Hall.

Carmichael, A. (1991). *The network marketing self-starter.* Reading, UK: Cox and Wyman.

Carmichael, A. (1993). *Network and multilevel marketing.* Reading, UK: Cox and Wyman.

Carr, C., Tomkins, C., & Bayliss, B. (1994). *Strategic investment decisions: A comparison of U.K. and German practices in the motor components industry* (Research Report to the Institute of Chartered Accountants in England and Wales). Aldershot: Avebury.

Carroll, J. D., Green, P. E., & Schaffer, C. M. (1987). Comparing interpoint distances in correspondence analysis. *Journal of Marketing Research, 24,* 445-450.

Carter, A. P. (1989). Know-how trading as economic exchange. *Research Policy, 18*, 155-163.

Centry, J. (1993). Strategic alliances in purchasing. *International Journal of Purchasing and Material Management, 29*, 10-17.

Christensen, A. (1983). Intervention. In H. H. Kelley (Ed.), *Close relationships* (pp. 397-448). New York: W. H. Freeman.

Christopher, M., Payne, A., & Ballantyne, D. (1991). *Relationship marketing: Bringing quality, customer service, and marketing together.* Oxford: Butterworth-Heinemann.

Clark, T., & Martin, C. L. (1994). Customer-to-customer: The forgotten relationship in relationship marketing. In J. N. Sheth & A. Parvatiyar (Eds.), *Relationship marketing: Theory, methods, and applications* (pp. 1-10). Atlanta, GA: Emory University, Center for Relationship Marketing.

Clegg, S. (1990). *Modern organizations.* Newbury Park, CA: Sage.

Clegg, S., Redding, G., & Carter, M. (Eds.). (1990). *Capitalism in contrasting cultures.* Berlin: De Gruyter.

Clothier, P. (1994). *Multilevel marketing* (2nd ed.). London: Kogan Page.

Coase, R. (1938). The nature of the firm. In G. J. Stigler & K. Boulding (Eds.), *Readings in price theory* (pp. 331-352). Homewood, IL: Irwin.

Cole, M. (1991). Conclusion. In L. Resnick, J. Levine, & S. Teasley (Eds.), *Perspectives on socially shared cognition* (pp. 398-417). Washington, DC: American Psychological Association.

Coleman, J. S. (1988). Social capital in the creation of human capital. *American Journal of Sociology, 94*, S95-S120.

Coleman, J. S., Katz, E., & Menzel, H. (1966). *Medical innovation.* New York: Bobbs-Merrill.

Coleman, J. S., Katz, E., & Menzel, H. (1969). The diffusion of an innovation among physicians. *Sociometry, 20*, 253-270.

Coleman, W. D. (1991). Fencing off: Central banks and networks in Canada and the United States. In B. Marin & R. Mayntz (Eds.), *Policy networks: Empirical evidence and theoretical considerations* (pp. 209-234). Frankfurt: Campus Verlag/Westview.

Colombo, R., Ehrenberg, A., & Sabavala, D. (1994). *The car challenge: Diversity in analyzing brand switching tables.* Unpublished manuscript.

Colombo, R. A., & Morrison, D. G. (1989), A brand switching model with implications for marketing strategies. *Marketing Science, 8*, 89-99.

Cook, K. S. (1977). Exchange and power in networks of interorganizational relations. *Sociological Quarterly, 18*, 62-82.

Cook, K. S. (1982). Network structures from an exchange perspective. In P. V. Marsden & N. Lin (Eds.), *Social structure and network analysis.* Beverly Hills, CA: Sage.

Cook, K., & Emerson, R. (1984). Exchange networks and the analysis of complex organizations. *Research in the Sociology of Organizations, 3*, 1-30.

Cook, K. S., & Emerson, R. M. (1978). Power, equity, and commitment in exchange networks. *American Sociological Review, 43*, 721-730.

Cooke, P., & Morgan, K. (1993). The network paradigm: New departures in corporate and regional development. *Environment and Planning: Society and Space, 11*, 543-564.

Coughlan, A., & Grayson, K. (1994, April). Multilevel marketing executives' survey. *Downline News*, pp. 1-5.

Cousins, P. (1994). *A framework for the selection, implementation, measurement, and management of partnership sourcing strategies.* Unpublished doctoral dissertation, University of Bath, U.K.

Cusumano, M. A., & Takeishi, A. (1991). Supplier relations and management: A survey of Japanese, Japanese-transplant, and U.S. auto plants. *Strategic Management Journal, 12*, 563-588.

Cyert, R. M., & March, J. G. (1963). *A behavioral theory of the firm*. Englewood Cliffs, NJ: Prentice Hall.

Czepiel, J. A. (1975). Patterns of interorganizational communication and diffusion of a major technological innovation in a competitive industrial community. *Academy of Management Journal, 18,* 6-24.

Czepiel, J. A. (1979). Communication networks and innovation in industrial communities. In M. J. Baker (Ed.), *Industrial innovation, technology, and policy* (pp. 399-416). New York: Macmillan.

Czepiel, J. A., Solomon, M. R., Surprenant, C. F., & Gutman, E. G. (1985). Service encounters: An overview. In J. A. Czepiel, M. R. Solomon, & C. F. Surprenant (Eds.), *The service encounter: Managing employee/customer interaction in service businesses* (pp. 3-15). Lexington, MA: Lexington Books.

von Daehne, N. (1994, December). Techno-boom. *Success,* pp. 43-46.

Daunton, M. J. (1983). *House and home in the Victorian city: Working-class housing 1850-1914.* London: Edward Arnold.

Davies, B., Baron, S., & Harris, K. (1995). *Observable oral participation in the servuction system: Toward a content and process model* (Unpublished working paper). Manchester: Manchester Metropolitan University.

Davis, G. F. (1991). Agents without principles? The spread of the poison pill through the intercorporate network. *Administrative Science Quarterly, 36,* 583-613.

Davis, M. S. (1971). That's interesting: Toward a phenomenology of sociology and a sociology of phenomenology. *Philosophy of Social Sciences, 1,* 309-344.

Day, G. S. (1994). The capabilities of market-driven organizations. *Journal of Marketing, 58,* 37-52.

Day, G. S. (in press). Assessing advantage: Frameworks for diagnosing the present and prospective competitive position. In G. S. Day & D. Reibstein (Eds.), *Wharton on dynamic competitive strategies.* New York: John Wiley.

Day, G. S., & Nedungadi, P. (1994). Managerial representations of competitive positioning. *Journal of Marketing, 58,* 31-44.

Day, G. S., Shocker A. D., & Srivastava, R. (1979), Customer-oriented approaches to identifying product-markets. *Journal of Marketing, 43,* 8-19.

DeBresson, C., & Amesse, F. (1991). Networks of innovators: A review and introduction to the issue. *Research Policy, 20,* 363-380.

Dierickx, I., & Cool, K. (1989). Asset stock accumulation and sustainability of competitive advantage. *Management Science, 35,* 1504-1511.

DiMaggio, P. J. (1986). Structural analysis of the organizational fields. *Research in Organizational Behavior, 8,* 335-370.

DiMaggio, P. J. (1988). Interest and agency in institutional theory. In L. G. Zucker (Ed.), *Institutional patterns and organizations* (pp. 3-21). Cambridge, MA: Ballinger.

DiMaggio, P. J., & Powell, W. W. (1983). The iron cage revisited: Institutional isomorphism and collective rationality in organizational fields. *American Sociological Review, 82,* 147-160.

Direct Selling Association/UK Research Unit. (1995). *The direct selling of consumer goods in the United Kingdom 1995 survey.* London: Direct Selling Association.

Direct Selling Association/USA. (1995). *1995 industrywide growth and outlook survey.* Washington, DC: Direct Selling Association.

Doebele, J. (1994, July 18). Global way. *Forbes,* p. 318.

Donaghu, M. T., & Barff, R. (1990). Nike just did it: International subcontracting and flexibility in international footwear. *Regional Studies, 24,* 537-552.

Donne, J. (1975). Devotions upon emergent occasions. In A. Raspa (Ed.), *John Donne, 1573-1631* (p. 86). Montreal: McGill-Queens University Press.

Donovan, R., & Rossiter, R. (1982). Store atmosphere: An environmental psychology approach. *Journal of Retailing, 58,* 34-57.

Dwyer, F. R., Schurr, P. H., & Oh, S. (1987). Developing buyer-seller relationships. *Journal of Marketing, 51,* 11-27.

Easton, G. (1992). Industrial networks: A review. In B. Axelsson & G. Easton (Eds.), *Industrial networks: A new view of reality* (pp. 3-27). London: Routledge.

Easton, G. (1995a). Methodology and industrial networks. In K. Moller & D. T. Wilson (Eds.), *Business networks* (pp. 411-492). Norwell, MA: Kluwer.

Easton, G. (1995b). Case research as a methodology for industrial networks: A realist apologia. In P. Turnbull, D. Yorke, & P. Naude (Eds.), *Proceedings of the 11th Industrial Marketing and Purchasing Conference, Vol. 1: Group, interaction, relationships, and networks* (pp. 368-391). Manchester: Manchester Federal School of Business and Management.

Easton, G., & Araujo, L. (1992). Industrial networks theory: A literary critique. In R. Salle, R. Spencer, & J.-P. Valla (Eds.), *Business networks in an international context: Recent research developments. Proceedings of the 8th Industrial Marketing and Purchasing (IMP) Conference, 2,* (pp. 101-118). Lyon, France: Lyon Graduate School of Business.

Easton, G., & Araujo, L. (1993). Language, metaphors, and networks. In D. Sharma (Ed.), *Advances in international marketing, 5* (pp. 67-85). Greenwich, CT: JAI.

Easton, G., & Araujo, L. (in press). Interfirm responses to heterogeneity of demand over time. In M. Ebers (Ed.), *Forms of interorganizational networks: Structures and processes.* Oxford: Oxford University Press.

Eccles, R. G., & Crane, D. B. (1988). *Doing deals: Investment banks at work.* Cambridge, MA: Harvard Business School Press.

Eiglier, P., Langeard, E., Lovelock, C. H., Bateson, J. E. G., & Young, R. F. (1977). *Marketing consumer services: New insights.* Cambridge, MA: Marketing Science Institute.

Emerson, R. M. (1962). Power-dependence relations. *American Sociological Review, 27,* 31-41.

Emirbayer, M., & Goodwin, J. (1994). Network analysis, culture, and the problem of agency. *American Journal of Sociology, 99,* 1411-1454.

Eskin, L. (1991, July 7). Marketing gem. *Chicago Tribune,* Section 1BSW, p. 1.

Etgar, M. (1976). Channel domination and countervailing power in distribution channels. *Journal of Marketing Research, 13,* 254-262.

Failla, D. (1984). *How to build a large successful multilevel marketing organization.* Gig Harbor, WA: MLM International.

Faulkner, D. (1995). *Strategic alliances.* London: McGraw-Hill.

Feick, L., & Price, L. (1987). The market maven: A diffuser of marketplace information. *Journal of Marketing, 51,* 83-97.

Feinberg, F. M., Kahn, B. E., & McAlister, L. (1994). Implications and relative fit of several first-order Markov models of consumer variety seeking. *European Journal of Operational Research, 76,* 309-320.

Fienberg, S. E. (1980). *The analysis of cross-classified categorical data* (2nd ed.). Cambridge: MIT Press.

Fisher, J. D., & Byrne, D. (1975). Close for comfort: Sex differences in response to invasions of personal space. *Journal of Personality and Social Psychology, 32,* 15-21.

Fisk, G. (1994). Reality tests for relationship marketing. In J. N. Sheth & A. Parvatiyar (Eds.), *Relationship marketing: Theory, methods, and applications* (pp. 1-5). Atlanta, GA: Emory University, Center for Relationship Marketing.

Fligstein, N. (1990). *The transformation of corporate control.* Cambridge, MA: Harvard University Press.

Fligstein N., & Brantley, P. (1992). Bank control, owner control, or organization dynamics: Who controls the modern corporation. *American Journal of Sociology, 98,* 280-307.

Foa, E. B., & Foa, U. G. (1980). Resource theory: Interpersonal behavior as exchange. In K. Gergen, M. S. Greenberg, & R. H. Willis (Eds.), *Social exchange advances in theory and research.* New York: Plenum.

Folkes, V. (1988). Recent attribution research in consumer behavior: A review and new directions. *Journal of Consumer Research, 51,* 83-97.

Fombrun, C. J. (1982). Strategies for network research in organizations. *Academy of Management Review, 7,* 280-291.

Fombrun, C. J. (1983). Attributions of power across a social network. *Human Relations, 36,* 493-508.

Ford, I. D. (1980). The development of buyer-seller relationships in industrial markets. *European Journal of Marketing, 14,* 291-353.

Ford, I. D. (1989, September). *One more time, what buyer-seller relationships are all about.* Paper presented at the Industrial Marketing and Purchasing (IMP) Conference, Pennsylvania State University, University Park.

Ford, I. D. (Ed.). (1990). *Understanding business markets.* San Diego, CA: Academic Press.

Ford, I. D. (1994, November). *Developing relationship strategy.* Paper presented at the 2nd International Colloquium in Relationship Marketing, Cranfield University, U.K.

Ford, I. D., Håkansson, H., & Johanson, J. (1986). How do companies interact? *Industrial Marketing and Purchasing, 1,* 26-41.

Forgas, J. (1983). What is social about social cognition? *British Journal of Social Psychology, 22,* 129-144.

Forsgren, M., & Kinch, N. (1970). *Företagets anpassning till förändringar i omgivande system. En studie i massa och pappersindustrin.* ACTA Universitatis Upsaliensis; Studia Oeconomica Negotiorum.

Frair, J., & Horwitch, M. (1985). The emergence of technology strategy: A new dimension of strategic management. *Technology in Society, 7,* 143-178.

Frazier, G., Spekman, R., & O'Neill, C. (1986). Just-in-time exchange relationships in industrial markets. *Journal of Marketing, 52,* 52-67.

Freeman, C. (1991). Networks of innovators: A synthesis of research issues. *Research Policy, 20,* 499-514.

Freeman, L. C. (1979). Centrality in social networks: Conceptual clarification. *Social Networks, 1,* 215-239.

Freeman, L. C., Borgatti, S. P., & White, D. R. (1991). Centrality in valued graphs: A measure of betweenness based on network flow. *Social Networks, 13,* 141-154.

Frenzen, J. K., & Davis, H. L. (1990). Purchasing behavior in embedded markets. *Journal of Consumer Research, 17,* 1-12.

Fruin, W. M. (1992). *The Japanese enterprise system: Competitive strategies and cooperative structures.* Oxford: Oxford University Press.

Gadde, L.-E., & Mattsson, L.-G. (1987). Stability and change in network relationships. *International Journal of Research in Marketing, 4,* 29-41.

Galaskiewicz, J. (1979). *Exchange networks and community politics.* Beverly Hills, CA: Sage.

Galaskiewicz, J. (1985a). *Social organization of an urban grants economy.* New York: Academic Press.

Galaskiewicz, J. (1985b). Professional networks and the institutionalization of the single mind set. *American Sociological Review, 50,* 639-658.

Galaskiewicz, J. (1995). *An urban grants economy revisited: Company contributions in the Twin Cities, 1979-1981, 1987-1989.* Minneapolis: University of Minnesota, Department of Sociology.

Galaskiewicz, J., & Burt, R. S. (1991). Interorganizational contagion in corporate philanthropy. *Administrative Science Quarterly, 36,* 88-105.

Galaskiewicz J., & Shatin, D. (1981). Leadership and networking among neighborhood human service organizations. *Administrative Science Quarterly, 26,* 434-448.

Galaskiewicz, J., & Wasserman, S. (1989). Mimetic processes within an interorganizational field: An empirical test. *Administrative Science Quarterly, 34,* 454-479.

Galaskiewicz, J., & Wasserman, S. (1993). Social network analysis: Concepts, methodology, and directions for the 1990s. *Sociological Methods and Research, 22,* 3-22.

Gallup, G., Jr. (1990). *The Gallup poll: Public opinion 1990.* Wilmington, DE: Scholarly Resources.

Galotti, K. (1989). Approaches to studying formal and everyday reasoning. *Psychological Bulletin, 105,* 331-345.

Gentner, D., & Stevens, A. (1983). *Mental models.* Hillsdale, NJ: Lawrence Erlbaum.

Gereffi, G. (1994). The organization of buyer-driven global commodity chains: How U.S. retailers shape overseas production networks. In G. Gereffi & M. Korzeniewicz (Eds.), *Commodity chains and global capitalism* (pp. 95-122). Westport, CT: Praeger.

Geribger, J. M., & Herbert, L. (1991). Measuring performance of international joint ventures. *Journal of International Business Studies, 22,* 249-264.

Gerlach, M. L. (1992). *Alliance capitalism.* Berkeley: University of California Press.

Gerlach, M. L., & Lincoln, J. R. (1992). The organization of business networks in the United States and Japan. In N. Nohria & R. G. Eccles (Eds.), *Networks and organizations: Structure, form, and action* (pp. 491-520). Boston: Harvard Business School Press.

Ger-ro-mar. (1974). *Federal Trade Commission Decisions, 84,* 95-162.

Ghoshal, S., & Bartlett, C. A. (1993). The multinational corporation as an interoganizational network. In S. Ghoshal & D. E. Westney (Eds.), *Organization theory and the multinational corporation.* New York: St. Martin's.

Givon, M., & Muller, E. (1994). Cyclical patterns in brand switching behavior: An issue of pattern recognition. *European Journal of Operational Research, 76,* 290-297.

Goffman, E. (1973). *The presentation of self in everyday life.* Woodstock, NY: Overlook. (Original work published 1959)

Gomes-Cassers, B. (1987, Summer). Joint venture instability: It is a problem. *Colombia Journal of World Business,* pp. 97-102.

Gouldner, A. W. (1954). *Patterns of industrial bureaucracy.* New York: Free Press.

Grafton, R., & Posey, C. (1990). Tax implications of fraudulent income earning schemes: Ponzi and others. *American Business Law Journal, 27,* 599-610.

Grandori, A., & Soda, G. (1995). Interfirm networks: Antecedents, mechanisms, and forms. *Organization Studies, 16,* 183-214.

Granovetter, M. (1973). The strength of weak ties: A network theory revisited. *American Journal of Sociology, 78,* 3-30.

Granovetter, M. (1985). Economic action and social structure: The problem of embeddedness. *American Journal of Sociology, 91,* 481-510.

Granovetter, M. (1995). *Getting a job: A study of contacts and careers* (2nd ed.), Chicago: University of Chicago Press.

Grant, R. M. (1991, Spring). The resource-based theory of competitive advantage: Implications for strategy formulation. *California Management Review,* pp. 112-135.

Gray, B. (1989). *Collaborating.* San Francisco: Jossey-Bass.

Grayson, K. (in press). Commercial activity at home: The private servicescape. In J. F. Sherry (Ed.), *Encountering servicescapes: Built environment and lived experience in contemporary marketplaces.* Lincolnwood, IL: NTC Publishing.

Greenacre, M., & Hastie, T. (1987). The geometric interpretation of correspondence analysis. *Journal of the American Statistical Association, 82,* 437-447.

Griffin, G. L. (1981). Missouri lottery law: Of promotional games and pyramids. *UMKC Law Review, 49,* 320-337.

Gronroos, C. (1981). Internal marketing: An integral part of marketing theory. In J. H. Donnelly & W. R. George (Eds.), *Marketing of services* (pp. 236-239). Chicago: American Marketing Association.

Gronroos, C. (1990). Relationship approach to marketing in service contexts: The marketing and organizational behavior interface. *Journal of Business Research, 20,* 3-11.

Grove, S. J., & Fisk, R. P. (1983). The dramaturgy of services exchange: An analytical framework for services marketing. In L. L. Berry, G. L. Shostack, & G. D. Upah (Eds.), *Emerging perspectives on services marketing* (pp. 45-49). Chicago: American Marketing Association.

Guetzkow, H. (1966). Relations among organizations. In R. V. Bowers (Ed.), *Studies in the behavior of organizations* (pp. 13-44). Athens: University of Georgia Press.

Gupta, A. K., & Lad, L. J. (1983). Industry self-regulation: An economic, organizational, and political analysis. *Academy of Management Review, 8,* 416-425.

Gutman, J. (1982). A means-end chain model based on consumer categorization processes. *Journal of Marketing, 46,* 60-72.

Gutman, J. (1991). Exploring the nature of linkages between consequences and values. *Journal of Business Research, 22,* 143-148.

Hage, P., & Harary, F. (1983). *Structural models in anthropology.* Cambridge: Cambridge University Press.

Hagg, I. (1992). On investments and accounting with a focus on international investments. In I. Hagg & E. Segelod (Eds.), *Issues in corporate investment research.* New York: North-Holland/Elsevier.

Håkansson, H. (Ed.). (1982). *International marketing and purchasing of industrial goods.* New York: John Wiley.

Håkansson, H. (Ed.). (1987). *Industrial technological development: A network approach.* London: Croom Helm.

Håkansson, H. (1989). *Corporate technological behavior: Cooperation and networks.* London: Routledge.

Håkansson, H., & Johanson, J. (1992). A model of industrial networks. In B. Axelsson & G. Easton (Eds.), *Industrial networks: A new view of reality* (pp. 28-34). London: Routledge.

Håkansson, H., & Lundgren, A. (1995). Industrial networks and technological innovation. In K. E. Möller & D. T. Wilson (Eds.), *Business marketing: An interaction and network approach.* Boston: PWS Kent.

Håkansson, H., & Snehota, I. (1989). No business is an island: The network concept of business strategy. *Scandanavian Journal of Management, 4,* 187-200.

Håkansson, H., & Snehota, I. (Eds.). (1995). *Developing relationships in business networks.* London: Routledge.

Halberstam, D. (1984). *The reckoning.* London: Bloomsbury.

Hall, E. T. (1966). *The hidden dimension.* Garden City, NY: Doubleday.

Hallen, L. (1986). A comparison of strategic marketing approaches. In P. W. Turnbull & J.-P. Valla (Eds.), *Strategies for international industrial marketing* (pp. 235-249). London: Croom Helm.

Hamel, G. (1991). Competition for competence and interpartner learning within international strategic alliances. *Strategic Management Journal, 12,* 83-103.

Hamilton, G. G. (1994). Civilizations and the organization of economies. In N. J. Smelser & R. Swedberg (Eds.), *The handbook of economic sociology* (pp. 183-205). Princeton, NJ: Princeton University Press.

Hamilton, G. G., & Biggart, N. W. (1988). Market culture and authority: A comparative analysis of management and organization in the Far East. *American Journal of Sociology, 94,* S52-S94.

Hamilton, G. G., Zeile, W., & Kim, W. J. (1990). The network structures of East Asian economies. In S. Clegg, G. Redding, & M. Carter (Eds.), *Capitalism in contrasting cultures* (pp. 105-129). Berlin: De Gruyter.

Hanf, K., & O'Toole, L. J., Jr. (1992). Revisiting old friends: Networks, implementation structures, and the management of interorganizational relations. *European Journal of Political Research, 21,* 163-180.

Hannan, M. T., & Freeman, J. (1977). The population ecology of organizations. *American Journal of Sociology, 82,* 929-964.

Harary, F. (1969). *Graph theory.* Reading, MA: Addison-Wesley.

Harary, F., Norman, Z., & Cartwright, D. (1965). *Structural models: An introduction to the theory of directed graphs.* New York: John Wiley.

Harrigan, K. R. (1988). Joint ventures and competitive strategies. *Strategic Management Journal, 9,* 141-158.

Harris, K., Baron, S., & Ratcliffe, J. (1995). Customers as oral participants in a service setting. *Journal of Services Marketing, 9,* 64-76.

Harrison, B. (1994). *Lean and mean: The changing landscape of corporate power in the age of flexibility.* New York: Basic Books.

Haunschild, P. R. (1993). Interoganizational imitation: The impact of interlocks on corporate acquisition activity. *Administrative Science Quarterly, 38,* 564-592.

Hayes, R., & Abernathy, W. (1980, July-August). Managing our way to economic decline. *Harvard Business Review,* pp. 67-77.

Haywood, K. M. (1989). Managing word of mouth communications. *Journal of Services Marketing, 3,* 55-68.

Hedaa, L. (1995). *Understanding portfolios of customers relations* (Working Paper 21). Copenhagen: Management Research Institute, Copenhagen Business School.

Hedlund, G. (1993). Assumptions of hierarchy and heterarchy, with application to the management of the multinational corporation. In S. Ghoshal & C. A. Bartlett (Eds.), *Organization theory and the multinational corporation* (pp. 211-236). New York: St. Martin's.

Heide, J. B. (1994). Interorganizational governance in marketing channels. *Journal of Marketing, 58,* 71-85.

Heide, J., & Miner, A. (1990). *The shadow of the future: The effect of the anticipated interaction and frequency of delivery on buyer-seller cooperation.* Unpublished manuscript.

Heider, S. (1958). *The psychology of interpersonal relations.* New York: John Wiley.

Heinz, J. P., Laumann, E. O., Nelson, R. L., & Salisbury, R. H. (1993). *The hollow core.* Cambridge, MA: Harvard University Press.

Hennart, J. F. (1993). Control in multinational firms: The role of price and hierarchy. In S. Ghoshal & D. E. Westney (Eds.), *Organization theory and the multinational corporation* (pp. 157-181). New York: St. Martin's.

Hertz, S. (1993). *The internationalization processes of freight transport companies: Toward a dynamic network model of internationalization.* Doctoral dissertation. Stockholm: Stockholm School of Economics, Economic Research Institute (EFI).

Hines, M. (1988). Multilevel distribution companies: Regulate under business opportunities act. *Legislative Review, 5,* 228-234.

Hoffman, D. L., & Franke, G. R. (1986). Correspondence analysis: Graphical representation of categorical data in marketing research. *Journal of Marketing Research, 23,* 213-217.

Holiday Magic. (1974). *Federal Trade Commission Decisions, 84,* 748-1078.

Hollingsworth, J. R., Schmitter, P. C., & Streeck, W. (Eds.). (1994). *Governing capitalist economies: Performance and control of economic sectors*. Oxford: Oxford University Press.

Hopkins, N., Henderson, G., & Iacobucci, D. (1995). Actor equivalence in networks: The business ties that bind. *Journal of Business-to-Business Marketing, 2*, 3-31.

Howard, J. (1994). A social cognitive conception of social structure. *Social Psychological Quarterly, 57*, 210-227.

Hubert, L. J. (1987). *Assignment methods in combinatorial data analysis*. New York: Marcel Dekker.

Hubert, L., & Baker, F. B. (1978). Evaluating the conformity of sociometric measurements. *Psychometrika, 43*, 31-41.

Huffman, C., & Houston, M. J. (1993). Goal-oriented experiences and the development of knowledge. *Journal of Consumer Research, 20*, 190-207.

Iacobucci, D. (1989). Modeling multivariate sequential dyadic interactions. *Social Networks, 11*, 315-362.

Iacobucci, D. (1994). Toward defining relationship marketing. In J. N. Sheth & A. Parvatiyar (Eds.), *Relationship marketing: Theory, methods, and applications* (pp. 1-10). Atlanta, GA: Emory University, Center for Relationship Marketing.

Iacobucci, D., & Grace, J. (1993). Interpretation of parameters from the Holland-Leinhardt stochastic network models. In D. W. Cravens & P. R. Dickson (Eds.), *Enhancing knowledge development in marketing, 4* (pp. 84-91). Chicago: American Marketing Association.

Iacobucci, D., & Hopkins, N. (1991). The relationship between the Scheiblechner model and the Holland-Leinhardt "p1" model. *Social Networks, 13*, 187-202.

Iacobucci, D., & Hopkins, N. (1992). Modeling dyadic interactions and networks in marketing. *Journal of Marketing Research, 29*, 5-17.

Iacobucci, D., & Hopkins, N. (1994). Detection of experimental effects in social network analysis. *Social Networks, 16*, 1-41.

Iacobucci, D., & Ostrom, A. (1993). Gender differences in the impact of "core" and "relational" aspects of services on the evaluation of service encounters. *Journal of Consumer Psychology, 2*, 257-286.

Iacobucci, D., & Ostrom, A. (1996). Commercial and interpersonal relationships: Using the structure of interpersonal relationships to understand individual-to-individual, individual-to-firm, and firm-to-firm relationships in commerce. *International Journal of Research in Marketing, 13*, 53-72.

Iacobucci, D., & Wasserman, S. (1987). Dyadic social interactions. *Psychological Bulletin, 102*, 293-306.

Iacobucci, D., & Wasserman, S. (1988). A general framework for the statistical analysis of sequential dyadic interaction data. *Psychological Bulletin, 103*, 379-390.

Ibarra, H. (1992). Structural alignments, individual strategies, and managerial action: Elements toward a network theory of getting things done. In N. Nohria & R. G. Eccles (Eds.), *Networks and organizations* (pp. 165-188). Boston: Harvard Business School Press.

Ibarra, H. (1993). Network centrality, power, and innovation management: Determinants of technical and administrative roles. *Academy of Management Journal, 36*, 471-501.

Ibarra, H., & Andrews, S. B. (1993). Power, social influence, and sensemaking: Effects of network centrality and proximity on employee perceptions. *Administrative Science Quarterly, 38*, 277-303.

International Customer Service Association (ICSA). (1995). *Building effective customer service teams*. Chicago: Author.

Imai, K. (1992). Japan's corporate networks. In S. Kumon & H. Rosovsky (Eds.), *The political economy of Japan: Cultural and social dynamics* (pp. 198-230). Palo Alto, CA: Stanford University Press.

Imai, K., & Itami, H. (1984). Interpenetration of organization and market. *International Journal of Industrial Organization, 2*, 285-310.

Inc. (1994, October). *The 1994 Inc. 500* [Special issue].

Jackson, B. B. (1985). *Winning and keeping industrial customers: The dynamics of customer relationships*. Lexington, MA: Lexington Books.

Jain, D. C., & Niu, S.-C. (1994). Analyzing household brand switching: A stochastic model. *European Journal of Operational Research, 76*, 298-308.

Jarillo, J. C. (1988). On strategic networks. *Strategic Management Journal, 9*, 31-41.

Jarillo, J. C. (1993). *Strategic networks: Creating the borderless organization*. Oxford: Butterworth-Heinemann.

Johanisson, B. (1994). *Entrepreneurial networks: Some conceptual and methodological notes* (Unpublished working paper). Lund: University of Lund, Institute of Economic Research.

Johanisson, B., Alexanderson, O., Nowicki, K., & Senneseth, K. (1994). Beyond anarchy and organization: Entrepreneurs in contextual networks. *Entrepreneurship and Regional Development, 6*, 329-356.

Johanson, J., & Mattsson, L.-G. (1987). Interorganizational relations in industrial systems: A network approach compared with a transactions cost approach. *International Studies of Management and Organization, 17*, 34-38.

Johanson, J., & Mattsson, L.-G. (1988). Interorganizational relations in industrial systems: A network approach. In N. Hood & Vahlne, J.-E. (Eds.), *Strategies in global competition* (pp. 287-314). New Hampshire: Croom Helm.

Johanson, J., & Mattsson, L.-G. (1992). Network positions and strategic action: An analytical framework. In B. Axelsson & G. Easton (Eds.), *Industrial networks: A new view of reality* (pp. 205-217). London: Routledge.

Johanson, J., & Mattsson, L.-G. (1994). The markets-as-networks tradition in Sweden. In G. Laurent, G. L. Lilien, & B. Pras (Eds.), *Research traditions in marketing* (pp. 321-342). Norwell, MA: Kluwer.

Johanson, J., & Vahlne, J.-E. (1977). The internationalization process of the firm: A model of knowledge development and increasing foreign market commitments. *Journal of International Business, 8*, 23-32.

John, G., & Reve, T. (1982). The reliability and validity of key informant data from dyadic relationships in marketing channels. *Journal of Marketing Research, 19*, 517-524.

Johnson, M. A. (1993). *The association between perceived customer-to-customer compatibility and selected characteristics of service/retail physical environments*. Unpublished master's thesis, Wichita State University, Wichita, KS.

Johnston, R., & Lawrence, P. R. (1988). Beyond vertical integration: The rise of the value-adding partnership. *Harvard Business Review, 88*, 94-101.

Johnston, W., & Spekman, R. (1982). Industrial buying behavior: A need for an integrated approach. *Journal of Business Research, 10*, 133-146.

Jonas, N. (1986, March 3). The hollow corporation. *Business Week*, pp. 56-59.

Jordan, G., & Schubert, K. (1992). A preliminary ordering of policy networks. *European Journal of Political Research, 21*, 7-27.

Kalawani, M. U., & Narayandas, N. (1995). Long-term manufacturer-supplier relationships: Do they pay off for supplier firms? *Journal of Marketing, 59*, 1-16.

Kaplan, R. S., & Atkinson, A. A. (1989). *Advanced management accounting* (2nd ed.). Englewood Cliffs, NJ: Prentice Hall

Kanter, R. M. (1989). *When giants learn to dance.* London: Simon & Schuster.

Kavanagh, D., & Araujo, L. (1995). Chronigami: Folding and unfolding time. *Accounting, Management, and Information Technologies, 5,* 103-121.

Kelley, H. H. (1983a). Perceived causal structures. In J. Jaspers, F. Fincham, & M. Hewstone (Eds.), *Attribution theory and research: Conceptual, developmental, and social dimensions* (pp. 343-370). London: Academic Press.

Kelley, H. H. (1983b). *Close relationships.* New York: W. H. Freeman.

Kenney, M., & Florida, R. (1993). *Beyond mass production: The Japanese system and its transfer to the U.S.* Oxford: Oxford University Press.

Kenny, D., & Judd, C. M. (1986). Consequences of violating the independence assumption in analysis of variance. *Psychological Bulletin, 99,* 422-431.

Kent, S. (1990). A cross-cultural study of segmentation, architecture and the use of space. In S. Kent (Ed.), *Domestic architecture and the use of space* (pp. 127-152). Cambridge: Cambridge University Press.

Kilduff, M. (1990). The interpersonal structure of decision-making: A social comparison approach to organizational choice. *Organizational Behavior and Human Decision Processes, 47,* 270-288.

Kilduff, M., & Krackhardt, D. (1994). Bringing the individual back in: A structural analysis of the internal market for reputation in organizations. *Academy of Management Journal, 37,* 87-108.

Killing, J. P. (1988). *Strategies for joint venture success.* Beckenham: Croom Helm.

Kinch, N. (1984). Strategy and structure of supplier relations in IKEA. In I. Hagg & F. Wiedersheim-Paul (Eds.), *Between market and hierarchy* (pp. 89-102). Uppsala: University of Uppsala.

Knights, D., Murray, F., & Willmott, H. (1993). Networking as knowledge: A study of strategic interorganizational development in the financial services industry. *Journal of Management Studies, 30,* 975-995.

Knoke, D. (1983). Organizational sponsorship and influence reputation of social influence associations. *Social Forces, 61,* 1065-1087.

Knoke, D., & Guilarte, M. (1994). Networks in organizational structures and strategies. *Current Perspectives in Social Theory, Suppl. 1,* 77-115.

Knoke, D., & Kuklinski, J. H. (1982). *Network analysis.* Beverly Hills, CA: Sage.

Knoke, D., & Rogers, D. L. (1979). A blockmodel analysis of interorganizational networks. *Sociology and Social Research, 64,* 28-52.

Knoke, D., & Wood, J. R.. (1981). *Organized for action.* New Brunswick, NJ: Rutgers University Press.

Kogut, B. (Ed.). (1993). *Country competitiveness: Technology and the organizing of work.* New York: Oxford University Press.

Koscot Interplanetary, Inc. (1975). *Federal Trade Commission Decisions, 86,* 1106-1192.

Kotler, P. (1973). Atmospherics as a marketing tool. *Journal of Retailing, 49,* 48-64.

Kotler, P., & Levy, S. J. (1969). Broadening the concept of marketing. *Journal of Marketing, 33,* 10-15.

Kosnik, R. D. (1987). Greenmail: A study of board performance in corporate governance. *Administrative Science Quarterly, 32,* 163-185.

Krackhardt, D. (1990). Assessing the political landscape: Structure, cognition, and power in organizations. *Administrative Science Quarterly, 35,* 342-369.

Krackhardt, D. (1992). The strength of strong ties: The importance of philos in organizations. In N. Nohria & R. G. Eccles (Eds.), *Networks and organizations: Structure, form, and action* (pp. 216-239). Cambridge, MA: Harvard Business School Press.

Krackhardt, D., & Brass, D. J. (1994). Intraorganizational networks: The micro side. In S. Wasserman & J. Galaskiewicz (Eds.), *Advances in social network analysis* (pp. 207-229). Thousand Oaks, CA: Sage.

Krackhardt, D., & Porter, L. (1986). The snowball effect: Turnover embedded in communications networks. *Journal of Applied Psychology, 71*, 50-55.

Krapfel, R. E., Salmond, D., & Spekman, R. (1991). A strategic approach to managing buyer-seller relationships. *European Journal of Marketing, 25*, 22-37.

Kumon, S. (1992). Japan as a network society. In S. Kumon & H. Rosovsky (Eds.), *The political economy of Japan: Cultural and social dynamics* (pp. 109-141). Palo Alto, CA: Stanford University Press.

Laage-Hellman, J. (1989). *Technological development in industrial networks.* Unpublished doctoral dissertation, University of Uppsala, Department of Business Administration.

Langeard, E., Bateson, J. E. G., Lovelock, C. H., & Eiglier, P. (1981). *Services marketing: New insights from consumers and managers.* Cambridge, MA: Marketing Science Institute.

Langlois, R. N., & Robertson, P. L. (1995). *Firms, markets, and economic change: A dynamic theory of business institutions.* London: Routledge.

Larsen, J., & Rogers, E. (1984). *Silicon Valley fever.* New York: Basic Books.

Larson, A. (1992). Network dyads in entrepreneurial settings: A study of the governance of exchange relationships. *Administrative Science Quarterly, 37*, 761-774.

Larson, A., & Starr, J. A. (1993). A network model of organization formation. *Entrepreneurship: Theory and Practice, 17*, 5-16.

Larson, J., & Christenson, C. (1993). Groups as problem-solving units: Toward a new meaning of social cognition. *British Journal of Social Psychology, 32*, 5-30.

Latour, B. (1987). *Science in action: How to follow scientists and engineers through society.* Cambridge, MA: Harvard University Press

Latour, B. (1988). *The Pasteurization of France.* Cambridge, MA: Harvard University Press.

Latour, B. (1993). *We have never been modern.* New York: Harvester Wheatsheaf.

Laumann, E. O., Galaskiewicz, J., & Marsden, P. V. (1978). Community structure as interorganizational linkages. *Annual Review of Sociology, 4*, 455-484.

Laumann, E. O., & Knoke, D. (1987). *The organizational state.* Madison: University of Wisconsin Press.

Laumann, E. O., & Pappi, F. (1976). *Networks of collective action.* New York: Academic Press.

Laumann, E. O., Tam, T., Heinz, J. P. (with R. L. Nelson & R. H. Salisbury). (1992). The social organization of the Washington establishment during the first Reagan administration: A network analysis. In G. Moore and J. A. Whitt (Eds.), *Research in politics and society, 4,* (pp. 161-188). Greenwich, CT: JAI.

Law, J. (1992a). Notes on a theory of actor-network: Ordering, strategy, and heterogeneity. *Systems Practice, 5*, 379-393.

Law, J. (1992b). The Olympus 320 engine: A case study in design, development, and organizational control. *Technology and Culture, 33*, 409-440.

Law, J. (1994). *Organizing modernity.* Oxford: Basil Blackwell.

Lawrence, P., & Lorsch, J. W. (1967). *Organization and environment: Managing differentiation and integration.* Homewood, IL: Irwin.

Lawrence, R. J. (1990). Public collective and private space: A study of urban housing in Switzerland. In S. Kent (Ed.), *Domestic architecture and the use of space* (pp. 73-91). Cambridge: Cambridge University Press.

Lazerson, M. (1995). A new Phoenix?: Modern putting-out in the Modena knitwear industry, *Administrative Science Quarterly, 40*, 34-59.

Lehmann, D. R. (1972). Judged similarity and brand-switching data as similarity measures. *Journal of Marketing Research, 9*, 331-334.

Lei, D., & Slocum, J. W. (1991). Global strategic alliances: Payoffs and pitfalls. *Organizational Dynamics, 12,* 44-62.

Leonard-Barton, D. (1992). Core capabilities and core rigidities: A paradox in managing new product development. *Strategic Management Journal, 13,* 111-125.

Levine, J. (1972). The sphere of influence. *American Sociological Review, 37,* 14-27.

Levine, R. V. (1993). Cities with heart. *American Demographics, 15,* 46-54.

Lewis, J. (1990). *Partnership for profit: Structuring and measuring strategic alliances.* New York: Free Press.

Li, Z. X. (1995). *The dynamics of export channels: A network approach.* Unpublished doctoral dissertation, University of Lancaster.

Liljegren, G. (1988). *Interdependens och dynamik i långsiktiga kundrelationer: Industriell försäljning i nätverksperspektiv.* Doctoral dissertation. Stockholm: Economic Research Institute (EFI)/Market Technology Center.

Lincoln, J. R. (1982). Intra- (and inter-) organizational networks. *Research in the Sociology of Organizations, 1,* 1-38.

Lincoln, J. R., Gerlach, M. L., & Takahashi, P. (1992). Keiretsu networks in the Japanese economy: A dyadic analysis of intercorporate ties. *American Sociological Review, 57,* 561-585.

Linden, D. W., & Stern, W. (1993, March 15). Betcherlife Herbalife. *Forbes,* pp. 46-48.

Litwak, E., & Hylon, L. (1962). Interorganizational analysis: A hypothesis on coordinating agencies. *Administrative Science Quarterly, 6,* 395-420.

Lorenzoni, G., & Ornati, O. A. (1988). Constellations of firms and new ventures. *Journal of Business Venturing, 3,* 41-57.

Luce, D., & Perry, A. (1949). A method of matrix analysis of group structure. *Psychometrika, 14,* 95-116.

Lundgren, A. (1995). *Technological innovation and network evolution.* London: Routledge.

Lunt, P., & Livingstone, S. (1991). Everyday explanations for personal debt: A network approach. *British Journal of Social Psychology, 30,* 309-323.

Maister, D. H. (1985). The psychology of waiting lines. In J. A. Czepiel, M. R. Solomon, & C. F. Surprenant (Eds.), *The service encounter: Managing employee/customer interaction in service businesses* (pp. 113-123). Lexington, MA: Lexington Books.

Malecki, E. J. (1994). Entrepreneurship in regional and local development. *International Regional Science Review, 16,* 119-153.

Marin, B., & Mayntz, R. (Eds.). (1991). *Policy networks: Empirical evidence and theoretical considerations.* Frankfurt: Campus Verlag/Westview.

Marsh, D., & Rhodes, R. A. W. (Eds.). (1992). *Policy networks in British government.* Oxford: Clarendon.

Martilla, J. A. (1971). Word of mouth communication in the industrial adoption process. *Journal of Marketing Research, 8,* 173-178.

Martin, C. L. (1993). New smoke signals. *Bowlers Journal International, 80,* 140-143.

Martin, C. L. (1995). The customer compatibility scale: Measuring service customers' perceptions of fellow customers. *Journal of Consumer Studies and Home Economics, 19,* 299-311.

Martin, C. L. (1996). *Owning and operating a service business.* Menlo Park, CA: Crisp.

Martin, C. L. (in press). Consumer-to-consumer relationships: Satisfaction with other consumers' public behavior. *Journal of Consumer Affairs.*

Martin, C. L., & Pranter, C. A. (1989). Compatibility management: Customer-to-customer relationships in service environments. *Journal of Services Marketing, 3,* 5-15.

Mattsson, L.-G. (1969). *Integration and efficiency in marketing systems.* Doctoral dissertation. Stockholm: Stockholm School of Economics, Economic Research Institute (EFI)/Norstedts & Söner.

Mattsson. L.-G. (1985). An application of a network approach to marketing: Defending and changing market positions. In N. Dholakia & J. Arndt (Eds.), *Changing the course of marketing: Alternative paradigms for widening market theory, 2*, (pp. 263-288). Greenwich, CT: JAI.

Mattsson, L.-G. (1986, September). *Indirect relationships in industrial networks: A conceptual analysis of their significance.* Paper presented at the 3rd Industrial Marketing and Purchasing (IMP) International Seminar, IRE, Lyon, France.

Mattsson, L.-G. (1987). Managing of strategic change in a "markets as networks" perspective. In A. Pettigrew (Ed.), *Management of strategic change* (pp. 236-255). London: Basil Blackwell.

Mattsson, L.-G. (1988, August). *Interaction strategies: A network approach.* Paper presented at the Summer Marketing Educators Conference, American Marketing Association, Chicago, IL.

Mayntz, R. (1993). Modernization and the logic of interorganizational networks. In J. Child, M. Crozier, & R. Mayntz (Eds.), *Societal change between market and organization* (pp. 3-18). Aldershot: Avebury.

McCarthy, B., & Straus, K. (1992). Tastes of America 1992. *Restaurants & Institutions, 102*, 24-29.

McCarthy, P. S., Kannan, P. K., Chandrasekharan, R., & Wright, G. P. (1992). Estimating brand loyalty and switching with an application to the automobile market. *Management Science, 38*, 1371-1393.

McKenna, R. (1991). *Relationship marketing: Successful strategies for the age of the customer.* Reading, MA: Addison-Wesley.

Mehrabian, A., & Russell, J. A. (1974). *An approach to environmental psychology.* Cambridge: MIT.

Miles, R. H. (1980). *Macro organizational behavior.* Glenview, IL: Scott, Foresman.

Miles, R., & Snow, C. C. (1986). Organizations: New concepts for new forms. *California Management Review, 28*, 62-73.

Miles, R., & Snow, C. C. (1992). Causes of failure of network organizations. *California Management Review, 34*, 53-72.

Miller, P., & O'Leary, T. (1994). The factory as a laboratory. *Science in Context, 7*, 469-496.

Mintz, B., & Schwartz, M. (1990). Capital flows and the process of financial hegemony. In S. Zukin & P. DiMaggio (Eds.), *Structures of capital: The social organization of the economy* (pp. 203-226). New York: Cambridge University Press.

Mintzberg, H. (1983). *Power in and around organizations.* Englewood Cliffs, NJ: Prentice Hall.

Mintzberg, H. (1991). Five ps for strategy. In H. Mintzberg & J. B. Quinn (Eds.), *The strategy process: Concepts, contexts, and cases* (pp. 12-19). Englewood Cliffs, NJ: Prentice Hall.

Mizruchi, M. (1992). *The structure of corporate political action.* Cambridge, MA: Harvard University Press.

Mizruchi, M. S. (1994). Social network analysis: Recent achievements and current controversies. *Acta Sociologica, 37*, 329-343.

Mizruchi, M. S., & Galaskiewicz, J. (1994). Networks of interorganizational relations. In S. Wasserman & J. Galaskiewicz (Eds.), *Advances in social network analysis* (pp. 230-253). Thousand Oaks, CA: Sage.

Mizruchi, M. S., Mariolis, P., Schwartz, M., & Mintz, B. (1986). Techniques for disaggregating centrality scores in social networks. In N. B. Tuma (Ed.), *Sociological methodology, 16* (pp. 26-48). Washington, DC: American Sociological Association.

Mizruchi, M. S., & Schwartz, M. S. (Eds.). (1987). *Intercorporate relations: The structural analysis of business.* Cambridge: Cambridge University Press.

Mizruchi, M. S., & Stearns, L. B. (1994). A longitudinal study of borrowing by large American corporations. *Administrative Science Quarterly, 39*, 118-140.

Mohr, J., & Spekman, R. (1994). Characteristics of partnership success: Partnership attributes, communications behavior, and conflict resolution techniques. *Strategic Management Journal, 15,* 135-152.

Moore, C. (1994). *Group techniques for idea building.* Thousand Oaks, CA: Sage.

Moore-Shag, E., & Wilkie, W. (1988). Recent developments in research on family decisions. *Advances in Consumer Research, 15,* 454-460.

Moorman, C., Zaltman, G., & Deshpande, R. (1992). Relationships between providers and users of marketing research: The dynamics of trust within and between organizations. *Journal of Marketing Research, 29,* 314-329.

Morgan, R. M., & Hunt, S. D. (1994). The commitment-trust theory of relationship marketing. *Journal of Marketing, 58,* 20-38.

Morgan, D., & Schwalbe, M. (1990). Mind and self in society: Linking social structures and social cognition. *Social Psychological Quarterly, 53,* 148-164.

Moxon, R. W., Roehl, T. W., & Truitt, J. F. (1988). International cooperative ventures in the commercial aircraft industry: Gains, sure, but what's my share. In F. Contractor & P. Lorange (Eds.), *Cooperative strategies in international business* (pp. 255-278). Lexington, MA: D. C. Heath.

Mulford, C. L. (1984). *Interorganizational relations.* New York: Human Sciences Press.

Mullin, B. J., Hardy, S., & Sutton, W. A. (1993). *Sport marketing.* Champaign, IL: Human Kinetics.

Murdoch, J. (1995). Actor-networks and the evolution of economic forms: Combining description and explanation in theories of regulation, flexible specialization and networks. *Environment and Planning A, 27,* 731-757.

Negandhi, A. R. (Ed.). (1980). *Interorganization theory.* Kent, OH: Kent State University Press.

Nelson, J. E. (1978). Children as information sources in the family decision to eat out. *Advances in Consumer Research, 6,* 419-423.

Nelson, R. R., & Winter, S. G. (1982). *An evolutionary theory of economic change.* Cambridge, MA: Belknap.

Nielson, R. P. (1988). Cooperative strategies. *Strategic Management Journal, 9,* 475-492.

Niederkofler, M. (1991). The evolution of strategic alliances: Opportunities for managerial influence. *Journal of Business Venturing, 6,* 237-257.

Nishiguchi, T. (1994). *Strategic industrial sourcing: The Japanese advantage.* New York: Oxford University Press.

Nohria, N. (1992). Is a network perspective a useful way of studying organizations? In N. Nohria & R. Eccles (Eds.), *Networks and organizations* (pp. 1-22). Cambridge, MA: Harvard Business School Press.

Nohria, N., & Eccles, R. G. (1992). Face-to-face: Making network organizations work. In N. Nohria & R. G. Eccles (Eds.), *Networks and organizations: Structure, form, and action* (pp. 262-287). Boston: Harvard Business School Press.

Nonaka, I., & Takeuchi, H. (1995). *The knowledge-creating company: How Japanese companies create the dynamics of innovation.* New York: Oxford University Press.

Noordewier, T. G., John, G., & Nevin, J. R. (1990). Performance outcomes of purchasing arrangements in industrial buyer-vendor relationships. *Journal of Marketing, 54,* 80-93.

Novak, T. P. (1993). Log-linear trees: Models of market structure in brand switching data. *Journal of Marketing Research, 30,* 267-287.

O'Reilly, C., III, & Chatmen, J. (1986). Organizational commitment and psychological attachment: The effects of compliance, identification and internalization on prosocial behavior. *Journal of Applied Psychology, 71,* 492-499.

Ogilvy, D. (1983). *Ogilvy on advertising.* New York: Random House.

Oliver, C. (1988). The collective strategy framework: An application to competing predications of isomorphism. *Administrative Science Quarterly, 33,* 543-561.

Oliver, C. (1990). Determinants of interorganizational relationships: Integration and future directions. *Academy of Managament Review, 15*(2), 241-265.

Oliver, N., & Wilkinson, B. (1988). *The Japanization of British industry.* Oxford: Basil Blackwell.

Olson, J. C. (1995). Introduction [Special issue]. *International Journal of Research in Marketing, 12,* 189-191.

Orrù, M., Hamilton, G. G., & Suzuki, M. (1989). Patterns of interfirm control in Japanese business. *Organization Studies, 10,* 549-574.

Palmer, D., Friedland, R., & Singh, J. V. (1986). The ties that bind: Organizational and class stability in a corporate interlock network. *American Sociological Review, 51,* 781-796.

Palmer, D. A., Jennings, P. D., & Zhou, X. G. (1993). Late adoption of the multidivisional form by large American corporations: Institutional, political, and economic accounts. *Administrative Science Quarterly, 38,* 100-131.

Park, S. O., & Markusen, A. (1995). Generalizing new industrial districts: A theoretical agenda and an application from a non-Western economy. *Environment and Planning A, 27,* 81-104.

Parkhe, A. (1991). Interfirm diversity, organizational learning, and longevity in global strategic alliances. *Journal of International Business Studies, 22,* 579-601.

Parkhe, A. (1993). Strategic alliance structuring: A game theory and transaction cost examination of interfirm cooperation, *Academy of Management Journal, 36,* 794-829.

Parvatiyar, A., & Sheth, J. N. (1992, June). *Paradigm shift in interfirm marketing relationships: Emerging research issues.* Paper presented at the Conference on Customer Relationship Management: Theory and practice, Emory University, Atlanta, GA.

Payne, A., & Rickard, J. (1994, November). *Relationship marketing, customer retention, and service firm profitability.* Paper presented at the 2nd International Colloquium in Relationship Marketing, Cranfield University, U.K.

Peven, D. E. (1968). The use of religious revival techniques to indoctrinate personnel: The home-party sales organizations. *Sociological Quarterly, Winter,* 97-106.

Pfeffer, J., & Leong, A. (1977). Resource allocations in united funds: Examination of power and dependence. *Social Forces, 55,* 775-790.

Pfeffer, J., & Salancik, G. R. (1974). Organizational decision making as political process: The case of a university budget. *Administrative Science Quarterly, 19,* 135-151.

Pfeffer, J., & Salancik, G. R. (1978). *The external control of organizations: A resource dependence perspective.* New York: Harper and Row.

Pickering, A. (Ed.). (1992). *Science as practice and culture.* Chicago: University of Chicago Press.

Piore, M., & Sabel, C. (1984). *The second industrial divide.* New York: Basic Books.

Podolny, J. M. (1994). Market uncertainty and the social character of economic exchange. *Administrative Science Quarterly, 39,* 458-483.

Porter, M. E. (1990). *The competitive advantage of nations.* New York: Free Press.

Powell, W. W. (1990). Neither market nor hierarchy: Network forms of organization. In L. Cummings & B. Staw (Eds.), *Research in organizational behavior* (pp. 295-336). Greenwich, CT: JAI.

Powell, W. W., & Brantley, P. (1992). Competitive cooperation in biotechnology: Learning through networks? In N. Nohria & R. Eccles (Eds.), *Networks and organizations* (pp. 366-394). Boston: Harvard Business School Press.

Powell, W. W., & Smith-Doerr, L. (1994). Networks and economic life. In N. J. Smelser & R. Swedberg (Eds.), *The handbook of economic sociology* (pp. 368-402). Princeton, NJ: Princeton University Press.

Prahalad, C. K., & Hamel, G. (1990, May-June). The core competence of the corporation. *Harvard Business Review*, pp. 79-91.

Pranter, C. A., & Martin, C. L. (1991). Compatibility management: Roles in service performances. *Journal of Services Marketing, 5*, 43-53.

Provan, K. G. (1984). Interorganization cooperation and decision-making autonomy in a consortium multihospital system. *Academy of Management Review, 9*, 494-504.

Provan, K. G., & Gassenheimer, J. B. (1994). Supplier commitment in relational contract exchanges with buyers: A study of interorganizational dependence and exercised power. *Journal of Management Studies, 31*, 55-68.

Provan, K. G., & Milward, H. B. (1995). A preliminary theory of interorganizational network effectiveness: A comparative study of four community mental health systems. *Administrative Science Quarterly, 40*, 1-33.

Putnam, R. D. (1995). Bowling alone: America's declining social capital. *Journal of Democracy, 6*, 65-78.

Quelch, J. A., & Ash, S. B. (1981). Consumer satisfaction with professional services. In J. H. Donnelly & W. R. George (Eds.), *Marketing of services* (pp. 82-85). Chicago: American Marketing Association.

Quinn, J. (1993). *The intelligent enterprise*. New York: Free Press.

Raye-Johnson, V. (1990). *Effective networking*. Menlo Park, CA: Crisp.

Read, M. D. (1992). Policy networks and issue networks: The politics of smoking. In D. Marsh & R. A. W. Rhodes (Eds.), *Policy networks in British government* (pp. 124-148). Oxford: Clarendon.

Redding, S. G. (1990). *The spirit of Chinese capitalism*. Berlin: Mouton de Gruyter.

Redding, S. G., & Whitley, R. D. (1990). Beyond bureaucracy: Toward a comparative analysis of forms of economic resource coordination and control. In S. Clegg, G. Redding, & M. Carter (Eds.), *Capitalism in contrasting cultures* (pp. 105-129). Berlin: De Gruyter.

Reingen, P. H., & Kernan, J. B. (1986). Analysis of referral networks in marketing: Methods and illustration. *Journal of Marketing Research, 23*, 370-378.

Rentsch, J. R. (1990). Climate and culture: Interaction and qualitative differences in organizational meanings. *Journal of Applied Psychology, 75*, 668-681.

Reve, T., & Stern, L. W. (1986). The relationships between interorganizational form, transaction climate, and economic performance in vertical interfirm dyads. In L. Pellegrini & S. Reddy (Eds.), *Marketing channels* (pp. 75-102). Lexington, MA: Lexington Books.

Reynolds, T. J., & Gutman, J. (1988, February-March,). Laddering theory, method, analysis, and interpretation. *Journal of Advertising Research*, pp. 11-31.

Rhodes, R. A. W., & Marsh, D. (1992a). Policy networks in British politics: A critique of existing approaches. In D. Marsh & R. A. W. Rhodes (Eds.), *Policy networks in British government*. Oxford: Clarendon.

Rhodes, R. A. W., & Marsh, D. (1992b). New directions in the study of policy networks. *European Journal of Political Research, 21*, 181-205.

Ring, P. S., & Van de Ven, A. H. (1994). Developmental processes of cooperative interorganizational relationships. *Academy of Management Review, 19*(1), 90-118.

Roehl, T. W., & Truitt, J. F. (1987). Stormy open marriages are better. *Columbia Journal of World Business, Summer*, 87-95.

Roethlisberger, F. J., & W. J. Dickson. (1939). *Management and the worker*. Cambridge, MA: Harvard University Press.

Rogers, D. L., & Whetten, D. A. (1982). *Interorganizational coordination: Theory, research, and implementation.* Ames: Iowa State University Press.

Rogers, E. M. (1962). *The diffusion of innovation.* New York: Free Press.

Roha, R. R. (1991, November). The ups and downs of "downlines." *Kiplinger's Personal Finance Magazine,* pp. 63-70.

Ronchetto, J. R., Hutt, M. D., & Reingen, P. H. (1989). Embedded influence patterns in organizational buying systems. *Journal of Marketing, 53,* 51-62.

Russell, C. (1993). The master trend. *American Demographics, 15,* 28-37.

Sabel, C. F. (1989). Flexible specialization and the re-emergence of regional economies. In P. Hirst & J. Zeitlin (Eds.), *Reversing industrial decline?: Industrial structure and policy in Britain and her competitors* (pp. 17-70). Oxford: Berg.

Sabel, C. F. (1991), Moebius-strip organizations and open labor markets: Some consequences of the reintegration of conception and execution in a volatile economy. In P. Bourdieu & J. S. Coleman (Eds.), *Social theory for a changing society* (pp. 23-54). Boulder, CO: Westview.

Sabel, C. F., & Zeitlin, J. (1985). Historical alternatives to mass production. *Past and Present, 108,* 133-176.

Sako, M. (1992). *Price, quality, and trust: An analysis of interfirm relations in Britain and Japan.* New York: Cambridge University Press.

Salancik, G. R. (1995). WANTED: A good network theory of organization. *Administrative Science Quarterly, 40,* 345-349.

Sarbin, T. R., & Allen, V. L. (1968). Role theory. In G. Lindzey & E. Aronson (Eds.), *The handbook of social psychology* (pp. 488-567). Reading, MA: Addison-Wesley.

Saxenian, A. (1989). In search of power: The organization of business interests in Silicon Valley and Route 128. *Economy and Society, 18,* 25-70.

Saxenian, A. L. (1994). *Regional advantage: Culture and competition in Silicon Valley and Route 128.* Cambridge, MA: Harvard University Press.

Sayer, A., & Walker, R. (1991). *The new social economy: Reworking the division of labor.* London: Basil Blackwell.

Schlissel, M. R. (1985). The consumer of household services in the marketplace: An empirical study. In J. A. Czepiel, M. R. Solomon, & C. F. Surprenant (Eds.), *The service encounter: Managing employee/customer interaction in service businesses* (pp. 303-319). Lexington, MA: Lexington Books.

Schneider, V. (1992). The structure of policy networks: A comparison of the "chemicals control" and the "telecommunications" policy domains in Germany. *European Journal of Political Research, 21,* 109-129.

Schouten, J., & Alexander, J. (1995). Subcultures of consumption: An ethnography of the new bikers. *Journal of Consumer Research, 22,* 43-61.

Schrader, S. (1991). Informal technology transfer between firms: Cooperation through information trading. *Research Policy, 20,* 153-170.

Schumpeter, J. (1934). *The theory of economic development.* Cambridge, MA: Harvard University Press.

Schutz, W. C. (1966). *The interpersonal underworld.* Palo Alto, CA: Science and Behavior Books.

Scott, J. (1991). *Social network analysis.* London: Sage.

Senge, P. (1992). *The fifth discipline.* New York: Century Publishing.

Shank, J. K. (in press). Analyzing technology investments: From NPV to SCM. *Management Accounting Research.*

Shaw, M. E. (1964). Communication networks. In L. L. Berkowitz (Ed.), *Advances in experimental social psychology* (pp. 111-147). New York: Academic Press.

Sheth, J. (1973). A model of industrial buyer behavior. *Journal of Marketing, 37,* 50-56.

Sheth, J. N., & Parvatiyar, A. (1993, June). *The evolution of relationship marketing*. Paper presented at the Conference on Historical Thought in Marketing, Atlanta, GA.

Shocker, A. D., Stewart, D. W., & Zahorik, A. J. (1990). Mapping competitive relationships: Practices, problems, and promise. In G. Day, B. Weitz, & R. Wensley (Eds.), *The interfaces of marketing and strategy* (pp. 9-56). Greenwich, CT: JAI.

Shorter, E. (1976). *The making of the modern family*. London: Collins.

Silk, A. J., & Kalwani, M. U. (1982). Measuring influence in organizational purchase decisions. *Journal of Marketing Research, 19*, 165-181.

Sirsi, A., Ward, J. C., & Reingen, P. H. (1996). Microcultural analysis of sharing and variation in consumption behavior. *Journal of Consumer Research, 22*, 345-372.

Smitka, M. (1991). *Competitive ties: Subcontracting in the Japanese automobile industry*. New York: Columbia University Press.

Snehota, I. (1993). Markets as networks and the nature of the market process. In D. Sharma (Ed.), *Advances in international marketing, 5* (pp. 31-41). Greenwich, CT: JAI.

Snyder, M. (1974). Self-monitoring of expressive behavior. *Journal of Personality and Social Psychology, 30*, 526-537.

Solomon, M. R. (1983). The role of products as social stimuli: A symbolic interactionism perspective. *Journal of Consumer Research, 10*, 319-329.

Sonquist, J. A., & Koenig, T. (1975). Interlocking directorates in the top U.S. corporations: A graph theory approach. *Insurgent Sociologist, 5*, 196-229.

Spekman, R. (1979). The purchasing audit: A guide for management. *Journal of Purchasing and Materials Management, 15*, 8-12.

Spekman, R., Forbes, T., Isabella, L., & MacAvoy, T. (in press). Creating strategic alliances that endure. *Long-Range Planning*.

Spekman, R., & Gronhaug, K. (1986). Conceptual and methodological issues in buying center research. *European Journal of Marketing, 20*, 50-64.

Spekman, R., & Johnston, W. (1986). Relationship management: Managing selling and buying centers. *Journal of Business Research, 14*, 519-531.

Spekman, R., & Salmond, D. (1992). *A working consensus to collaborate: A field study of manufacturer and supplier dyads*. (MSI Working Paper, Report 92-134). Cambridge, MA: Marketing Science Institute.

Sriram, V., Krapfel, R., & Spekman, R. (1992). Antecedents to buyer seller collaboration: An analysis from the buyer's perspective. *Journal of Business Research, 25*, 303-320.

Srivastava, R. K., Alpert, M. I., & Shocker, A. D. (1984). A customer-oriented approach for determining market structures. *Journal of Marketing, 48*, 32-45.

Stalk, G., Evans, P., & Schulman, L. E. (1992). Competing on capabilities: The new rules of corporate strategy. *Harvard Business Review, 70*, 57-69.

Starbuck, W. H. (1976). Organizations and their environments. In M. D. Dunnette (Ed.), *Handbook of industrial and organizational psychology* (pp. 1089-1123). Chicago: Rand McNally.

Stearns, L. B., & Mizruchi, M. (1993). Board composition and corporate financing: The impact of financial institution representation on type of borrowing. *Academy of Management Journal, 36*, 603-618.

Stephenson, K., & Zelen, M. (1989). Rethinking centrality: Methods and examples. *Social Networks, 11*, 1-37.

Stern, L. W., & A. El-Ansary. (1992). *Marketing channels* (4th ed.). Englewood Cliffs, NJ: Prentice Hall.

Stern, L. W., & Scheer, L. K. (1991). Power and influence in marketing channel research: Observations on the state of the art. In G. Frazier (Ed.), *Advances in distribution channel research* (pp. 259-275). Greenwich, CT: JAI.

Sternthal, B., Tybout, A. M., & Calder, B. J. (1987). Confirmatory versus comparative approaches to judging theory tests. *Journal of Consumer Research, 14,* 114-125.

Stinchcombe, A. L. (1965). Social structures in organizations. In J. G. March (Ed.), *Handbook of organizations* (pp. 316-338). Chicago: Rand McNally.

Stilley-Hopper, J. (1995). Family financial decision making: Implications for marketing strategy. *Journal of Services Marketing, 9,* 24-32.

Stone, R. E., & Steiner, J. M., Jr. (1984). The Federal Trade Commission and pyramid sales schemes. *Pacific Law Journal, 15,* 879-897.

Storper, M., & Harrison, B. (1991). Flexibility, hierarchy, and regional development: The changing structure of industrial production systems and their forms of governance in the 1990s. *Research Policy, 20,* 407-422.

Streeck, W., & Schmitter, P. (Eds.). (1985). *Private interest government: Beyond market and state.* London: Sage.

Sverisson, A. (1994). Making sense of chaos: Socio-technical networks, careers, and entrepreneurs. *Acta Sociologica, 37,* 401-417.

Tam, S. (1990). Centrifugal versus centripetal growth processes: Contrasting ideal types for conceptualizing the developmental patterns of Chinese and Japanese firms. In S. Clegg, G. Redding, & M. Carter (Eds.), *Capitalism in contrasting cultures* (pp. 105-129). Berlin: De Gruyter.

Tauber, E. M. (1972). Why do people shop? *Journal of Marketing, 36,* 46-49.

Teece, D. (1986). Profiting from technological innovation: Implications for integration, collaboration, licensing, and public policy. *Research Policy, 15,* 285-305.

Telser, L. G. (1980). A theory of self-enforcing agreements. *Journal of Business, 53,* 27-44.

Thibaut, J. W., & Kelly, H. K. (1959). *The social psychology of groups.* New York: John Wiley.

Thomas, J. B., & Trevino, L. K. (1993). Information processing in strategic alliances: A multiple case approach. *Journal of Management Studies, 30,* 779-814.

Thompson, R. (1987, November). Ready, fire, aim. *Nation's Business,* pp. 77-78.

Thorelli, H. B. (1986). Networks: Between markets and hierarchies. *Strategic Management Journal, 7,* 37-51.

Thurman, B. (1979). In the office: Networks and coalitions. *Social Networks, 2,* 47-64.

Treacy, M., & Wiersema, R. (1995). *The discipline of market leaders.* Reading, MA: Addison-Wesley.

Trivedi, M., Bass, F. M., & Rao, R. C. (1994). A model of stochastic variety-seeking. *Marketing Science, 13,* 274-297.

Turley, L. W., & Fugate, D. L. (1992). The multidimensional nature of service facilities: Viewpoints and recommendations. *Journal of Services Marketing, 6,* 37-45.

Turnbull, P. W., & Topcu, S. (1994, September). *Customer profitability in relationships life cycles.* Paper presented at the 10th Industrial Marketing and Purchasing (IMP) Conference, Groningen.

Turnbull, P. W., & Valla, J. P. (Eds.). (1986). *Strategies for international industrial marketing.* London: Croom Helm.

Turnbull, P. W., & Zolkiewski, J. M. (1995, September). *Customer portfolios: Sales costs and profitability.* Paper presented at the 11th Industrial Marketing and Purchasing (IMP) International Conference, Manchester, U.K.

Turner, J. H. (1987). Toward a sociological theory of motivation. *American Sociological Review, 52,* 15-27.

Tushman, M. L., & Romanelli, E. (1983). Uncertainty, social location, and influence in decision making: A sociometric analysis. *Management Science, 29,* 12-23.

Tyebjee, T. T. (1988). Japan's joint ventures in the United States. In F. Contractor & P. Lorange (Eds.), *Cooperative strategies in international business* (pp. 457-472). Lexington, MA: D. C. Heath.

Uncles, M. D., Hammond, K. A., Ehrenberg, A. S. C., & Davis R. E. (1994). A replication study of two brand-loyalty measures. *European Journal of Operational Research, 76*, 375-384.

Urban, G. L., Johnson, P. L., & Hauser, J. R. (1984). Testing competitive market structure. *Marketing Science, 3*, 83-112.

Valley, K., White, S., & Iacobucci, D. (1992). The process of assisted negotiations: A network analysis. *Group Decision and Negotiation, 2*, 117-135.

Van de Ven, A. H. (1976). On the nature, formation, and maintenance of relations among organizations. *Academy of Management Review, 1*(4), 24-36.

Van de Ven, A., & Ferry, D. L. (1980). *Measuring and assessing organizations.* New York: John Wiley.

Van de Ven, A. H., Venkataraman, S., Polley, D., & Garud, R. (1989). Process of new business creation in different organizational settings. In A. Van de Ven, H. Angle, & M. S. Poole (Eds.), *Research on the management of innovation: The Minnesota studies* (pp. 221-298). New York: Ballinger/Harper & Row.

Van de Ven, A. H., & Walker, G. (1984). The dynamics of interorganizational cooperation. *Administrative Science Quarterly, 29*, 598-621.

Van Waarden, F. (1992a). Emergence and development of business interest associations: An example from the Netherlands. *Organization Studies, 13*, 521-562.

Van Waarden, F. (1992b). Dimensions and types of policy networks. *European Journal of Political Research, 21*, 29-52.

Vavra, T. G. (1992). *After-marketing: How to keep customers for life through relationship marketing.* Homewood, IL: Irwin.

Vogel, M. (1992, August 23). When friends turn flack. *The Washington Post*, p. C5.

Von Hippel, E. (1987). Cooperation between rivals: Informal know-how trading. *Research Policy, 16*, 291-302.

Von Hippel, E. (1988). *The sources of innovation.* Oxford: Oxford University Press.

Wade, J., O'Reilly, C. A., III, & Chandratat, I. (1990). Golden parachutes: CEOs and the exercise of social influence. *Administrative Science Quarterly, 35*, 587-603.

Wakefield, K. L., & Blodgett, J. G. (1994). The importance of servicescapes in leisure service settings. *Journal of Services Marketing, 8*, 66-76.

Walker, B. A., & Olson, J. C. (1991). Means-end chains: Connecting products with self. *Journal of Business Research, 22*, 111-118.

Ward, J. C., & Reingen, P. (1990). Sociocognitive analysis of group decision making among consumers. *Journal of Consumer Research, 17*, 245-262.

Warren, R. L. (1967). The interorganizational field as a focus for investigation. *Administrative Quarterly, 12*, 396-419.

Warren, R. L., Rose, S. M., & Bergunder, A. F. (1974). *The structure of urban reform.* Lexington, MA: Lexington Books.

Wasserman, D. (1985). *How to get your first copywriting job.* New York: Center for the Advancement of Advertising.

Wasserman, S. (1987). Conformity of two sociometric relations. *Psychometrika, 52*, 3-18.

Wasserman, S., & Faust, K. (1994). *Social network analysis.* New York: Cambridge University Press.

Wasserman, S., & Galaskiewicz, J. (Eds.). (1994). *Advances in social network analysis: Research in the social and behavioral sciences.* Thousand Oaks, CA: Sage.

Wasserman, S., & Iacobucci, D. (1986). Statistical analysis of discrete relational data. *British Journal of Mathematical and Statistical Psychology, 39*, 41-64.

Wasserman, S., & Iacobucci, D. (1988). Sequential social network data. *Psychometrika, 53*, 261-282.

Webster, F. E., Jr. (1992). The changing role of marketing in the corporation. *Journal of Marketing, 56,* 1-17.

Webster, F., & Wind, Y. (1972). A general model for understanding organizational buying behavior. *Journal of Marketing, 36,* 12-19.

Wegner, D. (1987). Transactive memory: A contemporary analysis of the group mind. In B. Mullen & G. A. Goethals (Eds.), *Theories of group behavior* (pp. 185-208). New York: Springer-Verlag.

Wellman, B. (1988). Structural analysis: From method and metaphor to theory and substance. In B. Wellman & S. D. Berkowitz (Eds.), *Social structures: A network approach* (pp. 19-61). Cambridge: Cambridge University Press.

Wellman, B., & Berkowitz, S. D. (Eds.). (1988). *Social structures: A network approach.* Cambridge: Cambridge University Press.

Wener, R. E. (1985). The environmental psychology of service encounters. In J. A. Czepiel, M. R. Solomon, & C. F. Surprenant (Eds.), *The service encounter: managing employee/customer interaction in service businesses* (pp. 101-112). Lexington, MA: Lexington Books.

Westbrook, R. A. (1980). A rating scale for measuring product/service satisfaction. *Journal of Marketing, 44,* 68-72.

Whetten, D. A. (1981). Interorganizational relations: A review of the field. *Journal of Higher Education, 52,* 1-28.

Whetten, D. A., & Aldrich, H. (1979). Organization set size and diversity: People-processing organizations and their environments. *Administration and Society, 11,* 251-281.

White, H. C. (1981). Where do markets come from? *American Journal of Sociology, 87,* 517-547.

White, H. C. (1992). *Identity and control.* Princeton, NJ: Princeton University Press.

White, H., Boorman, S., & Breiger, R. (1976). Social structure from multiple networks. I. blockmodels of roles and positions. *American Journal of Sociology, 81,* 730-779.

Whitley, R. (1990). Eastern Asian enterprise structures and the comparative analysis of business enterprise. *Organization Studies, 11,* 47-74.

Whitley, R. (Ed.). (1992). *European business systems: Firms and markets in their national contexts.* London: Sage.

Whitley, R. (1995). Academic knowledge and work jurisdiction in management. *Organization Studies, 16,* 81-105.

Williamson, O. (1975). *Markets and hierarchies.* New York: Free Press.

Williamson, O. (1985). *The economic institution of capitalism.* New York: Free Press.

Williamson, O. E. (1981). The economics of organization: The transaction-cost approach. *American Journal of Sociology, 87,* 548-577.

Wilson, D. T. (1994). Commentary on J. Johanson and L.-G. Mattsson's *The markets-as-networks tradition in Sweden.* In G. Laurent, G. L. Lilien, & B. Pras (Eds.), *Research traditions in marketing* (pp. 343-346). London: Croom Helm.

Wilson, D. T. (1995). An integrated model of buyer-seller relationships. *Journal of the Academy of Marketing Science, 23,* 336-346.

Wilson, D. T., & Jantrania, S. (1994). Understanding the value of a relationship. *Asia-Australia Marketing Journal, 2,* 55-66.

Wilson, D. T., & Moller, C. E. (1991). Buyer-seller relationships: Alternative conceptualizations. In S. J. Paliwoda (Ed.), *New perspectives on international marketing* (pp. 87-107). New York: Routledge: New York.

Womack, J. P., Jones, D. T., & Roos, D. (1990). *The machine that changed the world.* New York: Rawson Associates.

Yamada, K. (1992, January 3). Nu Skin to adopt new sales policies in pact with states. *Wall Street Journal,* p. C17.

Yeung, H. W. C. (1994). Critical reviews of geographic perspectives on business organizations and the organization of production: Toward a network approach. *Progress in Human Geography, 18,* 460-490.

Young, L. (1992). *The role of trust in interorganizational relationships in marketing channels.* Unpublished doctoral dissertation, University of New South Wales, Australia.

Zahorik, A. (1994). A nonhierarchical brand switching model for inferring market structure. *European Journal of Operational Research, 76,* 344-358.

Zajac, E. J., & Olsen, C. P. (1993). From transaction cost to transactional value analysis: Implications for the study of interorganizational strategies. *Journal of Management Studies, 30*(1), 131-145.

Zeitz, G. (1980). Interorganizational dialectics. *Administrative Science Quarterly, 25,* 72-88.

Zenor, M. J., & Srivastava, R. K. (1993). Inferring market structure with aggregate data: A latent segment logit model. *Journal of Marketing Research, 30,* 369-379.

Zerrillo, P. (1995). *Interorganizational properties and interorganizational perceptual agreement: A model and empirical test in marketing channel relations.* Unpublished doctoral dissertation, Northwestern University, Evanston, IL.

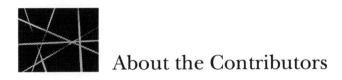

About the Contributors

Luis Araujo
Department of Marketing
The Management School
Lancaster University
Lancaster, UK LA1 4YX

Richard P. Bagozzi
Department of Marketing
School of Business Administration
University of Michigan
Ann Arbor, MI 48109-1234
E-mail: bagozzi@umich.edu

Ronald S. Burt
Graduate School of Business
University of Chicago
1101 E. 58th Street
Chicago, IL 60637
E-mail: ron.burt@gsb.uchicago.edu

Alexandra J. Campbell
Department of Marketing
York University
4700 Keele St.
North York, Ontario, Canada M3J 1P3

Jennifer E. Chang
Department of Marketing
Kellogg Graduate School of Management
Northwestern University
2001 Sheridan Rd.
Evanston, IL 60208

Terry Clark
Department of Marketing
Goizueta Business School
Emory University
Atlanta, GA 30322

Pratibha A. Dabholkar
Department of Marketing
307 Stokely Management Center
University of Tennessee
Knoxville, TN 37996-0530
E-mail: pa146028@utvm1

Geoffrey Easton
Department of Marketing
The Management School
Lancaster University
Lancaster, UK LA1 4YX

David Ford
Department of Marketing
School of Management
University of Bath
Claverton Down
Bath, UK BA2 7A4

Joseph Galaskiewicz
Department of Sociology and Management
909 Social Sciences Bldg.
University of Minnesota
Minneapolis, MN 55455

Kent Grayson
London Business School
Sussex Place
Regent's Park
London, UK NW1 4SA
E-mail: kgrayson@lbs.lon.ac.uk

Håkan Håkansson
Department of Marketing
Uppsala University
Box 513
751 20 Uppsala
Sweden

Geraldine Henderson
Department of Marketing
Fuqua Graduate School of Management
Duke University
Durham, NC 22706

Susanne Hertz
Department of Marketing and Distribution
Stockholm School of Economics
Hollandargatan 32
Box 6501
11383 Stockholm
Sweden

Dawn Iacobucci
  Department of Marketing
  Kellogg Graduate School of Management
  Northwestern University
  2001 Sheridan Rd.
  Evanston, IL 60208
  E-mail: d-iacobucci@nwu.edu

Gregory A. Janicik
  Graduate School of Business
  University of Chicago
  1101 E. 58th Street
  Chicago, IL 60637

David Krackhardt
  Public Policy and Management
  Carnegie Mellon University
  Pittsburgh, PA 15213
  E-mail: krack@cmu.edu

Alberto Marcati
  Diparimento Di Discipline Economico-Aziendali
  Universita Degli Studi Di Bologna
  Piazza Scaravilli 2
  40126 Bologna
  Italy

Charles L. Martin
  Department of Marketing
  1845 Fairmont
  Wichita State University
  Wichita, KS 67260-0084

Raymond McDowell
  Department of Marketing
  School of Management
  University of Bath
  Claverton Down
  Bath, UK BA2 7A4

Ravi Raina
Department of Marketing
University of Texas
Austin, TX 78712

Peter Reingen
Department of Marketing
College of Business
Arizona State University
Tempe, AZ 85287

D. Deo Sharma
Department of Marketing
Uppsala University
Box 513
751 20 Uppsala
Sweden

Robert E. Spekman
Department of Marketing
Darden School of Business
University of Virginia
Charlottesville, VA 22906
E-mail: spekmanr@darden.gbus.virginia.edu

Louis W. Stern
Department of Marketing
Kellogg Graduate School of Management
Northwestern University
2001 Sheridan Rd.
Evanston, IL 60208
E-mail: lwstern@merle.acns.nwu.edu

Cyril Tomkins
Department of Marketing
School of Management
University of Bath
Claverton Down
Bath, UK BA2 7A4

James C. Ward
Department of Marketing
College of Business
Arizona State University
Tempe, AZ 85287
E-mail: atjcw@asuvm.inre.asu.edu

David T. Wilson
Department of Marketing
Pennsylvania State University
402 Business Administration Bldg.
University Park, PA 16802-3004

Philip C. Zerrillo, Sr.
Department of Marketing
University of Texas
Austin, TX 78712
E-mail: bubbaz@utxvms.cc.utexas.edu